MEMORIALS

AND

CORRESPONDENCE

OF

CHARLES JAMES FOX.

MEMORIALS

AND

CORRESPONDENCE

OF

CHARLES JAMES FOX.

EDITED

BY LORD JOHN RUSSELL.

VOLUME IV.

AMS PRESS
NEW YORK

Reprinted from the edition of 1857, London
First AMS EDITION published 1970
Manufactured in the United States of America

International Standard Book Number:
  complete set: 0-404-05470-6
  volume 4: 0-404-05474-9

Library of Congress Catalog Card Number: 75-115362

AMS PRESS, INC.
NEW YORK, N.Y. 10003

CORRESPONDENCE OF

CHARLES JAMES FOX.

BOOK THE SEVENTH.

I HAVE now arrived at the last period of the correspondence of Mr. Fox, and I shall preface it by a very few remarks.

Some letters of 1803, and of the early part of 1804, which had been omitted, are here inserted.

From the time when Mr. Fox returned to active politics in 1804 till the period of his coming into office in 1806, his correspondence with Lord Grey, Lord Lauderdale, Lord Holland, and General Fitzpatrick is very full. The period is one of so much interest, and the conduct of such a man is of so much importance, that I have retrenched little of this correspondence. Some repetitions I have, however, omitted.

Mr. Fox explains so clearly, and so openly, as his manner was, his views to his friends, that I shall not here attempt any further explanation of them.

Lord Holland, in his memoirs of the Whig party, after relating the circumstances of Mr. Fox's death, adds, "His character could be best delineated by a narrative of the leading events of his political life, by a reference to his speeches and writings, by a publication of many of his private letters, a description of his domestic life, and such fragments of his conversation as the memory of his friends might supply.   Such a work I have long meditated."   At a later period Lord Holland, busy with politics, and immersed in society, limited his hopes to the plan of forming a collection of materials for the life of Mr. Fox. He was not sanguine with respect to the completion of even so much of his task, and he said to me one day, "I suppose I shall not be able to finish my book : I shall leave it to you to complete."   Unfortunately his labours carried him only to the period when his own recollections of Mr. Fox's conversation became distinct, and his own interest in politics lively and intelligent.   The present Lord Holland says in a note, "My father abandoned this work at a later period of his life.   The late Mr. Allen commenced it, but also gave it up.   The ample materials left by my father are now in Lord John Russell's hands for that purpose."

Political employments still more absorbing than those of the late Lord Holland have hitherto prevented my doing more than publishing the collections made by Lord Holland and Mr. Allen, with such comments as I thought essential, and with the assistance of some valuable notes furnished me by a friend, in illustration of the letters to Lord Holland published in the third volume. I shall endeavour, in a separate form, to place in a connected narrative the relation of Mr. Fox's political career, and an account of his times. In that manner the great events of his life will be prominently set forth, and his public policy fully discussed.

TO R. ADAIR, ESQ.

" January, 1803.

" Dear Adair,

" I send you back your newspaper, which, I confess, I do not admire so much as you do. I certainly think it too anti-Gallican, as it seems to look to hopes from time which, at present, there is no ground to form. I look upon Europe as much lost to us as America, and all notions of recovering it, unless some unexpected alterations happen, as visionary. However, if Perry * had been so strong on the other side that a circuitous route was necessary to come round, I think the papers (for he has sent me the preceding one) very judicious in that view.

" I am more afraid for peace than ever ; Bonaparte's insolence to us in his speech to the Swiss Delegates is not only grating in itself, but is a symptom that the nonsense talked here has produced a strong effect upon his mind. I still hope, however, that his interest will determine him to be in no

---

* Mr. Perry, the honest and able editor of the " Morning Chronicle," which seems to be the newspaper referred to.

degree the aggressor, and that our government will
not be quite foolish enough to put him in the right
by any violent act on their part. The business of
sending Moore does appear to have been very absurd
indeed, and one cannot wonder that Bonaparte
should consider it as more seriously meant than in
fact it probably was.* The Ministers, instead of
avoiding, ought to have sought an opportunity of
explaining themselves upon this point; but one of
their grand errors was that they spoke entirely with a
view to the Opposition, and not at all to the Consul.
A few civil words would have done all.

" Yours ever,
" C. J. FOX."

" St. Ann's Hill, *Tuesday.*"

TO SAME.

" 1803.

" Dear Adair,

           " I have just received your letter and the
Duchess's,† and can only say that if the P. of W.
wants to see me it will of course be my duty to wait
upon him, either in London, or wherever else he
chooses to appoint: but that as to attending Parliament at present, it appears to me impossible that
any good can come of it. It is, as the P. very
properly says, respecting the war, both too soon and
too late; too soon for anything like a junction and
strength, and too late for opposing the Defence Bill,

---

* This alludes probably to the mission of a confidential agent of the
British government to the borders of Switzerland. See " Alison's History
of Europe," vol. vi. p. 171.   † Probably the Duchess of Devonshire.

&c. &c. At the same time you may tell his R. H.
that I am very happy to find that my general
opinions are nearly the same as his. To add the
conscripts to the regulars would be far the best plan,
but whether his mode of raising recruits be at all
right, even for the purpose which I best like of a
regular army, is another question. If the conduct of
Ministers respecting Hanover be as blameable as
H. R. H. supposes, (and I have little doubt but he is
right,) a motion of inquiry may certainly be made on
that subject; and indeed this is the only thing like a
parliamentary measure that can be now taken; and
remark how very unfavourable for such a motion the
time of the session and other circumstances are. It
ought not to be made without a perfect concert
between persons who are not in the habit of
concerting, and this alone would take some time.

"The part of the P.'s opinions in which I most
heartily concur is that which relates to the propriety he
thinks there would have been in waiting for some cause
of war in which other nations would have concurred.
Now as to men, you know I have no objection to any
set, and to some of those mentioned I have something
like partiality; but you know the strong impressions
which many of my friends entertain against Windham, and everything of the name of Grenville. That
these prejudices must, if there is occasion, be resisted,
I am most ready to admit; but *until* there seems some
opportunity of doing good, there is no use in doing
violence to the feelings of friends. Lord Spencer's
influence with the K. I suspect to exist only in the

P.'s imagination, nor do I conceive that any influence can turn him against a ministry made in a manner so agreeable to him.   What then is to be done?   Alas! I know not; but I think the best chance is to wait for the effect which these violent measures and outward events will produce, and then if much discontent should arise, a junction, such as the P. seems to wish, may be produced, and the exertion of his R. H.'s influence may very much contribute to give strength —ay, and cordiality too,—to such a junction.

" One thing, however, it may be necessary to pre-mise, viz.: that I cannot be one of any party who do not see both the possibility and the eligibility of being at peace with Bonaparte upon certain conditions. The only question with me at all doubtful is, whether in the expectation of the propriety of such a junction as has been hinted at, *hereafter*, it might not be advisable soon to have some concert provisionally, if I may so express myself, between the P. and some at least of the Grenvilles, Lord Spencer, &c., in order that our respective modes of conduct might be such as at least not to create new difficulties, if not to facilitate a union next session.   One good consequence of such an understanding might be to put a stop to Moira's rhodomontades, and other things of the kind.   I am sensible all this is a proceeding far too slow for the Prince's impetuosity, an impetuosity which upon this occasion, however, is much to his credit.   If he and those most immediately connected with him can suggest any plan of more rapid operation, I am sure I have no unwillingness to listen to it with all

imaginable deference.   In the meantime pray say
everything from me to his R. H. that is respectful
and affectionate, and if I might venture one piece of
advice, it would be to take great care not to say or do
anything that can tend to declare a personal enmity
between him and Bonaparte.   I am sure this advice
is unnecessary, but the follies of ———— and ————
make one feel an inclination to give it.

"Let me repeat, that with respect to men, I have
no objection.   With Lord Moira, however I may
disapprove of his late speeches, I always have lived,
and wish still to live, in friendship.   Tom Grenville
and Windham I like, and Lord Grenville and Lord
Spencer are persons to me quite unexceptionable; of
the abilities of the former I have also a very high
opinion.   I have, I think, explained to you all my
feelings and opinions, and you will communicate as
much of them as you think proper.

"Yours ever,

"C. J. FOX.

"St. Ann's Hill, *Monday.*

"P.S. I observe I have said nothing of the blockade
of the Elbe.   Upon the face of it, it appears a very
injudicious measure; but the secret history *may*,
though I hardly think it *will*, make some difference.

"If I must go to the P., remember that to-morrow,
Friday, and Monday, would be the most inconvenient
days to me; but surely there is no reason for my
going at all."

MR. FOX TO MR. O'BRIEN.*

"St. Ann's Hill, *June 26th*, 1803.

" I shall hardly have time to answer your two letters to-day, and, therefore, very briefly. I still think as I did about the attack upon the Grenvilles, and especially upon Lord Grenville. To prove how impolitic it is, it is only necessary to observe that we are exactly doing the work of the Court: Are not they abusing the Grenvilles every day? have they not had even the impudence to call them bloodhounds? and that too when they were about to make a more unnecessary, if not a more odious, war than the last? Even the milk-and-water Addington gets to something like invective when he speaks of them. And why are *we* to attack them? as warriors? are not they the true warriors who make a wicked war, rather than those who talk absurdly against peace? Besides, has not Lord G. said distinctly, 1st, that bad as the Peace of Amiens was, your sole object ought to have been to keep the Consul to it; 2ndly, that the Ministers, however blameable for what *he* calls former submissions, are still more so for bringing on war at this time, and upon this question? You will not suspect me of denying that we have sufficient cause of complaint against the Grenvilles; but, alas, against whom have we not? and is this the moment—when the Court is in direct and bitter

---

* Dennis O'Brien, Esq., a gentleman connected with the press. He was a warm adherent of Mr. Fox., but much distrusted by many of his friends.

hostility to them, and when, moreover, Pitt and they seem to be every day getting further distant from each other,—is *this* the moment for us to attack them? At the beginning of the session the case was far different; there were then hopes with regard to the conduct of the present Ministers which have now vanished, and I cannot help thinking that, among the different corps of the enemy, these Grenvilles are those that have preserved most of something like a trifle of reputation, and that, for that very reason, they are most run down by the Court. Now ought we to assist the Court in this? I think not. On the contrary, I think we ought to contend that there is not the smallest reason for distinguishing any one of these gangs as at all more set upon war than another. Pitt is as bad in that respect as Windham, and Addington as either of them; with this difference, that the latter by his folly has contrived to lay bare the injustice of our cause, more perhaps than the others would have done in his place. . . . .

" You are quite right in your system of doing *nothing*. It is as wise as it is agreeable. I am very far from wishing to make any coalition at this time, but neither would I throw unnecessary impediments in the way of any future one with any persons who are capable of acting in *real* opposition. Pitt has shown decidedly that *he* is not.

" Yours ever,

" C. J. FOX."

TO SAME.

"July 6th, 1803.

" I. AM glad you agree to what I say concerning the Grenvilles, &c., but shall be sorry if it makes you wholly abandon your ill-fated book.*   My reasons are rather strengthened by the insolent manner with which I hear Addington, now he thinks he is safe from Pitt, attacks Windham in the House of Commons. As to our difference concerning invasion and its consequences, I still think they cannot venture it, but I own the language of the French towns, &c., which I suppose to be approved by Bonaparte, has a face the other way, and if they do come, the extreme folly of our Ministers and their measures makes me tremble for London.   However, I am one of those who think that it is *not* true, that London lost, all is lost. My main dependence is still upon the difficulty of escaping our fleet so as to land in numbers,—a difficulty which must, I think, deter Bonaparte from the undertaking, and the rather because it is of a nature not to be surmounted by exertion, but by *chance* only.   If it does not deter him, it will make me think him not bold but rash, and I think the probabilities are ten to one against his succeeding even so far as to land."

---

* Probably some pamphlet that Mr. O'Brien was writing.

TO SAME.

"ST. ANN'S HILL, *August 12th*, 1803.

" I WILL not say anything of public affairs, but
Sheridan has outdone his usual outdoings. Folly
beyond all the past; but what degree of folly will
not extreme levity and vanity be capable of producing? The P.'s offer, and the refusal of it, ought,
I repeat, to be noticed more than it is. Cannot
you, without troubling yourself, give a hint to some
friend that it should be done ? "

TO SAME.

"ST. ANN'S HILL, *December 30th*, 1803.

" MANY thanks for your letter, and pray write what
you hear of the intended invasion. I still think they
will find it very difficult to get out of their ports, and
still more so to reach England and land in safety; and
upon these difficulties my boldness rests. You do not
argue so logically as you usually do. Bonaparte is not
a fool, and would not, say you, attempt such an enterprise without reasonable hopes of success ; but in the
very next sentence, you say he has no other means of
making war *but* by invasion ; if this is so, it accounts
for his taking a mode by no means eligible in itself,
and where the chances are much against him ; for a
wise man will take bad means if he has no better.
This blowing weather, if it blows off our ships from his
coast, will also, in all probability, disperse his ships,
and still more his boats and floats, &c., if they put to

sea. In short, I am bold, very bold, as long as they
are on the other side of the water or on the seas. If
they land, I am not in the same state of confidence ;
but even then, and supposing the enemy were to be
victorious, I hope—nay, I think—he will grievously
feel his want of communication with the Continent.
Remember, that in your favourite instance, Carthage
was not conquered till Rome had obtained a superiority by sea as well as by land."*

TO MR. ADAIR.

" *December* 28*th*, 1803.

"DEAR ADAIR,
        "I had a letter by the same post from the
Duchess of D., relating merely to some general wish
of communication. I told her that if I had intended
to bring on the Irish business, I should have communicated ; but now there was nothing to communicate. Letters from Grattan and Ponsonby have
dissuaded me (though I remain wholly unconvinced)
from bringing on that business now, but I still
think, as I did before, that it is desirable that such
of our friends as are *for*, should make their opinions
known, at least to me."

---

* In these opinions about the chances of invasion, Mr. Fox came on one
side to nearly the same conclusions which Napoleon did on the other.
Napoleon's combinations, in order to become master of the sea, were
exceedingly able, and had it not been for two circumstances might have
succeeded. These two circumstances were, that operations by sea, to be
performed by sailing vessels, cannot be reduced to the same certainty as
marches by land ; and secondly, that Villeneuve, and not Napoleon, was
to direct them. Had the French landed, they might have caused a good
deal of confusion, but would easily have been cut off by sea, and must, in
all probability, have surrendered.—See Thiers, and Napoleon's conversation
with Lord Whitworth in the " Parliamentary Papers."

TO GENERAL FITZPATRICK.

"January 1st, 1804.

" YESTERDAY, and not before, died James, Duke of Monmouth, &c. It will be well if the historian has not made as bungling a piece of work with him as the hangman.

"The accounts from London all are that an attempt is to be expected immediately : if the troops in Holland are really (as is said) embarked, it looks serious; but I hope, and believe, too, that between sailing and landing πολλὰ μεταξύ. I find the Dublin papers are open-mouthed against my brother.* I have not heard from *him,* but I understand by a letter from Admiral Berkeley, there was something going on to make him easy. He either had seen, or was to see, Addington ; but Berkeley did not think matters could be amicably settled. I rather wish they could, if it can be done properly, and that somebody should bring on the affair of the 23rd of July, which is in no shape connected with him."†

" ST. ANN'S HILL, *Sunday.*"

* General Fox. He was replaced by Lord Cathcart. See Life of Lord Sidmouth. "It may be considered as settled, that your present commander-in-chief is to have a command in the Mediterranean, for which he is better calculated than for his present situation, being certainly an excellent officer, and a most valuable man ; and that Lord Cathcart is to succeed him in Ireland." Mr. Addington to Lord Hardwicke, August 25, 1803.

† The 23rd of July was the day of the murder of Lord Kilwarden by a savage mob at Dublin.

TO SAME.

"January 6th, 1804.

" I DO not yet give up the bringing on of the Irish question: the Duke of Bedford has written me a letter strongly in favour of it, and something is said of the English Catholics wishing me to bring on their claims ; with respect to this last circumstance, I shall know more in a few days. If the thing is to be done, Grey will come to move it. I have heard nothing more since I wrote to you, except that the invasion is to be this week or the next. Did you see the Moniteur's observations on the King's Speech ? They were in the Morning Chronicle about ten days or a fortnight ago, and are excellent."

" St. Ann's Hill, *Friday*."

TO MR. O'BRIEN.

" St. Ann's Hill, *January 22nd*, 1804.

"DEPEND on it, there is no truth in any treaty at present—(I mean these last nine months)—with Pitt or for Pitt.* I suspect there *is* foundation for what Cobbett says of his concealment; indeed, I always thought the confidence among the resigners was partial; certainly neither Lord Spencer or Windham were completely trusted, still less Lord Cornwallis or Lord Castlereagh : I think it equally certain that Dundas *was;* with respect to Lord Grenville, I should

---

* Mr. Fox was quite mistaken. See Life of Lord Sidmouth.

think it most doubtful. I suspect there were shades and degrees, and that he was less trusted than Dundas, and more than the others; but of all this more when we meet. At present, I can only guess at these things; I may by-and-by know more, but it is more matter of curiosity than of interest."

TO GENERAL FITZPATRICK.

"*January* 27*th*, 1804.

" Dear Dick,

"I thought to have heard from you before now, but should nevertheless have written if I had come to any determination concerning the Irish business. I hear George Ponsonby says to others that it is only delay which he recommends, but I have not yet had his promised letter, nor have I yet had what I shortly expect, an account of Lord Fingal's wishes upon the occasion; so I should naturally remain upon this point in the same irresolution as when I wrote last. But in the meantime a proposition has been made to me, concerning which it is expected I should give an answer, and indeed the fairness and openness with which it has been made entitles the makers of it to explicitness on my part. I have a message by our old friend T. G.,* from his family and friends, stating their wish to co-operate with me (and friends, of course) in a systematic opposition for the purpose of destroying the Doctor's Administration, and

* Mr. Thomas Grenville.

of substituting in its place one upon the most comprehensive basis possible. The first object (first in
point of time) is to oppose the bill which Ministers
are to bring in on the Volunteer business, and to
propose a general system of arming the people upon
the principles I approve, reducing the Militia to its
old quantum, putting an end to bidding for substitutes
&c., with many details which I am to see. When I
say this is the first in point of time, I ought to observe
that so it appears to me, for *they* stated a doubt
whether some inquiry relative to the 23rd of July, to
be moved by some friend of ours, might not precede
everything. I mention this to show that there is no
point of precedence as to which wing should begin
the attacks; but to return, some inquiry into the
management of foreign politics is also suggested, and
more particularly if the war with Spain takes place, of
which I much doubt. Ireland and the Catholics are
left to my judgment. Upon their connection with
Pitt, I understand them to be quite explicit; that it
is over, and that his opinions are no further to be
considered or looked to, than in a prudential view
with respect to the questions in which he might or
not join us. P. and Lord G. have had full explanations; the same proposal was made to him as is now
made to me. His answer was, that the present
Ministry is weak and inadequate to the crisis; that
their dismission will be a benefit to the country; that
in case of such an event an Administration should be
formed upon the broadest possible basis; that if
His Majesty were on such an occasion to send for him,

he should think it right to endeavour to comprehend
in the arrangement all parties, and even those who
had been most hostile to him; (N.B. This tallies exactly
with what we heard before;) that in many points he
would support the new Opposition if it took place, but
that he was *determined* not to engage either with
Ministers or their opponents systematically. In short
he could not be what is called *in Opposition.* He
hinted too that these men might probably die of their
own weakness, an opinion too absurd I think for him
to entertain seriously. The truth seems to be that he
cannot give up the hope of being in some way
acceptable at Court;* like Sancho he cannot quite give
up his hopes of the island, in which however he has
no faith whatever. As to measures he seems, as I am
told, not averse to the measure of new modelling
Volunteers', Military Defence, &c., but is against
inquiry into the 23rd of July, as that is a *retrospec-
tive* measure. And this I think will be the rule of his
conduct. He will oppose Ministers in cases where
there is a pretence to say, we are suggesting better
measures *to be* pursued, but oppose inquiries as their
object is to censure the past, rather than to provide
for the future. *Censures lead to removals, removal is
the King's prerogative :* mind, however, this reasoning
is what I impute to him, not what he avowed. If the
report is true, that Ministers are to bring in a
Declaratory Bill, justifying the Attorney-General's
opinion, and of course condemning Erskine's, it would

---

* This remark resembles one which Burke made on Lord Chatham :—
"A peep into that closet intoxicates him."

be the best possible opportunity of commencing operations. Erskine would not only be safe with us, but furious, and the more so as he says the whole bar or nearly is with him ; and even Sheridan will not like to take a part which will be generally considered as hostile to the liberty of the volunteers ; of course Tierney and the Southwark volunteers *entreront en jeu.* In short, it would be a better question for us than any we could devise, if we had a friend to advise the Doctor for us. But though this report is universally credited, and though it is difficult for anything to be too foolish for the Doctor, I confess I doubt it very much, and the more so because I see in to day's paper, that Erskine has got a *certiorari* by which means the question will shortly come before the King's Bench. However, if they do not bring a Declaratory Bill, they will certainly bring in *some* bill, which will be distasteful to a great number of the volunteers, relative to the *election* of officers, *fines for absence, &c.*

" My answer was that, I thought with them upon all the subjects discussed, and that I felt no repugnance to agree to the proposal, at least in some degree, but that I must have some days before I could answer. Now what is your advice ? If Grey would come to town to stay and engage heartily, (of which, if he would come, I have no doubt,) perhaps it would be right to say *yes*, perhaps it is *right* even now. But the inconvenience is terrible, for to do the thing thoroughly without a stay in London is impossible, and then expense, interruption to history, &c. &c.,

where after all there is no chance of success; it is very hard to encounter all this. Suppose I were to answer that I will give them all occasional help in my power, but that I cannot alter my plan of life so as to give a regular attendance in Parliament, and that I am afraid Grey can hardly be induced to come up. I must finish now, though I have omitted several circumstances, and among others a very important one, that our old friend * sees the possibility, nay the probability, that if we succeed in ousting the Doctor, P. may return to power, and after having proposed terms in vain to some of the *Opposition*, may put himself at the head of the present Administration, or one like it, and this is admitted to be an objection to the plan. I do not feel this so much as he does, but many others will.†

　　　　　　　" Yours affectionately,

　　　　　　　　　　　　　　" C. J. F.

" St. Ann's Hill, *Friday.*"

TO SAME.

　　　　　　　" *January 28th*, 1804.

" I was interrupted in my letter yesterday, and have an opportunity of sending this to London, so I will add a little supplement, the most material part of which is to say, pray come as soon as you can. Mrs. F. says I should say nothing but *come, come, come*, and she would say it down on her knees. You know she thinks there is no adviser but you. Pray by return of post say when you come exactly. I

* Mr. Thomas Grenville.　　　† It is exactly what happened.

should have mentioned yesterday, that our friend was very distinct as to the persons who were parties to the proposal—*i.e.* all of his own name and family, Lord Spencer, Windham, &c. He had seen Carlisle, and he was much for it, and thought he could answer for Morpeth. Of Fitzwilliam, of course, there could be no doubt. He knew nothing of Canning or Lord Granville,* but rather guessed that Lord Stafford would hang off with Pitt; of Lord Melville he knows no more than we do. He thinks that *if* Pitt offered to stay in without Catholic Emancipation, (and by what I hear of Charles Long's pamphlet, that *if*, is now a certainty,) he concealed the circumstance from *all* his colleagues, except Dundas. I hear Cobbett asserts this positively. You and I, you know, always suspected some concealment, but such a circumstance as this, and concealed from Lord Grenville too! *quel homme!* adieu, write and come.

" Yours affectionately,
" C. J. FOX.

" St. Ann's Hill, *Saturday*."

TO D. O'BRIEN, ESQ.

" *January 29th*, 1804.

" I do think, as Perry does, that Publicus † comes from some friends of Pitt's, but among the different sections, which is entitled to the appellation of bosom friends, I know not; my opinion is, that he is a man incapable of reposing thorough confidence in any

---

* Lord Granville Leveson Gower, afterwards Earl Granville.

† A letter in the "Public Advertiser" with that signature.

friend. I dare say he did not see it himself, but I have good reason to believe that he would approve far the greater part of the letter. I rather think if he had looked it over, he would have erased the incivility to me, and put the question more upon the impropriety of his going into Opposition at all, than upon the associates he was to engage with in such a business ; but perhaps I am too candid. Rose and his creatures are the set of P.'s friends who have, I believe, most to say to the ' True Briton,' and are, besides, those from whom such sentiments as those of Publicus are most likely to come. I have reason to believe the meeting you heard of between P. and Lord Grenville was *political*, but not with the view you heard.* I suspect it was for the purpose of a final explanation, before they took their different roads, and that Lord G. is very much dissatisfied. P. will not go into Opposition systematically, though he means to take opportunities of discrediting the Doctor, while the other, on the contrary, wishes to make and join in as extensive and systematical an Opposition as can be formed. It will, therefore, I think, be shortly understood, that all political connection between them is over. Mind all this is in confidence, though I hope and believe it will soon be known. What part will be taken by Canning and his (friends), I have no guess, though I know their inclination is for action, but whether or not they will have leave, remains to be seen. They say that P. has a notion that these Ministers must go, and that, in that case, he may

---

* See "Courts and Cabinets," &c. vol. iii. p. 342.

return to power, without the odium at Court of
having been in Opposition; I cannot think he
can be weak enough to have such a hope, " but Love
will hope where reason would despair," and Sancho
Panza could never quite give up the idea of his island
after he had discovered the vanity and illusion of his
master's plan.   It is certain that, *if* he offered to stay
in without Catholic Emancipation, the offer was concealed from all his colleagues except Dundas.   I say
if, because I am told the pamphlet does not make
that point so clear as you suppose ; I have, however,
no doubt of the fact nor ever had."

TO GENERAL FITZPATRICK.

" *February* 24*th,* 1804.

" I suppose the system of sliding, as you call it,
into a junction must be adopted, but you must
recollect that one great advantage is lost by that
method, I mean that it puts an end to that decisive
disconnection with Pitt, which the other mode would
nail.   Besides, in cases where he joins them (as I
suppose he will in the course of the Volunteer Bill)
they will appear rather following him than us.   But
it cannot be helped—whatever prejudices Plumer and
other good men may have, surely they must see that
in case of junction, we have so very decisively the
lead in the House of Commons, that there can be no
doubt upon that point.

" Yours, affectionately,

"C. J. F.

" *Friday.*"

TO SAME.

"February 25th, 1804.

" DEAR DICK,

"I shall be in town Monday, and at the House, though there will be probably nothing to do there. I hope I shall see Lord Grenville on Tuesday, and then I shall be able to tell my friends (pretty unreasonable friends they are) something of the matter. I have a letter from Whitbread, and it will probably be as he wishes, but do not you see that by this mode, the objection (which others lay more stress on than I do), of Pitt's taking advantage, gains tenfold strength? He can, in this case, (if the King will let him,) come in with just as many, or as few, of his old colleagues as he chooses, and they will have no motive to withhold them from following him. If a real junction had taken place, he must be driven to the alternative of coming in with the present men, or not at all. That there should be some divisions and debates previous to any regular junction may be right, but if it does not take place no good can be done, " nor if it does " you may answer, and I cannot easily reply ; but one likes to have done for the best. I think the style of this letter will sufficiently inform you that Mrs. F. is quite well again.

"Yours affectionately,

"C. J. F.

" Saturday morning."

TO THE EARL OF LAUDERDALE.

"*March 15th*, 1804.

"Dear Lauderdale,

"I write to you as you desire it, though I have little worth communicating. The K. is, I believe, recovering, but certainly not recovered as yet. They go on just as if he was as well as ever, and for the present this is endured without any very general impatience. That it will be long so endured, I can hardly believe, because even now, and much more a fortnight ago, I have perceived what appear to me to be symptoms of some dissatisfaction upon this head. That the Ministers will venture everything for their places, I always believed, and it now seems certain. Three years ago, after the K. had recovered sufficiently to invest them in their offices, it is known, and now scarcely disavowed, that he had a severe relapse, and was for weeks at Kew, in such a state as neither to see Ministers or family; and yet these very men, from whose timidity so much is expected, ventured to conceal this relapse, and even to deny it, and went on just as if nothing had happened! The K. is now, I really believe, much better than he has been, as far as quiet and composure go, but I suspect they are as much afraid as ever of letting him see his family, or talking to him of any real business.

" Grey went on Tuesday, and I think I shall go on Sunday, but to come back for a day if there is anything more before Easter. You will perceive that the Doctor is much weaker in numbers than one could

have imagined, but it looks as if this was not so
much owing to our strength, as to speculations among
their friends concerning the K., and Pitt's ambiguous situation.   However, it has this good effect, that
it makes him (the Doctor) more and more contemned
every day; indeed the contempt, both with respect to
the degree and universality of it, is beyond what was
ever known.   Not *one* unpaid defender, unless you
reckon Dallas, who is impatient for the Solicitor-
Generalship.   It is not merely old partiality that
makes me say that your brother has been by far his
best man.   Sheridan will appear for him to-day in
the Admiralty business, in which Ld. St. V. has been
so ill-advised as to refuse papers and thus to force me
and others to vote what will be called against him.
If he had granted the papers, Pitt must have moved
a vote of censure, and the division would have been
in every respect, both with respect to names and
numbers and also to the nature of the question, far
more honourable and satisfactory to him.   I am not
sure that Sheridan is not the cause of this for the
purpose of giving him the opportunity of making a
speech, he has a fancy for making.   Ld. Holland's
arm was broken on the 6th of February, and there
are letters from Ly. Holland as late as the 21st,
saying it has been set perfectly well, and that everything goes on rightly.   As to the Paris news, I know
nothing more than what you see in the papers.   It
seems incredible that Moreau should have ventured on
such a bottom, but I am afraid he has.   I have great
curiosity to hear more.   Now I have despatched the

general topics, let me tell you that I have read all you
have sent me of your book, but I am sorry to say
that I am confirmed in my opinion respecting the
science.* Your refutations are almost always satisfactory, but not so to my mind your own theories;
and after all, on the particular point of paying off
debt, the most you do is making it a question merely
of degree, and what ground is there for fixing the
point beyond which it is mischievous? If Sir R.
Walpole was right, that in his time we could bear the
operation of a million, surely on the face of the thing
six millions would not be too much now, but the
whole of your reasoning on this point appears to me
to be very uncertain. I should like to argue it with
you in talk, but in writing it is too much trouble;
yet I am not sure that I shall not try. The part
I agree most with you in, is the statement of the
means by which capital operates in the production and
increase of wealth. I never saw that point so intelligibly stated before."

TO SAME.

March 25th, 1804.

"Dear Lauderdale,

"When I said it was a question of degree,
I did not mean that I admitted all sinking funds to
be evils in a more tolerable, or a more intolerable
degree, but that there might be a degree of sinking
fund which is useful, a greater which is tolerable, and

* Political Economy. This letter and the next refer to Lord Lauderdale's work on Public Wealth. See Vol. iii. p. 241.

possibly a still greater might be mischievous; mind,
I only say *possibly*, because you give no proof that as
yet any degree of it has been injurious. You show
indeed, that it had great effect in lowering interest,
but the lowering of interest being attended with
the increase of canals, inclosures, &c., is a strong
presumption the other way. It is impossible without writing volumes, to carry on this controversy by
letter; but I may just observe that your proposition
that parsimony cannot increase national wealth
appears to me wholly unproved. If parsimony can
accumulate capital, and capital is one of the sources
of wealth, surely that which increases the source *may*
(I do not say necessarily does) increase through that
medium the wealth derived from such source. You
admit that in some cases it has the effect, viz., if you
lessened your consumption for the purposes of
furnishing the country with spades, ploughs, &c.,
where implements of this sort are not in sufficient
abundance. Why not, therefore, in increasing other
species of capital? It may be true that there is a
point beyond which accumulation of capital may be
hurtful, though, by the way, I know of no instance
where it ever was so. If there is a superabundance
of capital it may be exported, you say, to France;
but have you shown that this would be an evil? and
have you not rather meanly mentioned this export to
France *ad captandum?* One of my grand objections
to this most nonsensical of all sciences is that none
of its definitions are to me intelligible. Your notions
(I do not mean yours only, but *vous autres*,) of value

seem to me to be stark nonsense. You use that as a positive term which never can be other than a relative term. We grammarians are much wiser; we say a thing is valuable, *i. e.*, capable of being valued or compared to some other thing. But we have no substantive to express value; we say such a thing is worth a shilling, or a pot of porter, &c., &c. I am very much in another place for preferring the French economists, who deduct the subsistence of the labourer from his produce, nor do I think any of you have answered them upon that point. I still approve highly your account of the manner in which capital operates, but I accept your defiance of denying the consequences you think follow. If capital should be increased beyond the possibility of applying it to the supplying the place of labour, what you say *might* be true (but even then it *might not*, as I will some day dispute with you,) but you must show that such is the case of the particular country to which you apply your reasoning. With respect to our own, it is a common expression, you say, that such a field has had all done for it that can be done; but with respect to how many fields and acres is this true, and where it is not true, does there not appear *primá facie* at least an unsatisfied demand for capital? That an increased produce of the land would increase national wealth, you are not yet so far gone in paradox as to deny; that increase of capital reduces interest is not denied either. He who borrows money to cultivate land must take into his calculation the rate of interest he is to pay, and consequently, the lower the interest the better he can afford to borrow for his agricultural enterprise ; which might answer at three per cent., and not at five per cent., and this reasoning is equally applicable to commercial enterprise. In short, I have nothing but doubts upon almost all your propositions, except that which I have mentioned. I cannot leave this subject without noticing your constant use of the word *supplant* where we should say *supply the place of* or *be a substitute* for. I remarked it the more because it occurred to me how unfortunate it would be, if, in recommending a Regency, you should have said that your intention was to *supplant* the personal exercise of the royal functions. This leads me to another part of your letter; I think of the King's health just as I did; and my reason for thinking it possible that some impatient symptoms will appear is this, that when he was generally believed to be very ill, impatience did appear ; that impatience has subsided, because there is a pretty general opinion that he is nearly well, and will, in a very short time, be quite so. When these hopes shall be disappointed, and we recur to the same state that we were in a month ago,—*i. e.*, that there is little hope of an efficient K. being to be soon produced, the same symptoms of impatience may reappear. However, this is all very uncertain speculation, and I shall not be surprised to find myself quite mistaken. I think we were wrong not to take up the question. My opinion for taking it up remained unchanged ; but I found the idea that Pitt would try, and succeed in making a violent

cry against us, had so strong an effect on many of
our friends that we could not have done it with any
heart or unanimity.   I think the only opinions that
were with me for action were those of Carlisle, Fitzwilliam, and T. Grenville, to some of which I know
you think much weight ought not to be given;
to these *I believe* (for he was not present) I might
add Lord Spencer; on the other hand, of our new
friends, Lord Grenville and Windham, and most of
our old ones, particularly Whitbread, were very much
for inaction, and Grey, though still of my opinion in
regard to what was right, grew every hour to think
it more inexpedient.   The P. wished something to
be done, and Moira would have supported us, but I
am convinced Sheridan would not; indeed, in order
to avoid being brought to the point, he strongly
dissuaded our moving at that time, though I suspect
he has since represented this matter somewhat
differently at Carlton House.

" As to general politics, my opinion is that things
will remain as they are for some time, though
Addington's friends say he means to go out as soon
as the K. is well enough to appoint a successor.   I
utterly disbelieve this; but I do suspect that the
Doctor has said as much, and the lamentable faces of
Tierney, and some others, seem to give credit to the
report.   After Easter I shall bring in some questions
myself, of which I will write at large to Grey in a
few days.   My guess is that Pitt will support me in
some and not in others, but he does not know
always his own mind, and much less can his friends

answer for him. His temper makes him more and more in Opposition, whatever his intentions may be. I suspect he has treated Castlereagh roughly ; but he (C.) will bear anything. The Doctor has exceeded, if possible, all his former lies in what he said about the Russian business. It is, I own, an ignoble chase, but I should have great pleasure in hunting down this vile fellow."

TO D. O'BRIEN, ESQ.

"ST. ANN'S HILL, *March 27th*, 1804.

" THE Doctor outdid his usual outdoings in his lie the other day on the subject of the Russian business. On the 22nd of November, he told me upon his legs distinctly, that the objection to the producing of the negociation consisted in circumstances which he expected to be of a temporary nature, and when they were over he should be happy to give me and the House the information which it was so natural that we should desire. He now says that he did indeed say that there were temporary circumstances which precluded him from giving the information then, but that he had added (then, on the 22nd November,) that even when those circumstances should no longer exist, it would not be the opinion, or at least it would be very doubtful whether it would be the opinion of the K.'s Ministers that the information should be given. Every person whom I have asked, is clear that he said no such thing, but nearly the contrary, as I have stated above : " That he should

be very happy when difficulties were removed," &c.
Now, how to convict him? I understand there are
coffee-houses where files are kept of all the principal
newspapers. These I wish to be examined, and to
have extracted out of them the account of the
Doctor's speech. I am not without hope that as
the speech was short, they may all agree in favour of
my statement of it; at any rate I should like to see.
The most material papers of course, will be those
most devoted to Ministry, "Times," "Morning Post,"
&c., but the more testimonies can be had, the
better." *

TO R. ADAIR, ESQ.

"*March*, 1804.

" DEAR ADAIR,

"I will be at the house to-morrow, and
will write by post to Windham, to apprise him of
my intention, but I write by the coach to you, in
order that there may be time to settle this future
business, if possible, before I leave the House ; but at
all events before I leave town on Friday morning,
which I shall do as early as I can. I am very
desirous of making some general motion, but my
difficulty is to frame one which will not in some view
be objectionable to Pitt. The state of the nation I

---

* "Tom asked me, and seemed to expect that I should learn from my
visitor, what the Doctor's mysterious declaration, in answer to Fox's
question, could possibly mean? It meant, as usual with the Doctor's
mysteries, nothing at all, and the whole assertion was, as is no less usual
with the Doctor's assertions, a lie."—Lord Grenville to the Marquis of
Buckingham, January 5, 1804. "Courts and Cabinets," vol. iii. p. 343.

should like best, directing my view to the defence of
the country, to the state of Ireland, to the state of
foreign politics, and to the personal exercise of the
royal functions, if the state of the K.'s health should
make that an object.   But I have heard it whispered
that Mr. Pitt's repeated opposition to the state of the
nation on former occasions might make that question
unpalatable to him.   The defence of the country alone
would not do, the naval defence having been already
taken up, and the land defence so repeatedly touched
upon on the Volunteer Bill, &c.   *Ireland* is an object
full large enough to be considered by itself, but of
that subject it is necessary to premise that the Catholic
question makes a principal part.   *Foreign politicks*,
though, God knows, a most important question, are
not at present in that sort of state, as to afford the
ground of any direct motion of importance.   The
chief blame with respect to them, except perhaps
some misconduct with regard to Hanover, with which I
am very imperfectly acquainted, is that the war was
unnecessarily made upon such a ground as to exclude
all hopes of assistance.   To this I should add at such
a time too,—I mean so early that Austria, whatever
your cause might be, was not sufficiently prepared to
engage with you.

" These things being so, I do not see what general
motion I can bring on, except the state of the nation
or Ireland.   I had once thought of an address to
request H. M. to take measures for increasing the
army, and a more general arming of the people ; but
the first of these objects is precluded by the two

pending propositions of Mr. Yorke and Mr. Pitt, and
the second alone will hardly do, as the fact may be
that there are no arms for the people. The result of
all this is that my present intention is to move soon
after the holidays a state of the nation, unless I hear
objections to that motion, and at the same time learn
that the same objections will not lie against some
other of the kind, Ireland for instance, or unless
some other be suggested to which I on my part have
no objection. The K.'s health of course is a separate
question, which must depend upon circumstances, and
which according to those circumstances may or may
not be thought necessary to take place of every other.
Now as to the time, I think it must be soon after
Easter, suppose the 12th; certainly I think not later
than Monday the 16th of April. The shortest public
notice is the best, but yet I think that public notice
must be given before the holidays—the very last day
will do. If you can find an opportunity of talking
this over with Lord Granville Leveson, or Canning, pray do, and there is nothing in this letter
which I wish to be kept from them. We shall meet
of course in the House, and it would be desirable that
I should be able to give private notice to as many
friends as I can see to-morrow, either at the House of
Commons or at Brooks's.

" Yours,

"C. J. F.

"St. Ann's Hill, Wednesday."

TO THE EARL OF LAUDERDALE.

"March 30*th,* 1804.

" I HEAR that several friends in Scotland are very violent against what they call my junction with the Grenvilles, and that they say you have declared you will never more take part in politics. I hope and believe the account is exaggerated with regard to you. You are unfortunately not now in a situation to be called upon to take any very active part in politics, therefore why determine ? and much more, why declare for the future ? All I can say is, that if you were to adhere to this supposed declaration, I must cut and run too ; for reduced as we have been, you and Grey are all that, for certain purposes, is left ; I might perhaps add Whitbread. My only objection to what has passed is that it was not junction enough. Can there be less of connection between persons who agree on particular questions, and in their hostility to Ministry, than that which consists only in such concert as is necessary to give their debates and divisions what strength they can ?

" I hear the K. has been much worse again, but my accounts are probably exaggerated. I dare say you agree with me in thinking the Doctor will not go out spontaneously, but perhaps you will not agree with me when I say there is a chance of his being forced out. What then ? you'll say. Why then there is an inroad upon the power of the real enemy, I mean the Court, happen what may afterwards. Give me for once a little credit; I am sure we are going as right as in the untoward circumstances of the time is possible. The worst would have been (and I believe you apprehended and perhaps still apprehend that it may happen), if the Doctor and P. had been reconciled, and the latter had come in by favour. I think that is now hardly possible. We have not heard anything here of Lord Melville's sentiments and language."

TO SAME.

"*April 2nd*, 1804.

"I HAVE read your fifth chapter, and like it by far the best; perhaps it is partly owing to my being refreshed by a passage of Xenophon amid all the scientific gibberish; but, seriously, I do like it far the best of any in the book; and think you have a complete triumph over A. Smith's division of labour : but of all this when I have more leisure.

"I think exactly as you do about the plot and ou. guilt, if (which I cannot doubt) we are concerned in it.* I rather suspect you over refine' on the conduct of the Doctor last year. When we believed he was inclined to peace we were imposed upon, not by our informant, but he was deceived by the Doctor. The truth seems to be, that the moment the Doctor found that the K.'s madness took the turn of wishing war against Bonaparte, he was determined to humour that on which his sole existence depended, viz., the K.'s madness. Now all the papers

---

* The royalist plot of Georges and his accomplices. Our government does not appear to have been concerned in it.

are before the public, you must observe that at the times when we were fools enough to believe in his pacific intentions, there never appears to have been one conciliatory expression, much less any instance of conciliatory conduct to the Consul. The reports are that the K. is much worse, and I think that question must come on. I shall always regret that we lost the best opportunity, which was that of the first exercise of the Royal function in the state in which he then was. I have a strong notion these men will act most desperately, but it will be impossible for us to submit quietly much longer. I hope to God, Grey will come ; and if you could without great inconvenience come too, it would be an excellent deed. Though out of Parliament you would not be out of Counsel, and in this case, perhaps, that is the most important place of the two. I have a great notion that if you had been with us we should not have acted so pusillanimously as we did."

TO SAME.

" April 3rd, 1804.

" Dear Lauderdale,

" Since I wrote yesterday I have received yours, and write a line because I think I did not say so much about the Paris plot as you would expect, and as I had intended. You cannot feel more indignation at it than I do ; and if there comes out any ground for supposing the Ministers encouraged it, I am for making a question of it, let who

will support or oppose me.   Of the distinction
between seizing forcibly and assassinating, I think
(in this case at least) as contemptibly as you do.   I
can CONCEIVE cases where there is a distinction,
possibly, but this is certainly not one of them.   I
am very sorry indeed Moira said what he did to you,
but I am inclined to believe he said more than he
knew, not perhaps more than he thought he knew.
I am still in hopes (not very well grounded hopes,
I admit) that Moreau is not so much implicated as
is said; and I learn that this is a very general
opinion at Paris.   He I believe once said, speaking of
his own safety, ' *Bonaparte est tyran, mais pas
assassin.*'   One would hardly think that he meant
to say he would show him the difference.   Is it not
possible that he may have had that sort of share in
this plot, that Russell, Essex, &c., had in the Ryehouse-Plot,—that is, supposing the Ryehouse-Plot
ever to have had an existence?   I have no time
to dispute with you on your book, but I cannot help
thinking that if a nation having a stock of wine,
instead of drinking it, changes it against ships to
carry on trade, or any other capital of that value,
such nation becomes more wealthy by such an act
of parsimony."

TO GENERAL FITZPATRICK.

"*April 3rd*, 1804.

"DEAR DICK,

        "I write now, though I have not positively
fixed the days for my different motions, to tell you

that I consider the campaign as opening on the 16th, and that we are sparing no pains to get all the attendance we can. I believe the other parts of the Opposition are doing the same, and it is very material, not only that we should be strong as a mass, but that our part should appear as considerable as may be.

" The accounts of the King are, I am told, very bad ; and I think in some shape *that* business must come on, perhaps sooner than the 16th. I go to town the 10th, to No. 9, Arlington Street.

" Yours affectionately,

"C. J. F.

"St. Ann's Hill, *Monday*."

TO THE EARL OF LAUDERDALE.

" *April 9th*, 1804.

"I had your letter yesterday. I should have thought you had lived long enough in the world not to be much surprised at a false report. One does not like to mention one's authors, however innocent we may think them of the original lie ; but I will say this much, that what I heard was from Scotland, and not in London. Your brother is so far from saying anything about you that he is often asking me news about you. I do not deny the truth of the objection *you* state to this junction, but it applies to all junctions of the kind, and would, if attended to, make all resistance to the Crown more impossible even than as it is. No strong confederacy since the Restoration, perhaps not before, ever did exist without the accession of obnoxious persons : Shaftesbury, Buckingham,

&c., in Charles II.'s time; Danby and many others at the time of the Revolution; after the Revolution many more, and even Sunderland himself. In our times, first the Grenvilles with Lord Rockingham, and afterwards Lord North with us. I know this last instance is always quoted against us because we were ultimately unsuccessful; but after all that can be said, it will be difficult to show when the power of the Whigs ever made so strong a struggle against the Crown, the Crown being thoroughly in earnest and exerting all its resources. In what you say of the hardship suffered in Scotland by our supporters I agree entirely with you, and that neither of us can come in with honour without obtaining redress for them. Whether such redress may be obtained by a partial instead of a thorough *overturn* of the present arrangements is a question upon which you can judge better than I. If we were to come in *with* Pitt, a partial overturn is probably all that could be obtained, and how far that would do would be for our consideration before we engaged; but if without Pitt, there could be no difficulty in a thorough overturn, for all the rest of our new allies are as adverse to Dundas as we are, or more. By the way, you have never told me what language he holds, or what he is at. I do not think Lord Dalkeith has ever voted with us. You think that the Court cannot now be forced; remember, all I have said is that there is a *chance* that it may; Pitt's utter incapacity to act like a man renders that chance much less than it would otherwise be."

TO THE HONOURABLE C. GREY.

"ARLINGTON STREET, 17th April, 1804.

" DEAR GREY,

"I write on the supposition that you are not coming. When I think of the extreme inconvenience to you of coming, I cannot be sorry that you stay; but I foresee events, which, if they should happen, will make me more regret your absence than ever. However, if things take the turn I augur, you may perhaps bring Mrs. Grey early in the next month, as I hear Mrs. Ponsonby is coming, and (you) would wish to meet her in London. The event I allude to is a speedy discomfiture of the Doctor; our division last night was 107 to 128,* and *IF* Pitt plays fair, we shall run him very hard indeed on my motion, and in one or two more probably give him his death blow, unless he runs away first. Now if this happens, it must of course follow that negotiations and propositions will take place, in which to act quite alone and without you will be distressing to me in the extreme. If Lauderdale were here it would be something. You will say there is Whitbread and Fitzpatrick, and that is a great deal; but there are cases where those who are to take the most active parts in case of arrangements are everything. I have not written my *IF* in great letters for nothing; and yet I rather think it will be right. As you are so far off I may let you into the secret, that my motion may probably, at

---

* On the Irish Militia Augmentation Bill, 16th April, 1804.—See Parliamentary Debates.

Pitt's earnest request (for reasons foolish and fanciful beyond belief), be put off till Monday, so that if you did think of coming, you would not be too late. It is impossible not to suspect Pitt from his ways of proceeding, and yet his interest is so evident, that I think he will do right. I defer the article " Sheridan " till another letter, only he is absurd as ever, to say no worse.

" Yours affectionately,

" C. J. FOX.

" The Grenvilles seem as steady and honourable as possible. What I have seen of Lord G. particularly confirms me in my opinion that he is a very direct man."

TO THE HONOURABLE C. GREY.

" ARLINGTON STREET, April 18th, 1804.

" DEAR GREY,

" P. sends me word that he hears the Doctor is determined to go in to the King and tell him he cannot go on, and to advise H. M. to send for Mr. P. to hear his ideas. P. seems to believe this, but agrees that it is no reason against our proceeding in our parliamentary measures. He likewise says that if it does happen, the first thing he shall say is, that he must communicate H. M.'s intentions to Lord Grenville and me, for the purpose of forming arrangements or consultation with us. I tell you all this just as his messenger Lord Gr. Leveson told it me an hour ago. I disbelieve the intelligence P. has had, for many reasons : 1st, the Doctor said the same as to his resigning, just after the division on the admiralty business, and so, I believe, did Tierney too : 2ndly, I doubt very much, whether he would, even in case of resigning, say anything in favour of P.'s being sent for, against whom I really believe, he feels all possible resentment : but 3rdly, and principally, I cannot believe the King to be in a state in which he would venture to make any proposition of the sort to him. It is certain that though better he is not well : that Doctor S. constantly attends him, and is present at his interviews with the Queen and his children. I therefore completely disbelieve the whole story; and the more so, because I can easily see reasons which might induce Lord Castlereagh and others to mislead P. on this subject. Lord Hawkesbury is said to be going off from the Doctor, but though this is generally reported, I know not on what foundation.

"I am afraid I shall be obliged to put off my motion till Monday, and that some of our friends will dislike the postponement, but it cannot be helped— and Monday at any rate it *shall* come on. Everything looks as if what I said in my yesterday's letter was right, and the Doctor will soon be done for, though for the reasons I have given, I disbelieve in his immediate resignation. I understand there is expectation of a great division against him to-morrow in the House of Lords. I should write my *if* in rather smaller letters to-day, but there is still an *if* upon the subject of P.

"Yours ever most affectionately,
"C. J. FOX."

TO THE SAME.

"Arlington Street, *Thursday, April 19th,* 1804.

"Dear Grey,

"I have to-day received yours of the 16th. As to your coming while Mrs. Grey's health is such as to give you any uneasiness, I am sure you will not suspect me of such a wish, for I hope I have pretty well adhered to a rule which I have always prescribed to myself, of not asking a friend to do what in similar circumstances I should myself refuse. I write to-day, chiefly because I have seen Lord Grenville, who gives me somewhat a different account from that given me yesterday by Lord G. L. I understood the latter that it was only *intelligence,* or at most an *intimation* that P. had received. I understand from Lord G. to-day that it was a *message* to which Pitt was to give an answer; and his answer was that if the K. sent for him *directly,* or through a *proper person,* meaning to exclude Addington, he would state his notions. With regard to what those notions are, they were stated to be pretty much the same as I heard yesterday from Lord G. L. Only I understood pretty distinctly from Lord G. to day, that if P. found H. M. impracticable upon the idea of an extended administration, he (P.) should feel himself bound to try one by himself. These were not the words, but nearly the substance, and exactly the same idea that we heard through the Duchess, of his having expressed to some of his friends before you left town. However, he (P.) agrees that our parliamentary measures must go on with the same vigour as if no such message had been brought him, and this is all I care for. Let the event be what it may, it is good to force the K. to change; and as to any arrangement in conjunction with Pitt, I see and feel the difficulties (amounting nearly to an impossibility) more and more every day. He is not a man capable of acting fairly, and on a footing of equality with his equals. Lord G. confirmed to me the extraordinary fact of Pitt never having told him of his offer to continue without Catholic Emancipation, in the year 1801. This subject, by the way, was one on which Lord G. wished to know my opinion, how far I thought it possible to make a Government without the Emancipation. I told him in perfect confidence what you and I have often agreed upon; that, *if* there was a Ministry cordially united on giving the Catholics substantial relief, and their full share (as far as the law will allow) in the government of the country, I thought some consideration, as far at least as delay went, might be had of the King's prejudices, especially in his present state. After all this I still disbelieve the intention of the Doctor to resign immediately, and though the K. is (I believe) a good deal better this week, I have no notion of his being well enough for the manœuvre. I began this letter five hours ago, and shall hardly be time enough for the post: but I have told you I think all that is material.

" Yours affectionately,

"C. J. FOX."

TO LORD GRENVILLE.*

"*April 20th,* 1804.

"My Dear Lord,

          "I will endeavour to have five minutes
conversation with you to day at the House of Lords,
but in case I should not have the opportunity, I must
trouble you with a few thoughts on what passed
between us yesterday. What I said, I meant to say
in perfect confidence, and not to go further than us
two. But upon recollection, I fear you must have
understood that it might be repeated to Mr. Pitt.
What I should wish to have said to him is, that the
inclination of my mind is to think Catholic Emancipation
absolutely necessary ; but that I am willing to consider
of the possibility of temporising, whenever by a *full*
knowledge of *all* the circumstances with which such
temporising is proposed to be accompanied, I shall be
enabled to give that question a fair consideration.
The concomitant circumstances must indeed be very
favourable to induce me to think even delay ad-
missible in this business. You will observe that
there is nothing in this answer inconsistent with what
I said to you in confidence, but it is something
different, and the difference appears to me to be not
immaterial. Upon the subject itself, the frankness you
have shown, in the short intercourse we have had
together, encourages me to take the liberty of suggesting some considerations which more immediately

---

* See Letter to Lord Grey, in which a copy of this was enclosed.

concern your Lordship, Lord Spencer, and Mr. Windham. In an administration under a Regent, the delay
of a measure, the discussion of which that Regent
might think likely to retard the returning health of his
father, would carry with (it) its own excuse in the
judgment of all reasonable men. But if in the present
circumstances you should consent to yield the very
point on which you resigned three years ago, will it
not be a submission on your part to the K. liable to
the worst construction? and when by such submission
you may have lost your public ground, how will it be
in your power to resist afterwards with success? The
removal of Lord Redesdale may be stipulated, but,
after that removal, there will be many measures, nay,
a constant succession of measures, necessary to operate
as a substitute for the Emancipation. If you are
thwarted in any of these, shall you not be almost
hopeless? Will you go out again? Will you not be
met then everywhere by the observation that so they
did before, and, after having taken their time, returned,
and so they will do again? This reasoning does not
apply in the same manner to me, because, if I were to
go out, in such a case, my conduct, I not having been
concerned in the former resignation, would not be
liable to such observations. If I have made this
statement with some freedom, I am sure you can
attribute my doing it to nothing but to that regard
which I always must feel for the honour and interest
of those with whom I am likely to be connected,
whether in administration or in opposition. Now, on
the other side, if you were to stand out on the

Emancipation, in which of course I should join you, and if Mr. Pitt, without any of us, should form an administration, giving up the point, is it not evident that you would stand upon the highest ground possible? that you would gain much in character with all men of right and honourable feelings, and all this, considering the state of the K.'s health and mind, by a very small sacrifice? If Pitt would think the same it would be best of all, but of that I have no hope; and if I had, I have no degree of intercourse with him which would justify my speaking to him as I do to you."

TO THE HONOURABLE C. GREY.

" Dear Grey,

"Upon thinking on what I had said to Lord G. yesterday, I was afraid I had appeared too yielding upon the point in question, and have written him a letter of which the inclosed is a copy. Send it back, as I have no other copy. You may take one if you think it worth while. Nothing new except the divisions in the House of Lords, 31 to 30 in one, 48 to 77 in the other. I have no time.

" Yours affectionately,

" C. J. FOX.

" *April 20th,* 1804."

TO THE HONOURABLE C. GREY.

"ARLINGTON STREET, *Monday, April* 23*rd*, 1804.*

" DEAR GREY,

"I have yours of the 20th, and I have little more to say than I had last week. I hardly remember what the tenor was of those letters of mine which you say will determine you. The Doctor is supposed to be given over; but my opinion is that the state of the King's health is such (though they say he is to have a Council to-day,) as to prevent the *close quarters* coming so soon as Pitt expects. With respect to the results, you and I do not much differ—but when they do come, you must perceive how I shall feel the want of you and Lauderdale—and come they certainly will, and propositions will be made, how honestly is another affair, and great circumspection will be necessary as to the manner, either of rejecting or accepting them. You will easily conceive I have not time to write much this day. Our division will, I believe, be very good. Pitt, I hear, talks of upwards of 200, but I shall be very well satisfied with 170. I think, before the end

---

* On this day, the 23rd of April, Mr. Fox moved, " That it be referred to a committee of the whole House, to revise the several bills for the defence of the country, and to consider of such further measures as may be necessary to make that defence more complete and permanent." This was in fact a motion to declare want of confidence. The division, in which Mr. Pitt's name appeared in the Minority was—

For Mr. Fox	204
Against	256
Majority for Ministers . . .	52

of the week, we shall divide 70 in the House of
Lords. I think I can steer clear of your objections
to-day; at least I will try.

" Yours affectionately,

" C. J. FOX."

TO THE SAME.

" ARLINGTON STREET, Tuesday, April 24th, 1804.

" DEAR GREY,

"If you are not set out, I hope you will
not long delay. We were last night 204 to 256, and
there will be a great division in the House of Lords
to-day, and a still greater on Friday. The King held
a Council yesterday, and looked and behaved very
well. It certainly will come to negotiation, and I think
it will go no further.

" Yours affectionately,

" C. J. FOX."

TO THE EARL OF LAUDERDALE.

" ARLINGTON STREET, April 24th, 1804.

" I REALLY cannot help saying that your coming just
now would be a most useful measure, and a very
obliging one to me. At the same time my opinion is
that nothing good will happen, further than the satisfaction of forcing out the Doctor. But negotiations
there probably will be, and to take everything quite
upon oneself, or even on Grey and myself, is very
unpleasant."

"April 27th, 1804.

" Dear Grey,

"I shall write to you very shortly, as well for want of time, as in hopes of your being set out. I agree with almost all your speculations, except two : — 1st, the possibility of Pitt's showing any mercy to the Doctor, and 2ndly, in the danger of getting something worse than a King Log. I do not think the Stork, (which, by the way, is Pitt's crest,) would be worse for reasons which we may discuss when we meet. Fitzpatrick, and he alone, thinks there is a probability of the Doctor's standing—but I so far agree with him, as to think there is a *chance.* The King is certainly much better, or rather he *was* so on Sunday or Monday, for I know nothing since. His pages, valets-de-chambre, &c., were restored to him on Sunday, and on Monday, at Council, he behaved perfectly well. Fitzpatrick grounds his opinion on H. M.'s getting well, and supporting the Doctor roundly—and that certainly will give a chance ; but I suspect his colleagues will not stand by him, and rather prefer their chance with Pitt, to that of victory with the Doctor. I have no time to go on ; only I think I shall about the middle of next week make a motion on the misconduct with respect to Hanover. My *opinion* is, Grenville will not engage without us—but this is opinion only.

" Yours affectionately,

"C. J. FOX.

" Division in House of Lords yesterday, 61 to 94.
" Division in House of Commons, 76 to 100."

TO THE SAME.

" April 28th, 1804.

" Dear Grey,

" I have just got yours of the 25th. I guess you are on the road, but if not, I hope you will not delay further. What will happen I know not—but certainly either a battle in which you would wish to fight, or a negotiation which *cannot* proceed without you. Reports are various, but I *know* nothing.

" Yours,

" C. J. FOX.

" Saturday, April 28th, 1804."

TO THE SAME.

" May 5th, 1804.

" Dear Grey,

" Pitt has not seen the King, but perhaps he may to-morrow. I shall put off my motion, because I hear that it is not expected by some to come on, and we should not be so well attended as on a later day; but I think it almost certain that it *will* come on Tuesday or Wednesday, probably the latter day. I hope I shall see you to-night, for I have more to tell you. I have a letter from Lauderdale, who probably set out on Thursday or yesterday. I think it will not be amiss for you to say at dinner, that the probability is that there will be some more struggle; at least that such is my opinion, as it really is.

" Yours ever,

" C. J. FOX.

" Half-past 5, Saturday, May 5th, 1804."

MR. GRENVILLE TO MR. FOX.

"CHARLES STREET, half-past 12, *May 6th*, 1804.

"DEAR CHARLES,

"I do not find your letter to-night till it is too late so to answer it as that you can hear from me before to-morrow morning. I will lose no time in communicating to my brother, to Lord Spencer, and to Windham, the sentiments which you wish them to know that you entertain respecting them, more especially because I consider that declaration from you in this moment as a valuable and honourable testimony of that fair and open and manly character which so much distinguishes you. It is true that the persons whom you name are unfettered by engagement; it is honourable in you to take this moment to declare that you consider them to be so, and it is gratifying to me to feel confident that (in the case of such an offer as you describe) their conduct will show the sincerity of the principles which they have avowed.

"I was with my brother when he sent to you this evening the note which he received from Pitt; I think it looks unpromising for the general result; but as long as I can I will hope that the more exclusive system will not be adopted by Pitt. I think, however, that in all events he will prolong the discussion, and that in both Houses some authentic communication will be made to obtain delay. There are opinions, and those very respectable, that the motion in our House should at all events come on on Tuesday; but I must confess that is not at present the course of my opinion, because I doubt if it would be possible to obtain the attention of the House to Hanover and the old Government, at the moment when that old Government is declared extinct, and the whole House alive only to the formation of a new one.

" Good night.

" Yours ever,

"T. GRENVILLE."

[From Courts and Cabinets of Geo. III.]

LORD GRENVILLE TO MR. PITT.

" May 8th, 1804.

" My dear Pitt,

" I have already apprised you that all the persons to whom, at your desire, I communicated what passed between us yesterday, agreed with me in the decided opinion that we ought not to engage in the administration which you are now employed in forming.

" We should be sincerely sorry, if by declining this proposal, we should appear less desirous than we must always be, of rendering to his Majesty to the utmost of our power any service of which he may be graciously pleased to think us capable. No consideration of personal ease or comfort, no apprehension of responsibility, or reluctance to meet the real situation into which the country has been brought, have any weight in this decision, nor are we fettered

with any engagements on the subject, either expressed
or implied; we rest our determination solely on our
strong sense of the impropriety of our becoming parties to a system of government, which is to be formed
at such a moment as the present on a principle of
exclusion.

" It is unnecessary to dwell on the mischiefs which
have already resulted from placing the great offices of
Government in weak and incapable hands. We see
no hope of any effectual remedy for these mischiefs,
but by uniting in the public service ' as large a proportion as possible of the weight, talents, and character, to be found in public men of all descriptions, and
without any exceptions.' This opinion I have already
had occasion to express to you in the same words,
and we have for some time been publicly acting in
conformity to it; nor can we, while we remain im-
pressed with that persuasion, concur in defeating an
object for which the circumstances of the present
times afford at once so strong an inducement, and so
favourable an occasion.

" An opportunity now offers, such as this country
has seldom seen, for giving to its government, in a
moment of peculiar difficulty, the full benefit of the
services of all those who, by the public voice and
sentiment, are judged most capable of contributing to
its prosperity and safety. The wishes of the public
on this subject are completely in unison with its interests, and the advantages which not this country
alone, but all Europe and the whole civilized world
might derive from the establishment of such an

administration at such a crisis, would probably have exceeded the most sanguine expectations.

" We are certainly not ignorant of the difficulties which might have obstructed the final accomplishment of such an object, however earnestly pursued. But when in the very first instance all trial of it is precluded, and when this denial is made the condition of all subsequent arrangements, we cannot but feel that there are no motives of whatever description which could justify our taking an active part in the establishment of a system so adverse to our deliberate and declared opinions.

" Believe me ever, my dear Pitt,

" Most affectionately yours,

" GRENVILLE." *

MR. FOX TO LORD HOLLAND.

" Cheltenham, *July* 24*th*, 1804.

" It is a long time, my dear young one, since I wrote to you; but till within these ten days we were, as well from your own letters as from Mr. Lambert's accounts, in constant expectation of you. We first heard the 22nd of May, and then the 1st of June was fixed for your leaving Madrid, and are of course disappointed at the new delay, and the sorrier because the reason seems but too good. We have been here about ten days.

---

* This letter of course put an end to the negotiation, and thenceforth Lord Grenville acted with Mr. Fox. Lord Malmesbury unfairly attributes to ambition the upright conduct of Lord Grenville.

"The Bishop of Down and family are here. He looks thin and yellow, but I think him in good spirits, and therefore am sanguine that he will do. As for politics, you will have learnt all from newspapers that I could tell you in a letter, for with all my disregard for secrecy, I cannot bring myself to write about very private transactions in letters that are sure to be opened. *In summá*, nothing could have fallen out more to my mind than what has happened: the party revived and strengthened, Pitt lowered, and, what is of more consequence in my view, the cause of *Royalism* (in the bad sense of the word) lowered too. There is a very general dissatisfaction which, in the present state of things, is the better for not being *violent*, for violence would produce *reaction*, and perhaps revive the royalist fanaticism. The conduct of our new friends has been such as to satisfy those who were most prejudiced against them, and, what could hardly be expected at his time of life, Windham has improved in speaking as much as any young man ever did in a session. You will have heard, of course, of Lord A. H.'s* pamphlet, if you have not got it. It is excellent, unless I am deceived by partiality to the exact orthodoxy of it as a Whig creed. As to other politicks, I hear an invasion is again expected from Boulogne, but I have no belief in it. If they do attempt anything, it will be Ireland, not England, and in ships, not boats; however, *nous verrons*. What do you think of the fuss that is made about acknowledging the new Emperor?

* Lord Archibald Hamilton.

Is there any folly like it in history? I do not recollect any. May not people give their own magistrate the name they choose? The only ground of refusing acknowledgment (that I have ever heard) is having a contradictory claim yourself, as in the case of Spain and the Netherlands, England and America, &c., or favouring others who have, as in the case of England and Philip V. of Spain, Louis XIV. and King William, &c. But in this case all Europe has done as much against the Bourbons in acknowledging Bonaparte as First Consul of France, as they could do in recognising him as Emperor. If we refuse this last, it is the Republican, or at least the Consular Government of which we make ourselves the champions. Yet they say Russia will peremptorily refuse; and it is remarked that Austria has not yet sent her congratulations. *Cela fait pitié!* Some here are foolish enough to hope that all this will produce an extension of the war—*bad politicks* in every sense; they are wrong, I believe, in fact, and much more wrong in thinking such an extension would be good for us just now. Prussia without Austria would be worse than nothing; and the latter in her present state could only be a burden upon us, and possibly, nay probably, furnish means of aggrandising both France and Prussia. A long bore this on politicks; but it is quite vexatious to see and hear such folly. Austria, with all her weakness, is the only effectual banner to look to in better times against France, at least so these politicians say; and yet they would in the most disadvantageous moment, and not called upon by any actual aggression on the part of France, risk her total annihilation.   There are two books of letters come out : ' Cowper,' third volume, and ' Richardson's Correspondence.'   The life of the latter, and the whole preface by Mrs. Barbauld, is excellent.   Hayley's preface to the third volume of Cowper, worse than usual.   I have no classical book here but the ' Odyssey,' which I delight in more and more.

" Yours affectionately,

" C. J. FOX."

TO THE HONOURABLE C. GREY.

"St. Ann's Hill, September 19th, 1804.

" I have long intended writing to you, though I had nothing to say, nor have I now indeed ; but if I were to wait till I had, I do not know when we should renew our correspondence.   You may think, perhaps, that I might have written on the Prince's negotiation, if it may be so called ; but I cannot make out the facts, and still less all the motives to my own satisfaction.   Lauderdale would, of course, tell you all he knew, when he left London, and I knew no more till my return from Cheltenham, when the thing was quite over, and I not sorry (as you may suppose) that I had no advice to answer for. It originated with Tierney ; and Sheridan was, I believe, kept out of it till quite towards the close. My judgment is, that if a reconciliation could have taken place by the Queen it was right, if by Pitt it was wrong; but Tierney saw no such distinction. The refusal to see the King had gone before I knew anything more than when I went to Cheltenham: I should not have advised it. It seems to be all over; and the only thing that is of any consequence is to know how far Moira acted fairly in it, or indeed how far he was concerned at all. His advice to the Prince to offer the young Princess to the King was certainly very bad; but I believe it was only folly; and the Prince has (upon good pretences enough) done away the offer completely. Some accounts from Weymouth say the King is very well, others the reverse. My way of reconciling them is, that he is better in health, but still insane. If continental politics should turn out to *be* as they appear, what a new scene a real union between France and Austria will exhibit! and all owing to this foolishest of all wars! I hope you and Mrs. Grey had a pleasant tour in Scotland: pray say whether in point of beauty it answered your expectations.

" The only news I hear is a talk of an expedition to Boulogne, which appears to me to be madness. Indeed I do not see any great use in the sort of skirmishes that have taken place. If they would fairly sail from Boulogne at a time when we are ready to meet them at sea, it would surely be the best event we could wish for. Have they attempted to execute Pitt's bill with you yet? Here they are just beginning; but it is not thought we shall get a man. My poor friend, the Bishop of Down, is almost gone; there are not the smallest hopes left. It is a melancholy thing.

" Yours ever affectionately,

"C. J. FOX."

TO MR. O'BRIEN.

"St. Ann's Hill, *November 15th*, 1804.

" You are I think over suspicious; besides, if one does feel suspicious in a matter of this sort, where is the use of indulging or discussing them? The P. is such as he is, and we cannot alter him. Moira will not do any act so flagrantly dishonourable, as going away from all his professions would be. Your most unjust suspicion is that of McMahon, whose *earwiggings*, as you call them, if they have any influence at all, will be on the right side. He appears to me to be a *very honest* man, grateful to Moira, as he ought to be, but wishing the P. to go quite straight."

TO THE HONOURABLE C. GREY.

"Southill, *November 18th*, 1804.

" Dear Grey,

" You may have heard that I went to town from Woburn last Monday, to see the Prince after his first interview with the King; and I intended writing to you, as far as I understood it, the state of things; but partly idleness, and partly a hope that in a few days I should be able to give you some

information to the purpose, made me put it off.
Now the letter-writing day is come, and I know no
more than I did. The P. sent for me to tell me of
the message he had had from the K., and of an interview which Lord Moira had had with Pitt. With
regard to the first, it seemed only a continuation of
what had passed before the Weymouth journey, and
when he did see the King (almost all the family
present) at Kew, he says there was no cordiality or
pretended affection, but common talk on weather,
scandal, &c.,—a great deal of the latter, and *as the
P. thought*, very idle and foolish in the manner, and
running wildly from topic to topic, though not
absolutely incoherent. With respect to Lord
Moira's meeting with Pitt, he said that Pitt had
expressed a particular desire of having him (Moira)
in the Cabinet, and a general wish to admit many of
the P.'s friends. I rather think Moira, whom I saw
separately, added hopes of time bringing about *all*.
That Moira had declared explicitly that he could do
nothing without me and my friends. I asked
whether it was considered that any proposition had
come from Pitt, to which either H. R. H. or I were
to give any answer ; this was answered by a most
explicit negative ; so that there was no difficulty for
us—nothing having been said *to* us, there was nothing
for us to say or do. Here there seemed to be an
end, and a very good end of all this folly ; but I
understood from Moira that he was again to see
either Pitt or Melville, and to know positively
whether or no the P. was to have a military com-

mand offered him. I did not much like this; but
you will feel with me that it would have been as
impolitic as indelicate in me to have attempted to
dissuade the measure. Since last Monday I have
not heard one word but from the newspapers, from
which I understand that the P.'s visit to Windsor,
Friday (of which by the way he had apprised me),
was prolonged till this day. Moira must, I think,
have seen Pitt by this time, as he said he was in a
hurry to return to Scotland. I saw Sheridan, and I
need not tell you that he was in a terrible fidget.
My opinion is that, notwithstanding all these in-
trigues, the P. will be in essentials quite steady. I
think, too, that Pitt and Melville will not be able to
get authority to offer him anything that will shake
him. I have this day intelligence (which I believe)
of an event which will bring all these matters to a
crisis—and which, on that, as well as many other
accounts, I shall think a very good one. I hear it
is quite certain that the Irish Catholics will petition
both Houses for complete Emancipation. Upon that
question, the P. and Moira must declare themselves,
and what will be most satisfactory to me, the Opposition will be marshalled together in a *cause* that is
not merely of a personal nature; for to have so much
stress laid upon my coming, or not coming, into office,
is, to say the least, very unpleasant. Tierney has, I
believe, been offered Ireland, but wishes to get the
Prince's consent to his acceptance. In this *I think*
he will fail; but failing, whether he will accept
without it, I have no means of judging. That Pitt

is very much afraid is plain. The state of the King, you will say, is a sufficient reason for his fear; but I believe he fears opposition too. The repeal of his foolish bill and the Catholic question will make two questions at the opening of Parliament as embarrassing and mortifying to him in different ways as can be conceived. It is said Ministers have hopes from the Continent; and, if what I see to-day in the papers about Prussia be true, there is more apparent foundation for their hopes than there has been for some time; but *I feel somehow* that it will not do. When I hear or know anything more concerning Carlton House, &c., I will write again. We came here yesterday and go to town Thursday, where, if not before, I shall probably learn something, though I shall stay only one night on my way home. They say here they have not heard from you for a long time, but they learn that you are all quite well. I am a good deal alarmed lest Lord Holland should be caught in Spain, and detained. I have a letter from him, Valladolid, 21st October, in which he speaks of the more or less probability of war, but does not seem to speculate on the possibility of the Spaniards being ordered to imitate Bonaparte with regard to the English. Mrs. F. desires to be remembered to you, as I do to Mrs. G.

"Yours ever most affectionately,

"C. J. FOX."

TO THE HONOURABLE C. GREY.

"SOUTHILL, *November* 19*th*, 1804.

"DEAR GREY,

"I add a line to my letter of yesterday to say that since I wrote it I have heard that all Moira's interviews have ended, as I expected, in nothing, and that he is going back to Scotland. I have not heard this from positive authority, but I believe it.*

"Yours affectionately,

"C. J. FOX."

TO LORD HOLLAND.

"ST. ANN'S HILL, *December* 12*th*, 1804.

"SINCE I wrote to you I have read the letters of Don Pedro,† which I think very interesting, and not un-useful to my period, which of course is to go down to the grant of the crown to William and Mary.

"The sum of politicks here is, that there is no prospect of peace at any period, be it never so distant, and that people seem to be making up their minds to per-petual war. There is a famous new argument (if I remember my logic) of a *Sorites.* Our prosperity is daily increasing; the more prosperous we are, the more we shall be envied; the more we are envied, the more enemies we shall have; the more enemies we have, the more necessary to be at war, in

* Lord Moira had persuaded the Prince to prefer Pitt as minister to Fox; but this secret was kept from Fox, both by the Prince and Lord Moira.

† Don Pedro Ronquillo. See Hist. of James II.

order to reduce their power, &c., &c. The fear of invasion is much diminished since Admiral Cornwallis has been able to stay off Brest in these gales of wind. The nonsense of the Volunteers is therefore less detrimental to the country than it would otherwise have been, but I think it is the worst system, as it has been managed, that ever was adopted, and Windham and I exposed it pretty well on Friday. The truth is, that while you are adding bad troops to the *army*, you are robbing the *country* of all its natural defence; besides that, you are teaching your new troops all the nonsense, and none of the useful parts of military discipline. I have not yet determined upon the Irish question, my own judgment is clear for it. Pitt spoke very flatly on Friday; his scheme seems to be to convert the Volunteers gradually into a real regular army. I think, as somebody said about universal suffrage, that the best thing about that plan is its utter impracticability. Lord King is gone to town to-day to support Lord Grenville against the Irish Martial Law Bill. Grey, at Howick, is as difficult to fetch to town, as you from Spain. If you were both here, I cannot help thinking some good moves might be made this Session, though of a check mate I have no hopes in almost any case. Pitt is in a strange situation, and I suspect that he feels that he is so. His friends will be more dissatisfied with him and his enemies fear him less every day.

"Yours affectionately,

"C. J. F."

TO THE EARL OF LAUDERDALE.

" December 13th, 1804.

" I AM glad you are going to publish on the subject you mention; from not hearing much of it lately I had supposed things were mending, but I dare say you are right.

" I shall write to Grey to-day or to-morrow to press him very much about coming up; pray assist me, for it is on every account most desirable that he should take his part in this session. The first business in point of time will probably be Pitt's foolish bill, &c., and the rupture with Spain. I know Grey likes both these subjects very much, and I think he is the proper person to take up that of Spain; but let him choose. I am afraid he thinks either of them, in a prudential view, a better question than the Catholic business, which, though, as I conceive, far the first in importance, will probably come on later in order of time."

TO LORD HOLLAND.

"December 17th, 1804.

" MY DEAR YOUNG ONE,

" After various reports of your having left Madrid with Frere, which from the dates of your Valladolid letters I totally disbelieved, I now learn from your letter to Caroline, that you were at Merida the 25th, and expected to be at Lisbon the 30th

of last month.   By this time, I hope you are
sailed for England, but in case you should not be, I
cannot refrain from telling you, how very anxious all
your friends, as well as myself, are, that you should
delay your voyage as little as possible.   Excepting,
and hardly excepting the last, I do not think there
ever was, or is likely to be, a session of Parliament,
which you would be so sorry to miss as the next.
The Catholic question will most probably come on in
the best possible mode, by a petition from the Catholics themselves; and there will be besides, on Pitt's
ridiculous Defence Bill, &c., and on the seizure of the
Spanish dollars, and on twenty other matters that one
cannot yet clearly state, questions that will be very
useful if well managed.   You will observe I do not
mention what there is always a chance of, questions
in which the Prince of Wales is particularly concerned.
Exclusive, however, of particular questions, you will
easily conceive how much a propitious outset is likely
to influence the future strength, character, and union
of this newly coalesced Opposition, and of what importance it is that such a party should be strong,
united, and powerful, he who thinks as we do cannot
doubt.   But in our view of things it is further very,
very desirable that its power, strength, and union
should appear considerable while out of office, in order
that if ever they should come in, it may be plain that
they have an existence of their own, and are not the
mere creatures of the Crown.   For all these, and
many more reasons, it is highly desirable that every
friend to good principles should shew himself this

session, and therefore it is that I must press you to come if possible. You will observe all these reasons are on public grounds, or with a view in some degree to my own consequence, but the reasons to be drawn from considerations respecting yourself, are full as strong, and this, I assure you, is the opinion of all your friends, as well as mine.

"Everybody here is mad about this Boy Actor,* even Uncle Dick is full of astonishment and admiration. We go to town to-morrow to see him, and from what I have heard, I own I shall be disappointed if he is not a prodigy.

"I received yours of the 4th ult., and despair of the Simancas papers. God knows, if I had them, when I should find time to make use of them. Those concerning the Cortes must be very curious and interesting.

"Yours affectionately,
"C. J. F."

TO THE HONOURABLE C. GREY.

"St. Ann's Hill, *December 17th,* 1804.

"Dear Grey,

"It is a long time that I have been deferring from day to day thanking you for your letter, and letting you know how matters stood at Carlton H. when I last saw the Prince, on the 28th of last month. The sum of it is that the Chancellor sent the Prince a message from the King, demanding the

* Master Betty.

young Princess upon the supposed acquiescence of
the Prince, an acquiescence which, in the last conversations between Lord Moira and Pitt, had been positively denied. The Prince expressed, in a written
note, his surprise that, after what had passed, such a
proposition should be made to him, and sent it back.
Both Pitt and the Chancellor replied, first insinuating
that the Prince ought to have shown more respect
to a paper coming directly from his Majesty, and
saying they had not understood Moira as the Prince
did. The Prince sent an answer disclaiming of
course all intentional disrespect to the King, refusing
peremptorily to give up his daughter, and for what
had passed referring them to Moira, to whom he
said he transmitted their notes. Luckily enough
Moira had left with the Prince a written summary
of what had passed between Pitt and him, which
entirely justified the Prince's interpretation. Since
this I have heard no more ; but I read in the newspaper that the preparations making for the Princess of
Wales and the child at Windsor are discontinued.
Whether this be true I know not. All this is so far
good, as it seems, in the present state of things,
nearly impossible that one should be teazed with any
more negotiations pretending to be of the amicable
kind. Now for your letter, of which I like the
greatest part as much as possible, *but* there is one
terrible sentence in it which seems to say that you
do not intend to come up. There never was a time
when, for the sake of the public, of the Party, (I do
not add your own, because I know your answer would

be that you have no wish to have anything to do with politicks,) and certainly for mine, your attendance was so desirable as it will be this session. Opposition *seems* now restored, at least to what it was before the Duke of Portland's desertion, and the other adverse circumstances of those times. Mind, I say *seems*, for if *you* stay away, it will be very far from being so; and whatever is gained, will be thought by all, and most certainly by me, a bad exchange for you. The great point is to show a union of all or nearly all the talents and character of the country, and in such a case the absence of a person much less considerable than you, would take much from the effect of any reasoning to be grounded on such a state of circumstances. Do, for God's sake, make up your mind to one unpleasant effort, and come for the first two months at least of the session. I understand you have a governess with whom Mrs. Grey can leave the younger children with satisfaction. The expense and trouble are, I know, not to be despised, but surely this is a time, if ever there was one, to make some sacrifices. With respect to particular questions the two first that will, I suppose, occur, will be Pitt's Defence Bill, and the Spanish War. I think, as you do, the latter a very good question, and only did not name it to you, because I waited to see how it would end. I now look on war as inevitable, but am told there is still an opinion in the city, that it is not certain. You may take up either this or the Defence question; but I should recommend the Spanish, because there are so many persons (among whom

Windham) ready enough to take the lead in the other. You will not be so sorry to hear, as I am to tell you, that I begin to doubt whether the Catholic Petition is so sure to be presented this year, as I once thought. However, in a day or two we must hear the proceedings of the Dublin meeting, which was to take place on Friday last, and they, I suppose, will be decisive. Everybody is mad about this young Roscius, and we go to town to-morrow to see him. The accounts of him sound incredible, but the opinion of him is nearly unanimous, and Fitzpatrick, who went strongly prepossessed against him, was perfectly astonished, and full of admiration. You may depend upon it, Burke was right, Idleness is the best of all earthly blessings, but even to that first of pleasures some additional relish may be given by occasional labour, provided, however, that that labour be neither too severe nor too long continued. I love idleness so much, and so dearly, that I have hardly the heart to say a word against it ; but something is due to one's station in life, something to friendship, something to the country. I have experience enough of the disagreeableness of being pressed, to hate pressing others, and most especially those I love ; but this once I feel myself bound and obliged to do it, by a sense of right that I cannot resist. Miss Fox has had a letter from Holland, dated Merida, the 25th of last month ; and they expected to be at Lisbon on the 30th. I hope they are sailed by this time, but in case they are not I write a pressing letter to him too.

"Yours affectionately,

"C. J. FOX."

TO THE HONOURABLE C. GREY.

"St. Ann's Hill, *January 7th,* 1805.

"Dear Grey,

"I got your letter at Woolbeding, Saturday, and being on the road yesterday had no time to write, so you have had a day's respite from plague more than I intended you should have. If I could alter my opinion I would, but I cannot, and indeed the more I consider the whole of the case, the more I feel it to be very important in every view, that you should be in town during the early part of the session. With respect to the very first day, I think it highly desirable, but if very inconvenient, it is certainly not so necessary as when questions come on. I have not seen the pamphlet you mention on the Spanish business. I had heard that Bentley, the author of the administration pamphlet last year, had advertised one, but I supposed the reconciliation might have prevented the publication. It is certain all the Doctor's friends, and he himself, condemned the conduct of Ministers very openly, but that will not signify. I hope you will bring it on yourself.

"Now, as you have addressed yourself to Mrs. Fox, let me do so to Mrs. Grey, and beg her not to think of your coming alone, or at least that she would follow very soon after. You know when you are in town without her, you are unfit for anything, with all your thoughts at Howick, and as the time for which your stay may be necessary must be uncertain, you will both be in constant fidget and misery. Indeed you must come *en famille*, and make up your mind to some stay. If you knew how very unpleasant I feel in pressing those I love against their inclination, you would be convinced that nothing but a rooted opinion that it is right in this case could induce me to do it. I have much to tell you in regard to foreign affairs that I cannot write by the post. I will only say, lest you should be disappointed hereafter, that I have little, if any, hopes of any good. On the other hand, if there were an honest, independent administration, I should have hopes. I believe you do not think the first of the above epithets belongs to the present, and how little the second does, every event speaks more clearly every day; indeed the reconciliation, if any were wanting, is damning proof. I am afraid the Doctor is not to have office—which I agree with you in thinking would have most effect on the public. I go to town Thursday to stay. If it is any comfort to you, you may be assured that I hate the going thither as much as you can do, or more.

" Yours affectionately,
" C. J. FOX.

" P.S. I think the question on Pitt's bill and the Spanish business must come on immediately, and perhaps notices be given in the first week. In short your best way by far is to come up for the day of meeting, unless by putting it off for a day or two, Mrs. Grey can come with you."

TO LORD HOLLAND.

"ARLINGTON STREET, *March* 19*th*, 1805.

" MY DEAR YOUNG ONE,

"I have no excuse for having been so long without writing, except the constant hurry of business in this odious place. I have made great sacrifices indeed in coming again into this scene of politicks, but as I do make them, I am determined to do the thing handsomely, and as far as the existence of some respectable standard against the dreadful power of the Crown is of advantage, I may flatter myself that I have been of great use. I have not time to discuss this question at large and in detail; suffice it to say, that even our enemies cannot deny that we are a respectable Opposition, and few now will dispute Pitt's being a contemptible Minister. He certainly gained more in numbers by his junction with the Doctor than I thought he would, but his loss in reputation from that and other causes is incalculable. The next two questions of importance will, if he has any feeling, hurt him beyond measure; 1st, the tenth Report of the Naval Commissioners against Lord Melville, 2nd, the Catholic question.

" Here have I been interrupted, and have but just time to write three words more. Lord Grenville and I are to present the petitions next Monday,* and in each House give notice that we shall move upon them on or about the 8th of May. Now if you are coming (as the good accounts we have of Lady Holland

---

* From the Roman Catholics.

make us hope) this spring, I think you would start a
week or fortnight sooner, in order to be in the House
of Lords on this question.   You have no notion how
anxious Lord Grenville is for you on all questions.   I
shall be too late if I do not finish ; so my love to Lady
Holland and God bless you all.

" Yours affectionately,

"C. J. F."

TO THE SAME.

" *March 26th*, 1805.

" MY DEAR YOUNG ONE,

　　　　"I have no time, nor do I know when
I shall have, to write you a comfortable letter,
but you will I am sure like to know about the
Catholic business.   Lord Grenville and I presented
the petitions yesterday.   I named the 9th of May
for my motion.   Lord G. fixed no day for his, but
I think it probable they will come on the same
day (which I should prefer), or at least within a few
days of each other.

" If postponing the motions for a very few days to
the 13th or 14th at latest would give us any additional
chance of your being present, it may be done, but if
that be the case, write without loss of time to say so.
I understand the time you think of embarking is the
23rd of April ; but it is possible, surely, you will think
it worth while to set out a week or ten days sooner,
for such an object as the Catholic question.   By the
bye, what fine time you will have on board ship to
think over your speech !   I think I foresee that the

lines taken in the two houses will be different (I mean by the enemy). In our house the objections will be chiefly to the time, in yours to the substance of the measure.

" At present the only political subject that engages attention is the 10th Report of the Naval Commissioners against Lord Melville. On that question we expect a great division.

" Yours affectionately,
"C. J. FOX."

TO THE SAME.

"ARLINGTON STREET, *April 9th*, 1805.

"DEAR YOUNG ONE,

" As I hope you will have sailed before this reaches Lisbon, I shall make it very short. I believe I told you in my last, that Lord Grenville has fixed the 10th for the Catholic Question, and I have now fixed on the same day. We beat Ministers by the speaker's casting vote last night, and Lord Melville has resigned to prevent our removing him by address to-morrow. Pitt will certainly not go out yet, and I am not one of those who think it impossible that he should last some time longer. Lord Henry * made a famous speech last night, far surpassing all his others.

" Yours affectionately,
"C. J. FOX."

* Lord Henry Petty.

TO THE SAME.

"ARLINGTON STREET, *April 26th*, 1805.

"DEAR YOUNG ONE,

"Of all the days among the many uncertain days we have had lately with regard to politics, I believe I am choosing the most uncertain to write to you, and consequently I have nothing worth telling you beyond what you will see in the newspapers. If I had written yesterday morning, I should have told you that Lord Sidmouth had resigned, having parted with Pitt on Saturday, declaring that all connection between them was at an end *for ever*. Now I understand that *for ever* lasted just 24 hours, and that yesterday there was a meeting between the said Lord S. and Pitt, in which all their differences were *finally* adjusted.* What interpretation may be given to *finally* I know not, but now for the worst of all uncertainties. The cry of all or almost all our friends is so strong against bringing on the Catholic question *now*, that I am afraid it is uncertain whether or not we shall be forced (most shamefully according to my feelings), to put it off till next session. Lord Grenville will I hope be in town to-day when it must be decided.

"What divisions we shall make this week on Lord Melville's business is also very uncertain; if good ones, I think it most probable that the Doctor will again fly off, and that it will be decisive on Pitt's Administration; if bad ones, things will continue for some time (though I think not very long) *as they are*."

* See "Life of Lord Sidmouth," vol. ii.

"ARLINGTON STREET, *May 2nd*, 1805.

"MY DEAR YOUNG ONE,

        "I cannot tell you how happy your letter
from Falmouth has made me.

"I shall write you again a line to Hartford
Bridge, lest this should miss you, but I write this to
tell you that (thank God and Lord G.'s and my
stoutness), the Catholic business will most certainly
come on the 10th in both Houses.

                "Yours affectionately,
                        "C. J. FOX.

"P.S. I have no chance of getting out of town."

TO MR. O'BRIEN.

"ST. ANN'S HILL, *June 23rd*, 1805.

"I RETURN you the paragraph in which 1 can safely
say there is not one word of truth, and the idea
attempted to be conveyed by it, is as false as the
words are different from mine.   First of all, the words
alluded to were not spoken in a low tone of voice
(the writer's pretence I suppose for his misrepre-
sentation), but distinctly and audibly to a House the
most silent and attentive that I ever witnessed : but
this is of little consequence.   I cannot recollect, nor
ever can, my exact words, but the sense of them was
as follows : ' Who can expect that we should give
extraordinary confidence, or that foreign nations
should give any confidence at all, to such an

Administration as the present? I am perhaps less
sanguine than others with respect to the good that
could be done by the best Administration, but I feel
myself sure that an Administration formed to
comprehend all that is respectable for rank, talents,
character and influence in the country, affords the only
chance of safety; and I trust that nobody can suppose
that any individual (however he may disapprove, as I
certainly do, the unconstitutional principle of exclusion)
would suffer any personal object of ambition, if
ambition he had, to stand in the way of the formation
of such a Ministry.' There might be something more,
either in words or perhaps only in manner that made
it clearly understood (as I meant it should) that *I*
would not stand in the way, &c. Now what does all
this mean? or what can it be tortured to mean
further than the words import? except perhaps to lay
an implied responsibility on Pitt, as *He* suffers considerations respecting *his* power or personal situation
to prevent the formation of such a Ministry as I hinted
at. I never meant to admit (nor do the words at all
convey such a meaning), that such a Ministry could
be made without my having a principal, or perhaps
the principal share in forming it, or that it could be
formed at all without Pitt's coming down from his
situation at the treasury, and in fact considering the
present Ministry as annihilated, in which case all such
persons as I alluded to might be consulted on the
formation of a new one. The strange misunder-
standing which has taken place on this occasion makes
me almost wish the words had never been spoken,

though I never was surer of anything than that they were the most judicious I ever uttered, and calculated to produce the best effects.   Nay, I think even now they will do good.   Pitt will possibly do *nothing* in consequence of them, and then the blame of there being no fit Administration rests wholly with him. If he applies to Opposition, he must either come down from his situation, or the thing will go off in such a manner as to show the public that the obstacle to a comprehensive system is no longer referable to any object of mine, or of any friends for me, but, on the contrary, to considerations respecting *his* personal power and situation.

"I confess I have been much mortified at the warmth some of my friends have expressed at my supposed offer of a coalition with Pitt in his present situation, than which nothing was ever further from my mind. I say I have been mortified, because it is hard after so many years of trial they should not have confidence enough in me to give me credit for not intending to do wrong till they see me do it."

TO THE HONOURABLE C. GREY.

"ARLINGTON STREET, *June 30th,* 1805.

"I AM going as I hope not to return this session, but if you think that it is *very* desirable that I should attend Jeffery's motion, I will.* A letter by Monday's

---

* Mr. Jeffery's motion related to the Naval Administration of Earl St. Vincent.   On the 1st of July, it was postponed till the next session.— Parliamentary Debates, 1805.

post, which I shall receive Tuesday morning, will
be time enough to fetch me; but it will be very inconvenient as well as unpleasant to me to come, and
in trusting to you, I hope I put myself into merciful
hands.   God bless you all!   I shall consider the
letter of attorney I talked of as given.   If the moment
were not so very critical to the country (I mean on
account of the pending transactions with the Continent,
where a false step may be irretrievable), how very satisfactory to us would be the determination of these
fellows to go on!   I do not know anything we could
do to prevent the other evils of the war; but we
might, I still think, either get a peace,—ay, and a
peace to which the continental powers might be
parties,—or at least show all the world that we have
done all in our power for that purpose.   In any other
view I think it is full as well for the country, and
infinitely better for us, that Pitt should disgrace himself more and more—which he undoubtedly will do
unless the King's death should save him.   I did not
intend all this prose.   Pray remember both Mrs. F.
and me kindly to Mrs. Grey and the little beauties.

" Yours affectionately,
" C. J. FOX."

TO THE HONOURABLE C. GREY.

"St. Ann's Hill, July 2nd, 1805.

" Dear Grey,

" I must write a line to say how excessively
obliged to you I am, and the more so, as I now feel

myself safe for the session. As to the next, *alors comme alors*, my favourite proverb. I repeat again that I consider the letter of attorney given, with such limitations only as I can guess; but if you think I cannot, you had better specify them. Putting all circumstances together, I do not think the French can do a great deal of mischief in the West Indies, but that they should be able to have such a force at sea is very bad. If the King bears his misfortune as you hear he does, nothing will be done soon; and his illness will be a reason (with which many will be satisfied) for the country's remaining without a government. It would be good poetical justice on us if we were actually to get our death by our extreme love of monarchy and monarchs. Pray write a line when you get home to say how you all are.

" Yours most affectionately,

" C. J. FOX."

TO THE HONOURABLE C. GREY.

" St. Ann's Hill, *July 6th*, 1805.

" DEAR GREY,

　　" You will have heard, before you receive this, of the Doctor's resignation. I believe it certainly did take place yesterday; but maybe he may be in again to-day. If, however, it is a serious and permanent breach, I think it certain, from what you and I know, that Pitt will immediately apply to Lord Grenville; the probability I think is that upon Lord G.'s answer he will stop short, but *if* he goes on, a negotiation may ensue, in which great difficulties and responsibility will fall upon me. I should feel frightened, particularly in the absence of you and Lauderdale and Fitzpatrick; but, if necessary, I would undertake it with a hope that, whether it were successful or abortive, I would give no reasonable man among our friends cause to complain. But I should like to know, in case I should be put into such a situation sooner than I expect, what your limitations are to your letter of attorney. I am sure you will feel that if any good can be done, it is not a time to let any particular predilections or dislikes have much weight with any of us.

" I feel a sort of confidence that if anything be attempted it will break off upon preliminary points, so as to save us from the very unpleasant difficulties of detailed negotiation; but yet it is right to be secretly prepared as well as one can. As to yourself you know my wishes; but if a great sacrifice were made (a sacrifice which I feel quite sure will never be made) on the other side, perhaps it would be expected that the nominal head should be a person less marked than you or I. It is said that the K. has agreed to undergo an operation, but is resolved to have his journeys to Birmingham and Weymouth first. I think the delay at Martinique looks as if the French had found some unexpected impediment, probably sickness.

" Yours ever affectionately,

"C. J. FOX."

TO R. ADAIR, ESQ.

"July, 1805.

" DEAR ADAIR,

" I have just received yours of yesterday. I should not like the proposal you have heard hinted, because there might be those who would think the rejection of it unreasonable ; and yet the argument on our side is short, clear, and intelligible, I should hope, to every fair person. It was understood last year that it was Pitt's intention, if he had been permitted, not to offer us places in *his* Administration, but to consult with us about the formation of one. Now, without blaming him for accepting as he did, surely we must be allowed to say that there was nothing in that act calculated to *increase* our confidence in him, and that in our view of things he has certainly gained no right to stand on *higher* ground than he did before. Again, would he have proposed Hawkesbury or even Castlereagh to us then ? I think hardly the latter, and certainly not the former ; and, if not then, it can hardly be supposed that the meanness of their subsequent conduct can make them more palatable to us now. Besides such Sticks in an arrangement which purposes to be a union of ability and character would be ridiculous. Our first principle ought to be *exclusive* (and in that sense only will I use or admit the idea) of underlings of all sorts. To this rule the retaining of Lord Chatham, if P. wishes it, should be the only exception.

" The great distinction, however, between acceding

to a Ministry and co-operating in the forming of a new one, is what is principally to be insisted on, and this distinction (clear, intelligible, as I think, to every man) is I know particularly felt and understood by Pitt ; as when there was a probability of our situations being reversed, I mean in the then expected event of a Regency or a new reign, Lord Gr. Leveson particularly stated how differently Pitt would feel in the different cases, supposing the proposition to come from us.

" Did you understand the K. to wish Lord Grenville to be the mediator of the domestic coalition, or of the foreign one ?   As to peerages, to the two mentioned must be added at least two more, Anson and Crewe, but I do not suspect that would make much difficulty. Nothing I suppose was said of Eldon or Chatham. If they were to be kept, Pitt, certainly in point of eminent friends the weakest of the three, would be nearly as strong in numbers as the Grenvilles and I put together.

" I have written all this chiefly for your own satisfaction, for I would not have it stated as coming from me to any one ; but if it can be useful to you in any loose conversation or *pour parler* on these matters, you are welcome to it."

MR. FOX TO LORD HOLLAND.

"*July 6th,* 1805.

" The Doctor has chosen a bad time for his resignation, as Pitt can certainly go on without him while

Parliament is not sitting, and by these means gains time for all sorts of negotiation. That all these negotiations will fail *I* am sure; but the Doctor could not be so, and therefore his folly in this, as in everything else, is beyond all ordinary conception. It looks as if the French would not be able to do much mischief in the West Indies."

TO MR. O'BRIEN.

"*July 7th*, 1805.

"So the Doctor is out at last, and has as usual taken the worst time possible for his manœuvre. Had he stuck to his first resignation in April, he must have destroyed Pitt: even three weeks ago he might have done it, but to wait for the close of the session, and to go out at a season when his retiring is rather an ease to his enemy than any additional difficulty, it is too foolish. What time does it not give Pitt for negotiation? and though I know that all such negotiations will be unsuccessful, probably the Doctor did not. If the accounts of to-day are true, and the places are to be filled up immediately, it looks indeed as if Pitt knew as well as I that he has no chance from negotiation; but, even supposing him to know it, I confess I am surprised that he should not make a *show* of attempting it. And so all our friends are for a coalition with the Doctor. I do not know that I shall be an enemy to it in proper time and circumstances, but remember your motto, *Softly John*, or a *word to the Warriors*. I apply it to the warriors against Pitt, who are for a *bellum inter-necinum* without any offer of reasonable conditions. The state of the case appears to me to be this : Pitt, though he may have still a bare majority, is too weak to carry on his Government as it is; at least we flatter ourselves so. What then must be his resource? either to get strength from *us*, which I hold to be impossible; to unite again with the Doctor, which is not likely; or, if he can do neither, to get some *cause* with the public upon which he may be able to stand his ground against all parties. Now what cause can he get? no possible other than the old cry against storming the Cabinet, imprisoning and dethroning the K., aristocratical faction, interested coalitions, &c. &c. &c. Now, what method so good for the purpose of cutting him off from this his only resource, as to show on our part every degree of moderation ? to show that we would do everything possible to soften the K.'s prejudices, and would by no means adopt ourselves those principles of exclusion which we condemn in others ? My speculation *was* that Pitt would immediately seek some intercourse with the Grenvilles, and that upon their answer he would give out that the whole Opposition was equally unreason-able, and would evidently be content with nothing less than unconditional submission on the part of the Court. In that view it would have been very ma-terial that the answer should have been such as to give the least possible colour to such an interpre-tation. But it looks now as if Pitt did not mean to give us the trouble of framing such an answer, but to

go on on his own strength, joined to that of the
King. I think this is best of all for us; for, if I am
not mistaken, the public wish for a comprehensive
Administration is very strong, and the want of it
must now lie altogether at Pitt's door. With this
view, too, the Doctor's resignation may do great good,
as furnishing evidence of the impossibility of Pitt's
going on with any set of Ministers who are not his
own mere creatures and tools. If the Doctor will
fall in with these views, I am sure I have no objection
to coalescing with him; on the contrary I should
like whatever would tend most to show that the
contest was between Pitt on one side, and *all* the men
of influence on the other. I mention *influence*, because
I think that is the only circumstance in which the
Doctor is considerable, and I am sadly afraid lest, by
mismanagement, he should lose what he has of that
kind in the House of Commons. Upon the whole, I
consider matters as in the best possible train, and yet
it does sometimes come across me (and I wish others
would not quite forget it) that the Ministry with
which this very Pitt set out in the year '84, was in
all respects as weak and contemptible as the present.
However, the circumstances are different, and in this
respect above all, that we may by moderate professions and conduct prevent the possibility of such a
cry as was raised against us at that time.

" Yours ever,
"C. J. FOX."

FROM MR. ADAIR TO MR. FOX.

" Sunday Morning, July 7th, 1805.

" I HAVE received a letter of so much importance in many respects, that I think it right to send you down the substance of it, together with a copy of my answer by the stage.

" The letter states to me (and I can depend on the writer's veracity as far as that is concerned) the substance of the King's conversation with Mr. Pitt at Windsor, on Sunday. I think I had better give it you in the writer's own words :

" ' It was not from Canning that I heard it, but from a person to whom the King reported the conversation. It was a strong representation to the King of the impossibility of going on without the assistance of Opposition, that the experiments the King wished for had both been made, and both completely failed, and that something else must be resorted to, for that he would go on no longer. The King mentioned Mr. Fox's speech : Pitt replied, it was a most noble one, and that the man who could make it was the fittest to be applied to for advice. On the King's asking whether some proposal might not be made to the Opposition without Mr. Fox, Pitt replied, " They ought not to listen to such proposals, and in my opinion their acceptance would be of very little use without him." He then argued the point for some time. The person to whom the King told all this, asked, what his Majesty had answered ?

The King said, he could not deny there was great
good sense in what Pitt said, and that the argument
stood on very different ground from what it did last
year ; " Addington has acted like a fool and lost
himself, and the Catholic question is laid asleep for
some time." He went on, saying, his chief objection
was that he thought Mr. Fox had a personal dislike
to him. The person answered, " Then your Majesty
has given a complete refusal to Mr. Pitt." The
King said, No, not that ; he had only taken time to
consider, and had told Pitt to patch up as well as he
could for the present ; but that Pitt was so obstinate
he would only offer terms which the Addingtons
could not accept, and they would probably go out ;
and then he added again, " What a fool Addington
has been ! "

" ' In consequence of this conversation Pitt sent
for Canning, whom he had not seen for some time.
Canning answered him by saying, " There is but
one hope of success. Send at once to Mr. Fox, and
speak to him yourself." This was good advice ; but
I was asked whether Mr. Fox would consent to such
an interview if it were asked for ? I ask you this as
your opinion only.'

" These are the very words of the letter. Whether
the intention be or be not to open any negotiation
with you, or, failing in that, to open one with any
others, I know not ; but as my opinion was asked on
one point, and as I can depend upon the fidelity of my
correspondent, I thought I was not advancing too far
in the following answer to the application :

" ' Sunday Night, July 7th.

" ' I received your letter late last night. I thank you for it, and only wish, for the sake of all the good objects it points to, that I had known the circumstances you state some days earlier. You will be sensible that it would be taking too great a responsibility upon myself were I to answer your question about Mr. Fox, in a case of so much importance as that of his consenting to an interview with Mr. Pitt ; and indeed I do not feel sufficiently authorised even to consult with him upon the subject, without further grounds to go upon than your letter contains. As to my own opinion, I have no objection to giving it to you freely ; assuring you at the same time upon my most sacred word of honour that I speak without any sort of authority from Mr. Fox, or any means whatever of knowing positively what would be his answer should such a proposal be made to him.

" ' If it be true, as your informant states, that the difficulties which obstructed the union of parties last year in the highest quarter appear to be giving way, I cannot conceal from you that the events which have taken place since Mr. Pitt's acceptance of office, as well as that acceptance itself under the circumstances under which it took place, have greatly increased those difficulties among a considerable portion of our oldest friends. What Mr. Pitt is stated to have replied to the King in speaking of proposals to the Opposition without Mr. Fox, namely, " That neither ought the Opposition to accept, nor would their acceptance be of much use without him," is handsome, and in the true character of Mr. Pitt; but what may be called the converse of the sentiment is perhaps equally true, namely, that Mr. Fox could not accept, nor could his acceptance be of much use, without his friends. How far Mr. Fox himself might be able to remove the difficulties which long and recently inflamed resentments opposed to an union so necessary for the country is more than I can pretend to say; but as far as my own observation extends, I should say that nothing short of putting affairs again into that situation in which they were previous to Mr. Pitt's going into the King's closet last year, can afford a hope of Mr. Fox's being able to negotiate successfully even with his most confidential, as well as with his oldest adherents. This is frankly my opinion; but again and again I must entreat you to consider it only as my opinion formed, as well as given to you, without communication with any one. Whether an interview, such as you allude to, would be of any use without some previous explanation upon the point I have touched upon may be worth considering; I can only say I am ready to assist on my part, *i. e.*, producing that explanation in any manner in which it may be thought desirable, &c. &c.'

"I hope you will not think I have done wrong in sending the above before consulting you. It was impossible for me to give a more distinct answer as to the point of interview, even although I was only asked my own opinion. If anything more comes of it, we shall at least have the benefit of knowing distinctly the grounds on which the interview will be proposed. Tell me what you wish me to do if I hear again from my correspondent.

" Ever yours,

" R. ADAIR."

TO R. ADAIR, ESQ.

"*July 8th,* 1805.

" DEAR ADAIR,

"I have just received by the stage yours of yesterday morning. Nothing can be properer than your answer, and I think it was full as well you should have written it without previous consultation with me. As I do not know who your correspondent is, I do not know exactly what to make of his intelligence : first, because intentional veracity alone is not a sure proof of a correct narrative ; next, because much may be inferred from the sort of person from whom he was likely to get his intelligence.

"My belief was that Pitt would attempt some negotiation more or less extensive ; but if the accounts, so generally credited, of his intention to fill up the vacant places immediately be true, I must suppose he has abandoned all thoughts of it, if indeed he ever entertained any. Write again when you hear anything. I am told that though the K. seemed to bear every thing very composedly at first, he has since shown many symptoms of flurry and agitation.

" Yours ever."

TO THE HONOURABLE C. GREY.

"St. Ann's Hill, *July 9th*, 1805.

" Dear Grey,

"Inclosed is some seed of the Anemone Pulsatilla, which Mrs. Fox sends Mrs. Grey. It should be put in light bog earth as soon as possible. Lord Grenville came over to me yesterday, and we agreed in all our speculations and opinions—but with regard to the former, it looks as if we were mistaken, as the general opinion is that the vacant places are to be filled up immediately : * Yorke to be Secretary of State, Camden President, Harrowby Chancellor of the Duchy. I still have my doubts as to the first of these appointments, though it may seem to tally with the circumstance of Pitt's having given up Foster to Lord Hardwicke.

" Yours ever,
"C. J. FOX."

TO THE HONOURABLE C. GREY.

"St. Ann's Hill, *Friday, July 12th*, 1805.

" Dear Grey,

"I got yesterday yours of the 7th, and am very happy to hear you are all so well after your journey. If I had written to you every day this week my speculations of each day would have been different from the former. I now think, as when I wrote to

---

* See letter of Lord Camden to Lord Grenville in " Courts and Cabinets," &c., vol. iii. p. 470.

you last, that no proposition will be made to us, and
I am quite sure it is best that it should be so—for
those who are anxious for union, will be more angry
with Pitt for making *no* proposal, than for making an
unreasonable one.　I refer to persons not connected
with us; for among ourselves there would be, I think,
the greatest unanimity in rejecting an improper offer.
My reason for thinking none will be made, rests
entirely on the filling up of the places, and especially
on the appointment of Castlereagh, whom I have
reason to think Pitt would in no case consent to
remove.　On the other hand, I learn from a quarter
which I credit, that Pitt has obtained H. M.'s consent to propose an extended Administration without
any exclusion, and that the idea was to propose the
admission of six of us into the Cabinet:　Grenville,
Spencer, Windham, Moira, you and me.　Now, I
should conceive that either this plan is abandoned, or
that such is the impudence of the man, that he conceives it not incompatible with this plan to insist on his
own remaining where he is, and continuing Hawkesbury
and Castlereagh Secretaries of State.—N.B. It was part
of my intelligence that these two were to be retained.
I can hardly think him audacious enough to make
such an overture; but if he does, I think it cannot
hurt us, for though any proposal ought to be, and
would be, rejected in which he was to be head, yet I
think the impudence of this will be more generally
felt.　With respect to the Doctor and his friends, I
hear they are ready enough for war, and I have had
a sort of a message from them, hinting at a union on

the ground of Pitt's conduct in screening delinquents, thwarting the inquiries of the Commissioners, and disgracing the House of Commons. My answer was, of course, civil and general.* I am told in London they consider it as certain that Nelson will overtake the enemy and beat him. A few days will show. The combined fleet must have suffered severely from sickness, perhaps among their sailors as well as their soldiers.

" Yours affectionately,

" C. J. FOX."

TO THE EARL OF LAUDERDALE.

" ST. ANN's HILL, *July 12th,* 1805.

" I HAVE been here near a fortnight, and Grey left town Wednesday se'nnight, so that of us three Whitbread is the only one who will have an opportunity of seeing your friend. The truth is, that I had determined not to be a manager,† and only lent my name on the express condition that I was not expected *ever* to attend.

" Concerning the state of politics here, accounts differ so from day to day, that it is quite useless to write about them. My speculations have varied more than once or twice in the last week. I *now* think, from the circumstance of the appointments, that Pitt will not make any proposal to opposition, but, on the other hand, I have good reason to think he mentioned to

---

* There seems to have been some mis-apprehension about this supposed message. See Life of Lord Sidmouth.

† On Lord Melville's impeachment.

the K. his intention of making what *he* (P.) thought a
very ample one, and that he obtained the King's
consent. What to make of this I cannot tell. I know
that nothing ought to be consented to unless he will
consider the present Ministry as annihilated in all its
parts, and consult about forming a new one. He will
not, I think, bring his mind to this, and yet his
weakness since the defection of the Doctor is extreme ;
however, that is his affair. The only thing that could
hurt us, would be an apparently fair offer on his part,
when, though we might be justified in refusing, we
might not be able to make the public see it in the
same light. On the other hand, I think I see every
disposition in the Addingtonians to join heartily
against him, and if they have as good a case as they
pretend, they will be pretty strong. The House of
Commons is evidently divided into four parties, nearly
upon a loose calculation, as follows ;—

Supporters of the Chancellor of the Exchequer for the time being	180
Opposition	150
Pitt	60
Addington	60
	450

There are, besides, several members who vote whim-
sically, or, in such case as Melville's, from fear of their
constituents, &c. ; and many, of course, who never or
very seldom attend. The first class, were it not for
the very precarious state of the K., would, I fear, be
much larger ; and the second, for the same reason, and
from the slowly increasing, but still increasing weight

of Carlton House, will much more likely gain ground
than lose any. The third class seems very unlikely to
increase at present; and the fourth will either gain or
lose,—first, according to the notions that will be entertained of the Doctor's being more or less well regarded
at Windsor; next, according to their success in setting
themselves up (which they will endeavour to do) as
opposers of corruption and guardians of the public
purse, &c. . . What is clearest of all is, that P. is very
low and does not seem to have any notion of what
plan he can follow to raise himself. Here is political
speculation enough of all conscience."

TO THE HONOURABLE C. GREY.

"St. Ann's Hill, *July* 16*th*, 1805.

" Dear Grey,

" Since I wrote last I have received yours
of the 10th, and, if occasion should happen (quod
procul a nobis, &c.), will certainly attend to it. My
wishes and opinions, with regard to situation for you,
remain unaltered; nor do I think that the precarious-
ness of your stay in the House of Commons is any
objection. My only fear was, and is, that if a negotiation of the sort alluded to, was to take place, it might
be expected that something less efficient would be
thought the proper compromise. The filling up of
the places seems to *me*, and on the first view must
appear so to everybody, to be a declaration that there is
no longer any intention to negotiate; but the Pittites
say it is not so meant, and I am told that we are to

H 2

consider Pitt's journey to Weymouth, whenever it shall take place, as a signal that the mischief is about to commence. I doubt this very much; but from all appearance, if any proposition is made, it will be such a one as may be instantly rejected, without any danger of our being blamed for it. If contrary to my expectations, and to the nature of the man, anything plausible should be proposed, I shall indeed be in difficulties, though by adhering to the sine quâ non, I should hope we should still be safe. It is worthy consideration, too, what security we could take, that he will not continue to use the influence in his hands to screen Melville, and to thwart further inquiries. It would be very unseemly if it could be said with any colour that we could acquiesce in measures on this point in which the Doctor could not. I hear the Addingtonians put the resignations entirely on the ground of this business; but whether they can make out their case clearly, I doubt. It seems to be admitted that Pitt's interview with the Doctor was the immediate cause that produced the resignations. Well, then, if that interview, which is also admitted to have been of Pitt's seeking, had not taken place, would not the Doctor have been still a member of Ministry, notwithstanding Leicester's motion, &c.? However, it is right, I think, to uphold the Doctor in his resignation, as far as we can, and, I think, Cobbett has taken the right line on this subject exactly. To be sure it is impudence hardly to be endured, considering the different shares that he and we have had in the business, that the Doctor should hold himself

out as the *sole* Centre, &c.   There is no truth in Lord
Grenville's having seen the K. T. Grenville was
here Sunday, and he is one of those who still think
there will be negotiation.   I have a letter from Lord
Moira, who concurs entirely in the opinion that this
Ministry must be given up, and considered as annihilated before anything can be done towards union;
nor indeed have I seen any one who does not think
the same.   We have had strange weather here, cold
and dark ; but everything looks well.

" Yours affectionately,
                "C. J. FOX."

TO MR. O'BRIEN.

"*July* 17*th,* 1805.

" THE Doctor, Lord help him, is a great fool,
and one whom experience cannot make wise.   His
whole consequence depends (for personally he is
nothing) on the number of votes in the House of
Commons, who seem at present inclined to go with
him, and nine out of ten of these he will lose by
talking the senseless language you hear of.   He will
then be reduced to absolute insignificance ; whereas,
if he was to manage well, and state publicly his
hostility to Ministers, bringing forward, as he might
do, good ostensible reasons, he might be a man of
much more consequence than it is fit such a man
should be.   I think Cobbett takes quite the right
line about the resignations, &c. ; but no man can do
anything for one who will not do anything for him-

self; nay, who on the contrary who will do everything *against* himself and for his enemies. I see no newspapers that speak of politics; but I think the tone of the paragraphs ought to be to treat with contempt the notion of Pitt's being able to carry on the Government as he is, or to gain any accession of strength; and Castlereagh's appointment ought to be stated as complete proof of his weakness and impotence in either view."

TO MR. O'BRIEN.

"St. Ann's Hill, *August 7th*, 1805.

" Without coalitions *nothing* can be done against the Crown; with them, God knows how little! As to the abuse which has been made of my civil expressions, as they are called, to Pitt, I always foresaw that they would be so used; but I am still positive that I was right, and do not repent one of them."

TO MR. O'BRIEN.

"St. Ann's Hill, *August 25th*, 1805.

"The combined fleets being out is, as you know, now certain; but for what particular object it is vain to guess. They generally have mismanaged at sea; so it is to be hoped they will continue to do. The Austrian Mediation, which is now so much talked of, *may* do a great deal, if well managed, but that it is not like to be. I like

to-day's 'Cobbett' very much, both on Invasion
and on Foreign Affairs. The failure of another
Continental coalition would be fatal, and this cannot
be too much beat into the heads of all rational
Anti-Gallicans."

TO THE EARL OF LAUDERDALE.

"St. Ann's Hill, *August 27th*, 1805.

" I AM inclined still to adhere to my opinion that
he (Pitt) will make no overture; but in this opinion
I find myself nearly single. However, none has
been as yet made; and I am told that you are to
look to Pitt's going to Weymouth as the signal that
something is about to be done. He has not yet
been there. In the meantime there is a belief that
war on the Continent will break out immediately,
though it is certain Austria has sent a paper to
Petersburg, Berlin, London, and Paris, stating her
wish that negotiations may be resumed, and offering
good offices.

" I have not seen the paper, but it is said to be
couched in very general terms; and many think
Napoleon will consider it merely as an artifice to
gain time, and begin the attack. I think the more
immediate cause of war, if war is to be, will be
the passage of Russian troops into Austrian ter-
ritories, and then it will once more be contrived
so as to put Bonaparte in the right. For he will
have good reason to say, that admitting Russian
troops at the moment she pretends to lament Russia's

having broken off the negotiation, is such a proof both of the ill-will and the insincerity of Austria, as to justify his choosing his time for going to war."

TO THE HONOURABLE C. GREY.

"ST. ANN'S HILL, *August 28th,* 1805.

" DEAR GREY,

" I received with great pleasure yours of the 23rd. We wish you heartily joy, and hope Mrs. Grey and the boy will continue as well as you have reason to expect.* It is a long while since I wrote, and I will not be so long again, but idleness, and having nothing new to tell you, were the reasons. The latter of these reasons still continues. There was a strong report (an absurd one on the face of it) that some proposition was to be sent to us at Stowe ;† this of course did not happen, and they who think some offer will be made, adhere to what was said some time ago, that Pitt's visit to Weymouth (where he has not yet been) would be the signal for the commencement of what I call the mischief. I have still a notion that no offer will be made, but I must confess I am nearly singular in that opinion. It is, I am sure, best for us that none should, unless it could be one through the channel you hint at, in which case, to reject it with indignation must be the course which every man would approve. You see I understand your letter, but should not do so unless I

---

* Hon. Frederick Grey born August, 1805.
† Mr. Fox met the Prince of Wales at Stowe.

had had one from Lauderdale explanatory of it. I
own I think it is absolutely impossible such a channel
should be attempted, and that whoever informed M.*
that it was intended must have been mistaken, or
meant to laugh at him. There could not be a measure
so calculated for making the refusal appear right in
the eyes of all mankind; whereas I presume the
intention is to endeavour to put us in the wrong, in
the opinions of as many people as possible: and in
this way, if Pitt were to manage dexterously, I should
fear he might have some success. I have strong
dependence however on his temper and character;
and suspect he will be more anxious to keep himself
clear of the imputation of what I should call modesty,
and he humiliation, than to fix upon us that of un-
reasonableness. I hear that to those who casually see
him, his appearance is just as it was in the House of
Commons—that of extreme uneasiness, and almost
misery. Most of his friends speak of the extreme
desireableness of a junction, and some even of the
absolute necessity of it: but then the friends I
speak of are such mere cyphers, that what they say is
of little moment, though they are in high offices.
Mulgrave, to my surprise, goes as far as any of them.
Harrowby is supposed to hold the stouter language,
and to say that Pitt must not let it be thought for a
moment that he is in any absolute want of us; and
with this view it is supposed that he advised the
immediate filling up of the places. Apropos of fillers
up; I hope you are delighted at Castlereagh's defeat.

* Lord Moira.

He seems in his speeches at Downpatrick to have made a worse figure, even than usual, with his reasons, first for his absence, then for his presence, and lastly for his being off. What a bother we have made with the sea-business ! Ministers blame Calder, and then intrust to him the command of the most important fleet we have ; they cannot be right in both. My notion is that if Calder and the enemy meet, there will be a bloody battle, with regard to which, considering the disparity of strength, I scarcely know how to be sanguine. But I think the most probable conjecture is, that the combined fleet is gone to the Mediterranean, in which case there will be a long time before any battle, and the best we can hope is that Collingwood and Bickerton may escape. Everybody expects immediate war on the Continent, and I am afraid there is but too much ground for the expectation. But yet it is certain that the Emperor of Austria has sent a paper to Petersburg, Berlin, London, and Paris ; wherein he expresses a strong desire that negotiations should recommence, and offers his good offices, &c. None of the answers are yet known ; but the fear is that Bonaparte, having strong evidence of the intentions of Austria to join Russia, will consider these pacific sentiments merely as means to gain time, and will begin the attack. I suspect too that the paper, which I have not yet seen, is in such vague and general terms, as to give but too much colour to the interpretation which it is feared Bonaparte will put upon it. The Austrians themselves admit that if they are attacked, there is nothing

but a victory over the French army that can stop it
from going directly to Vienna. No fortified places,
no strong positions to be taken. Their only resource
is to fight, and beat the enemy; and if their first
victory is not a decisive one, they must fight again
and again; if victorious, they compel the French to
retreat; if beaten in any one great battle, the enemy
must be at Vienna. A pleasant game to play this!
The alarm of invasion here was most certainly a
groundless one, and raised for some political purpose
by the Ministers; but, whether there may not be on
the cards a possibility of some naval events which may
render the alarm a most serious one, is another
question. I still however feel bold; that is to say
about the improbability of their being able to come;
not with regard to what would happen if they were to
land in force. In such a case I should feel quite the
reverse of bold. Upon the whole, a slow death by
the continuation of the war appears to be more
probable than a violent one. Could matters still be
remedied? God knows—but I think something better
than the present system might be tried; and nothing
worse is possible. I hear too that in military matters
everything is going on worse and worse: fortifications
and canals making at an enormous expense, that will
be worse than useless, and everything relative to the
army in the old track; it could not be in a worse.
Sir Charles Pole told a friend of mine that after the
12th or 13th report (I forget which) the Commissioners were to desist on the ground of the impossibility of conquering the obstacles thrown in their

way by all persons connected with Government. They should be careful, if such be their intention, to make a good case. Here are politics enough for a week; and yet upon reading over my letter, I do not think you will be much the wiser for anything it contains. By your not mentioning Lord Grey, I hope he is quite well again.

" Yours affectionately,
" C. J. FOX."

TO LORD HOLLAND.

" ST. ANN'S HILL, *September 4th,* 1805.

" WHAT I said about the Austrian proposition was not exactly represented, though partly so. I certainly have strong reason to think that our Court will state itself to be ready to comply with the wish expressed in the Austrian Circular Paper for the resumption of negotiations; at the same time I believe it to be the expectation of all parties, and perhaps the wish of most, that the war will commence almost immediately. The Austrians either do not expect, or pretend not to expect, that the attack will be made by Bonaparte upon the ground of their intimate connection with Russia, and of their supposed acquiescence in the Russian troops passing through the Austrian territory. You are to observe that I do *not* understand the Austrian paper to contain a distinct proposition of mediation, but on the contrary that the offer of good offices is very vaguely worded, and that when I spoke of these offers being well received I spoke of our

Court only.   I am totally ignorant what answers will be given by Russia, Prussia, or France.   Perhaps the whole is merely a device, and, as I should think, a very shallow device to gain time.

" Yours affectionately,
" C. J. FOX."

TO LORD HOLLAND

" September, 1805.

" A THOUSAND thanks, my dear young one, for your dear little boy.   I have not yet time to read your Vienna letter, but what you mention regarding the intention of forcing Prussia is not new to me.   It is intolerable, and will, if executed, make us odious to all mankind.   In *this* view too it is very foolish ; but, on the other hand, to leave Prussia in a state to join the French on the first favourable occasion for crushing Austria is liable to objections too.   These are among the fundamental and incurable difficulties.

" Yours,
" C. J. FOX."

TO THE HONOURABLE C. GREY.

" St. Ann's Hill, September 11th, 1805.

" DEAR GREY,

" I write one line to tell you that I hear, from pretty good authority, that Pitt goes down to Weymouth this week ; and consequently now or never will come on this cursed negotiation.   I still hope there will be nothing, but I find my opinion is not the general one; and there are circumstances which make me afraid. At any rate I have strong confidence in the insolence of his character, making him offer such a basis, as everybody will see the propriety of immediately rejecting. I hope Mrs. Grey and the young fry are all as well as we wish them.

" Yours ever affectionately,

" C. J. FOX.

" P.S. Fitzwilliam's attack was certainly paralytic; but Dr. Pitcairn says it was the slightest possible of the kind, nor has he been, as I understand, in any danger." *

TO THE EARL OF LAUDERDALE.

"September 17th, 1805.

" I HEAR from all quarters so much of an intended proposition, that I am forced to abandon my opinion, which was, that none would be made. As I feel myself quite sure that no good can come of it, the object with me is to consider of the best way of parrying it. To refuse absolutely having anything to do with Pitt, would, after all that has passed, be hardly justifiable, or at least it would require so much explanation to the public as to make it a very unadvisable party measure. But to refuse having to do with any negotiation in which the *whole* formation of a *new* Ministry is not perfectly open, would, I think, be so reasonable that every unprejudiced man must

---

* Lord Fitzwilliam lived till 1833.

see the propriety of it. Here, therefore, we may safely make our stand ; but if Pitt (which, however, I think very unlikely) should give way on this point, why then we must manage the negotiation as well as we can, and my difficulties will be very great. It would be unreasonable indeed to ask you to come up on such an occasion, and therefore it is, I suppose, out of the question ; but yet I feel that no occasion can occur in which I should so much want advice, and that there is no advice I should think so useful as yours. I think that, even if P. should like to have the appearance of giving way, there would be preliminaries very difficult, if not impossible, to be adjusted. Naval commanders, Melville, Redesdale, &c. &c. If P. went to Weymouth yesterday, as I learn that he intended to do, we shall soon know whether any offer is to be made, and, if any, what it is to be. I understand there are still great difficulties in regard to Austria, but the general opinion is that Bonaparte will cut that knot by making an almost immediate attack, and I think it very likely. Dissolution is more talked of than ever, but I believe in it less and less."

TO THE HONOURABLE C. GREY.

"St. Ann's Hill, *September 29th*, 1805.

"Dear Grey,

"I was very happy to get your letter on
my return home on Friday, as I had heard both
Mrs. Grey and one of the girls had been ill, but
nothing certain about it. I hope to God, they are
both by this time quite recovered, and that I shall
soon hear from you that they are so. Pitt has been
now some days returned from Weymouth, and no
news of overture. I am quite sanguine again that
none will come; but I own that about a fortnight
ago I was almost beat out of my opinion by the
concurrent opinion of all whom I saw or heard of.
In case any overture had been made, all you say
about communication of plans, &c., had been thought
of; but I always believed that everything would be
off upon preliminaries, and consequently before such
communications could be asked. Bonaparte does, I
think, appear very uneasy about the war; but this
gives me little hopes. 'O Navis, referent in mare
te novi fluctus!' is a sentence that cannot be pronounced by any thinking man without anxiety.
Our papers are, of course, all sanguine, and state
the accession of Bavaria to the League, as they call
it; but it is possible that this accession is only, in
fact, submission to the first army that appears in their
country; but we shall soon see. The disavowal on
the part of Austria and Russia of any interference in

the internal concerns of France is, I think, very judicious. *They* say, too, that our sentiments are similar; but surely this ought to be distinctly expressed, and not left to others to say for us, as if we were ashamed of it. Everything, except partridges, here is as abundant as you describe it to be with you.

" Yours affectionately,

" C. J. FOX."

TO THE EARL OF LAUDERDALE.

"*September* 30*th*, 1805.

" I AM very much obliged to you indeed for what you say in your second about coming. I never meant to express even a wish about it, unless the negotiation was fairly *entamé*, and I agree with you that even in that case there is something unpleasant and ridiculous in coming up for a business which is sure to end in nothing. The considerations in your last letter are by no means new to me; so far am I from thinking them immaterial, that the re-establishing of old interests, and especially where the persons to whom they belong have been steady to us, is, without exception, my first and principal object in wishing for any degree, more or less, of personal power, and therefore in any arrangement, whether by means of coalition or otherwise, it is what I shall most anxiously look to. Eighteen months ago, when there was a *possibility* of a junction with Pitt, I thought this would not be (as far as relates to England) a very difficult point.

The line seemed to me pretty clear, i. e., that
there should be an equitable division between our
friends and those few who had stuck by Pitt, *against*
Government. At that time he could have no *inclination*, as I should think, but certainly no duty
incumbent on him to protect those who had just been
fighting under the King's and the Doctor's banners
against him and us united. The difficulty in Scotland was greater, because Dundas had done so much
for Pitt against Government, that it would have been
impossible not to allow him very great weight indeed
in Scotland. At the same time we must have insisted
as a *sine quá non* on the support of such of our
friends as had uniformly stuck by us, which would
not have been a very great number. As to those
who had *sold* themselves and their interest, one
should have had less delicacy. This was my general
view of the matter last year. I have thought the
less about it this year, because I have all along held
a junction with Pitt to be not improbable but impossible ; but still as many things that I deemed
impossibilities have happened, I have not been quite
inattentive to the change of circumstances both in
England and Scotland since last year. Pitt would
now certainly have the *desire*, and he would pretend,
perhaps, too, that he was *bound in honour* to protect
many who were the most adverse to him when he
was out, and who are, properly speaking, the *âmes
damnées* of the Court of Corruption. This must be
guarded against ; but I think no letter or explanation
would afford so good a guard in this case as the

having the office of First Lord of the Treasury in proper hands, and this must, therefore, be insisted on.   Grey would be best, Fitzwilliam next, and Moira the least good of any that I could propose. In case the latter were the person, which, because he is the least eligible, would be the most likely, I should in that case think it necessary to have a complete explanation with *him*, and I have little doubt but he would act fairly ; indeed it would be so much his interest to do so, that he could not do otherwise. So far for England : with respect to Scotland, I should hope that what has passed must have so far lessened the Melville, that the difficulties of last year must be nearly smoothed, and at all events now, Melville, as a Minister at least, is out of the question, and the management of the Scotch patronage would be put in a great measure into your hands and those of the Hamiltons.   If this was not consented to in words, it would in fact take place ; indeed the mere circumstance of your being in office, and Melville out, would go a great way to insure things taking a right course.

" Now, after all this speculation, my opinion again is that no offer of any kind will be made.   Even those who were most sure that it would, begin now to think with me, and especially since Pitt has been so long returned from Weymouth without doing anything.   I shall be very glad if I am right, though I do not think there would be any great difficulty in bringing forward one or two preliminaries, which would put a stop to the negotiation in a manner far from disreputable to us; I do not recollect when I last wrote to you; but I believe it is since I was in town (Saturday fortnight) for a few hours. The universal opinion *there* did, I own, shake mine considerably, and particularly as it was certain that Pitt's friends gave out as a matter of certainty that something would be done.

"I know nothing more of the breaking out of the war than I learn from the newspapers. Bonaparte seems disturbed, but I cannot help thinking the Austrians will have the worst of it."

TO LORD HOLLAND.

"*September*, 1805.

"Dear Young One,

"I send you back your dear little boy, who has made us both more and more fond of him. He seems very well, thank God. I forgot to send the Vienna letter by yesterday's post, so send it now. The contents of it exactly correspond with what were my notions at the time it was written. Bad as the war is, the general reluctance with which it is entered into will make it worse if it takes place: but let us hope that some further attempts at peace will be made, and if they are made with any tolerable management, I am very sanguine about their success. I feel quite sure that Bonaparte would like peace if we would give way in anything.

"We should have gone with Hen. E.* to-day if we

---

* The present Lord Holland.

had not so arranged our visits that we must be at
Goodwood on Monday. We hope now Hen. E.
has been here once, that Lady Holland and you will
let him visit us now and then, as change of air must
be good for him, and it is the greatest gratification
to us. Notwithstanding the universal opinion, my
fancy is that Pitt will not make any proposition (at
least none in which he is serious) unless he means
foreign pacific negotiation. In that case I really
believe he would *wish* a junction ; but whether he
could bring his mind to the sacrifices necessary for
it, is another question."

TO R. ADAIR, ESQ.

" *October 6th,* 1805.

" DEAR ADAIR,

" I have just received yours of the 4th.
Depend upon business enough next session if you are
inclined that way. *My* opinion for refusing the
subsidy is clear ; whether Bonaparte actually gets it
in money or in money's worth, that is, increase of
greatness and dominion, it comes to the same thing.
But, mind, I only mention this as my opinion ;
to-morrow I go over to Dropmore, and shall learn
more of that of others. Concerning the conduct of
the war there can be no difference ; but the truth is,
that any war at this time, unless well concerted and
directed rather to future successes than to the
present, and more in the nature of a *sap* than a *coup
de main,* is nonsense, and for such a war neither we
nor our allies are by any means prepared."

TO THE EARL OF LAUDERDALE.

" October 10*th,* 1805.

" .   .   .   It is very curious to see what part Prussia will take, though I think the only hesitation can be between neutrality and open alliance with France. Her situation seems to me to have its difficulties. What seems to me clear, is, that she or Austria will be the great victim of this war, according as success attends France or the Allies. If the Cabinet of Berlin see this as I do, they will of course give the most efficacious assistance they can to France; but, on the other hand, there is something plausible in neutrality. Some say that Russia and Austria will not consent to Prussian neutrality, and, if they cannot have Prussia *with* them, will force her to be *against* them. This would be a stronger act of national tyranny than any that is imputed to France. I suppose we shall have to pay enormously. I know our Allies have said that 5,000,000*l.* will by no means do. Let me have your speculations. I think the most probable event is the success of the French, and a second treaty of Campo Formio in a few months, but it is possible it may be otherwise, and that the Allies may begin with successes; if so, the war and the ruinous expense attending it may go on for many years. There is a third case, viz., that the advantages of this campaign may be balanced. In this case, I believe both the French and the Austrians would be inclined to negotiation; but should we and the Russians allow them to follow their inclinations?"

TO LORD HOLLAND.

"St. Ann's Hill, *October 25th*, 1805.

" Dear Young One,

"I am very happy indeed to hear Charles is so well again. Little Hen. E. is perfectly well, and a delight to us all. He says 'Pity the sorrows' very well; but I cannot get him to learn anything new to say to you. I wait with some curiosity to know about Prussia. One should think it impossible he should put himself in the power of Austria and Russia, but as it is evident the Austrian Cabinet is mad, why not the Prussian too? What if Prussia were to seize this moment, when she is least suspected of partiality to France, to propose an effectual mediation? *Non lo farà*, but if she would, it would be a good thing.

" Yours affectionately,
" C. J. FOX."

TO MR. O'BRIEN.

"St. Ann's Hill, *October 31st*, 1805.

" I have received your letter, and would gladly do what you desire if I could, but I have no remembrance of the words, nor even of the manner in which the opinion you refer to was introduced. The sentiment I remember perfectly, and indeed it has been the uppermost in my mind ever since I first heard that there was a probability of the Austrians joining. I am sure I expressed the opinion of the danger strongly, and perhaps what may be worth Cobbett's while to recollect, that Pitt made the very foolish answer 'that all war was attended with danger.' I replied that they were not the general dangers of war that I referred to, but the peculiar danger of Austria in the *existing circumstances.*'

TO MR. O'BRIEN.

"St. Ann's Hill, *November 6th*, 1805.

"Many thanks for the Courier. These are wonders indeed, but they are not *much* more than I expected.* Now for a domestic speculation. Will the country bear all this? I fear they will bear everything, but I allow they never were tried quite so high before. I take for granted that there is no chance *now* of the K. of Prussia joining, but that there should be persons mad enough to wish it (and I hear Ministers do wish it,) is an instance of infatuation and stupid determination not to act by experience unexampled in the annals of the world. It is not enough to have laid Austria at Bonaparte's feet, but they want to sacrifice Prussia to him also. If the greater power could do nothing against him, taken by surprise, as in some degree she certainly was, let us try what a lesser power can do.

* The campaign of 1805, Ulm, &c.

TO LORD HOLLAND.

"*November 7th*, 1805.

" THANK you, my dear Young One, for your packet which I received. It is a great event,* and by its solid as well as brilliant advantages, far more than compensates for the temporary succour which it will certainly afford to Pitt in his distress.

" I am very sorry for poor Nelson ; for though his conduct at Naples was atrocious, I believe he was at bottom a good man, and it is hard he should not enjoy (and no man would have enjoyed it more,) the popularity and glory of this last business. We have been so occupied with Madoc that we have not yet looked at Lope, but we will begin immediately. A paper I have seen says that the Prussians jointly with the Russians have entered Hanover, and that the Emperor A. is at Potsdam. If this be so, I suppose the K. of Prussia is in for it, and I dare say our wise Ministers are quite happy at the prospect of offering up another victim to Bonaparte's shrine. They will never be satisfied till they have destroyed all possible means of continental resistance to France. I am sorry Hutchinson goes, because I have a great liking to him. I have heard nothing of the offer to Moira, and you do not mention what answer he has made.

Yours affectionately,

"C. J. FOX."

---

* The news of the Battle of Trafalgar.

TO THE HONOURABLE C. GREY.

"ST. ANN'S HILL, *December* 3rd, 1805.

" DEAR GREY,

"What an age it is since I have heard from
you! Perhaps you may make me the same reproach,
but I rather think mine was the last letter. I have
deferred writing these ten days, thinking that some
news would come which would clear up matters on
the continent to the conviction of everybody; to mine
they are too clear already, and indeed have been so
for some time. I should hope you cannot disagree
with me, in thinking that Pitt ought to be fallen on
without mercy, for having set on foot the ill-timed,
rash, and ill-constructed attack of the Austrians,
without waiting either for Prussia, or even for the
Russian armies, that were to form so main a part of
the strength. However, I am sorry to say that some
among our new Allies, are far from ready for such an
attack, which (by very weak arguments as I think,)
they maintain, would tend to destroy all hope and
spirit here. So things stand at present; but if events
should occur (and most probably they will,) which
will extinguish all hope of Austria continuing the
contest, then I think our friends will come nearly
right; for during the short time when Kickhort's
letter was believed, I know they considered all continental attempts as necessarily to be renounced. At
any rate, however desirable union may be, these are
points too important to sacrifice even for that object;

at least I feel them so; and could not answer it to
myself, if I did not make some effort to stop a system
which, if it goes on one or two years longer, must end
in making Bonaparte as much in effect monarch of
Germany as he is of France.

"I saw John Ponsonby at Lord Paget's, who gave
me a very good account of Mrs. Grey, little Bessy,
and all of you ; and from him I was confirmed in what
I had before heard, that you were coming up. I had
concluded that for several reasons, the impeachment
among others, you would feel it necessary to do so,
and therefore have forborne teasing you; all I shall
now press you for is, that it should be early, for the
first day if possible, for on the address itself there
must be a most interesting debate, and probably even
a division. Besides the general scheme of the war,
there is our own particular conduct in it for discussion; the *timing* of our expedition from home, and
the employment of our Mediterranean force in making
at least a most useless invasion of Naples. The
Parish Bill, and other subjects connected with it will
be brought on immediately, the first possible day after
the meeting ; and there we expect to be very strong,
as there will on that subject not only be a complete unanimity among ourselves, but as I hear, and
believe, we shall be fairly supported by the Addingtons.

"If you chance to see Lauderdale, pray tell him
that I wrote him near a fortnight since a letter which
I desired he would answer by return of post, about
some vine cuttings, &c.   Mrs. Fox desires to be kindly

remembered to you all, and so do I, and wish you a merry Christmas and happy new year,

Yours affectionately

"C. J. FOX."

"P.S. Are not you struck with the extreme impudence of our ministerial bulletins? The assertion that the convention between Murat and the Russians, and the correspondence of Palfi were forgeries, was sent to the newspapers by Ward, of the Secretary of State's office. They say the extreme follies they have been guilty of in this way lately, are owing to Pitt's being out of town."

MR. FOX TO LORD HOLLAND.

"*December 7th,* 1805.

"DEAR YOUNG ONE,

"I was very bad in not answering your letters at Woolbeding, but I was always either shooting or at chess.

"I will do all I can for attendance, but with respect to what is to be done, I can say nothing positive till after to-morrow, when I shall see Lord Grenville. My own inclination is for the strongest and plainest measures, such as refusal of subsidy, but I have little hope of getting others to agree in this.

"The disapprobation of the manner and time of the attack on France must I think be very general. As to *pacific language* which is your phrase, I own I doubt very much whether this is a time even for us, (exclusive of new friends) to hold out that there is much chance of obtaining any tolerable peace just now. I think we ought more than ever to deal in retrospect rather than prospect.

"Yours ever,

"C. J. FOX."

MR. FOX TO MR. O'BRIEN.

"ST. ANN'S HILL, *December 3rd*, 1805.

"THRICE have I determined to trouble you with a commission, and thrice have I forgotten it. It is this, if an article in the papers is true that there is a book opened somewhere (at the Herald's office I think), to receive the names of those who purpose attending Lord Nelson's funeral, I should like my name to be set down. I shall attend if I am no further from town than here, but at any rate I should like to have my name set down."

TO THE EARL OF LAUDERDALE.

"*December 17th*, 1805.

"THE folly of the newspapers is indeed beyond credibility, but what is more extraordinary is that they are certainly encouraged in holding out these foolish and false hopes by the Ministers, who cannot I should think seriously entertain them. I will tell you a very strong instance of this. You have seen probably paragraphs in almost all the papers stating the Russian offer of capitulation, and the correspondence

with the Archduke Palatine to be forgeries; now
these paragraphs were sent to the different newspapers
(the 'Morning Chronicle' included) by Ward of the
Secretary of State's office; and this as I am assured,
without the shadow of reason for thinking them
forgeries, except possibly their own foolish belief.
As to Pitt's illness, I heard in general that he was
not well, but till this day I never heard that anything
serious was apprehended. Letters from London
to-day mention reports of his being in great danger
with the gout in his stomach, but these are only
reports, and I do not believe them. That he has
had, and probably has stomach complaints is I believe
true. I believe his meeting Melville at Bath will
cause much scandal. I hear the Doctor talks of it
with uplifted eyes, and says he cannot believe it.
What do you think Pitt's death would produce just
now? My speculation is, a new edition of an
Addington Administration, Peace of Amiens and all."

TO MR. O'BRIEN.

"*December* 26th, 1805.

"I return you the *Lucius*. I remember it's coming
out very well, and that it was afterwards the general
opinion that Junius was from the same pen, as also
some letters signed Atticus. I do not think much of
it, but you know I am no great idolizer of Junius."

TO LORD HOLLAND.

"*January 1st,* 1806.

"DEAR YOUNG ONE,

"I could not conceive what you meant by asking how I made out the news, when from the "Morning Post," which was sent to me, it appeared all clear enough, God knows; but I now suppose you had not seen that paper, nor heard what was to be in the evening ones. I think these events do make a great change in the question of Amendment, and I should hope will have much influence on those of our friends whom I thought most unwilling, as their principal argument was the fear of discouraging future exertions on the continent. Such exertions are now out of the question. I think now that an amendment there must be; and I wish you and Lord Henry would try your hands without loss of time in sketching out one. My only objection is, an apprehension that others will use the phrase you do, of a *trial of strength*, and I am sure it will not be a favourable trial of strength for us. But this objection must yield to other reasons; and I have told those to whom I have written that there would be a division. I have done all I can for attendance. Between the two sorts of amendment proposed I am pretty indifferent, but rather incline to a strong one, that is, unless we should have reason *to know*, that a soft one will gain us a dozen or two in numbers. Say, therefore, to everybody that there will be an Amendment and Division, and I shall be for risking one whatever our probable numbers may be. I will fairly own that, though I have some hope, I am not very sanguine about being able so to word it as to make Lord Grenville support it. If he does not, it will be a sad affair, not only with respect to the House of Lords, but with reference to the influence of his conduct in the House of Commons ; but sad as it is, this appears to me to be a moment when no *great* sacrifice ought to be made, even for the purpose of unanimity among ourselves, a purpose which I am disposed to think as important as anybody else can. When I go to town for the funeral I will endeavour to see both Lord G. and Tom, and see what I can make of them ; but I have a dread of arguing much with obstinate men, lest one rivet them faster in their absurdities. N.B. Pray do not repeat any part of the above sentence to anybody. If we fail in getting a strong support on the Amendment, I would not despond, but bring on without loss of time either the Friday or the Monday after the meeting, the Parish Bill, and other circumstances connected with Land Military Force ; whether we are to continue the war or to treat for peace, a respectable army is equally neces- sary, and not only this is a subject on which Pitt is particularly vulnerable ; but it is one on which we shall probably have the *full* support of the Addingtons, as well as that of all our friends. Lord Henry ought, with as little delay as possible, to bring on his Scotch jobs, and especially Melville's additional salary.* In

---

* Lord Melville holding the sinecure place of Keeper of the Privy Seal of Scotland, with a large salary, obtained a large addition to it, without any duties to perform.

short, we ought to act as vigorously as possible in the
early part of the session, as I know it is the general
wish, and there may be hopes of keeping some in
town whom it would be more difficult to bring back.
I had a letter from Windham about a week ago, and
I was sorry to see a disposition in him upon any even
slight appearance of success to form new hopes for a
coalition.   However, that evil must be now quite
done away, and his desire to blame Ministers is as
strong, I think, as that of any of us.   Pray write a
line before you go to Bedfordshire, to say what impression the news seems to make.

" P.S.—I mean the substance of this letter, all
indeed except the one *tabooed* sentence, for Lord
Henry as well as you.   You and he must work this
session like drayhorses. It would not be amiss if you
would get made, for yourselves as well as for me, a
catalogue of all the subsidiary treaties since the
revolution. I wish you would look, too, at the famous
passage in Demosthenes, to which yesterday's ' Morning Post' refers, and tell me where it is.   I remember it very well, but not all the circumstances of
the case to which it is applied, nor am I sure in what
oration it is.   I rather think in the περι στεφανου."

TO SAME.

"*January 2nd*, 1806.

" I am very much surprised at your letter, which
I have just received, as both Mr. Knap and I wrote

yesterday. Mine was a very long, and if I may say so, a very wise and instructive letter which, if it has not reached you, your loss is as great as it is irreparable.

" As to your news I must know Pitt's resignation for certain before I believe it.

" I am told that it is reported Parliament is *not* to meet on the 21st, but I suppose there is no ground for this report. Putting off in Pitt's present circumstances would be fatal to him. If there *be* any truth in the report of his going out, for God's sake do all you can to prevent our friends from being eager to come in, until they are sure of being quite and entirely masters. The taking of anything short of complete power, would be worse than anything that has as yet happened, and most especially for the Prince. The Fish's* turning Foxite is a strong circumstance, but still I am incredulous as to P.'s going out voluntarily.

" Yours affectionately,

"C. J. FOX."

TO HON. CHARLES GREY.

" *January* 10*th*, 1806.

" DEAR GREY,

" I received yours of the 5th on my return hither to-day, and too late for the post; but as you wish me so much to write again, I just write a few lines to tell you that I am more sanguine than I was

---

* John Crauford, Esq., of Piccadilly.

about our all agreeing to march in one column, though God knows, far enough from anything like certainty. I do not think any of our friends, or even the Ministry, are quite mad enough to wish for another campaign in Germany, even with the Russians or Prussians; but the difficulties will be of a minor kind, and arising from apprehensions, which I deem unseasonable, lest the condemnation of the particular attempt should imply a condemnation of the general system, &c., &c. Though I have mentioned Ministers, one can know little or nothing of their opinions. Pitt has been seriously ill, and, as I believe, too much so to attend to these matters; and without him, what are the rest? It is now said, that Sir Walter Farquhar, who went to Bath for him, is now coming back *with him* to London, but for this I will not vouch.

" Concerning the delusions of the Courier, bulletins, &c., I should hope and believe there can be no difference among us; and perhaps this is of all the most important point for the House of Commons. Tom Grenville comes here to-morrow, and when I have seen him I shall be able to say more; but unless I send this time enough to get into to-morrow's post, it will hardly reach you by the 16th. I will write Sunday or Monday, and direct to you to the post-office, Doncaster, to be left till called for. I am very happy to hear Mrs. Grey and the children come, but I could almost wish you would leave them a day behind you, rather than not be in London on the 19th. Between the 19th and 20th there is a

great difference, especially to me.   Mrs. Fox desires
to be kindly remembered to you all.

" Yours ever,

" C. J. FOX."

The following letters and extracts are taken from
the correspondence of Mr. Fox with my father, John,
Duke of Bedford, during the time that he was Lord
Lieutenant of Ireland, and Mr. Fox Secretary of State.
The latest of these letters, it will be seen, is dated
June 16th.

TO THE DUKE OF BEDFORD.

" *April* 13*th*, 1806.

" FIRST let me beg a line to say how the Duchess
is, for we have been uneasy at the accounts in the
newspapers.

" I do not yet hear whether or not the report of
the Bishop of Limerick's death is confirmed.   If he is,
Dean Warburton, I suppose, will be the new bishop ;
but if this should give an opening to any translation, I
should be very happy if the Bishop of Killala should
get a step.   He is one of the few bishops who are eminent for their learning, and I have good reason to think
has been kept down chiefly on account of the im-
partial narrative he gave of the landing of the French.
I have no acquaintance with him whatever, but I
think it would be a creditable thing to do, and that it
is a little incumbent on us not to let a man suffer

from his having abstained from the violent and abusive language, which has done so much mischief.

"I hear great complaints of the bad example shown in retaining Marsden, who is represented as a man willing, and, from his situation, capable of doing all manner of mischief to you and your friends; but of this I know nothing; in my brother's business he certainly behaved very ill. There are, besides, complaints of many torturers and persecutors being left in power, but of this you must be able to get far better information than I. My advice is, if you cannot steer quite even, rather to risk offending those attached to the old system than our real friends.

"With regard to us here, our bed of roses * is not very comfortable. This Prussian war, which we had no means of avoiding, but by a submission equal to that of the King of Prussia himself, will be very injurious to our commerce, and of course cause great discontent; and if there be a bad harvest, the evil will be incalculable. The best way of seeing it is, that if Russia joins heartily, we may make some impression; if not, there will be a pretence for a separate peace.

"Our budget gets a little unpopular, as was natural to expect; on the other hand I hear that Windham's plans are pretty generally approved. However, they will certainly be fought with all the strength of our opponents in three parts. First, the repeal of the Parish Bill; secondly, the limited term of service; thirdly, the abridging the allowances

* A phrase of Lord Castlereagh's.

to volunteers. It is, therefore, most desirable that we should then, if we can, not only get a large proportional majority, but large positive numbers. I hope you will desire Elliot to bring or send us as great a reinforcement from Ireland as possible. Next week and the week following will probably be the time they will be most wanted. Some of the bills may, probably, be read a second time to-morrow and Tuesday se'nnight, but the Committees and the Report scarcely till the week following. Pray let me know whether the Archbishop of Dublin is recovered, and give me in general as early notice as possible, when anything of importance becomes vacant, together with your wishes on the matter. To prevent omissions on either side of lesser points, I will agree, if you will, to write regularly once a-week, suppose Saturdays, to each other, and this to hold even if we have nothing more to say than common news. Pray remember Mrs. Fox and me in the kindest manner to the Duchess."

TO THE SAME.

"*April 20th*, 1806.

"Whitbread opened the business capitally yesterday. Our division to-night will be of the utmost importance."

TO THE SAME.

"*April 26th*, 1806.

" I HAVE received yours of the 19th, and am much obliged to you for it.   I will keep steady to a weekly correspondence.   With respect to Hardy's case, it is merely this, that he was sometime in the Irish parliament, always supported our principles without a single deviation, was a distinguished speaker there, and is in very indifferent circumstances.   He is a friend of Grattan's and of Lord Moira's, and though I am but little acquainted with him, I have an excellent opinion of him, and a regard for him for the Bishop of Down's sake, whose brother-in-law he was. I certainly did mention him to Elliot, and I believe to you, for an office, but stronger claims stood in his way.   An opportunity may offer, and he is really a most deserving man.

" I am much obliged to you for what you say about the Bishop of Killala.   You know my motives.   He is, I know, a very moderate man respecting the Catholics, but is more a man of learning than a politician.

" With respect to Mr. Evans's, a case which I think of the greatest importance, I have burnt or mislaid his son's original letter, but I enclose you his reply to my answer.   He was offered leave to return if he would retract his former opinions.   This he will not do, and is, I think, quite right in his determination.   But he promises future quiet obedience, and can give any security that may reasonably be demanded. He is an old man. His son is a man of most excellent character, and the rightest dispositions in all respects, and has, I have reason to believe, more influence with the Catholics and the remainder of the rebels than any other person. This influence he has used, and is still using for the best purposes, as far as he can venture to use it at all. If some lenity, especially in cases where, as in this, nothing is required, is not used, I have no hopes of any solid union among the different classes of Irishmen. The word rebel must not frighten us, and whenever there is reason to think the intentions for the future good, such intentions ought to be encouraged. I mentioned Evans to Elliot, as well as to you. Lord H. Petty knows the son very well, and the Parnells, especially William, who is one of the best as well as one of the cleverest men I ever knew, can give you a more full account of him. With respect to the divisions among the Catholic body, they are to be lamented, but remember the names first in rank are not the first in influence. Upon this point, too, you would do well to consult Wm. Parnell.

" I have no time to add anything about affairs here. All negotiation with France is now, I understand, at an end. We insisted on negotiating jointly with Russia; they on a separate negotiation. The difference between us is, therefore, plain and intelligible, but nothing of this ought *yet* to be mentioned publicly. You will be happy to hear that it occasioned no difference or even shade of difference in the cabinet."

TO THE SAME.

" *May 3rd,* 1806.

" PARTICULARLY in regard to Curran I know that he, more than anybody, feels the necessity of marking strongly the favour of government to him. I am afraid what you say is true, that Curran's private character does not stand so high as one might wish, but his public conduct, his resisting of temptations, his support of the cause of justice and humanity, when few, very few dared support it, are merits which cannot be overlooked without disgrace to us, more especially as the reasons against making him Attorney-General (very weak ones in my judgment) cannot be alleged. I most anxiously hope, therefore, that the negotiation you allude to will soon be brought to bear.

" I hope and believe that on all these points Elliot will be right, but I am sure that the Chancellor * and you cannot be wrong. There is no man. of more sound and excellent judgment than the Chancellor ; my only apprehension is, that he should attend too much to what his enemies may tell him will be the public sense on his conduct and that of the government. When you two thoroughly agree, do not let yourselves be shaken."

---

* Right Hon. George Ponsonby, afterwards leader of the Whig Party in the House of Commons.

TO THE DUKE OF BEDFORD.

"*May* 13*th*, 1806.

" I COULD not resist going to hear Romilly sum up on Saturday, which is the day I wish usually to allot to writing to you, and I have not had a moment since. I am very glad indeed to hear Evans's request is to be granted, and will write without delay to his son, to desire him to make a proper application. I entirely concur with you in thinking it right, that in case the first vacant see should not be of the very first class Dean Warburton should have it, but when the case of translation does occur, I still feel anxious for Stock. There is something in what you say of translation, but yet it is hard, when a man of merit happens (which is mere chance) to get a poor bishopric at first, he should not be preferred. Stock and Hamilton are, I believe, of all the Irish bishops the only two eminent for learning, which you know both with Lord G. and myself is a matter of great weight.

" Perhaps you are right on the subject of Sir R. Musgrave, and I am sure most of my colleagues are of the same opinion with you. I cannot help retaining my old prejudices on matters of this sort, and am already most exceedingly sorry that I have been porsuaded to acquiesce so much as I have done in what is called a conciliatory system here. The bad effects of it to my eyes are becoming every day more visible. We have permitted persons to think that they may be considered as friendly, though they reserve to themselves the intention of opposing us on particular questions, where Pitt's memory and what not is concerned. The consequence of this is, that our friends are (and in many cases most reasonably) discontented, and say, ' Surely if enemies are indulged with such reserves, much more we.' Thus every fancy any man takes about volunteers, limited service, &c., makes him vote against us, or stay away, saying that his opposition is confined to that question, and there are many who think we shall not be able to carry through Windham's plan in its most essential parts, in which case, whatever people may fancy, there must be an end of the administration. The leading men in rank and property among the Catholics must certainly be the great object of attention, only it is good to be aware, not for the purpose of slackening that attention, but for that of extending it to others, that their influence is not what one could wish.

" As to English matters you will guess from what I have said above, that we are not in a very easy state. Many of our friends are clamorous with us to give way on that part of Windham's plan which to him and me seems the most essential. If we give it up I shall consider all as lost, and the best thing to do is to break up the Ministry at once; but if a different opinion prevails, which is most likely, we may stay a little longer, but with an absolute certainty of having some other struggle with the King and the D. of Y. in which we shall be defeated. I hope and trust, therefore, that we shall not give up anything material,

but then we must expect hard fighting, and I have
little doubt but that in the course of the business the
enemy will muster towards 180.

" News is come of peace in India, and it seems as
if the Porte would certainly adhere to Russia and
Great Britain.   The state of Sicily is very bad, but I
hope we shall be able to retain it.   Sir J. Craig is
returned on account of bad health, and my brother
has orders to replace him.   There are reinforcements
sent, but if they are out of the channel yet, it is as
much as can be expected."

TO THE SAME.

" STABLE-YARD, May 21st.

" I AM very well satisfied with our division last
night in the House of Lords, 97 to 40, but I am told
others are not."

TO THE SAME.

" LORD SPENCER'S OFFICE, June 8th.

" I MEAN to write to-morrow, but I must avail
myself of an express Lord Spencer is sending to write
two lines.   I am afraid from what you said it will be
an object to Dean Warburton to have Limerick at
once, and if so, I give up ; but if not, I must again
mention Stock, who has been introduced to me since
I wrote last to you, and whose wish to be removed
from Killala is *very* strong.   I believe the difference
in income between the two is not very considerable,

and the more I enquire, the more I am confirmed in my belief that Stock has been much discountenanced by the late Ministers on account of his moderation and humanity. Tavistock has been with us some days, and we are quite delighted with him."

TO THE SAME.

"STABLE-YARD, *June 9th.*

" I have terribly failed in my weekly engagement, but I really have not had half an hour's quiet I do not know when. I have now before me your letters the 24th, the 25th, 26th, and 31st of last month, and will answer them in order, though, if you have no copies of your own letters, there may be some of my observations you may not understand.

' " In yours of the 24th, you begin with expressing your dissatisfaction at the division in the Lords. I own I was very well pleased with it, for I never did imagine that this opposition had not considerable strength in each House, and I heartily wish we may not have more divisions to send you an account of this week. Lord Grenville thinks there will not be more than forty. I shall be satisfied if they do not exceed sixty. Whether we shall have fair support from the quarter you allude to I much doubt, but I believe we at least shall not be thwarted there, and unless some marked occurrence at Court, or a near division in the House of Commons should make it justifiable, I think we could not answer to the country the leaving government at such a time as this to the

miserable administration which alone could succeed
us.   On the subject of instructions to the commander-
in-chief, I imagine Lord Spencer has already written
to you as fully as he is enabled to do at present.   The
Duke of York was three hours with him yesterday,
and will probably be as long with Lord Grenville
to-day, but I trust nothing material will be conceded
on this or any other occasion.   I will not conceal
from you that I am very glad that Marsden is going
out, and it is not necessary to say anything more on
the subject. Pray let me know as soon as you have fixed
his successor; the less connection he has had with the
old castle the better.   I think what you had conveyed
to Sir Richard Musgrave was quite right.   If I was
desirous of turning him out it was because, knowing
and feeling every day what we have lost by the fear of
being thought persecutors, I apprehend the like effects
with you.   If we had completely routed the Melvil-
lites, do you think they would have the courage or the
means to be endeavouring openly to preserve and
even increase their party power in Scotland ?

" In yours of the 25th you say if our majority is
small you think we ought to give up, and this was
strongly my opinion, but the divisions, though not so
good as one could wish, were too good to bring that
point in question.

" I am very happy indeed to find from your note
of the 26th, how thoroughly you are pleased with
Elliot.   I knew it would be so.   I have the highest
opinion of him in every respect, and though I *wish*
he had not been in the castle during Lord Camden's

and Lord Cornwallis' lieutenancies, I am perfectly convinced that he has come out (a most rare instance) uncontaminated from that sink of iniquity. There is something in my eyes of liberality, honour, and gentlemanlike feeling in him that I have seldom seen equalled, and not unmixed with a fair show of prudence.

"I am very happy indeed to learn by yours of the 31st, that Evans's business is in so fair a way. You have never said whether you have seen, any of you, William Parnell. He is perhaps rather romantic, but is an excellent man with great talents, and if he takes a right turn may be of great service to you."

TO THE DUKE OF BEDFORD.

"St. Ann's Hill, *June* 16*th.*

"A JOB and a fraud are very different things, and you may as well look for an Irishman free from the brogue as one free from job.

"Your statement of the comparative value of the bishoprics, as well as what related to Dean Warburton's present preferment, makes my requesting him to give way quite out of the question. So no more *at present* about Dr. Stock, but on the next occasion I shall return to the charge. As to his not attending much to the duty of a diocese where there are no Protestants, I do not value that much; while on the other hand I do value very highly his learning and particularly his edition of Demosthenes. If I had my

own way, except in very particular cases, I never
would make a man a bishop, who was not eminent in
some branch of learning. I do not care which, but
classical learning is of course my favourite. Besides,
I must repeat, it is our duty to recompense, at least
with our countenance, those who have been oppressed
on account of their moderation; and that he has been
so vexed on account of his narrative is a fact in which
not only Lord Hutchinson, but all those with whom
I have conversed, are agreed.

"With regard to our general situation I own I feel
now very confident. From the moment of our
first division on the Limited Service Bill, 254 to 129,
I began to be sanguine, and was not much staggered
by the reports circulated. You must consider that
the letting the men go during a war was not liked
among many of our best friends, and that the name
of *Windham's Plan* studiously connected with volunteers, &c., was for a time very unpopular. I mention
this to show that we came to our divisions under great
disadvantages. There was at one time a shout of
rage against Windham from the shabby feeling that
some of all parties are but too apt to entertain, and
which makes them hate any man who proposes anything bold, and which may lead to turn them out.
To this sentiment Pitt almost always yielded. That
we may be in some cases obliged to do so too I fear,
but I trust *very* seldom, and this will make the great
distinctive feature of this administration compared
with former ones. Hopes were afterwards entertained
by the opposition that they should have assistance in

the House of Lords.   These hopes are now at an
end ; 91 to 34 is a great division without proxies.

" Tavistock and his brothers left us on Friday
evening, and we were highly pleased with them all.
And now adieu : only in perfect confidence, and to you
only, let me add that I think things look something
better for peace than they did.   Here we have had
two charming days of idleness and enjoyment, but
must return to town to-day."

The private correspondence ends here.   I add
the official correspondence in French and English
relating to the negotiation of 1806.   The French
copies are printed from the Archives of the Foreign
Office at Paris; the English dispatches from the
Papers laid before Parliament.   It will be seen that
each has passages which are omitted in the other.
For instance, the French government omit the letter
of M. de Talleyrand, containing an extract of the
Emperor's speech, and the papers laid before parliament omit some of the phrases which do homage to
the virtues and character of Mr. Fox.

MR. FOX TO M. DE TALLEYRAND.

"DOWNING STREET, *le* 20 *Février*, 1806.

" MONSIEUR LE MINISTRE,

" Je crois de mon devoir, en qualité d'hon-
nête homme, de vous faire part, le plutôt possible,
d'une circonstance assez étrange qui est venue à ma

connoissance. Le plus court sera de vous narrer tout
simplement le fait comme il est arrivé.

" Il y a quelques jours qu'un quidam m'annonça
qu'il venait de débarquer à Gravesend sans passe-
port, et qu'il me pria de lui en envoyer un, parce qu'il
venait récemment de Paris, et qu'il avait des choses
à m'apprendre *qui me feraient plaisir*. Je l'en-
tretins tout seul dans mon cabinet, où après quelques
discours peu importans, ce scélérat eut l'audace de
me dire que, pour tranquilliser toutes les couronnes,
il fallait faire mourir le chef des Francais, et que,
pour cet objet, on avait loué une maison à Passy,
d'où l'on pouvait à coup sûr et sans risque exécuter
ce projet détestable. Je n'ai pas bien entendu si ce
devait être par le moyen des fusils en usage ou bien
par des armes à feu d'une construction nouvelle.
Je n'ai pas honte de vous avouer, à vous, Monsieur
le Ministre, qui me connoissez, que ma confusion
était extrême de me trouver dans le cas de con-
verser avec un assassin déclaré. Par une suite de
cette confusion, je lui ordonnai de me quitter instam-
ment, donnant en même temps des instructions à
l'officier de Police qui le gardait, de le faire sortir du
royaume au plutôt. Après avoir réfléchi plus mûre-
ment sur ce que je venais de faire, je reconnus la
faute que j'avais faite en le laissant partir avant que
vous en fussiez informé, et je le fis retenir.

" Il y a apparence que tout ceci n'est rien, et que
ce misérable n'a eu autre chose en vue que de faire
le fanfaron, en promettant des choses qui, d'après sa
facon de penser, *me feraient plaisir*.

" En tout cas, j'ai cru qu'il fallait vous avertir de
ce qui s'est passé, avant que je le renvoyasse.   Nos
lois ne nous permettent pas de le détenir longtemps,
mais il ne partira qu' après que vous aurez eu tout
le temps de vous mettre en garde contre ses atten-
tats.   Supposé qu'il ait encore de mauvais desseins,
lorsqu'il partira, j'aurai soin qu'il ne débarque que
dans quelque point le plus éloigné possible de la
France.   Il s'est appelé ici Guillet de la Gervillière :
mais je pense que c'est un faux nom.   Il n'avait pas
un chiffon de papier à me montrer, et à son premier
abord, je lui fis l'honneur de le croire espion.   J'ai
l'honneur d'être, avec le plus parfait attachement,
Monsieur le Ministre, votre très-obéissant serviteur,

(Signé)

"C. J. FOX."

M. DE TALLEYRAND, PRINCE DE BÉNÉVENT, TO MR. FOX.

" 5 Mars, 1806.

" MONSIEUR,

" J'ai mis la lettre de votre Excellence sous
les yeux de sa Majesté.   Son premier mot, après en
avoir achevé la lecture, a été : ' Je reconnais là les
principes d'honneur et de vertu qui ont toujours
animé M. Fox.'   Elle a ajouté : ' Remerciez-le de
ma part, et dites-lui que soit que la politique de son
souverain nous fasse rester encore long-temps en
guerre, soit qu'une querelle aussi inutile pour l'humanité ait un terme aussi rapproché que les deux
nations doivent le désirer, je me rejouis du nouveau
caractère que, par cette démarche, la guerre a déjà

pris, et qui est le présage de ce qu'on peut attendre d'un cabinet dont je me plais à apprécier les principes, d'après ceux de M. Fox, un des hommes les plus faits pour sentir en toutes choses ce qui est beau, ce qui est vraiment grand.'

"Je ne me permettrai pas, monsieur, d'ajouter rien aux propres expressions de sa Majesté impériale et royale. Je vous prie seulement d'agréer l'assurance de ma haute considération.

(Signé,)

"CH. MAU. DE TALLEYRAND,
PRINCE DE BÉNÉVENT."

MR. FOX TO M. DE TALLEYRAND.

"DOWNING STREET, 26 *Mars*, 1806.

"MONSIEUR,

"L'avis que votre Excellence m'a donné des dispositions pacifiques de votre gouvernement m'a induit à fixer particulièrement l'attention du Roi sur cette partie de la lettre de votre Excellence.

"Sa Majesté a déclaré plus d'une fois à son parlement son désir sincère d'embrasser la première occasion de rétablir la paix sur des bases solides, qui pourront se concilier avec les intérêts et la sûreté permanente de son peuple.

"Ses dispositions sont toujours pacifiques : mais c'est à une paix sûre et durable que sa Majesté vise, non à une trève incertaine, et par là même inquiétante tant pour les parties contractantes que pour le reste de l'Europe.

"Quant aux stipulations du traité d'Amiens qui

pourraient être proposées comme base de la négociation, on a remarqué que cette phrase peut être
interprété de trois ou quatre différentes manières, et
que par conséquent des explications ultérieures
seraient nécessaires ; ce qui ne manquerait pas de
causer un grand délai : quand même il n'y aurait
pas d'autres objections.

" La véritable base d'une telle négociation entre
deux grandes puissances qui dédaignent également
toute idée de chicane, devrait être une reconnoissance
réciproque de part et d'autre du principe suivant ;
savoir : que les deux parties auraient pour objet que
la paix soit honorable pour toutes les deux et leurs
alliés respectifs, et en même temps de nature à
assurer, autant qu'il est en leur pouvoir, le repos
futur de l'Europe.

" L'Angleterre ne peut négliger les intérêts
d'aucun de ses alliés, et elle se trouve unie à la Russie
par des liens si étroits, qu'elle ne voudrait rien traiter,
bien moins conclure, que de concert avec l'Empereur
Alexandre ; mais, en attendant l'intervention actuelle
d'un plénipotentiaire Russe, on pourrait toujours
discuter et même arranger provisoirement quelques-
uns des points principaux.

" Il pourrait sembler que la Russie, à cause de sa
position éloignée, ait moins d'intérêts immédiats que
les autres puissances à discuter avec la France ; mais
cette cour, à tous égards si respectable, s'intéresse
comme l'Angleterre vivement à tout ce qui regarde le
sort plus ou moins indépendant des différens princes
et états de l'Europe.

"Vous voyez, monsieur, comme on est disposé ici
d'aplanir toutes les difficultés qui pourront retarder
la discussion dont il s'agit.   Ce n'est pas assurément
qu'avec les ressources que nous avons, nous ayons à
craindre, pour ce qui nous regarde, la continuation de
la guerre.   La nation Anglaise est de toute l'Europe
celle qui souffre le moins de sa durée, mais nous n'en
plaignons pas moins les maux d'autrui.

"Faisons donc ce que nous pouvons pour les finir :
et tâchons, s'il se peut, de concilier les intérêts respectifs et la gloire des deux pays avec la tranquillité
de l'Europe et la félicité du genre humain.

"J'ai l'honneur d'être avec la plus haute considération, monsieur, de votre Excellence le très-humble
et très-obéissant serviteur,

(Signé)

"C. J. FOX."

M. DE TALLEYRAND TO MR. FOX.

"1er Avril, 1806.

"Monsieur,

"A l'heure même où j'ai reçu votre lettre
du 26 Mars, je me suis rendu auprès de sa Majesté,
et je me trouve heureux de vous informer qu'elle m'a
autorisé à vous faire sans délai la réponse suivante :—

"L'Empereur n'a rien à désirer de ce que possède
l'Angleterre.   La paix avec la France est possible et
peut être perpétuelle, quand on ne s'immiscera pas
dans ses affaires intérieures, et qu'on ne voudra ni

la contraindre dans la législation de ses douanes et dans les droits de son commerce, ni faire supporter aucune insulte à son pavillon.

" Ce n'est pas vous, monsieur, qui avez montré, dans un grand nombre de discussions publiques, une connoissance exacte des affaires générales de l'Europe et de celles de la France, qu'il faut convaincre que la France n'a rien à désirer que du repos, et une situation qui lui permette de se livrer, sans aucun obstacle, aux travaux de son industrie.

" L'Empereur ne pense pas que tel ou tel article du traité d'Amiens ait été la cause de la guerre. Il est convaincu que la véritable cause a été le refus de faire un traité de commerce nécessairement nuisible aux manufactures et à l'industrie de ses sujets.

" Vos prédécesseurs nous accusaient de vouloir tout envahir. En France, on accuse aussi l'Angleterre. Eh bien ! nous ne demandons que l'égalité ; nous ne vous demanderons jamais compte de ce que vous ferez chez vous, pourvu qu'à votre tour vous ne nous demandiez jamais compte de ce que nous ferons chez nous. Ce principe est d'une réciprocité juste, raisonnable, et respectivement avantageuse.

" Vous exprimez le désir que la négociation n'aboutisse pas à une paix sans durée. La France est plus intéressée qu' aucune autre puissance à ce que la paix soit stable. Ce n'est point une trève qu'elle a intérêt de faire, car une trève ne ferait que lui préparer de nouvelles pertes. Vous savez très-bien que les nations, semblables en ce point à chaque homme considéré individuellement, s'accoutument à une

situation de guerre comme à une situation de paix.
Toutes les pertes que la France pouvait faire, elle
les a faites ; elle les fera toujours dans les six premiers
mois de la guerre.   Aujourd'hui notre commerce et
notre industrie se sont repliés sur eux-mêmes, et se
sont adaptés à notre situation de guerre.   Dès-lors
une trève de deux ou trois ans serait en même
temps tout ce qu'il y aurait de plus contraire à nos
intérêts commerciaux et à la politique de l'Empereur.

    " Quant à l'intervention d'une puissance étrangère,
l'Empereur pourrait accepter la médiation d'une
puissance qui aurait de grandes forces maritimes ; car
alors sa participation à la paix serait réglée par les
mêmes intérêts que nous avons à discuter avec vous ;
mais la médiation dont vous parlez n'est pas de
cette nature.   Vous ne voulez pas nous tromper et
vous sentez bien qu'il n'y a pas d'égalité entre vous
et nous dans la garantie d'une puissance qui a trois
cent mille hommes sur pied, et qui n'a pas d'armée
de mer.   Du reste, monsieur, votre communication
a un caractère de franchise et de précision que nous
n'avons pas encore vu dans les rapports de votre
cour avec nous.   Je me ferai un devoir de mettre la
même franchise et la même clarté dans mes réponses.
Nous sommes prêts à faire la paix avec tout le
monde.   Nous ne voulons en imposer à personne,
mais nous ne voulons pas qu'on nous en impose ; et
personne n'a ni la puissance ne les moyens de le faire.
Il n'est au pouvoir de personne de nous faire revenir
sur des traités qui sont exécutés.   L'intégrité, l'indépendance entière, absolue, de l'empire ottoman, sont

non-seulement le désir le plus vrai de l'Empereur, mais le point le plus constant de sa politique.

"Deux nations éclairées et voisines l'une de l'autre manqueraient à l'opinion qu'elles doivent avoir de leur puissance et de leur sagesse, si elles appelaient dans la discussion des grands intérêts qui les divisent, des interventions étrangères et éloignées.   Aussi, monsieur, la paix peut être traitée et conclue immédiatement, si votre cour a véritablement le désir d'y arriver.

"Nos intérêts sont conciliables par cela même qu'ils sont distincts.   Vous êtes les souverains des mers ; vos forces maritimes égalent celles de tous les souverains du monde réunies.   Nous sommes une grande puissance continentale ; mais il en est plusieurs qui ont autant de forces que nous sur terre ; et votre prépondérance sur les mers mettra toujours notre commerce à la disposition de vos escadres, dès la première déclaration de guerre que vous voudrez faire.   Pensez-vous qu'il soit raisonnable d'attendre que l'Empereur consente jamais à se mettre aussi pour les affaires du continent à votre discrétion ? Si, maîtres de la mer par votre puissance propre, vous voulez l'être aussi de la terre par une puissance combinée, la paix n'est pas possible ; car alors vous voulez y arriver par des résultats que vous ne pourrez jamais atteindre.

"L'Empereur, tout accoutumé qu'il est à courir toutes les chances qui présentent des perspectives de grandeur et de gloire, désire la paix avec l'Angleterre.   Il est homme.   Après tant de fatigues, il

voudrait aussi du repos.   Père de ses sujets, il sou-
haite, autant que cela peut être compatible avec leur
honneur et avec les garanties de l'avenir, leur procurer
les douceurs de la paix, et les avantages d'un commerce heureux et tranquille.

" Si donc, monsieur, sa Majesté le Roi d'Angleterre
veut réellement la paix avec la France, elle nommera
un plénipotentiaire pour se rendre à Lille.   J'ai
l'honneur de vous adresser des passe-ports pour cet
objet.   Aussitôt que sa Majesté l'Empereur aura
appris l'arrivée du ministre de votre cour, elle en
nommera et en enverra un sans délai.   L'Empereur
est prêt à faire toutes les concessions que, par
l'étendue de vos forces navales et votre prépondérance, vous pouvez désirer d'obtenir.   Je ne crois pas
que vous puissiez refuser d'adopter aussi le principe
de lui faire des propositions conformes à l'honneur de
sa couronne et aux droits du commerce de ses états.
Si vous êtes justes, si vous ne voulez que ce qu'il vous
est possible de faire, la paix sera bientôt conclue.

" Je termine en vous déclarant que sa Majesté
adopte entièrement le principe exposé dans votre
dépêche, et présenté comme base de la negociation,
que la paix proposée doit être honorable pour les
deux cours et pour leur alliés respectifs.

" J'ai l'honneur d'être avec la plus haute considération, monsieur, de votre Excellence le très-humble
et très-obéissant serviteur,

(Signé),

" CH. MAUR. DE TALLEYRAND,
Prince de Bénévent."

MR. FOX TO M. DE TALLEYRAND.

"Downing Street, *ce* 8 *Avril*, 1806.

" Monsieur,

" Je n'ai reçu qu'hier au soir votre dépêche du 1ᵉʳ courant. Avant d'y répondre, permettez-moi d'assurer votre Excellence que la franchise et le ton obligeant qu'on y remarque ont fait ici le plus grand plaisir. Un esprit conciliatoire, manifesté de part et d'autre, est déjà un grand pas vers la paix.

" Si ce que votre Excellence dit, par rapport aux affaires intérieures, regarde les affaires politiques, une réponse n'est guère nécessaire ; nous ne nous y immisçons pas en temps de guerre ; à plus forte raison, nous ne le ferons pas en temps de paix ; et rien n'est plus éloigné des idées qui prévalent chez nous, que de vouloir ou nous mêler des lois intérieures que vous jugerez propres à régler vos douanes et soutenir les droits de votre commerce, ou insulter à votre pavillon.

" Quant à un traité de commerce, l'Angleterre croit n'avoir aucun intérêt à le désirer plus que les autres nations. Il y a beaucoup de gens qui pensent qu'un pareil traité entre la France et la Grande-Bretagne serait également utile aux deux parties contractantes ; mais c'est une question sur laquelle chaque gouvernement doit juger d'après ses propres aperçus ; et celui qui le refuse n'offense pas, ni n'a aucun compte à rendre à celui qui le propose.

" Ce n'est, monsieur, pas moi seulement, mais tout homme raisonnable doit reconnaître que le véritable intérêt de la France, c'est la paix ; et que, par consé-

quent, c'est sur sa conservation que doit être fondée
la vraie gloire de ceux qui la gouvernent.

"Il est vrai que nous nous sommes mutuellement
accusés; mais il ne sert à rien, dans ce moment-ci, de
discuter les argumens sur lesquels ces accusations ont
été fondées.   Nous desirons comme vous l'égalité.
Nous ne sommes pas assurément comptables l'un à
l'autre de ce que nous faisons chez nous ; et le principe de réciprocité à cet égard, que votre Excellence a
proposé, paraît juste et raisonnable.

"On ne peut pas disconvenir de ce que vos raison-
nemens sur l'inconvénient qu'aurait pour la France
une paix sans durée, ne soient bien fondés ; mais, de
l'autre côté, celui que nous éprouverions serait aussi
très considérable.   Il est peut-être naturel que, dans
de pareils cas, chaque nation exagère ses propres
dangers, ou qu'au moins elle les regarde de plus près
et d'un œil plus clairvoyant que ceux d'autrui.

"Quant à l'intervention d'une puissance étrangère,
il faut d'abord remarquer que, pour ce qui regarde la
paix et la guerre entre la France et l'Angleterre, la
Russie ne peut être censée puissance *étrangère*, en ce
qu'elle est actuellement en alliance avec l'Angleterre
et en guerre avec la France.   C'est pourquoi, dans
ma lettre, c'etait comme partie, non comme médiateur,
qu'on a proposé de faire intervenir l'Empereur
Alexandre.

"Votre Excellence, dans la dernière clause de la
dépêche, reconnaît que la paix doit être honorable tant
pour la France et l'Angleterre que pour leur alliés
respectifs.   Si cela est, il nous paraît être impossible,

vu l'étroite alliance qui subsiste entre les deux gouvernemens que celui de l'Angleterre puisse commencer
une négociation, sinon provisoire, sans la concurrence
ou tout au moins le consentement préalable de son
allié.

" Pour ce qui est de l'intégrité et de l'indépendance
de l'empire ottoman, aucune difficulté ne peut s'offrir,
ces objets étant également chers à toutes les parties
intéressées à la discussion dont il est question.

" Il est peut-être vrai que la puissance de la France
sur terre, comparée à celle du reste de l'Europe,
n'est pas égale à la supériorité que nous possédons
sur mer, envisagée sous le même point de vue ; mais
il ne faut plus se dissimuler que le projet de combiner
toute l'Europe contre la France est chimérique au
dernier point.   Au reste, c'est en vérité pousser un
peu trop loin les appréhensions pour l'avenir, que
d'envisager l'alliance entre la Russie et l'Angleterre
(les deux puissances de l'Europe les moins faites pour
attaquer la France par terre) comme tendant à pro-
duire un résultat pareil.

" L'intervention de la Russie à la négociation ne
peut non plus être regardée comme la formation
d'un congrés, ni pour la forme ni pour la chose,
d'autant qu'il n'y aura que deux parties ; la Russie
et l'Angleterre d'un côté, et la France de l'autre.
Un congrés pourrait être bon, à beaucoup d'égards,
après la signature des préliminaires, en cas que toutes
les parties contractantes soient de cet avis ; mais c'est
un projet a discuter librement et amicalement, après
que l'affaire principale aura été arrangée.

" Voila, monsieur, que je vous ai exposé, avec toute la clarté que j'ai pu, les sentimens du ministère Britannique sur les notions que votre Excellence a suggréées.   Je me plais à croire qu'il n'y a qu'un seul point essentiel sur lequel nous ne sommes pas d'accord.

" Dès que vous consentirez que nous traitions provisoirement jusqu' à ce que la Russie puisse intervenir, et dès-lors conjointement avec elle, nous sommes prêts à commencer, sans différer d'un seul jour, la négociation en tel lieu et en telle forme que les deux parties jugeront les plus propres à conduire à bon escient l'objet de nos travaux, le plus promptement possible.

" J'ai l'honneur d'être avec la considération la plus distinguée, monsieur, de votre Excellence le très-humble et très-obéissant serviteur,

"C. J. FOX."

M. DE TALLEYRAND TO MR FOX.

"Paris, *le* 16 *Avril,* 1806.

" Monsieur,

" Je viens de prendre les ordres de sa Majesté l'Empereur et Roi, sous les yeux de qui je m'étais empressé de mettre la dépêche que votre Excellence m'a fait l'honneur de m'écrire, en date du 8 Avril.

" Il a paru à sa Majesté, qu'en admettant, comme vous le faites, le principe de l'égalité, vous persistiez cependant à demander une forme de négociation qui ne peut s'accorder avec ce principe. Lorsque entre deux puissances égales, une d'elles réclame l'intervention d'un tiers, il est évident qu'elle tend à rompre cet équilibre si favorable à la juste et libre discussion de leurs intérêts. Il est manifeste qu'elle ne veut pas se contenter des avantages et des droits de l'égalité. J'ose croire, monsieur, qu'en revenant une dernière fois sur cette discussion, je parviendrai à persuader à votre Excellence qu'à aucun titre et pour aucun motif, la Russie ne doit être appelée dans la négociation proposée entre la France et l'Angleterre.

" Lorsque la guerre à éclaté entre les deux états, la Russie était en paix avec la France. Cette guerre n'a rien changé dans les rapports qui existaient entre elle et nous. Elle a d'abord proposé sa médiation; et ensuite, par des circonstances étrangères à la guerre qui nous divise, des froideurs étant survenues entre les deux cabinets de Saint Pétersbourg et des Tuileries, l'Empereur Alexandre a jugé à propos de suspendre ses relations politiques avec la France, mais en même temps il a déclaré, de la manière la plus positive, qu'il était dans l'intention de rester étranger aux débats existant entre nous et l'Angleterre.

" Nous ne pensons pas que la conduite que la Russie a tenue depuis cette époque, ait rien changé à cette détermination. Elle a, il est vrai, conclu un traité d'alliance avec vous, mais ce traité, il est aisé d'en juger par ce qui en a été rendu public, par l'objet qu'il avait en vue et plus encore par les résultats, n'avait aucun rapport avec la guerre qui existait depuis près de deux ans entre nous et l'Angleterre. Ce traité était

un pacte de participation à une guerre d'une nature
différente, plus étendue et plus générale que la première. C'est de cette guerre qu'est née la troisième
coalition, dans laquelle l'Autriche était puissance principale et la Russie puissance auxiliaire. L'Angleterre
n'a participé qu'en projet à cette guerre ; jamais nous
n'avons eu à combattre ses forces réunies à celles de
ses alliés. La Russie ne s'y est montrée que secon-
dairement. Aucune déclaration adressée à la France
n'est venue nous apprendre qu'elle était en guerre
avec nous, et ce n'est que sur les champs de bataille
où la troisième coalition a été détruite, que nous avons
été officiellement informés que la Russie en avait fait
partie.

" Lorsque sa Majesté Britannique a déclaré la guerre
à la France, elle avait un but qu'elle a fait connaître
par ses manifestes. Ce but constitue la nature de la
guerre. Lorsque, dix-huit mois après, sa majesté
Britannique s'est alliée avec l'Autriche, la Russie, et
la Suède, elle eut d'autres objets en vue ; ce fut une
nouvelle guerre dont il faut chercher les motifs dans
les pièces officielles qui ont été publiées par les diverses
puissances. Dans ces motifs, il n'est jamais question
des intérêts directs de l'Angleterre, ces deux guerres
n'ont donc aucun rapport ensemble : l'Angleterre n'a
point participé réellement à celle qui est terminée : la
Russie n'a jamais pris de part ni directe ni indirecte
à celle qui dure encore. Il n'y a donc aucune raison
pour que l'Angleterre ne termine pas seule la guerre
que seule elle a faite avec nous.

" Si sa Majesté l'Empereur adoptait le principe de

négocier maintenant avec l'Angleterre unie à ses nouveaux alliés, elle admettrait implicitement que la troisième coalition existe encore, que la guerre d'Allemagne n'est pas finie, que cette guerre est la même que celle que la France soutient contre l'Angleterre : elle accepterait implicitement pour base de la négociation les conditions de M. de Novosilzoff, qui ont excité l'étonnement de l'Europe et soulevé le caractère français : et de vainqueur de la coalition, l'Empereur se placerait volontairement dans la position du vaincu.

"Aujourd'hui l'Empereur n'a plus rien à débattre avec la coalition : il est en droit de méconnaître les rapports que vous avez eus avec elle ; et en traitant avec vous, il ne peut être question que du but et des intérêts de la guerre entreprise antérieurement à vos alliances et qui leur a survécu.

"Quoiqu'il n'y ait que six mois que le voile qui couvrait les combinaisons secrètes de la dernière guerre a été déchiré, il est cependant vrai que le continent est en paix. Le principal des vos alliés, l'Autriche, a fait sa paix séparée. La Prusse, dont les armes ont été pendant quelque temps sur le pied de guerre, a fait avec nous un traité d'alliance offensive et défensive. La Suède ne mérite aucune mention. Quant à la Russie, il existe entre elle et nous des propositions directes de négociation. Par sa puissance, elle n'a besoin de la protection de personne, et elle ne peut réclamer l'intervention d'aucune cour pour terminer les différens qui nous divisent. Par sa distance elle est tellement hors de notre portée, comme de tout moyen de nuire, que l'état de guerre ou l'état de paix ne produit dans nos rapports respectifs que des changemens purement diplomatiques. Si, dans une telle situation, l'Empereur acceptait de négocier conjointement avec l'Angleterre et la Russie, n'en méconnâitrait-il pas tous les avantages! ne supposerait-il pas l'existence d'une guerre qu'il a glorieusement terminée! n'abandonnerait-il pas enfin de lui à l'Angleterre le principe d'une égalité déjà convenue entre nous! Pour peu, monsieur, que vous vouliez examiner, avec le discernement qui vous appartient, les considérations que j'ai l'honneur de vous exposer, vous conviendrez qu'une telle négociation nous serait beaucoup plus préjudiciable que la guerre et même qu'un congrès.

"En effet dans un congrès, si l'Angleterre, la Suède, et la Russie débattaient pour faire prévaloir les principes qui ont servi de fondement à la troisième coalition, la Prusse, le Danemarck, la Porte, la Perse, et l'Amérique réclameraient contre ces principes et demanderaient des lois égales de navigation et un juste partage dans le domaine de la mer. Sans doute, dans cette discussion, on voterait souvent la diminution du pouvoir de l'Angleterre. Des puissances réclameraient l'équilibre du midi de l'Europe, mais d'autres aussi réclameraient l'équilibre du nord. Un grand nombre s'occuperaient de l'équilibre de l'Asie : toutes s'intéresseraient à l'équilibre des mers : et si, du sein de tant de discussions orageuses et compliquées, il est possible d'espérer qu'il en sortît un résultat, ce resultat serait juste, parce qu'il serait complet. Et certes, sa majesté l'a déclaré dans toutes les circonstances. Elle n'aura point de répugnance à faire des sacrifices pour la tranquillité publique, lorsque l'Angleterre, la Russie et toutes les grandes puissances seront chacune disposées à reconnaitre les droits établis, à protéger les états faibles, et à adopter des principes de justice, de modération, et d'égalité : mais l'Empereur connait trop les hommes pour se laisser séduire par des chimères, et il connait que ce serait s'égarer que de chercher la paix dans un dédale de dix ans de débats, qui pendant ce temps, perpétueraient la guerre et ne feraient que rendre son terme plus incertain et plus difficile à atteindre. Il faudrait alors changer de route, et faire comme on fit à Utrecht, laisser les alliés se morfondre dans des débats interminables et inutiles, traiter seul à seul, discuter, comme on fit alors, les intérêts des deux puissances et ceux de leurs alliés respectifs : faire enfin la paix pour soi, et la faire assez équitable et assez honorable pour qu'elle ne pût manquer d'être agréée par toutes les puissances intéressées. Voilà comme il convient, non pas dans dix ans, mais aujourd'hui, que deux puissances telles que l'Angleterre et la France terminent les différens qui les divisent, et établissent en même temps la règle de leurs droits et celle des intérêts de leurs amis.

"Pour me résumer, Monsieur, je ne vois dans la négociation proposée que trois formes possibles de discussion : négociation avec l'Angleterre et les alliés qu'elle a acquis lors de la formation de la troisième coalition ; négociation avec toutes les puissances de l'Europe, en y joignant les Américains ; négociation avec l'Angleterre seule. La première de ces formes est inadmissible, parce qu'elle soumettrait l'Empereur à l'influence de la troisième coalition, qui n'existe plus.   L'Empereur eût négocié ainsi, s'il eût été battu.   La seconde forme de négociation éterniserait la guerre, si les incidens inévitables qu'elle multiplierait à tous les instans, et les passions qu'elle déchainerait sans mesure, ne faisaient pas rompre avec éclat la discussion peu d'années après qu'elle aurait été établie.   La troisième est donc la seule que doivent désirer ceux qui veulent véritablement la paix.   Sa Majesté est persuadée que les dispositions justes et modérées qu'elle aime à reconnaitre dans le ton et le langage du ministère de sa Majesté Britannique, secondant, au gré de ses désirs, les sentimens pacifiques dont elle est plus que jamais déterminée à donner des preuves à ses amis et même à ses ennemis, les peuples, épuisés des efforts d'une guerre dont l'intérêt est aussi difficile à sentir que la véritable objet en est difficile à connaître, verront enfin sortir de la négociation proposée une paix qui est réclamée par tous leurs besoins et par tous leurs vœux.

" Agréez, Monsieur, &c.

(Signé),

"CH. MAUR. DE TALLEYRAND,
Prince de Bénévent."

"Downing Street, *ce* 21 *Avril*, 1806.

" Monsieur,

" J'ai reçu avant-hier la dépêche de votre Excellence, du 16 de ce mois.

" Après l'avoir lue et relue avec toute l'attention

possible, je n'y trouve aucun argument suffisant pour induire notre gouvernement à changer l'opinion qu'il a déjà énoncée, savoir, que toute négociation où la Russie ne serait pas comprise comme partie, est absolument inadmissible. Nous voulons la paix : mais nous ne pouvons rien vouloir qui puisse porter atteinte, où à la dignité de notre souverain, où à l'honneur et aux intérêts de la nation.

" Or, si nous traitions sans la Russie, vu les liens étroits qui nous unissent à cette puissance, nous nous croirions exposés au reproche d'avoir manqué à cette fidélité scrupuleuse dans nos engagemens, dont nous nous faisons gloire, tandis que, de l'autre côté, en persistant dans notre demande que la Russie soit admise, nous ne croyons rien faire qui soit contraire au principe d'égalité que nous réclamons tous les deux.

" Lorsque les trois plénipotentiaires se trouveront ensemble, comment croire qu'on pût rien emporter par la pluralité des voix, ou même qu'une assemblée pareille eût rien de commun avec un congrès général ! Il n'y existerait effectivement que deux parties, d'un côté, la France : de l'autre, les deux puissances alliées.

" Au surplus, si l'on voit tant d'avantages dans une affaire de cette nature à se trouver deux contre un, il n'y aurait aucune objection à ce que vous fissiez intervenir celui de vos alliés que vous jugeriez à propos.

" Désirant sincèrement d'éviter des disputes inutiles, je ne me permets pas d'entrer dans la dis-

cussion des conséquences que votre Excellence tire
des événemens de la dernière campagne.

"Je remarquerai seulement, en passant, que je ne
vois pas par quelle raison une alliance doit être
envisagée comme nulle, par rapport aux puissances
qui y tiennent, parce qu'une de celles qui la compo-
saient en a été détachée par les malheurs de la guerre.

"Quant à l'ouverture que la Russie vous a faite,
nous ne savons ce qui en est : mais quelle qu'en soit
la nature, nous sommes persuadés que cette cour ne
se conduira jamais de manière à compromettre la
loyauté reconnue de son caractère, ou d'affaiblir les
liens d'amitié et de confiance qui subsistent entre
elle et l'Angleterre.

"Pour revenir au point, votre excellence dit que
dans la négociation proposée, elle ne voit que trois
formes possibles de discussion : la première vous paraît
inadmissible.

"D'après ce que j'ai eu l'honneur de vous écrire,
vous devez juger, Monsieur, que la troisième est
incompatible, tant avec nos idées fondamentales de
la justice et d'honneur, qu'avec notre aperçu des
intérêts de notre pays. La seconde n'est pas peut-
être mauvaise dans son principe ; mais, outre les
délais qu'elle causerait, elle ne serait guère prati-
cable dans la conjoncture actuelle.

"C'est donc avec bien du regret que je dois déclarer nettement à votre Excellence que je ne vois
nul espoir de paix dans ce moment-ci, à moins que
chez vous on ne se dispose à traiter dans la forme que
nous avons proposée.

" Je crois devoir ajouter que cette forme nous est essentielle, non seulement pour les raisons que j'ai eu l'honneur de développer à votre Excellence, mais en tant que tout autre pourrait faire naître des soupçons que de fait vous entreteniez le projet chimérique qu'on vous reproche (à tort, comme j'aime à le croire) de nous exclure de toute relation avec les puissances du Continent de l'Europe ; et même qu'une telle idée est moins révoltante pour nous qu'elle ne devrait l'être et qu'elle ne l'est en effet. Ce n'est pas à un ministre aussi éclairé que votre Excellence qu'il puisse être nécessaire de déclarer que l'Angleterre ne peut jamais consentir à une exclusion qui la dégraderait du rang qu'elle a tenu jusqu'ici, et qu'elle croit pouvoir toujours tenir parmi les nations du monde.

" La chose enfin se trouve réduite à un seul point : veut-on traiter conjointement avec la Russie ! oui ; veut-on que nous traitions séparément ! non.

" Bien que nous n'ayons pas réussi dans le grand objet que nous nous sommes proposé, les deux gouvernemens n'ont qu'à se louer de l'honnêteté et de la franchise qui ont caractérisé la discussion de leurs différens : et je vous dois sur mon compte particulier, Monsieur, des remerciemens de la manière obligeante dont votre Excellence s'exprime à mon égard.

" Je vous prie d'agréer les assurances de ma considération la plus distinguée.

" J'ai l'honneur d'être, de votre Excellence, le très-humble et très-obéissant serviteur,

(Signé),   " C. J. FOX."

"PARIS, le 2 *Juin*, 1806.

" MONSIEUR,

     " J'ai mis sous les yeux de l'Empereur la
dernière lettre que votre Excellence m'a fait l'honneur
de m'écrire.   Je ne puis que vous répéter, d'après
ses ordres, qu'exiger de la France qu'elle traite avec
vous sur le principe de votre alliance avec la Russie,
c'est vouloir nous réduire à une forme de discussion
forcée, et nous supposer dans un état d'abaissement
où nous ne nous sommes jamais trouvés.   On ne doit
jamais se flatter d'imposer à la France ni des conditions de paix, ni un mode de négociation contraire aux
usages.   L'exigence sur l'un où l'autre de ces points
affecte également le caractère français : et je ne crains
pas de dire que, pour triompher à cet égard de toutes
nos répugnances, ce ne serait pas trop qu'une armée
Anglaise eût envahi la Belgique et fût à la veille de
pénétrer en Picardie par les débouchés de la Somme.

     " Je dois encore vous répéter, Monsieur, que dans
la vérité sa Majesté désire la paix : et pourquoi
n'ajouterais-je pas ce que nous avons pu dire, ce que
nous avons réellement dit à toutes les époques où les
negociations ont été rompues, que la prolongation de là
guerre n'a jamais été préjudiciable à la grandeur fran-
çaise, et qu'en temps de paix un grand état ne peut faire
usage de ses forces que pour se maintenir et pour conserver telles qu'elles sont ses relations avec ses voisins !

     " La France ne vous conteste pas le droit de choisir
et de conserver vos amis ; dans la guerre, elle n'a pas le
choix de ses ennemis, et il faut bien qu'elle les combatte

unis ou séparés, selon qu'il leur convient de se concerter
pour accomplir leurs vues d'agression et de résistance,
et de former des alliances si peu conformes à la véritable politique de leur pays, que la première clause de
ces alliances a toujours été de les tenir secrètes.

" Parce que nous voulons suivre, dans cette circonstance, la forme de négociation qui a été en usage
dans tous les temps et dans tous les pays, vous en
concluez que nous ne voulons pas que vous ayez des
liaisons sur le continent.   Je ne pense pas que nous
ayons jamais donné lieu à une telle induction.   Il
ne dépend de nous d'empêcher aucun gouvernement
de se lier avec vous, et nous ne pouvons vouloir, ni
ce qui est injuste, ni ce qui est absurde : mais autre
chose est que vous formiez des liaisons à votre choix,
et autre chose que nous y concourions, et que nous
vous aidions à les contracter.   Or consentir à traiter sur
les principes de vos alliances et les admettre dans la
discussion des intérêts directs et intermédiats qui nous
divisent, c'est plus que les souffrir et les reconnaître,
c'est en quelque sorte les consacrer, les cimenter, et
les garantir.   Je vous l'ai déjà fait observer, monsieur,
nous ne pouvons céder sur ce point, parce que le
principe est pour nous.   Toutefois, pour ne laisser
lieu désormais à aucun malentendu, je crois de mon
devoir de vous proposer, 1. De négocier dans les
mêmes formes préliminaires qui furent adoptées sous le
ministère de M. le Marquis de Rockingham en 1782,
formes qui ne furent pas si heureusement renouvelées
pour les négociation de Lille, mais qui eurent un
plein succès dans la négociation qui précéda le traité

d'Amiens.   2. D'établir pour bases deux principes
fondamentaux ; le premier, que je tire de votre lettre
du 26 Mars, savoir, ' que les deux états auront pour
objet que la paix soit honorable pour eux et pour les
alliés respectifs, en même temps que cette paix sera
de nature à assurer, autant qu'ils le pourront, le repos
futur de l'Europe.'

" Le second principe sera une reconnaisance, en
faveur de l'une et de l'autre puissance, de tout droit
d'intervention et de garantie pour les affaires continentales, et pour les affaires maritimes. Non-seulement sa majesté ne répugne pas à faire un tel aveu,
elle aime à l'ériger en principe : et en vous exposant
ainsi ses véritables intentions, je crois vous avoir
donné une preuve décisive de ces dispositions pacifiques.   Sa Majesté se persuade, en même temps,
qu'en prévenant pour toujours à cet égard tout sujet
de plaintes, d'inquiétudes et de déclamations, elle a
fait, sur un point qui intéresse essentiellement le bien
de l'humanité, son devoir d'homme et de souverain.

" Ce serait, Monsieur, avec regret que je verrais
finir une discussion qui a commencé sous de si bons
présages.   J'aurais toutefois, en perdant une espé-
rance qui m'est bien chère, la consolation de penser
que la tort de l'avoir fait évanouir ne saurait être
imputé à la France, puisqu'elle ne demande et ne
veut que ce qui est raisonnable et juste.

" Agréez, Monsieur, l'assurance de ma plus haute
considération.

　　　　(Signé),　　　　　"CH. M. DE TALLEYRAND,
　　　　　　　　　　　　　　PRINCE DE BÉNÉVENT."

" MONSIEUR,

 " J'ai reçu, il y a quelques jours, la dépêche de votre Excellence en date du 2 du mois courant.

 " Je ne conçois pas comment, en traitant avec la Russie et nous conjointement, vous ayez à reconnaître le principe de l'alliance entre elle et nous. Tout au plus vous ne reconnaissez que le fait.

 " Encore moins puis-je deviner comment cette manière de traiter vous suppose dans un état d'abaissement quelconque.   Nous ne prétendons nullement imposer à la France ni les conditions de la paix, ni un mode de négociation contraire aux usages.   En 1782, époque que votre Excellence cite elle-même dans sa dépêche, nous ne nous croyions pas dans un état d'avilissement : cependant, lorsque M. de Vergennes nous dit qu'il fallait, pour l'honneur de sa cour, que nous traitassions conjointement avec elle, la Hollande, et l'Espagne, nous adoptâmes, sans croire en aucun sens nous dégrader, le mode auquel ce ministre paraissait attacher tant de prix.   Votre gouvernement veut sincèrement la paix : ici on la désire également : et je pourrais cependant dire de l'Angleterre ce que votre Excellence dit de la France, que la prolongation de la guerre n'a jamais été préjudiciable ni à sa gloire ni à sa grandeur : à ses vrais intérêts permanens peut-être bien, mais également à ceux de la France.

 " Quant à ce qu'il y a eu de secret dans notre traité d'alliance avec la Russie, votre Excellence est trop éclairée pour ne pas reconnaître que, pour ce qui regardait la guerre et les propositions qu'on aurait à faire à la Prusse et à l'Autriche, le secret était nécessaire. Tout cela est passé. Agir de concert pour procurer en premier lieu le repos à l'Europe et pour le lui conserver après, c'est le principal, je pourrais même dire l'unique objet de nos liaisons.

" Après la manière franche dont vous désavouez l'intention qu'on vous a imputée à tort, par rapport à ce qui regarde nos liaisons continentales, il ne peut plus exister le moindre doute sur ce point essentiel ; et il n'en serait que plus fâcheux que les difficultés qui regardent la forme plutôt que la chose fissent continuer une guerre que les deux gouvernements souhaitent également de terminer.

" Venons à ce que votre Excellence propose. La forme qui eut lieu dans le ministère du Marquis de Rockingham m'est d'autant plus présente à la mémoire, que j'occupais alors le même poste dont sa majesté a bien voulu récemment m'honorer. Que la France et l'Angleterre changent de position, et c'est précisément celle que j'ai proposée. Nous traitions alors avec la France et ses alliés : que la France traite à cette heure avec nous et les nôtres.

" Les bases offertes dans votre seconde proposition sont parfaitement conformes aux vues de notre gouvernement ; bien entendu que, lorsque nous reconnaissons mutuellement nos droits respectifs d'intervention et de garantie pour les affaires de l'Europe, nous convenons aussi mutuellement de s'abstenir de tout empiétement de part et d'autre sur les états plus ou moins puissans qui la composent.

" Je ne regretterais pas moins que votre Excellence que cette discussion finît. Pour peu que nous puissions agir de façon qu'on ne puisse pas nous reprocher d'avoir manqué à la bonne foi vis-à-vis d'un allié qui mérite à tous égards une confiance entière de notre part, nous serons contens; d'autant plus que nous savons qu'une paix honorable ne serait pas moins conforme aux vœux de la Russie qu'à ceux de la France et de l'Angleterre.

" J'ai l'honneur d'être, avec la considération la plus distinguée, de votre Excellence, le très-humble et très-obéissant serviteur.

(Signé),

"C. J. FOX."

" Monsieur, je ne vous écris que deux mots pour vous dire combien je suis satisfait du désir que vous avez témoigné pour la paix.—Au surplus, Lord Yarmouth a toute ma confiance : tout ce qu'il vous dira, vous pouvez croire que c'est moi-même qui vous le dis.—Le temps presse. Agréez tous mes hommages.

"C. J. FOX.

" *Londres, ce* 14 *Juin*, 1806."

I give no more of these despatches. The remainder of the volume will comprise official letters relating to the negociation of 1782, the correspondence of Mr. Fox with Gilbert Wakefield, already published, a few letters from Mr. Fox to Mr. Trotter contained in that gentleman's Memoirs of Fox, and some letters from Mr. Fox to the Duke of Portland, for which I am indebted to the kindness of the present Duke.

MR. FOX TO MR. GRENVILLE.

"St. James's, *April* 30*th*, 1782.

" Sir,

"Although from the conversation we have
had together upon the objects of your journey to Paris,
I have no doubt but you are perfectly master of the
line of conduct which you are wished to follow there,
yet as it may be a satisfaction to you to have some
written instructions upon the subject, I am commanded by His Majesty to acquaint you that it is his
pleasure that you should proceed in the following
manner. When you arrive at Paris, you will endeavour to see Mr. Oswald as soon as possible, who will
probably have announced your arrival, and from whom
you may possibly collect whether the sentiments of
Mons. de Vergennes and Dr. Franklin continue to be
the same as they appeared to him in the first interview he had with them; you will then go to Mons. de
Vergennes, with whom your conversation will be more
or less open, as you find him (either from previous
information or otherwise) more or less inclined to
entertain sentiments favourable to the object of your
journey. You will first of all assure him of His Majesty's sincere and ardent wishes for the blessings of
a general peace, and acquaint him, that in order to
save the effusion of human blood, His Majesty wishes
the time and place of treating to be those which are
most likely to bring matters to a speedy issue. With
this view you will name Paris, provided it can be so
managed as to give no cause of offence to the Courts

of Vienna and Petersburgh. With respect to time, you will inform him that you are ready to send over hither for plenipotentiary powers, whenever matters shall appear to be ripe for such a measure. These things being settled, you will naturally propose to him to state to you some general outlines of his ideas on the subject of general pacification, which, if he should refuse, as there is too much reason to suppose he will, you will naturally enough be led to throw out yours; but with what degree of authority you are to state them, whether as merely your own, or as those which from your intimacy and confidence with me, you know me to share in common with you, or as those of His Majesty and his Ministers, must be left entirely to your discretion, which will of course be guided in a great measure by what you see and hear upon the spot, and by the degree of sincerity which you suppose to be in Mons. de Vergennes's pacific professions,—as to the manner, therefore, you are to judge, but the substance must be this: That His Majesty is willing to cede to His Most Christian Majesty, and his allies, the point which they, at various times, and upon various occasions, declared to be *the subject of the war*, and particularly in the last answer from the Court of Versailles to the mediating Courts; that is to say, to accede to the complete independency of the thirteen American States, and in order to make the peace, if it should take place, solid and durable, to cede to said States, the towns of New York and Charlestown, together with the province of Georgia, including the town of Savannah,

all which are still in His Majesty's possession,—
provided, that in all other respects, such a general
and reciprocal restitution shall take place in every
quarter of the globe, on the part of the belligerent
Powers, as shall restore things to the state they were
placed in by the treaty of Paris, 1763. When this
is stated as the basis of the intended treaty, you will
of course understand and explain if necessary that it
does not exclude any exchange of possessions which may
be made to the mutual satisfaction of both the Parties.
You will not fail to dwell upon the importance of those
places, which we should be ready to restore, upon
such a treaty taking place. The acquisitions in the
East Indies, St. Pierre, and Miquelon, places so necessary to their fisheries, and above all Stᵉ. Lucie, must
be principally insisted upon. The importance of this
last can scarcely be exaggerated beyond the opinion
which I have reason to think they entertain upon the
subject. After having seen Mons. de Vergennes,
you will go to Dr. Franklin, to whom you will hold
the same language as to the former, and, as far as his
country is concerned, there can be no difficulty in
showing him that there is no longer any subject of
dispute, and that if, unhappily, this treaty should
break off, his countrymen will be engaged in a war,
in which they can have no interest whatever, either
immediate or remote. It will be very material that,
during your stay at Paris, and in the various opportunities you may have of conversing with this gentleman, you should endeavour to discover whether, if the
treaty should break off, or be found impracticable on

account of points in which America has no concern, there may not in that case be a prospect of a separate peace between Great Britain and America, which after such an event must be so evidently for the mutual interests of both countries. As the *direct* object of your journey, at present, is rather to fix the time and place of a treaty, than to treat, it is not certainly necessary that you should communicate with the Count d'Aranda in this stage of the business; but whether it may not be advisable, is a question of some doubt, and perhaps you cannot do better than to consult the French Minister upon the subject. This step will be attended with this advantage at least, that it will take away all suspicion of our attempting any separate peace with Spain, and show a degree of confidence, which is always useful in business. I need not say that it is His Majesty's wish to have as frequent and exact accounts as may be of anything material that may pass between you and any of those with whom you are instructed to treat, as well as any interesting intelligence you may be able to procure with respect to the state of the French Cabinet, and the influence that most prevails there. I have nothing further to add but to acquaint you that His Majesty relies with the utmost confidence upon your abilities, for the dexterous management of a business upon which the situation of this country may so much depend.

"I have the honour to be, &c.

"P. S.—It may not be amiss if your first introduction to Mons. de Vergennes should be through Dr. Franklin himself, with whom you may have as much previous conversation as you may think advisable."

MR. FOX TO MONS. DE VERGENNES.

"St. James's, *April 30th*, 1782.

" Monsieur,

" Monsieur Grenville, qui a eu l'honneur de vous être presenté par Milord Stormont du tems de son Ambassade à Paris aura celui de remettre cette lettre à Votre Excellence. Après le rapport que Mons. Oswald nous a fait ici des sentimens favorables pour la paix que Votre Excellence lui temoigna dans l'entretien qu'il a eu à Versailles avec Votre Excellence et Mons. Franklin, je n'ai pas cru devoir differer un moment d'envoyer chez vous quelqu'un qui pût vous assurer des sentimens de cette cour à cet egard—Le nom, et j'ose ajouter le caractère distingué de celui que nous vous envoyons, fournisseut la preuve la moins equivoque de la bonne foi dont nous agissons, et si Mons. Grenville n'est pas encore revêtu d'une autorité formelle, ce n'est que parce que les circonstances ou se trouvent actuellement les choses ne paroissent pas justifier une pareille démarche de notre part.—Au reste je crois pouvoir assurer Votre Excellence qu'il est on ne peut pas plus dans la confiance des Ministres du Roi, que vous pouvez compter sur tout ce qu'il aura l'honneur de vous dire, et qu'il ne manquera pas de nous rapporter avec l'exactitude

la plus scrupuleuse tout ce que vous lui ferez celui
de lui communiquer.—Quant à moi, je prie Votre
Excellence de me faire la justice de croire que je ne
me trouverais que trop heureux si cette négociation
pût prendre entre mes mains une tournure conforme à
l'esprit d'humanité qui anime les deux Souverains, et
que la modération du Roi d'un coté, et la justice et la
magnanimité de S. M. T. C. de l'autre semblent
devoir promettre. — Permettez-moi Monsieur de ne
pas finir cette lettre sans vous marquer les sentimens
d'estime la plus parfaite avec les-quels j'ai l'honneur
d'être Monsieur votre très humble et obéissant serviteur."

MR. FOX TO MARQUIS DE CASTRIES.

" St. James's, *April* 30*th*, 1782.

"Je profite avec empressement, Monsieur, du départ
de Mons. Grenville pour vous temoigner ma recon-
naissance de l'échange de Mons. Stanhope, et des
sentimens aussi flatteurs pour moi, que Mons. Walpole
m'a fait l'honneur de me communiquer de la part de
Votre Excellence.   Mons. Grenville qui aura celui
de vous remettre cette lettre, vous expliquera plus
au large, Monsieur, le motif de son voyage, et je
connais trop les sentimens d'humanité de Votre
Excellence, et les vues justes et étenduës qu'elle a
des vrais intérêts de sa patrie pour ne pas m'assurer
de ses vœux pour l'heureux succès de la commission
dont il est chargé.

" J'ai l'honneur d'être."

MR. GRENVILLE TO MR. FOX.

"Paris, *May* 10th, 1782.

" Sir,

" Having arrived at Paris on the 7th, I accompanied Mr. Oswald on the 8th to Mr. Franklin at Passy. Mr. Franklin told me that Mr. Laurens, Mr. Jay, Mr. Adams, and himself had full powers, all or any of them that should be present, to bind Congress by any treaty to which they should subscribe; that Mr. Adams was very much busied in forming a treaty with the Dutch, and therefore could not come to Paris, but that he expected Mr. Laurens and Mr. Jay very soon; that as to the connections of America with France, America was free from any sort of engagement, but those which existed in the two public treaties of commerce and alliance, and that those two treaties were such as any other nation was free to make with America; that America had been greatly obliged to France, and must show her good faith in the observance of her treaties. I said that the extent of that obligation was what I wished him to consider, and whether, in the independence of America, if that should be the basis of a treaty, he did not see gratification enough for France. He said it was a great deal, but that Spain might want something,—he supposed, would want Gibraltar, and that perhaps it would be of little use to us, now we had lost Minorca and had less commerce to defend. I told him I hoped Spain would

be found to entertain no such idea; that the opinion
of the whole nation and those who understood its
interests best, was, I believed, so decided upon that
subject, that I hoped it would make no part of any
negociation that looked to a prosperous conclusion:
he immediately said it was nothing to America, who
kept or who had Gibraltar. I trusted therefore, I
said, that things foreign to the subject of the
quarrel would not be permitted to break off a treaty,
and lead America on in a war where she could find
no interest, particularly as I could not help believing
there was still in America a good disposition towards
England. He said there were *roots*, that they would
want a good deal of management; that, knowing
much of both countries, he believed he could give
good counsel upon the subject; that he wished
reconciliation as well as peace, — that he thought
there were circumstances in the power of England
which might bring it about, that showing kindness
to the American prisoners, particularly those now
going home; that enabling those persons whose
houses had been wantonly burnt to rebuild them,
such things, if spontaneously done, would, he was
sure, have the greatest effect to a real reconciliation.
I could only answer, that every *practicable* measure
would probably be taken to bring about a reconciliation, by those who desired so sincerely to bring
about a peace: in this as well as in a subsequent conversation, his language, in manner, as well as substance, expressed a very earnest and unaffected wish
for peace, though always accompanied with pro-

fessions of strict adherence to the treaties America had made.

" Yesterday morning I carried your letter, Sir, to Versailles, and, by Mons. de Vergennes' desire, Mr. Franklin went with me. As soon as I had stated to Mons. de Vergennes, his Majesty's sincere wish and disposition to put an end to the calamities of war, and the concurrence he was pleased to give that Paris should be the place of treaty, he said he could assure me that the King his master had the same good dispositions to peace, but that regarding as the first object his good faith to his Allies, H. M. C. M. could do nothing without them, and must, previously to any thing else, send to Madrid and Holland for persons authorised to confer with me. I answered that he must have been aware in reading Mr. Fox's letter, that I had no formal authority whatever, but that I had conceived it could not but be useful, previous to the necessary arrangements of a treaty, to have that sort of communication by conversation with him, which might show some general ideas upon which both parties might enough agree, to find in them the basis of a treaty.

" He said he could make no overtures, nor any answer to mine, till after a communication with the King his master's Allies. I told him I was now only looking to those general points which might supply a prospect sufficient to the foundation of a negociation, and went on to say that one naturally looked towards that which had been the motive of the war, and avowed to be such by France as well as

America; and that, was that cause of contest removed, it seemed perfectly just, that in every other instance, things should be placed exactly in the same state in which they were before the contest existed. He said he could not allow the independence of America to be the only cause of war, for that France had found, and not made, America independent; but even supposing that true, I must not forget that though the last war began only upon the subject of Nova Scotia, we had not confined ourselves to that at the Peace. I answered that the comparison did not appear to me just, for that the independence of America would be a point gained more essential to the interests of France, in the separation of Thirteen Provinces from England, than any acquisition we had made by the last peace had been to us. When I mentioned the important possessions we had to restore, he interrupted me, in speaking of St. Pierre and Miquelon, by crying out 'Oh, pour la pêche, nous allons arranger cela bien d'une autre manière.' He said we had checked and constrained the French in all the quarters of the world, that he wished for a treaty of peace more just and durable than the last, and that the two principal objects they should attend to, were justice and dignity. I answered, that in any treaty to be made, he must not forget, that justice and dignity were as essential objects to one great nation as another. I did not find it easy to make him advert to Ste. Lucie and to the East Indies; he contenting himself with saying, I did not tell him all (he saw) at the first word, and finished the conversation by telling me he would see

me the next morning, and that the Spanish Ambassador should meet me; and going out of the
room said, he did not foresee that what had now been
talked of would be the basis of a treaty.

" When I saw Mons. de Vergennes again this
morning, he told me he had his master's orders to
say that H. M. C. M. partook very sincerely of those
dispositions, which his Britannic Majesty felt, to put
an end to the calamities of war, and would do everything in his power to facilitate that end, but that
having indissoluble engagements with his Allies, he
could not enter into any treaty without their participation, but would, in conjunction with them, listen to
any overtures, as soon as persons empowered by them
could be here. He then informed me that the Spanish
Ambassador would immediately send for powers to
Madrid, and that there would be time for me to send
for powers, that I might be ready when the others
were; the Spanish Ambassador added that H. C. M.
had the same good dispositions towards peace with
H. M. C. M. I said I would communicate to Mr.
Fox what they had told me,—there was then pretty
near the same discussion with that of the day before;
the Spanish Ambassador insisting still more strongly
that his master's griefs were totally distinct from the
independence of America, and that to make a durable
peace, we must begin, he said, from the point at
which we now are. At my suggesting again to-day the
idea of ceding to H. M. C. M. and his Allies, the
independence of America, Mons. de Vergennes, with
great earnestness, said that the King his master could

not in any treaty consider the independence of America, as ceded to him, and that to do so would be to hurt the dignity of his Britannic Majesty; which idea I conceive to be thrown out only to lessen the value of the sacrifice by disclaiming all share in it.

" Mons. de Vergennes was more explicit than yesterday about the East Indies. He asked why we should not content ourselves with Bengal; said it was a great and rich province; that our arms were grown too long for our body, that the French had experienced from us in India every sort of indignity, and that, chiefly owing to the terms of the last peace; that for his part he could not read the last peace without shuddering (sans frémir), and that in making a new treaty they must be relieved from every circumstance in which their dignity had been hurt.

" Having thus, Sir, endeavoured to state to you the most material parts of the conversations I have had in the three days that I have passed here, you will not, I am persuaded, expect much comment upon them; perhaps however it may not be unnecessary to add, that Mons. de Vergennes's manner expressed a very strong persuasion that England must make infinitely more important and extensive sacrifices, to give to a negociation much prospect of success; the line of the last peace seeming to be that which of all others both he and Mons. Aranda are most intent upon excluding from the present negociation.

" Permit me, Sir, only further to observe, that it did not appear to me that anything could be facilitated by using the latitude which was given to me, of making a direct proposition, and therefore confined whatever I said to mere matter of conversation ; and of that conversation I have already related to you everything that seemed in the least respect worth leaving to your consideration.

"I have the honour to be,

"With great truth and regard,

"Sir, your very obedient

"Humble servant,

"THOMAS GRENVILLE."

MR. FRANKLIN TO MR. FOX.

"Passy, *May* 10*th*, 1782.

"Sir,

"I received the letter you did me the honour of writing to- me, by Mr. Grenville, whom I find to be a very sensible, judicious, and amiable Gentleman. The name, I assure you, does not with me lessen the regard his excellent qualities inspire. I introduced him as soon as possible to Mons. de Vergennes ; he will himself give you an account of his reception. I hope his coming may forward the blessed work of Pacification, in which, for the sake of humanity, no time should be lost ; no reasonable cause, as you observe, existing at present, for the continuance of this abominable war.

"Be assured of my best endeavour to put an end to it. I am much flattered by the good opinion of a person whom I have long highly esteemed, and I hope

it will not be lessened by my conduct in the affair
that has given rise to our correspondence.

"With great respect,

"I have the honour, &c.,

"B. FRANKLIN.

"RIGHT HON. C. J. FOX, ESQ.,
    "*Secretary of State, &c.*"

MR. FRANKLIN TO LORD SHELBURNE.

"PASSY, 13*th May*, 1782.

"I DID myself the honour of writing to your Lordship a few days since, by Mr. Grenville's courier,
acknowledging the receipt of yours of the 28th past,
by Mr. Oswald. I then hoped that gentleman would
have remained here some time; but his affairs, it
seems, recall him sooner than he imagined. I hope
he will return again, as I esteem him more, the more
I am acquainted with him; and his moderation,
prudent councils, and sound judgement may contribute much not only to the speedy conclusion of a
peace, but to the framing such a peace as may be
firm and long-lasting.

"With great respect, I am, &c.,

"B. FRANKLIN.

"EARL OF SHELBURNE, &c. &c."

MR. GRENVILLE TO MR. FOX.

"PARIS, *May* 14*th*, 1782.

"SIR,

"The letter which I sent to England, by
Lauzun, will, I flatter myself, have engaged your
attention to those difficulties, that seemed, from what

could be collected from Mons. de Vergennes' conversation, to attend the very first step in this business. Upon further considering those difficulties, they seem to demand such extraordinary attention to the form and nature of the first proposition which His Majesty's Ministers may be disposed to make, that I shall presume to trouble you with a few lines upon the subject, and have very readily concurred in the inclination Mr. Oswald has expressed, to go himself to London, in order to state them as fully as he is capable of doing.

"Everything that I have hitherto seen and heard, leads me to believe, that the demands of France and Spain will be found such as it will be difficult, perhaps impossible, for England to comply with, as they are at present conceived; that Spain looks to Florida and Gibraltar; that France looks to very essential alterations in the state of the Newfoundland Fishery, to perhaps more than Grenada in the West Indies, and to very extensive surrenders of commerce, and territory in the East Indies. It is from the expectation the Courts of Madrid and Versailles entertain of being supported by America in these claims, that they will derive the greatest confidence in making them, and if so, whatever measure could be found practicable to weaken that support, or to give to France and Spain even the apprehension of *losing* it, would be to take from them the strongest ground of their pretensions in a negociation; and could it be effectually done, would put them more within our reach in the prosecution of a war.

"It is true, that the present state of America's connection with France, and the good faith she professes to observe in it, has given no prospect for proposing to make with her a separate and distinct treaty; but, whether by giving in the first instance independence to America, instead of making it a conditional article of general treaty, we might not gain the effects, though not the form of a separate treaty; whether more would not be gained in well-founded expectation, than would be lost in substance; whether America once actually possessed of her great object would not be infinitely less likely to lend herself to other claims, than if that object should remain to be blended with every other, and stand part of a common interest; whether the American Commissioners would think themselves warranted, after such a measure, in adhering to the demands of France and Spain, or whether, supposing that they should, the Thirteen Provinces would consent to the carrying on the war upon such motives: whether too, the treaty now forming with Holland, would not so be baffled in its object, and that we should have, as it were, concluded with America before she had finally engaged herself with Holland. All these are questions which seem of immediate and important consideration, and I must say, for my apology in venturing to state them, arise more from the critical situation of things, than from any opinion I can presume to form about them. Should I not, however, add that Mr. Franklin's conversation has, at different times, appeared to me to glance towards these ideas? While

he was with me this morning, he went so far as to
say, that when we had allowed the independence of
America, the treaty she had made with France for
gaining it, ended; and none remained but that of
commerce, which we, too, might make, if we pleased.
He repeated, that he did not know what France
would ask, or would expect to be proposed; but
mentioning immediately the article of Dunkirk, I
confess that by putting his conversation together,
I was distantly led to suppose that in case of
America's being first satisfied, she might be more
likely to save the honour of her good faith by supporting France in such articles as that of Dunkirk,
than in the more essential claims upon the East
Indies.   He ended by saying, that he saw the consideration of *so many* interests, might make the
business very tedious; but assured me that whatever
influence he had at this Court should be used to
accommodate things; he had, too, once before said
that, in forming a treaty, there should, he thought,
without doubt, be a difference in a treaty between
England and America, and one between England
and France, that had always been at enmity: in
these expressions, as well as in a former one, where
he rested much upon the great effect that would be
obtained by some things being done *spontaneously*
from England, I think you will perhaps trace something not altogether wide of those ideas which I
suppose have weighed with him.   What weight they
will have in your better judgment, is not for me
to consider.   I conceived it important to state them;

and after that, have but to receive your orders upon the subject, repeating only, that as yet there seems little hope of a successful negociation with France, and that America, which was the road to the war, seems to offer the most practicable mode of getting out of it,—perhaps, too, threatens the greatest danger if she continues to assist the prosecution of it. I have the honour to be, Sir, your very obedient humble servant,

"THOMAS GRENVILLE."

MR. FOX TO MR. GRENVILLE.

" St. James's, May 21st, 1782.

" Sir,

" I have received your letter by Lauzun the messenger, and laid it before the King. His Majesty was pleased to refer it to the consideration of his confidential servants, and, in consequence of their advice, has thought proper to invest you with the full powers, and to give you the instructions which accompany this despatch. From the tenor of those instructions, you will, I trust, easily perceive what line of conduct you are expected to hold with respect to the direct object of your mission ; but as it may be of much advantage that you should be acquainted with the general designs and views which have influenced the conduct of the King's servants upon this occasion, in order that you may shape yours accordingly, his Majesty has directed me to explain them to you more fully. Upon reading your letter it was impossible not to perceive that the whole cast and complexion of the French Minister's conversation was very unfavourable to the expectation of any fair or equitable peace in the present moment, and it was therefore the principal concern of the King's servants, what steps should be taken to enable them to turn to account the probable failure of this nego-ciation. The two objects that suggested themselves first to their view, were, 1st, To detach from France, if possible, some of her present allies; 2nd, To gain some for this country. To these two might be added a third, viz., To draw forth the exertions of this country, and to induce the people to bear their heavy burdens with patience, by showing them that, if the war continues, it is not for want of reasonable endeavours to make peace, on the part of the Crown. To all these objects the same means seemed appli-cable, and there appeared nothing for us to do, but to convince the world of the sincerity of our wishes for Peace, and our readiness to make reasonable sacrifices, and to contrast these dispositions with the ambitious views of our enemies, which it must be our business as much as possible to unmask. No better method could be thought of, for compassing those ends, than by authorising you to make, in the King's name, the propositions contained in your first instructions, as a basis for a treaty, and, in case of that proposal not being agreed to, to solicit some proposition on their part. If they should make any that wears in any degree the appearance of reason and moderation, you will undoubtedly be instructed to negociate upon it, and to enter into a discussion of those points in which it may differ from our ideas; if on the contrary, they should make one consisting of exorbitant and absurd demands, or refuse to make any, it will then surely be in our power to convince the world in general, and America and Holland in particular, that everything has been done on our part, towards reconciliation; and that if they still persist in the war, they persist in it without any interest of their own, and for the sole, and at last avowed purpose of aggrandizing the House of Bourbon. You will easily perceive how consistent [it is] with those views, that you should cultivate Dr. Franklin and the Dutch Minister in a peculiar manner; the former of whom, there is all reason to believe, very sincere in his wishes for peace. If in the course of this negociation a foundation could be laid for a separate one afterwards either with Holland or America, or both, it will have been a most fortunate undertaking. You will, no doubt, make all the use possible of the advantageous time in which you are authorised to make these overtures, immediately after the most important and decisive victory that has happened during the war, which, though it has undoubtedly given the greatest satisfaction to his Majesty and the most important turn to his affairs, has nevertheless made no alteration in those sentiments of moderation and humanity, which incline his Majesty to make so many sacrifices for the sake of Peace. The very different face of things from that which they lately wore with respect to the prospect of the West Indian Campaign, might surely furnish abundant lessons of moderation to those who think of grounding high and unreasonable demands upon the good fortune they have hitherto experienced in war. I need say no more upon this topic, as I am sure it would be superfluous to observe, that with the more modesty, and even delicacy, you speak of this great event, the more the weight of it will be felt by those with whom you are to converse upon it. I send you inclosed the Gazette containing Sir George Rodney's letters, and the account of the advantages gained in the East Indies. I am commanded by his Majesty to send you the inclosed case of Mr. Parker into which it is his Majesty's pleasure that you should inquire, and give him all the assistance possible. I am likewise commanded by his Majesty to authorise you to agree to the revival of the intercourse between Dover and Calais by Packet Boats, if such a measure should be (as there is reason to suppose) agreeable to the French Court. I have nothing more to add, but to signify to you the King's approbation of the manner in which you have hitherto conducted yourself, and of the very clear and distinct account which you have given of your conversations with the different ministers.—I have the honour to be," &c.

Instructions for Our Trusty and Wellbeloved Thomas Grenville, Esq., whom we have appointed Our Minister to our Good Brother, the most Christian King; given at our Court, at St. James's, the 21st Day of May, 1792, in the twenty-second year of Our Reign.

Whereas, in consequence of Our earnest desire to put an

end to the calamities of war, in which Our Kingdoms are engaged by the aggression of Our Enemies, we have thought fit to direct you to repair to the Court of France; and have already directed you to be furnished with such papers and information as may have enabled you to make overtures of Peace, and to explain to the Ministers of Our Good Brother, the Most Christian King, the basis on which a negociation for the purpose of concluding a Peace between us and Our said Good Brother can be entered upon; and you having reported to one of Our principal Secretaries of State, for Our information, what passed in the conference with the Count de Vergennes; We have now thought proper to give you the following Instructions for your conduct in the execution of the important trust We have reposed in You.

1. On the receipt of these Our Instructions, together with Our Full Power and credential letter to the Most Christian King, you are to desire an audience of the Count de Vergennes, Minister and Secretary of State for Foreign Affairs, in which you will inform him that you are furnished with a credential letter as Our Minister to His Most Christian Majesty; but you are not to deliver it (with its copy) to the Count de Vergennes, 'till you shall receive Our further Instructions from one of Our principal Secretaries of State.

2. You will, in this audience of the Count de Vergennes, express Our regard for the Most Christian King, and Our sincere desire to see a speedy and happy end put to the evils of a war which has so long subsisted between the Two Crowns; and you will likewise acquaint the Count de Vergennes that you have a full power from Us; a copy whereof you will deliver to that Minister; at the same time declaring that you are ready to produce the Original when desired.

3. For your better guidance and direction in this important Negociation, We have judged proper to lay down, and fix the following essential points, by which you are to govern yourself in your future conferences with the Count de Vergennes.

4. You will repeat in Our Name the assurances which you have already given of Our desire to prevent the further effusion of human blood, and Our wish is that the time and place of treating may be those which are most likely to bring matters to a speedy issue.   With this view you will again name Paris, provided it can be so managed as to give no cause of offence to the Courts of Vienna and Petersbourg.   With respect to the time, you will inform the French Minister that you are authorized by us to present your letter of Credence whenever, our Good Brother, the Most Christian King shall name a person on his part, to repair to Our Court in quality of Minister from the said Most Christian King.

5. If the Court of France should declare their intention of naming such a person, you will declare that you are ready and desirous to learn any ideas and intentions they may have for carrying into effect with more speed and certainty, Our earnest wishes to restore Peace and Amity between the Two Crowns.

6. You will acquaint the Count de Vergennes that, in order to attain this desirable end, We are willing to declare Our intentions to cede to His Most Christian Majesty and His Allies, the point which they have, at various times and upon various occasions, declared to be the subject of the War, and particularly in the last answer from the Court of Versailles to the Mediating Courts ; that is to say, to accede to the complete Independency of the Thirteen American States ; and in order to make the Peace, if it should take place, solid and durable, to cede to the said States the Towns of New York and Charlestown, together with the Province of Georgia, including the Town of Savannah, all which are still in His Majesty's possession ; provided that in all other respects such a general and reciprocal restitution shall take place in every quarter of the Globe, on the part of the Belligerent Powers, as shall restore things to the state they were placed in by the Treaty of Paris, 1763.

7. This being the Basis of the intended Treaty of Peace,

you will explain to the French Minister, that it does not exclude any exchange of possessions which may be made to the mutual satisfaction of both parties.

8. You will not fail to dwell upon the importance of those places which We should be [have] to restore upon such a Treaty taking place—The acquisitions in the East Indies, St. Pierre, and Miquelon, places so necessary to their Fisheries; and above all, St. Lucie must be principally insisted on.

9. In case Monsieur de Vergennes should not consider your Overture as a sufficient Basis to form a Treaty upon, or should reject the Terms offered by you as inadmissible, you will acquaint him that We having, on Our part, made such a proposal as appeared to Us reasonable, We expect on theirs, either a concurrence in Our ideas, or some proposition of their own; and you will immediately transmit to one of Our Principal Secretaries of State, for Our information, the French Minister's answer to this request. You will observe to him how idle it would be for both Countries, that much time should be spent in this Negociation, unless there are some hopes of agreement; and therefore press for as little delay as possible, in giving an answer to your Proposition, declaring that if that answer should be a refusal without any suggestion of proposals on their part, We cannot avoid considering such a conduct as a proof that there is no real desire, in the Court of Versailles, to put an end to the war at present.

10. With regard to any Openings, Insinuations, or Ideas which may be thrown out by the Count de Vergennes, either relative to the particular Peace of the Two Crowns, or in reference to any views òr notions France may entertain for conciliating the other Belligerent Powers, our Will and Pleasure is, that you do receive all such matters *ad referendum,* promising to transmit the same faithfully to your Court, and taking care to hold such language as may best avoid giving room to the Court of France to take umbrage or offence at

your reserve, and making use of all those arguments which your prudence and address will suggest.

11. Notwithstanding you are by Our Full Power authorized to conclude and sign anything that may be agreed on between the Two Courts, it is Our express Will and Pleasure, that you do not, in virtue of the said Power, proceed to the signature of any Act whatever with the Court of France, without first having Our special orders for the purpose from one of Our Principal Secretaries of State.

12. If it shall be agreed between the Two Courts, that you and the person to be nominated by His Most Christian Majesty shall respectively enjoy in France and in England all the Rights, Prerogatives, Franchises, and Liberties belonging to your characters, as if the Two Courts were in full Peace, you are to be duly attentive to maintain Our Dignity in all things touching the same, and to take care that you be treated in the same manner as Ministers of your rank, from Spain or any other Crowned Head, except as to the form of not delivering Our Credential yourself to the Most Christian King in an audience.

13. You shall use your particular endeavours to inform yourself of the Interior situation of the Court of France, and of the actual state and dispositions of the French Nation. You will also give a watchful attention to the conduct and motions of the Spanish and Dutch Ambassadors, and also to those of the Minister or Agents from the American Congress there; and of all matters which may be of consequence, and worthy of our knowledge, you shall constantly give an account to Us by one of Our Principal Secretaries of State, from whom you will receive such further Instructions and Directions as We shall think fit to send you, which you are to observe accordingly.

GEORGE III. TO THE KING OF FRANCE.

[COPIE.]

[" MONSIEUR MON FRERE,]

　　" Ayant fait choix du Sieur Grenville, pour
se rendre à votre Cour en qualité de mon Ministre,
Je vous prie de donner une entière créance à tout
ce qu'il vous dira de ma part, et sur-tout aux assurances qu'il vous donnera de mon estime singulière
pour vous, et de mon desir sincère de voir heureusement rétablir entre nous une amitié ferme et durable.

　　[" Je suis, Monsieur mon frère,

　　　　　" Votre bon frère,

　　　　　　　" GEORGE R.]*

[" À S. JAMES, *ce* 21*st Maii*, 1782."]

MR. FOX .TO MR. GRENVILLE.

" ST. JAMES'S, *May* 21*st*, 1782.

" SIR,

　　" Mr. Oswald is just arrived with your letter of
the 14th inst., which I shall immediately lay before
the King.　As I do not see anything in the contents
of it, or in the account Mr. Oswald gives of the state
of affairs at Paris, which makes the sending of the full
powers and instructions to you less necessary, I shall
immediately despatch the messenger as I had intended,
in order that there may be no loss of time in taking
the first steps in this business.　The only new observation which I think myself at present authorised to
make, is that it may not be improper for you to

---

* It is the custom in letters from one Sovereign to another, that the parts
here enclosed in brackets should be written in the Sovereign's own hand.

mark, as distinctly as possible, that if Spain and Holland are brought into this negociation, it is not by your desire, but by that of the Court of Versailles; and that you should make this understood to the American Ministers in particular, in order that they may see clearly how difficult it will be for us to come to an agreement with them (even supposing us to be agreed upon the terms), if in the first place they think it necessary to have France included in the negociation, and France afterwards thinks proper that every other power should be considered as her ally, even though such power should be totally without any connexion with the Thirteen Colonies, of any kind whatever. It will surely be easy enough to show the Americans how very unreasonable it is that, in a negociation for peace, they should be encumbered by powers who have never assisted them during the war, and who have even refused to acknowledge their independence.

" I have the honour to be," &c.

LORD SHELBURNE TO RICHARD OSWALD, ESQ.

" WHITEHALL, *May* 21*st*, 1782.

" SIR,

" I have had the honour to lay your letter of the 10th inst., before the King, and I have his Majesty's commands to signify to you his approbation of your conduct hitherto.

" Mr. Grenville will, I make no doubt, acquaint you of the powers sent him by the present messenger, together with all such other matters as may be

necessary to govern your intercourse with Dr. Franklin and with the other American Commissioners,
which you will continue to cultivate by all fair and
honourable means, avoiding to give cause of jealousy
to the Court of France. It is his Majesty's pleasure
that you should furnish Mr. Grenville any lights which
may occur to you in the course of your communication
with any of these gentlemen, which may be useful to
him in his transactions with the French Ministers, or
those of any of the other powers of Europe who may
be to enter into the proposed negociation; and I must
recommend to you to omit no opportunity of letting
it be understood, that there subsists the strictest union
in his Majesty's Council upon the great subject of
peace and war.

" I am sorry to observe that the French Minister
gives very little reason to expect that his Court is
likely to make good their professions, which they
made through so many channels, of a desire of peace
upon terms becoming this country to accept, upon the
strength of which Dr. Franklin invited the present
negociation. I have that entire confidence in Dr.
Franklin's integrity and strict honour that, if the
Court of France have other views, and that they have
been throwing out false lures to support the appearance of moderation throughout Europe, and in the
hope of misleading and the chance of dividing us, I
am satisfied that he must have been himself deceived;
and in such a case I trust that, if this shall be proved
in the course of the present negociation, he will consider himself and his constituents freed from the ties

which will appear to have been founded on no ideas of common interest. We shall, however, I hope speedily ascertain the real purposes of France, by their conduct in the future progress of this negociation, which the King will not suffer to go into any length.

"In the mean time you will govern your conversation with the American Commissioners with all possible prudence, collecting their sentiments and every other information which you conceive may hereafter prove useful; and I have his Majesty's commands to acquaint you, that it is his pleasure you should continue at Paris, 'till you receive his orders to return, of which you will acquaint Dr. Franklin and Mons. le Comte de Vergennes.

"I am, &c.,

"SHELBURNE."

"P.S.—I send you inclosed a copy of my letter to Dr. Franklin; likewise the copy of a paper from an American (now in London), relative to the state of confiscations on that continent; though it may not be proper to go into such detail at present, yet it may be useful to consider this matter in as many views as possible, in order to be prepared, whenever things are sufficiently advanced, to enter upon such particulars.

"S."

LORD SHELBURNE TO MR. OSWALD.

"WHITEHALL, May 21st, 1782.

"Sir,

"It has reached me, that Mr. Walpole esteems

himself much injured by your going to Paris, and
that he conceives that it was a measure of mine
intended to take the present negociation with the
Court of France out of his hands, which he conceives
to have been previously commenced through his
channel by Mr. Fox. I must desire that you will
have the goodness to call upon Mr. Walpole, and
explain to him distinctly how very little foundation
there is for such an unjust suspicion, as I knew of no
such intercourse; Mr. Fox declares he considered
what had passed between him and Mr. Walpole, of a
mere private nature not sufficiently material to mention to the King or his cabinet, and will write to
Mr. Walpole to explain this distinctly to him; but if
you find the least suspicion of the kind has reached
Dr. Franklin, or Mons. le Comte de Vergennes,
I desire this matter may be clearly explained to
both. I have too much friendship for Dr. Franklin,
and too much respect for the character of Mons.
le Comte de Vergennes, with which I am perfectly
acquainted, to be so indifferent to the good opinion
of either as to suffer them to believe me capable
of an intrigue, where I have both professed and
observed a direct opposite conduct. In truth, I hold
it in such perfect contempt, that however proud I may
be to serve the King in my present station or in any
other, and however anxious I may be to serve my
country, I should not hesitate a moment about retiring
from any situation which required such services. But
I must do the King the justice to say that his
Majesty abhors them, and I need not tell you that it

is my fixed principle that no country in any moment
can be advantaged by them.

" I am, &c.

" SHELBURNE."

LORD SHELBURNE TO BENJAMIN FRANKLIN, ESQ.

" WHITEHALL, *May* 21*st*, 1782.

" SIR,

" I am honoured with your letter of the 10th
instant, and am very glad to find that the conduct
which the King has empowered me to observe
towards Mr. Laurens and the American prisoners, has
given you pleasure. I have signified to Mr. Oswald
his Majesty's pleasure that he shall continue at Paris
'till he receives orders from hence to return.

" In the present state of this business there is
nothing left for me to add, but my sincere wishes for
a happy issue, and to repeat my assurances that
nothing shall be wanting on my part, that can contribute to it.

" I am, &c.,

" SHELBURNE."

MR. GRENVILLE TO MR. FOX.

" PARIS, *May* 23*rd*, 1782.

" DEAR SIR,

" I enclose to you the copies of two letters from
Mons. de Vergennes, and my answers to them, written
in consequence of my applying to him for a passport
for Ogg the courier. I confess that I am little pleased

with the insinuations contained in Mons. de Vergennes's letters, and am the more suprised, as I have endeavoured by every attention in my power to have avoided giving the slightest ground for the suspicions he seems to have entertained. He must, one should think, have seen how natural it was for me to wish to have a constant communication with you, and how impossible it was for me to think of depending for it on the French post; to that however I commit these few lines, and the copies I allude to, which though opened will perhaps be allowed to pass to you. I hope that in reading them you will think that I have said what was requisite upon so unpleasant a subject, and I trust not more than was necessary to it.

" Monsieur de la Fayette desired me when I wrote to England to let Lord Cornwallis know that both Mr. Franklin and himself have written to Congress to endeavour to procure his discharge, I apprehend in return for that of Mr. Laurens. I expect every day to hear from you, and am with great truth,

         " Dear Sir,
                " Your very faithful and obedient
                        humble servant,
                                " THOMAS GRENVILLE."

                LORD SHELBURNE TO MR. FRANKLIN.

                              " WHITEHALL, *May 5th,* 1782.
" SIR,
        " I have the honour to receive your letter of the 13th of May, by Mr. Oswald. It gives me great pleasure to find my opinion of the moderation,

prudence, and judgment of that gentleman confirmed by your concurrence.   For I am glad to assure you that we likewise concur in hoping that those qualities may enable him to contribute to the speedy conclusion of a peace, and such a peace as may be firm and long-lasting.   With that view he has the King's orders to return immediately to Paris ; and you will find him, I trust, properly instructed to co-operate to the accomplishment of so desirable an object.

" I am, &c.,
" SHELBURNE.

" Benjamin Franklin, Esq."

MR. FOX TO MR. GRENVILLE.

" St. James's, May 26th, 1782.

" Sir,

" I had the honour of laying your letter of the 14th inst., before the King.   His Majesty was pleased to refer it to the consideration of his confidential servants, and in consequence of their advice has commanded me to signify to you his pleasure that you should lose no time in taking all the advantage possible of the concession which his Majesty has from his ardent desire of peace been induced to make, with respect to the independency of the Thirteen States ; and in order to this end, I have it in command from his Majesty to authorise you to make the offer of the said independency in the first instance, instead of making it a conditional article of a general treaty.   I need not point out to you the use that may be made of this method of commencing the business, as you

seem to have a very just idea of the advantages that
may be derived from it. The principal one appears
to me to be this, that the American agents must
clearly perceive, if there should now be any obstacle
to the recognition which they have so much at heart,
and which after all must be a matter infinitely interesting to them, that the difficulty comes from the
Court of Versailles, and not from hence ; and that it is
chiefly owing to the number of allies with which that
Court thinks fit to encumber America in the negociation for a peace, although she was never benefited by
their assistance during the war. When this point shall
have been reasoned and understood, I cannot help
flattering myself that it will appear upon the face of
the thing unreasonable and intolerable to any honest
American, that they, having gained the point for
which they contested, should voluntarily and unnecessarily submit to all the calamities of war, without
an object, 'till all the Powers in Europe shall have
settled all the various claims and differences which
they may have one with the other, and in which it is
not even pretended that America has any interest
whatever, either near or remote. You will not fail to
press Mr. Franklin's own idea, that the object of the
Treaty of Alliance with France being obtained, the
Treaty determines, to which if that gentleman should
adhere, we may fairly consider one of the ends of your
mission as attained. As to the good faith which is
supposed to be pledged by Congress to France not to
make a separate peace, I think it can only be understood that Congress is bound not to enter into any

Treaty separately, or without the knowledge and consent of France; but surely not that, when a general
peace is proposed, Congress is bound to support every
claim set up by the Court of Versailles and her Allies,
which would be a kind of engagement that never was, I
believe, entered into by any State at any time. It has
often been stipulated between two Allied Powers, that
one shall not make peace 'till the other has attained
some specific object named in the Treaty; but that
one country should bind herself to another to make
war 'till her ally shall be satisfied with respect to all
the claims she may think fit to set up, claims un-
defined and perhaps unthought of at the time of
making the engagement, would be a species of Treaty
as new, I believe, as it would be monstrous. If this
view of the thing should produce the effects you seem
inclined to hope from it, I need not observe to you
how greatly all the advantages of a separate peace
would be increased by the late events in the West
Indies; but I have the satisfaction to assure you that
those events have in no degree abated his Majesty's
most ardent and sincere desire for a general pacification, and I concur with you in your conjecture, that
the extravagance of the French expectations arises
chiefly from the support they expect from America,
and consequently will be considerably abated whenever they see reason to fear the loss of that support;
so that if things should take a right turn with respect
to the American agents, the best road may probably
be opened to a general as well as a separate peace. I
send you inclosed last night's Gazette, containing an

account of two more ships of the line and one frigate, which Sir Samuel Hood has taken from the enemy. I am commanded by his Majesty to direct you to communicate with Mr. Oswald, with the greatest freedom and openness, upon the concerns of your mission, which are connected more and more every day with the business of America. With respect to Mr. Franklin, if he continues in those friendly dispositions which your letter and Mr. Oswald's account seems to indicate, the more confidence you show to him the better chance there will be of bringing this business, either in one way or in the other, to a successful issue.

" I am, Sir," &c.

MR. GRENVILLE TO MR. FOX.

" Paris, May 30th, 1782.

" Sir,

" I received on the 25th your two letters of the 21st, together with the instructions and full power which accompanied them, and at the same time the account of the glorious victory obtained by his Majesty's arms in the West Indies, and the important acquisitions in the East, upon which great events I beg leave to offer my most humble but hearty congratulations.

" I saw Mons. de Vergennes on the 26th, and, having informed him that I had a credential letter which I should be authorised to deliver whenever H. M. C. M. should name a person in quality of Minister

on his part, I gave him, at the same time, a copy of
the full power which I had received; in reading it,
he immediately made the objection I had expected
from him, viz., that the full power enabled me only
to treat with the French Minister, whereas H. M. C.
M. had already declared that he could only treat in
conjunction with the other belligerent powers, and
that he was connected by the ties of blood to Spain,
and by friendship to Holland, who had been thrown
into this war.   I took this opportunity of complying
with your instructions by reminding Mons. de Vergennes, that to include Spain and Holland in this
negociation had not been the desire of the Court of
London, but that of the Court of Versailles; and
when he observed that a general peace was the most
essential object, I agreed that it was so, but said that
it might perhaps be most easily produced by not com-
plicating those interests, which, the more simple they
were kept, the more easily they would be discussed;
he said he would send for me another day to inform
me of the King, his master's, answer, but seemed to
think this in the first step an insurmountable difficulty: I, however, went on to tell him that I was authorised by his Majesty to make those propositions as
the basis of a treaty, which I had in a former conversation spoken of as probable to occur; and I did this,
notwithstanding his previously declining to answer
what I should state, because I conceived it to be your
wish that no time should be lost in making a direct
proposition, independent of the manner in which it
might be received.   It was not until this morning

that I received Mons. de Vergennes' answer. He told me that H. M. C. M. had found the full power sent to me very insufficient, as it did not enable me to treat with the Ministers of the other belligerent powers, without whose concurrence he had already declared he could enter into no treaty. Mons. de Vergennes then explained that H. M. C. M. did not require that all the parties should be included in one full power, but that at least I should have sufficient separate authorities to treat with them; he mentioned Spain and America as allies, and, speaking of Holland, I desired him to explain himself accurately, whether or no he considered Holland as an ally; he said, certainly not, but they were *en communauté de guerre*, and that his master was too noble in his sentiments to think of treating without giving Holland an oppor-tunity of making peace at the same time if she chose. I reminded him, upon this, that the objection therefore now made was not matter of obligation on the part of France, but of choice. The business then rests upon this difficulty, and waits your answer to it.

" I have not, I own, at these conversations, dwelt much upon the late glorious victory—an event so decisive best speaks its own importance, and the pro-positions I was charged with, unaltered by that success, perhaps in being so, most strongly speak the temper and moderation of his Majesty's councils. Indeed, added to this, it has been and still is so sorely felt here, that it would not be very easy to allude to it with sufficient delicacy. I wish I could say that the sensation it creates seemed likely to assist the business of pacification, but the reverse is so much the truth that public opinion looks less than ever favourable to it, and this I am persuaded a good deal owing to some public expressions of the King's, which are adopted and repeated with great earnestness :—'Il faut être fâché mais non pas consterné ; J'ai perdu *cinq* vaisseaux, je ferai faire quinze à leur place, et on ne me trouvera pas pour ceci plus traitable à la paix.' It does not seem improbable that this loss may prove fatal to Mons. de Castries's situation, whose influence is now supposed so weak that Mons. de Chatelet is much talked of to succeed him.

" I am to inform you, Sir, with respect to the proposed re-establishment of the passage from Dover to Calais, that this Court is ready to accede to it, provided that there shall be permitted as many French packet-boats as English. Mons. de Castries has likewise written to St. Malo's upon the subject of Mr. Parker, and I will not fail to communicate his answer as soon as I shall receive it.

" Mr. Franklin's conversation continues to express a strong desire for peace, a constant attention to the idea of establishing a solid union between England and America, but I must add does not lose sight of that part of America's treaty with France, which restrains either party from making peace or truce without the consent of the other ; he appears to be intent upon keeping the treaties of peace distinct between the several parties, though going on at the same time, and to this idea which seems to correspond

in part with your intentions, I give every encouragement I can. I have reason to think that when I see
him next in two or three days, he may be something
more explicit; but there has been already so much
delay in sending this courier, notwithstanding my
pressing for a speedy answer, that I will no longer
retard him, but reserve for a future occasion what I
may learn more from Mr. Franklin. Permit me, Sir,
to remind you, that I shall not perhaps be allowed to
send you another courier till I shall have received
your answer from London; and I should add that it
is clear, from Mons. de Vergennes' conversation, that
the French Court are determined not to consider the
independence of America as in any respect ceded to
them, and that such will be the principal part of
their first answer to your propositions, should the
previous difficulty about the full power be got over
by any alteration made in it.

" I have only farther to express how highly sensible
I am of the honour done me by His Majesty's approbation of my conduct.

" I have the honour to be,

" Sir,

" Your very obedient, humble servant,

"THOMAS GRENVILLE."

MR. GRENVILLE TO MR. FOX.

"PARIS, *June 4th*, 1782.

" SIR,

" Mr. Oswald arrived here on the 31st, the

day after Ogg was gone, and I received from him the honour of your letter of the 26th.

" You will have seen, by my last of the 30th, that Mons. de Vergennes' objections to the full power are such as while they subsist preclude any further discussion of business. I have, therefore, with regard to him, nothing new to inform you of. It cannot, however, Sir, have escaped your notice, that the offer of independence in the first instance, instead of making it a conditional article of general treaty, necessarily changes part of the propositions I had in charge to make to Mons. de Vergennes. I take it for granted, therefore, that in any future conversation with the French Minister, it was your intention that I should omit the mention of independence, and confine myself simply to the peace of 1763, as the basis of a treaty; but, as I should be very sorry to misinterpret this or any part of your instructions, I flatter myself that you will have the goodness to direct me upon this subject; the doubt which has arisen from Mons. de Vergennes and Mr. Franklin about the full power, gives sufficient time for this explanation without any additional delay. It is, I see, in the sense I mention that Mr. Franklin wishes it, for when I spoke to him of the offer your last letter would authorise me to make, he expressed very great satisfaction at its being kept out of the treaty with France, adding that the more good England did to America, the more America would assist this business. To repeat, therefore, the same offer as a proposition to France would defeat its purpose with America. I hope soon to receive your orders upon this as upon the subject of my last letter, in which I ought to have added that Mr. Franklin seemed not a little jealous of there being no powers yet sent to treat with America.

    " I have the honour to be,
      " Sir, with great truth,
          " Your most obedient and most
            " humble servant,
                " THOMAS GRENVILLE."

MR. OSWALD TO LORD SHELBURNE.

                         " PARIS, *June 9th,* 1782.

" MY LORD,
    " I had the honour of your Lordship's letter by Major Ross, which I carried immediately to Dr. Franklin; upon the perusal of it, he expressed some concern that he had received no such powers as would authorise him to discharge Lord Cornwallis of his parole, and said that the only commission he had of that kind related to General Burgoyne. However, upon my telling him that Mr. Laurens, while in the Tower, had undertaken (on condition of his being set at liberty) to procure Lord Cornwallis's discharge, and that I delivered the said obligation to his Majesty's Ministers of State, the Doctor said, that upon my writing him a letter to that purpose, he would venture to do the business without orders. I accordingly sent him the letter, and Major Ross will be in possession of the discharge, I suppose, to-morrow. I am very well pleased that it is done, and I imagine the Doctor

is equally so, that he has this opportunity of showing respect to your Lordship's recommendation.

" I have nothing of business to trouble your Lordship with, only that upon one occasion, since my last
arrival, the Doctor said, they, the Americans, had
been totally left out in Mr. Grenville's powers, as they
extended only to treating with the Minister of France.
I told him that the deficiency would no doubt be
supplied in due time, as might be supposed, since, in
the meanwhile, they had been assured by Mr. Grenville that his Majesty had agreed to grant independence *in the first instance*. The Doctor said it
was true, and he was glad of it, and supposed that
was all that could be done until the Act depending in
Parliament was passed.

" He then talked of treaties, and said he thought
the best way to come at a general peace was to treat
separately with each party, and under distinct commissions, to one and the same, or different persons.
By this method, he said, many difficulties which must
arise in discussing a variety of subjects not strictly
relative to each other, under the same commission,
and to which all the several parties are called, would
be in a great measure avoided ; and then, at least,
there will only remain to consolidate these several
settlements into one general and conclusive treaty of
pacification, which, upon inquiry, I found he understood to be the indispensable mode of final
accommodation.

" However material that part of the question
might be (regarding the possibility of an equitable

coalescence of so many different propositions and settlements), there was no explanation offered as to the extent of their relative dependence upon each other, and I did not think proper to ask for it. He only explained as to the commissions, that there might be one to treat with France, one for the colonies, one for Spain, and, he added, one for Holland, if it should be thought proper. Mr. Grenville being very well with the Doctor, he has no doubt mentioned the same things to him, yet I thought it my duty to communicate to him the substance of this conversation.

"The only other thing I shall trouble your Lordship with, relates to the answer, said to be brought over by Mr. Forth from this Court, to the late Administration. I asked Dr. Franklin about it, and having mentioned some of the particulars as reported to my friend Mr. Udney, the Doctor said the representation was a mistake from the beginning to the end ; that he had seen a copy of the answer which the Minister gave to Mr. Forth, which was this :—' That his most Christian Majesty was happy to find the King of Great Britain so well disposed to peace, which was equally his desire, and that in the progress of the business he would convince his Britannic Majesty of his intentions faithfully to perform what he should undertake for, by the punctuality which he would show in the discharge of his engagements to his present allies.' The Doctor said, there was not one word more of significancy in the whole paper, and that the Count de Vergennes to prevent mistakes took the precaution to make Mr. Forth quote the identity of the copy, with his own hand, upon the margin.

" It is said the Marquis de la Fayette is going out directly to America. Major Ross, by whom this goes, has been frequently with him, and some other French officers of his acquaintance ; and may possibly be able to give your Lordship some useful information from what he has learned among them in the short time he has been here. I am much mistaken if your Lordship will not find him an intelligent officer in relation to American affairs, as I believe him in other respects a gentleman of good sense and great worth.

" I have the honour to be,

" My Lord,

" Your Lordship's most obedient

" humble servant,

"RICHARD OSWALD."

MR. FOX TO MR. GRENVILLE.

" St. James's, *June* 10*th*, 1782.

" Sir,

" I have received your two despatches by Ogg and Lauzun the messengers, and laid them before the King. As it is his Majesty's intention that nothing shall be wanting on his part that may be supposed to facilitate the great work of peace, he has been graciously pleased to order further full powers to be made out, by which you will be authorised to treat and conclude not only with H. M. C. M., but with any other of the enemies of Great Britain, and these full powers I have the honour of sending herewith inclosed. With respect to the contents of your last despatch, you certainly conceive it rightly, that you are no longer to mention the independence of America as a cession to France, or as a conditional article of a general treaty; but, at the same time, you will not fail to observe to the French Ministry that the independence of America *is* proposed to be acknowledged, and to remark that this being done spontaneously, which they have at different times, and particularly in their last answer to the Imperial Courts, emphatically called the object of the war, little difficulty ought to remain with regard to other points which may be considered rather as collateral and incidental than as principal in this present dispute. The war was begun on their part, as they profess, not for the sake of conquest, but for the purpose of protecting their trade with America. All restraint upon that trade being now out of the question, and perfect liberty of commerce with North America being proposed as the basis of a treaty, the cause of the war is gone, and the war ought to cease. I am sensible how little argument and reasoning are likely to avail in this sort of business, and my object in pointing out to you those topics which appear to me most plausible and most unanswerable in our favour, is not so much with a view to any effect they may have on the success of the negociation, as for the purpose of being able to show clearly to all the world, and to America in particular, what are the real designs and motives of the Court of Versailles, and to whom the blame of the continuation of the war, (if it must continue,) ought to be imputed. I should have sent you the full power earlier, if I had not judged it advisable to wait for those private letters by General Murray, to which you seemed to refer, and which I did not receive till yesterday. It is his Majesty's pleasure that the passage between Dover and Calais should be re-established. You will, therefore, settle this business as speedily as possible, upon the footing proposed, of an equal number of packet-boats of each country.

" I am, Sir," &c.

MR. GRENVILLE TO MR. FOX.

"PARIS, *June* 21*st*, 1782.

" SIR,

" Having received on the 14th the honour of your letter of the 10th, I took a copy of the full power which accompanied it, and gave it to Mons. de Vergennes on the next day, the 15th; as he did not object to it, though he seemed to think it might have been more satisfactory to have named the parties, I lost no time in telling him that I was commissioned formally to propose to him the Peace of Paris, as the basis of a treaty, adding, more than once, the very reasonable expectation the Court of London now entertained that, should the proposition already made by them not be accepted at Versailles, some others would be stated in return by the French Minister, and further I observed to him, according to your direc-

tions, that it is proposed spontaneously to acknowledge the independence of the American States.

" It was not till this morning that I received Mons.
de Vergennes' answer, which I send you inclosed,
having copied it at Versailles; the object of it appears
to me to be the keeping in view the former general
expressions of a pacific disposition, though perhaps
the articles it includes seem to threaten that extensive
and wide scope in their demands which I have always
thought I have traced in every conversation about the
Peace of Paris. A strong expression of Mons. de
Vergennes upon this subject lately was, that in any
new treaty which should refer to that of 1763,
instead of saying that the Treaty of Paris should
stand good, except in certain specified articles, he
would rather express it that the Treaty of Paris should
be annulled except in certain specified articles—no
very promising qualifications of what now stands as
the proposed basis of the intended negociation; but
you will see, Sir, in the paper which I enclose, that
the French Minister does not at present enter into
any detail, so that I cannot add more for your information than you will have in reading his answer. I
must, however, observe to you that the Spanish ambassador is by no means satisfied with the full power.
He told me that the King his master, though an ally
of France, had made war on his own account; and
that his Court would, without doubt, object to the
French King's being named in the full power, without any particular mention being equally made of the
King of Spain. He said he mentioned this now, as

much time might be lost, if that difficulty was not now removed, which might be done in three modes, either by the giving a general power without naming any one of the parties, a power naming both of them, that is the Kings of France and Spain, or a power separate and distinct for each. Should it, therefore, be his Majesty's pleasure to proceed further in this business, and to remove this objection, you will excuse me for observing that if either the second or third of the expedients proposed should be adopted, a similar requisition will probably be made by Holland and America. I have already felt myself under some embarrassment respecting Mr. Franklin, not seeing precisely how far the expressions "*Princes* and *States*," in the full power, can apply to America till the independence is acknowledged, and knowing that he finds and expresses much doubt about it himself, and some disposition to ask a more explicit description. Indeed I have purposely avoided seeing him, till I had got Mons. de Vergennes' answer, which it seemed important to your views to transmit immediately, lest Mr. Franklin might have made a formal objection to me about the full power, and perhaps have stood in the way of the answer from Versailles till his objection shall have been removed. I have not lately had so much communication with Mr. Franklin, or been able to draw from him any satisfactory information. The last time I saw him he contented himself with observing, that the sooner the independence was declared, the less would the business be retarded. The Government of this country is still wavering, and [there are] daily reports and expectations of some change, but they talk confidently of the intended addition to their navy, and say they have already received the promise of nineteen millions of livres in voluntary contributions, four of which will come from the clergy. They have likewise some hopes in the East Indies, that their reinforcement, which was to be at Ceylon the first of February, will have got there before the Bombay ships joined Sir E. Hughes.

" I have the honour to enclose to you the answer respecting Mr. Parker, and I have agreed with Mons. de Castries, according to his Majesty's orders, that six or eight English packet-boats and as many French shall respectively sail from Dover and Calais, each having on board both an English and French passport, so that as soon as I receive the English passports, Sir, from you, I shall have the same number of French passports to transmit to your office.

　　　" I have the honour to be,
　　　　　" With great truth and sincerity,
　　　　　　　　" Sir,
　　　" Your most obedient, humble servant,
　　　　　　　　　　" THOMAS GRENVILLE."

LORD SHELBURNE TO RICHARD OSWALD, ESQ.

　　　　　　　　　　" WHITEHALL, *June* 30*th*, 1782.
" SIR,
　　" I received on the 17th inst. your letter of the 9th, and am very glad to acknowledge your care and assiduity respecting the discharge of Lord Cornwallis from his parole.

" I must own that I have been disappointed in not receiving any letter from you by two messengers who brought despatches from Mr. Grenville, especially as at this moment it is very essential to have early and regular intelligence. I take it, however, for granted, that you had nothing of business to communicate, which would indeed be naturally suspended, till the passing of the Act in question enabled me to send the necessary powers. This was completed the end of last week, and I lost no time in taking the King's commands for directing a commission to be made out conformable to the powers given to his Majesty.

" I hope to receive early assurance from you that my confidence in the sincerity and good faith of Mr. Franklin has not been misplaced, and that he will concur with you in endeavouring to render effectual the great work in which our hearts and wishes are so equally interested. You will observe that we have adopted his idea of the best method to come at a general pacification by treating separately with each party. I cannot but entertain a firm reliance that the appointment of the particular Commissioners will be no less satisfactory to him. He has very lately warranted me to depend upon that effect in the instance of your nomination, and he will not be surprised at the choice of your colleague, Mr. Jackson, when he considers how very conversant Mr. Jackson is with the subject of America, and how very sincere a friend he has uniformly shown himself to the re-establishment of peace and harmony between that country and this.

" It cannot have escaped Mr. Franklin's memory, that when I was formerly engaged in the same employment which I have now the honour to hold, and was accustomed, with so much satisfaction and advantage to myself, to converse freely with him upon all American subjects, I was, at the same time, in habits of similar intimacy with Mr. Jackson, whose particular acquaintance with these subjects recommended him to the office of Counsel to the Board of Trade. I persuade myself that you will find him an agreeable associate to yourself; and as far as can depend upon the choice of men, that I shall find your joint labours useful to the public. It will be altogether unnecessary for me to give you any additional instructions to those accompanying the Commission with Mr. Jackson, especially as he will communicate to you the substance of a full and confidential conversation I have had with him on the subject. In regard to Mr. Digges, you may assure Dr. Franklin, that he need be under no uneasiness about his connection with, or attendance upon Sir Guy Carleton. The fact is, he is now in London, and the amount of my knowledge of him is merely this. He had been, it seems, employed by the late Administration in an indirect commission to sound Mr. Adams at the Hague, which scheme appears to have had no consequence resulting from it. The man was afterwards recommended to me; but having heard by accident a very indifferent account of his character, and particularly that Mr. Franklin had a bad opinion of him, I from that moment resolved to have nothing to do with him. You will add my compliments to Mr. Franklin; and assure him, that as in this case I really had regard to his opinion, I shall not be less influenced by it in any other instance which may occur; and I beg him to believe, that I have no idea or design in acting towards him and his associates, but in the most liberal and honourable manner.

" I am, &c.,

"SHELBURNE."

LORD SHELBURNE TO MR. THOS. GRENVILLE.

"WHITEHALL, *July 5th*, 1782.

" SIR,

" His Majesty having thought proper to entrust me with the seals of the Foreign Department, upon the resignation of Mr. Secretary Fox, I take the earliest opportunity of notifying it to you. I am at the same time to signify to you the King's commands, that you should without delay acquaint the French Minister and Dr. Franklin, that neither the death of Lord Rockingham, nor the resignation of Mr. Fox, will make any change in the measures of his Majesty's Government, particularly in his ardent desire of peace upon terms which may consist with the dignity of his crown, and the welfare of his people; nor are they likely to be followed by any further changes in the persons of his Ministers. You will make the same communication to the Minister of any other power with whom you may have had intercourse in consequence of your instructions.

"You will be acquainted of the arrangements which may be to take place in consequence of what has passed, the moment they are finally determined, which will be in the course of a very few days. His Majesty being graciously pleased to command my services at the Board of Treasury, will probably deprive me of any other official occasion of assuring you of every personal regard and confidence. In the mean time, his Majesty desires that you will acquaint me of the state of your negociation, together with every light which may enable his Ministers to form a judgement of its possible success.

"I am, &c.,
"SHELBURNE."

MR. OSWALD TO LORD SHELBURNE.

"PARIS, July 8th, 1782.

" MY LORD,

"I beg leave to trouble your Lordship with the inclosed letter from Dr. Franklin to me, which he sent me on the day it is dated. He had mentioned his intention, some days before, of writing me such a letter, and that I might send it home, if I thought fit. Notwithstanding that option, I think it proper to forward it; since I cannot see for what other purpose it should be sent to me, and I hope its coming through my hands will be understood as rather intended to convey the Doctor's sentiments and wishes on this occasion of public concern, than with a view

of my availing myself of the compliments he is pleased
to bestow upon me.

> " I have the honour to be,
>> " My Lord,
>>> " Your Lordship's most obedient
>>> " humble servant,
>>>> "RICHARD OSWALD."

MR. OSWALD TO LORD SHELBURNE.

" PARIS, *Monday, July 8th*, 1782.

" MY LORD,

" I beg leave under this cover to transmit to
your Lordship a letter directed to myself from Dr.
Franklin, which he sent me ten days ago, on the day
it is dated; and I will also take notice of what passed
between him and me in consequence of it.

" Two days before that letter was sent to me, the
Doctor called upon me, and said that, agreeable to the
memorandum I showed him, he had wrote me a letter
which I might send your Lordship, if I thought fit.
Upon the perusal of it, I observed, he said, that I
might be appointed singly for the Colonies, or jointly
with Mr. Grenville, or included in Mr. Grenville's
general commission, to treat with all parties concerned
in the war.   To this last part I objected, for various
reasons needless to be here taken notice of.   The
Doctor acquiesced respecting foreign nations, and said
he would alter the letter; and accordingly, on the
27th of last month, he sent me the one inclosed.

" I have kept it in my hands until now, to go by

the return of the first courier that arrives, which Mr.
Grenville has been expecting daily.   But as none had
appeared, and thinking that the Doctor could have no
meaning in putting such a letter into my hands, but
with a view of its being forwarded to your Lordship,
and perhaps might be disappointed or disobliged if
delayed, I thought it right to let him know that it
was not sent, and the reason of its still remaining in
my hands.   On that account, and wishing to have an
opportunity of talking to him on the subject of it, I
went out to his house on Saturday the 6th, and stayed
with him about an hour.

"After thanking him for his good opinion of me
as expressed in that letter, and giving the reason for
its not being forwarded, I told him that this interval of
delay had given occasion to sundry questions in my
own mind, as to the business we should have to treat
about, in case I should be appointed, and should
undertake the office he was pleased to recommend in
that letter.   With France and the other parties I was
sensible there must be many points to be settled.
But with respect to the Colonies, I told him I could
not easily conceive how there could arise any variety
of subjects to treat on.   That as to a final conclusion,
the Treaty with France might make it necessary to
wait the event of a determination as to them, so as
both might be included in one settlement; but until
then, I could not see there would be much field for
negociation between Great Britain and the Commissioners for the Colonies, after their Independence
had been granted; and which being in a manner

acknowledged, I had been in hopes there remained
no questions of either side that would require much
discussion ; if he thought it would be otherwise, I told
him I would be much obliged to him to give me a
hint of them, as the question could not but be material
to me, in considering whether I might venture upon
such a charge ; that this I would request of him as a
friend, and I hoped I might also expect of him as a
friend to England, which I must still suppose him to
be, and in which I was not singular, believing it was
the universal opinion at home, and particularly with
regard to your Lordship, who, I had reason to be
assured, had the greatest confidence in his good intentions towards our country.   That I did not just then
desire or expect an answer ; but if he would name any
other day, I should wait on him, in hopes of having
his opinion and advice upon the particular subject of
this Colony Treaty, and his sentiments in general upon
the whole of these affairs, which I was certain would
be of service in guiding us how to proceed in the
safest and quickest course, to a final conclusion of this
unhappy business.   That I had too just a notion of
his character to expect any information, but such as
would not be inconsistent with particular engagements ; but where that did not interfere, his granting
the favour I asked, might be doing a good office to all
parties concerned ; for I could not help thinking that
the Commissioners of the Colonies had it much in
their power to give despatch to the General Treaty,
and to end it on just and reasonable terms, even
notwithstanding their particular Treaty with France.

Upon this the Doctor said they had no Treaty
with France, but what was published. I said I was
glad it was so, since I saw nothing there, however
guarded, against a separate peace, that should direct
or control the conditions of a Treaty between them
and Great Britain, excepting the provision for the
great article of independence, which was now out of
the question; that I was happy to be told by Mr.
Laurens, soon after he was discharged from the
Tower, that when they should obtain their Independence, their Treaty with France was at an end. I did
not on this occasion think it proper to quote what
Mr. Grenville said the Doctor himself told him, on
11th or 12th of May last, to the same purpose, and so
said nothing of it. I went on and said, that with
respect to France, whatever she might desire beyond
the separation of the Thirteen Colonies, would be more
than she had just reason to expect, being abundantly
indemnified thereby for the amount of all her expenses
in the present war; that hereafter she had nothing to
fear from England, but England had now much to
fear from France, as would be seen in a few years
after the first peace; since we might then be assured
that she would begin again with us whenever she
thought we were weakest, and I could have no doubt
the East Indies would be the next scene of contest;
and upon the whole, that the terms of the approaching
settlement were of the most interesting consequence
to our future safety; that whatever advice or hints
regarding that purpose, the Doctor would be pleased
to give me, I would make no indiscreet use of, but

would pledge my honour that they should be strictly kept under such directions of communication as he should think fit to prescribe. After allowing me to go on in this way, he said, there were some things, which he wished England to think of, or to agree to (I forget which), and yet he should not like that they were known to have been suggested by him. At last he told me, if I would come out to his house on Wednesday the 10th, he would show me a minute of some things which he thought might be deserving of notice upon the occasion. If we agreed in our opinions, it was so far well; if not, that I should let him know, and he would be glad to have my opinion; and where we agreed, I might make use of his sentiments as my own, to any good purpose I might think proper.

"I shall go out accordingly on Wednesday, and shall in a subsequent letter by the same conveyance, make a report of what had passed, and as I may be at liberty to do so. Meanwhile, I thought this previous explanation not improper to be laid before your Lordship; as in case there should be any advantage in the result, whether by advice or information, it may appear how it has been brought about, and may be some guide in farther proceedings in the same way. If no good should come of it, there is no help; the trial can do no harm. When the Doctor mentioned his not wishing that any particular things he should say, should be repeated as coming from him, I said, that was certainly right, and I supposed there would be no occasion that it should be known to any body here, that I had made this particular application to him, for which I could assure him I had neither orders nor instructions. To this I did not observe any direct answer was given.

"Amongst other things, in the course of this conversation I said, that people might talk as they pleased of a speedy conclusion of the war; but that I could not see it in that light, as if the Treaty could be finished in any short time, for many reasons; amongst other things, on account of the uncertainty of what was doing or like to be done in North America. In that the Doctor did not seem to differ from my opinion; meanwhile, he read to me some late resolutions of the Assembly of Maryland in May, just come to hand, declaring against a separate peace, or peace of any kind with England, until their Independence is acknowledged.

" He likewise mentioned two other pieces of news they have just received; Monsieur Guichen taking and carrying into Brest fourteen ships of our Quebec fleet, and the blowing up a great magazine and a bastion at Gibraltar. Talking of there being no courier from England, the Doctor said perhaps there might be some hesitation in his Majesty's Councils, on account of the late victory in the West Indies, and that Mr. Grenville as yet had been able to make no progress in his business.

"It is said Count de Grasse has wrote home, and confessed he was wrong in fighting, as he certainly was, until he got to leeward. But he says he saw the French colours surrounded by the enemy, which was too much for him, and he flew to their assist-ance.

> "I have the honour to be with much respect,
>> "My Lord,
>>> "Your Lordship's most obedient
>>> "humble servant,
>>>> "RICHARD OSWALD.

"P.S. I forgot to mention, that I told the Doctor that I would write to your Lordship by the first courier, for leave to return for some time to England; and wished he might give me something to carry, that would be acceptable to your Lordship. I shall be better able to judge after I have seen him on Wednesday. He again mentioned the affair of Canada, and said there would be no solid peace, while it remained an English colony."

MR. FRANKLIN TO MR. OSWALD.

"PASSY, *June 27th*, 1782.

"SIR,

"The opinion I have of your candour, probity, good understanding, and good will to both countries, made me hope that you would have been vested with the character of Plenipotentiary to treat with those from America. When Mr. Grenville produced his first Commission, which was only to treat with France, I did imagine that the other to treat with us was reserved for you, and kept back only till the Enabling Bill should be passed. Mr. Grenville has since received a second Commission, which, as he informs me, has additional words, impowering him to treat with the Ministers of any other prince or state whom it may concern; and he seems to understand, that those general words comprehend the United States of America. There may be no doubt that they comprehend Spain and Holland; but as there exist various public acts by which the Government of Great Britain denies us to be states, and none in which they acknowledge us to be such, it seems hardly clear that we could be intended, at the time that Commission was given, the Enabling Act not being then passed. So that though I can have no objection to Mr. Grenville, nor right to make it if I had any; yet as your long residence in America has given you a knowledge of that country, its people, circumstances, commerce, &c., which, added to your experience in business, may be useful to both sides in facilitating and expediting the negociation, I cannot but hope, that it is still intended to vest you with the character above mentioned, respecting the Treaty with America, either separately, or in conjunction with Mr. Grenville, as to the wisdom of your Ministers may seem best. Be it as it may, I beg you would accept this line, as a testimony of the sincere esteem and respect with which I have the honour to be, Sir,

" Your most obedient humble servant,
"B. FRANKLIN."

MR. GRENVILLE TO LORD SHELBURNE.

"Paris, *July 9th*, 1782.

" My Lord,

" I received last night the honour of your Lordship's letter of the 5th inst.; and in obedience to his Majesty's commands, have acquainted the French Minister, the Spanish Ambassador, and Mr. Franklin, that no change will be made in the measures of his Majesty's Government, particularly in his Majesty's ardent desire of peace, upon terms which may be consistent with the dignity of his crown, and the welfare of his people.

" I have had no intercourse with the Ministers of any other foreign powers.   From the interference of the Court of Russia, in order to bring about a particular peace with Holland, and there having been till a very few days since, no positive declaration of the Dutch being determined only to treat in conjunction with France, it appeared to me most prudent, and most agreeable to the spirit of my instructions, to avoid, as long as it was possible, the including Holland in this negociation; and I have consequently taken every opportunity to remind Mons. de Vergennes, that it had not been our desire to include Holland in this business.   I learned however from him to-day, that the Dutch having formally requested of the Court of Versailles to make no peace, but in common with them, every assurance of that nature had by the French King's orders been given to them.   Your Lordship will perhaps have learned from the official letters I have at times sent to

Mr. Fox, that the French Minister has not gone into
any detail as yet; the state of the negociation is, therefore, exactly what it was when I had the honour of
transmitting the written answer I copied at Versailles,
on the 21st ult., which consents to a future explanation,
provided the general grounds there stated, should be
adopted in England; of that, however, I took the
liberty of expressing some doubt by my last of the
21st, as I observed in them that very wide extent,
which, from my first coming here to this moment,
I have uniformly considered as a most unpromising
feature in the proposed pacification. It is not easy to
weigh the precise sense of general terms; but a new
treaty of commerce is always foremost in the conversation of the French, Spanish, and American Ministers.
Mons. d'Aranda dwells incessantly upon our giving
up Gibraltar, notwithstanding the little disposition he
finds in me to that discussion, and only varies what
he says upon it by stating, that if we give it by
Treaty, we shall get something for it; whereas if it
should be taken, the Court of Madrid can never hear
of its being reclaimed by us. Mr. Franklin, the other
day for the first time, gave me to understand that
America must be to have her share in the Newfoundland fishery, and that the limits of Canada would
likewise be a subject for arrangement; he seems
much disinclined to an idea he expects to be stated,
of going into an examination for the mutual compen-
sation of the losses of individuals, insisting, perhaps
with reason, upon the endless detail that would be
produced by it; nor does he cease to give the most

decided discouragement to any possible plan of
arrangement with America, short of complete and
distinct Independence in its fullest sense; when I
last saw him, he read to me upon this subject the
resolutions of the 16th of May last, that passed
unanimously both houses of Assembly in Maryland,
against making any peace, but in concert with France,
and with an admission of independence; resolutions,
he said, occasioned by Sir Guy Carleton's supposed
commission, and which spoke the determination, he
was sure, of all the Thirteen Provinces.

"Having touched, my Lord, upon those few circumstances that seem in any way important to this
business, I forbear to enlarge upon them, in full
trust that I shall be permitted to come (incessantly)
to London, where his Majesty's Ministers will
certainly command the little information I can have
to give them; it being my fixed purpose, firmly,
though as humbly and respectfully as it is possible,
to decline any further prosecution of this business. I
have therefore to request of your Lordship, as speedily
as may be, to lay before his Majesty in every
expression of duty and humility my earnest and
unalterable prayer, that his Majesty will be graciously
pleased to recall from me the Commission I am
honoured with at Paris. I am highly sensible to the
very flattering expressions of your Lordship's regard;
and have the honour to be, with great truth and
respect, My Lord,

            "Your Lordship's most obedient and most
                "humble servant,
                    "THOMAS GRENVILLE."

MR. OSWALD TO LORD SHELBURNE.

"PARIS, *Wednesday, July 10th*, 1782.

" MY LORD,

" In consequence of Dr. Franklin's appointment, as mentioned in my letter of the 8th, under this cover, I went out to his house this morning, and stayed near two hours with him, with a view of obtaining the information and advice I wished for, as to the terms and conditions upon which he thought a Treaty betweeen Great Britain and the Commissioners of the Colonies might be carried on and proceed to a conclusion. Having reminded him of what he in a manner promised on this head on the 6th, he took out a minute, and from it read a few hints or articles, some, he said, as necessary for them to insist on, others which he could not say he had any orders about, or were not absolutely demanded, and yet such as it would be advisable for England to offer for the sake of reconciliation and her future interest, viz. :—

" 1st. Of the first class *necessary* to be granted, Independence full and complete in every sense, to the Thirteen States, and all troops to be withdrawn from thence.

" 2nd. A settlement of the boundaries of *their* colonies and the loyal colonies.

" 3rd. A confinement of the boundaries of Canada; at least, to what they were before the last Act of Parliament, I think in 1774, if not to a still more contracted state, on an ancient footing.

" 4th. A freedom of fishing on the Banks of New-foundland and elsewhere, as well for fish as whales.

" I own I wondered he should have thought it necessary to ask for this privilege ; he did not mention the leave of drying fish on shore at New-foundland, and I said nothing of it. I don't remember any more articles which he said they would insist on, or what he called necessary for them to be granted.

" Then as to the advisable articles, or such as he would, as a friend, recommend to be offered by England, viz. :—

" 1st. To indemnify many people who had been ruined by towns burned and destroyed, the whole might not exceed the sum of five or six hundred thousand pounds. I was struck at this. However, the Doctor said, though it was a large sum, it would not be ill-bestowed, as it would conciliate the resentment of a multitude of poor sufferers, who could have no other remedy, and who without some relief would keep up a spirit of secret revenge and animosity, for a long time to come, against Great Britain ; whereas voluntary offer of such reparation would diffuse a universal calm and conciliation over the whole country.

" 2nd. Some sort of acknowledgment, in some public Act of Parliament, or otherwise, of our error in distressing those countries so much as we had done. A few words of that kind, the Doctor said, would do more good than people could imagine.

" 3rd. Colony ships and trade to be received, and have the same privileges in Great Britain and Ireland, as British ships and trade. I did not ask any

explanation on that head for the present. British
and Irish ships in the Colonies to be, in like manner,
on the same footing with their own ships.

" 4th. Giving up every part of Canada.

" If there were any other Articles of either kind, I
can't now recollect them ; but I don't think there
were any of material consequence, and I was perhaps
the less attentive in the enumeration, that it had been
agreed to give me the whole in writing ; but after
some reflection, the Doctor said he did not much like
giving such writing out of his hands, and, hesitating
a good deal about it, asked me if I had seen Mr. Jay,
the other Commissioner, lately come from Madrid. I
said, I had not. He then told me it would be proper I
should see him, and he would fix a time for our meeting ;
and seemed to think he should want to confer with
him himself, before he gave a final answer. I told
him, if I had such final answer, and had leave, I would
carry it over to England. He said, that would be
right, but that as Mr. Grenville told him he expected
another courier in four or five days, I had better wait
so long, and he would write along with me.

" Upon the whole, the Doctor expressed himself in
a friendly way towards England, and was not without
hopes, that if we should settle on this occasion in the
way he wished, England would not only have a beneficial intercourse with the Colonies, but at last it might
end in a fœderal union between them. In the mean
time we ought to take care, not to force them into the
hands of other people. He showed me a copy of the
Enabling Bill as it is called ; and said, he observed

the word ' revolted ' was left out, and likewise added,
that the purpose of it was to dispense with Acts of
Parliament which they were indifferent about, *and
that* now they were better prepared for war, and more
able to carry it on, than ever they were ; that he had
heard, we entertained some expectation of retaining
some sort of sovereignty over them, as his Majesty
had of Ireland, and that if we thought so, we should
find ourselves much disappointed, for they would
yield to nothing of that sort.

" He then showed me a state of their account with
this Government, and his contract with them for the
several loans the Congress had had of them,—beginning in 1778, and running on at the rate of two, three,
and four millions per annum, amounting in the whole
to eighteen millions of livres (or £750,000 sterling,
at 10*d*. per livre), payable with interest at five per
cent. from the time of the advance.   But, by a subsequent and late concession of the King, the whole preceding interest is given up, and to continue so until
the first day of the Peace;   and then the interest
again to commence.   He said, that would be a trifle
upon the whole, as their taxes would now come in fast;
that they had borrowed a sum, in Holland, at four
per cent., for which the King of France was guarantee.
I forgot the sum, but I think it was three millions of
guilders, about £275,000.

" The Doctor is Judge Admiral here for all prizes
brought into France by American vessels, and
determines their causes as such.   He received a
packet of these papers while I was sitting with him.

" From this conversation, I have some hopes, my Lord, that it is possible to put an end to the American quarrel in a short time, and when that is done, I have a notion, that a treaty with the other Powers will go more smoothly on. The Doctor did not, in the course of the above conversation, hesitate as to a conclusion with them, on account of any connection with those other States; and in general seemed to think their American affair must be ended by a separate commission.

" On these occasions I said, I supposed in case of such commission he meant that the power of granting Independence would be therein expressly mentioned. He said, No doubt: I hinted this, thinking it better in the power of treating to include Independence, than to grant Independence separately, and then to treat about other matters, with the Commissioners of such Independent States, who by such grant are on the same footing with the Ministers of the other Powers. By anything the Doctor said, I did not perceive he made any account of this distinction; and I did not think it proper to say anything more about it. I forgot one thing the Doctor said with respect to some provision or reparation to those called the Loyal Sufferers :—It would be impossible to make any such provision; they were so numerous and their cases so various, that he could not see that it could make any part of the treaty. There might be particular cases that deserved compassion; these being left to the several States, they might perhaps do something for them, but they, as Commissioners, could do nothing.

" He then read to me the Order in Carolina for confiscating and selling of estates, under the direction of the military, by which so great a number of families had been ruined, and which the people there felt so much, as would stifle their compassion for the sufferers on the other side. I remember, the Doctor, in a former proposal in April, hinted that a cession of the back lands of Canada would raise a sum which would make some reparation to the sufferers on both sides. Now, he says, one of the *necessary* articles is a cession of these back lands, without any stipulation for the Loyal Sufferers ; and as an *advisable* Article, a gift of five or six hundred thousand pounds, to indemnify the sufferers on their side. I should hope he would be persuaded to alter that part of the plan.

" I have the honour to be,

" My Lord,

" Your Lordship's most obedient

" humble servant,

"RICHARD OSWALD."

MR. OSWALD TO LORD SHELBURNE.

" PARIS, *July* 11*th*, 1782.

" MY LORD,

" Referring to my letter of yesterday's date, here inclosed, relative to my conversation with Dr. Franklin, on the subject of a treaty to the Colonies, I am now to own receipt of your Lordship's letter of the 5th, by the Courier Hog, which came to hand on the 8th. I don't know how far such a load of business will

be supportable to your Lordship, but I think I
may safely congratulate your country, on your taking
up this last charge, and sincerely wish your Lordship much satisfaction and success in the discharge
of it.

"When I went out yesterday to Dr. Franklin, I
read to him such parts of the above letter as you
desired to be communicated to him.

"I thank your Lordship for the caution with
respect to Gibraltar, or any affairs under Mr. Grenville's direction. As to the first, it was proposed by
the Doctor in such a way as I understood it to be an
express commission from the French Minister, and,
having an opportunity of Major Ross, I put it down
in my letter, as it seemed to show that this Court
would be glad to be excused taking a part in the
attempts of recovering the place in any other way.
In answer, it is true, I said territorial possession was
the only proper equivalent, if England chose to part
with it, and I happened to mention Porto Rico as
what in such case would be agreeable to many
people. That passed in the way of conversation,
although the proposal, I supposed, was designedly
prompted as above mentioned. I never heard anything more on the subject. As to Mr. Grenville's
business, it would have been quite wrong in me to
meddle in it in any shape, and so cautious was I, that
I scarce asked him any question as to the progress of
his affairs ; thinking it sufficient, if by an intercourse
with Dr. Franklin I could help to bring on a settlement with the Colonies, upon which, I always believed,

a conclusion with the other parties would in a great measure depend, both as to despatch and conditions.

" Even in this business I had scarce taken any steps, since my last coming over in the end of May. It was impossible to do so, as Mr. Franklin seemed to attend to the expectation and issue of Mr. Grenville's Powers and Instructions, which, he said, were imperfect at first, and not completed at last to his satisfaction with respect to them, so that the Doctor did not incline to talk of business to me, and I had nothing to write, even if I had known at times, when Mr. Grenville's couriers were despatched. The situation was not agreeable, but I could not help it, and I believe the Doctor was not pleased, although he said little to me on the subject. However, at last, being I suppose desirous that something should be done in their affairs, he very unexpectedly put his letter into my hands, of the 27th of June, which goes under cover with this. When I received it, I thought it my duty to take the steps mentioned in my letter of the 8th in consequence of it. If after seeing Mr. Jay, I can procure from those gentlemen, some sketch in writing of what they demand, I will talk to them on the subject, and try to bring it into some form of a settled Agreement, or rather Propositions, to be submitted to discussion at home, as necessary in the like cases. Upon that foundation a Commission may be granted to carry on the treaty to a conclusion ; for I plainly see the Doctor inclines that their business should be done under a separate

Commission.   As to any information I can give, in
relation to these affairs, which your Lordship recommends to me, I beg leave to say, that although I had
better opportunities of conversation than I have, there
is very little to be got here.   I will, however, not
scruple to give my opinion as things occur to me,
viz.:—That the more anxious we appear to be for
Peace, the more backward the people here will be,
or the harder in their terms, which is much the same
thing; and that having fully satisfied this Court of
our desire to put an end to the war, as has been done,
the more vigorously our exertions are pushed in the
interim, we shall come sooner to our purpose, and on
better terms.   With respect to the Commissioners for
the Colonies, our conduct towards them, I think, ought
to be of a style somewhat different; they have shown a
desire to treat, and to end with us on a separate
footing from the other Powers, and I must say, in a
more liberal way, or at least with a greater appearance
of feeling for the future interests and connections of
Great Britain, than I expected.   I speak so from the
text of the last conversation I had with Mr. Franklin,
as mentioned in my letter of yesterday.   And therefore
we ought to deal with them tenderly, and as supposed
conciliated friends, or at least well disposed to conciliation ; and not as if we had anything to give them,
that we can keep from them, or that they are very
anxious to have.   Even Dr. Franklin himself, as the
subject happened to lead that way, as good as told
me, yesterday, that they were their own Masters,
and seemed to make no account of the grant of Inde-

pendence as a favour.   I was so much satisfied beforehand of their ideas on that head, that I will own to
your Lordship, I did not read to the Doctor that
part of your letter, wherein you mention that grant,
as if it in some shape challenged a return on their
part.   When the Doctor pointed at the object of the
Enabling Bill, as singly resting upon a dispensation of
Acts of Parliament they cared not for, I thought it
enough for me to say they had been binding and
acknowledged ; to which no answer was made.
When the Doctor mentioned the report, as if there
was an expectation of retaining the sovereignty, I
ventured a little further (though with a guarded
caution) to touch him on the only tender side of their
supposed present emancipation, and said, that such
report was probably owing to the imaginations of
people, upon hearing of the rejoicings in America, on
the cessation of war, change of the Ministry, &c. &c.,
which they might conclude would have some effect
in dividing the provinces, and giving a different turn
to affairs ; as no doubt there was a great proportion
of the people, notwithstanding all that had happened,
who, from considerations of original affinity, correspondence, and other circumstances, were still strongly
attached to England, &c. &c.

" To this, also, there was no answer made.   At the
same time, I cannot but say, I was much pleased,
upon the whole, with what passed upon the occasion
of this interview.   And I really believe the Doctor
sincerely wishes for a speedy settlement ; and that
after the loss of Dependence, we may lose no more ;

but, on the contrary, that a cordial reconciliation may take place over all that country.

" Amongst other things, I was pleased at his showing me a state of the aids they had received from France, as it looked as if he wanted I should see the amount of the obligations to their Ally ; and as if it was the only foundation of the ties France had over them, excepting gratitude, which the Doctor owned in so many words; but at the same time said, the debt would be punctually and easily discharged, France having given to 1788 to pay it.

" The Doctor also particularly took notice of the discharge of the interest, to the term of the Peace, which he said was kind and generous.

" It is possible I may make a wrong estimate of the situation of this American business, and of the chance of a total or partial recovery being desperate. In that case, my opinion will have no weight, and so will do no hurt. Yet, in my present sentiments, I cannot help offering it, as thinking that circumstances are in that situation, that I heartily wish we were done with these people, and as quickly as possible, since we have much to fear from them, in case of their taking the pet; and throwing themselves into more close connection with this Court and our other enemies. I make no doubt, my Lord, but you will find fault with my troubling you with so much writing at a time, which must come very unseasonably, in the midst of so much other business, but we are so imprisoned here in our correspondence, that we cannot divide it, as in other countries.

" To write everything by post would be to no
purpose, so that everything must go by a messenger
on purpose, licensed by a passport obtained by the
formality of an address to the Minister at Versailles.

  " I have the honour to be,

    " My Lord,

      " Your Lordship's most obedient,

       " humble servant,

        "RICHARD OSWALD.

" P.S. I beg leave to repeat what was mentioned in
a former letter, that in my late conversations with Dr.
Franklin, I could not perceive that he meant that the
progress and conclusion of their treaty was to have
any connection, or would be influenced by what was
doing in the treaties with the other Powers ; but that
the Colony Commissioners were free agents and independent of these Powers. And consequently I
suppose they consider themselves restrained by their
alliance with France, only in the point of ratification ;
which indeed infers, that until we agree with France,
we can have neither peace or truce with the Colonies.
But then if we settle terms with the Colonies, and
France is unreasonable, the Colonies may interpose ;
or France may not choose to risk the possibility of
such an arbitration. At the same time I am entirely
persuaded, that Dr. Franklin does not take the least
step in their own affairs, even in such as his late communication with me, but what has been settled
between him and the Count de Vergennes : and
consequently, if from such communication it may be

presumed that the Doctor wishes for a conclusion of their treaty, it may be supposed, that the French are in like manner disposed with respect to theirs.

" I asked Dr. Franklin, as to the answer Mr. Grenville had from this Court to his last memorials, and he told me that the proposition from England being, to take the treaty of 1763 for the basis, it was answered, that it should be so, and that the sundry Articles of said treaty should be gone over, and suitable alterations should be made as a foundation or conditions of the present treaty. Since writing the above, I am told by a friend who had some conversation with Dr. Franklin this morning, that he (the Doctor) had received a letter from some person in England, who is no friend to the late changes, giving, among other things, an account as if the new Administration were not so well disposed to end so quickly and agreeably with the Colonies, as those who have left it, &c.

" This, the gentleman told me, led the Doctor to express himself very strong as to his desire of quick despatch, as he wanted much to go home, and have the chance of a few years' repose, having but a short time to live in the world, and had also much private business to do.

" I should therefore hope it may be possible soon to bring their business near to a final close, and that they will not be any way stiff as to those Articles he calls *advisable*, or will drop them altogether. Those he calls necessary will hardly be any obstacle. I shall be able to make a better guess when I have another meeting with him, jointly with Mr. Jay, which I hope to have by the time this courier returns. Allow me, my Lord, to observe, that if I continue here any time, I would wish to have a messenger attending. This Potter is a proper man."

MR. GRENVILLE TO LORD SHELBURNE.

"Paris, *July* 12*th*, 1782.

" My Lord,

" I profit by the opportunity, which Mr. Oswald's messenger offers, to add a very few lines to those which I had the honour to address to your Lordship on the 9th, and still upon the subject of that immediate return, for which I have made such urgent requisitions; should any difficulty occur upon the idea of the negociation being left unfinished, by such a measure, may I be excused for suggesting that Mr. Oswald or Mr. Walpole, who are both upon the spot, could much more than supply my place for any purpose that might be wished, and for keeping this business still ostensibly on foot by giving an answer to the French paper I had transmitted, should such be the intention of his Majesty ? Your Lordship will, I flatter myself, forgive my annexing so much import-ance, and so many words, to a subject of such infinitely little importance, and will be persuaded, I trust, that if I repeat the utter impossibility of my remaining here in any circumstances, it is not from the vanity of supposing it can be any object that I should, but from that earnestness which makes it natural to (press) any resolution finally and decisively taken. I will not, however, unnecessarily intrude upon the better employment of your Lordship's time, having nothing to add upon the subject of the negociation, further than the humble assurances, which, if I might so presume, I would wish to be conveyed to his Majesty, that I have not been wanting in zeal during my stay here, neither as I hope in duty to his Majesty by my respectful though invariable entreaty to return.

" I have the honour to be with the greatest respect,
" My Lord,
" Your Lordship's most obedient and
" most humble servant,
" THOMAS GRENVILLE.

"P.S. I have the honour to enclose to your Lordship a memorial I this instant received from Versailles, with a copy of Mons. de Vergennes' to me upon the same subject.

" T. G."

MR. OSWALD TO LORD SHELBURNE.

" PARIS, *July* 12*th*, 1782.
(3 Afternoon.)

" MY LORD,
" The courier has been in waiting some time for Dr. Franklin's letters. They are just come to hand, with one for myself, which I think proper to send to your Lordship, with the Maryland paper that was inclosed in it.

" I am glad to see by the Doctor's letter, as if he

wishes a settlement with them may not be stopped; I think that may be presumed from his sending me this letter, and the explanations therein mentioned. On the other hand, I cannot but be concerned at this report, which has been conveyed to him, of a reserve intended in the grant of Independence, being the first time I ever heard of it; at least, Mr. Grenville did not tell me that his signification on that head was accompanied by any such reservation, and upon the faith of that, I have in my letters to your Lordship, and in conversation with Dr. Franklin, always supposed, that the grant was meant to be absolute and unconditional, which last, however, is a term I never used, thinking such qualification unnecessary. Its being given out that a difference subsisted, and resignations happened on this account, must naturally occasion this hesitation in the Commissioners of the Colonies; and so I see by the Doctor's letter to me he puts a sort of stoppage upon the preliminaries of settlement with them, which had been pretty well sketched out, and defined in his conversation with me on the 10th instant; and until there is a further explanation under your Lordship's authority, on the said head of Independence, I am, in a manner forbid in the Doctor's letter, to go back upon the plan of that conference, and to claim any right to the propositions thereof, which, if complete Independence was meant to be granted, is a little unlucky; and there is reason to regret, that anybody should have been so wicked, as to throw this stumbling-block in the way, by which, not only Peace with the Colonies is obstructed, but the general treaty is suspended, which, I cannot help still thinking, hangs upon a settlement with the Colonies. And so by this unlucky interjection the peace of the country at home is disturbed, and the blame thrown upon the new Administration, and upon your Lordship by name.

" If before the return of the courier I should meet with the Doctor again and Mr. Jay, I will conduct myself in the best manner I can, according to circumstances, so as to lose no part of the ground that has been gained, although I am sensible there is no proceeding further, and it would be improper to attempt it, until there are fresh instructions from your Lordship. If your Lordship should think them material to be instantly communicated, the sooner they come perhaps, the better. I am perfectly ashamed of troubling with so much writing at one time, but this last letter I could not possibly help, the Doctor's letter not having come until the other packets were sealed up.

" I have the honour to be,

" My Lord,

" Your Lordship's most obedient,

" humble servant,

"RICHARD OSWALD.

" P.S. 1 shan't be surprised if the next meeting with the Doctor should turn out more unfavourably than the former. Your Lordship will, no doubt, do what is necessary to prevent it."

MR. OSWALD TO LORD SHELBURNE.

"PARIS, *July* 12*th*, 1782.

" MY LORD,

" Mr. Grenville having called upon me yesterday evening, and on my asking him as to his last answer from the French Minister, he informed me of it as far as he could remember, and I was sorry to find it of a style so much above the pitch of moderation ; that our Court, after taking the treaty of 1763 for the basis of the new treaty, must agree to material alterations respecting the four quarters of the world, and that before they proceed further, this must be assented to, without any further explanation as to the particulars of such alterations. Mr. Grenville did not say he remembered the words exactly, and I may have quoted him wrong.

" However, there is enough to show upon what an unlucky footing that matter stands ; and that Peace is likely to be at a greater distance than was expected. Some time last month with a view to this kind of possibility, and having nothing to do, I wrote out some minutes, as they occurred to me, of some things that I thought might be of use, in the present case, if the war should go on, or would concern the safety of England on future occasions. I intended them for your Lordship if you had continued in the other department, but now, in the hurry of such a multitude of affairs, I can hardly expect you will take up your time with such things. However, I have sent the

packet over by the bearer, to Mrs. Oswald, to lie in
her hands for the present.

"They would take better than an hour in the
perusal. In case your Lordship should desire to see
them, Mrs. Oswald will send the packet, upon receiving a card or other message from your Lordship; by
taking the papers to the country perhaps your Lordship may have leisure to give them a fair perusal.
Unless that can be done, I would rather they lie
where I have ordered them. Another thing I should
not like, that they should go into any other hands
than your own, while I continue in this place, and
there are so many Spaniards here. If your Lordship
should call for them, I can get them back, when I
return to England. I shall make no apology for this
freedom, since I by no means solicit your Lordship's
attention to the thing, doubting myself whether it is
deserving of it, and all the favour I ask is, that in
case the packet is called for, it may have a perusal at
your leisure.

　　　　"I am with much respect,
　　　　　　"My Lord,
　　　　　　　　"Your Lordship's most obedient
　　　　　　　　　　"humble servant,
　　　　　　　　　　　　"RICHARD OSWALD.

"I have sent notice to Mr. Grenville, that he may
have his packets ready. The copy I send is wrote
out fair and plain by Mr. Whiteford, so that the
papers will be more easily read, than if they had been
in my hand."

MR. FRANKLIN TO MR. OSWALD.

"Passy, *July* 12*th*, 1782.

" SIR,

"I inclose a letter for Lord Shelburne, to go by your courier, with some others, of which I request his care; they may be put into the Penny Post. I have received a note informing me, that 'some opposition given by his Lordship to Mr. Fox's decided *plan of unequivocally acknowledging American Independency*, was one cause of that gentleman's resignation;' this, from what you have told me, appears improbable,—it is farther said, 'that Mr. Grenville thinks Mr. Fox's resignation will be fatal to the present negociation.' This perhaps is as groundless as the former. Mr. Grenville's next courier, will probably clear up matters. I did understand from him that such an acknowledgement was intended before the commencement of the treaty; and until it is made and the treaty formally begun, propositions, and discussions seem, on consideration, to be untimely, nor can I enter into particulars without Mr. Jay, who is now ill with the influenza. My letter, therefore, to his Lordship, is merely complimentary on his late appointment.

"I wish a continuance of your health, in that at present sickly city, being with sincere esteem, Sir,

"Your most obedient and most humble servant,
"B. FRANKLIN.

"P.S.—I send you inclosed the late Resolutions

of the State of Maryland, by which the general disposition of people in America may be guessed respecting any Treaty to be proposed by General Carleton, if intended, which I do not believe."

MR. FRANKLIN TO LORD SHELBURNE.

"PASSY, *July 12th*, 1782.

"MY LORD,

"Mr. Oswald informing me that he is about to dispatch a courier, I embrace the opportunity of congratulating your Lordship on your appointment to the Treasury. It is an extension of your power to do good, and in that view, if in no other, it must increase your happiness, which I heartily wish, being with great and sincere respect,

"My Lord,

"Your Lordship's most obedient and most "humble servant,

"B. FRANKLIN.

"RIGHT HON. THE EARL OF SHELBURNE."

LORD SHELBURNE TO MR. GRENVILLE.

"ST. JAMES'S, *July 13th*, 1782.

"SIR,

"I have the honour to receive your letter of the 9th, containing a very clear state of the several negociations committed to your care. Your very earnest desire of being recalled, will be taken into consideration, the moment a Secretary of State is appointed, which will take place on Wednesday. In the mean time, as I collect from your letter, and

understand more particularly from Lord Temple,
that your wish is to return as soon as possible, I
have his Majesty's commands, to desire that you will
acquaint the French Minister, and others, with whom
you are in Treaty, that it is his Majesty's pleasure,
that you should return to receive such fresh instructions, as the change of the department may render
necessary, taking care to leave no suspicion on their
mind, that it is meant to relax in any respect from
the intention and spirit with which the negociations
have been hitherto carried on, by repeating the
assurances you were before directed to make to these
ministers, of his Majesty's sincere desire of peace,
upon safe, honourable, and permanent terms. I have
great satisfaction in relying on your discretion and
honour, that you will take care that his Majesty's
service shall not suffer in any respect by your
departure.

" I am, &c."

LORD SHELBURNE TO MR. OSWALD.

" July 13th, 1782.

[PRIVATE.]

" DEAR SIR,
            " The King has given Mr. Grenville leave
to return, and directed him to acquaint the French
minister, Dr. Franklin, &c., that it is for the purpose
of receiving fresh instructions, which will be necessary
on the change of the department, taking care to
repeat every assurance of the King's desire for peace,

and not to leave any impression on the minds of those with whom he is in treaty, of the least relaxation from the intention and spirit of the negociation, as hitherto carried on. I have the firmest reliance on Mr. Grenville's honour, that he will take care that the King's service shall not suffer in any respect by his departure : and I must strictly enjoin you not to mention to any person whatever this communication, till Mr. Grenville himself communicates his intentions and instructions, and in his own manner.

" I have nothing more to add, except that I am surprised at not hearing from you, that the present state of things makes it more necessary than ever that we should be fully instructed in all points leading to a general, or a separate peace, that though you are not instructed to talk upon points regarding France, Spain, and Holland, it does not prevent your endeavouring to gain all possible insight into their intentions and dispositions.

" I am, &c.

" Richard Oswald, Esq."

MR. OSWALD TO LORD SHELBURNE.

"Paris, Tuesday, July 16th, 1782.

" My Lord,
          " I had this morning the honour of your Lordship's letter of the 13th, by the messenger Hog. Having heard by different persons that Mr. Grenville is to set out for London to-morrow morning, I write this to inform your Lordship that I wrote you sundry

letters by the messenger Potter, who left this place on Friday last, the 12th.

"To those letters I have nothing to add relative to business, and am of opinion it would be improper for the present to attempt to take up afresh with Dr. Franklin the subject mentioned in my last letters. I will, however, observe, that having called upon him last Sunday, I showed him, from your Lordship's letter of the 5th, that paragraph relating to independence, which, on a former occasion, I had not read to him, as believing he was satisfied it was intended in the way he wished.

"I have the honour to be,
"My Lord,
"Your Lordship's most obedient,
"humble servant,
"RICHARD OSWALD."

RICHARD OSWALD, ESQ.

"Commission, *July 25th*, 1782.

GEORGE R.,

Our Will and Pleasure is, and We do hereby authorize and command you forthwith to prepare a Bill for our Signature, to pass Our Great Seal of Great Britain, in the words, or to the effect following, viz. :

George the Third, by the Grace of God, King of Great Britain, France, and Ireland, Defender of the Faith, &c., To Our Trusty and Wellbeloved Richard Oswald, of Our City of London, Esq., Greeting : Whereas by virtue of an Act passed in the last Session of Parliament, intituled, "An Act passed to enable His Majesty to conclude a Peace or Truce with certain Colonies in North America therein mentioned," it

is recited, " that it is essential to the Interest, Welfare, and
Prosperity of Great Britain, and the Colonies or Plantations
of New Hampshire, Massachusetts Bay, Rhode Island, Con-
necticut, New York, New Jersey, Pennsylvania, the three
lower Counties on Delaware, Maryland, Virginia, North
Carolina, South Carolina, and Georgia in North America,
that Peace, Intercourse, Trade, and Commerce should be
restored between them."

Therefore, and for a full Manifestation of Our earnest
Wish and Desire, and of that of Our Parliament, to put an
end to the calamities of War, it is enacted, that it should
and might be lawful for Us, to treat, consult of, agree, and
conclude with any Commissioner or Commissioners named, or
to be named, by the said Colonies or Plantations, or with
any Body or Bodies, Corporate or Politic, or any Assembly or
Assemblies, or Description of Men, or any Person or Persons
whatsoever, a Peace or a Truce with the said Colonies or
Plantations, or any of them, or any part or parts thereof,
any Law, Act or Acts of Parliament, Matter or Thing to the
contrary in any wise notwithstanding.

Now Know ye, That We reposing especial Trust in your
Wisdom, Loyalty, Diligence, and Circumspection in the
management of the Affairs to be hereby committed to your
charge, have nominated and appointed, and assigned, and by
these presents do nominate and appoint, constitute and
assign, you, the said Richard Oswald, to be our Commissioner
in that behalf, to Use and Exercise all and every the Powers
and Authorities hereby entrusted and committed to you, the
said Richard Oswald, and to do, perform, and execute all
other Matters and Things hereby enjoined and committed to
your care during Our Will and Pleasure, and no longer,
according to the Tenor of these Our Letters Patent.

And it is Our Royal Will and Pleasure, and We do
hereby authorize, empower, and require you, the said Richard
Oswald, to treat, consult of, and conclude with any Commis-

sioner or Commissioners named, or to be named by the said
Colonies or Plantations, and any Body or Bodies, Corporate
or Politic, or any Assembly or Assemblies, Description of
Men, or any Person or Persons whatsoever, a Peace or a
Truce with the said Colonies or Plantations, or any of them,
or any part or parts thereof, any Law, Act or Acts of
Parliament, Matter or Thing to the contrary in any wise
notwithstanding.

And it is Our further Will and Pleasure, that every Regulation, Provision, Matter, or Thing which shall have been
agreed upon between you, the said Richard Oswald, and such
Commissioner or Commissioners, Body or Bodies, Corporate
or Politic, Assembly or Assemblies, Description of Men,
Person or Persons, as aforesaid, with whom you shall have
judged meet and sufficient to enter into such Agreement,
shall be fully and distinctly set forth in Writing and authenticated by your Hand and Seal, on one side, and by such Seals,
or other Signature on the other, as the occasion may require,
and as may be suitable to the Character and Authority of the
Commissioner or Commissioners, &c., as aforesaid so agreeing. And such Instrument so authenticated, shall be by you
transmitted to Us, through one of Our Principal Secretaries
of State. And it is our further Will and Pleasure, that you
the said Richard Oswald, shall promise and engage for Us,
and in Our Royal Name and Word, that every Regulation,
Provision, Matter, or Thing, which may be agreed to, and
concluded by you, Our said Commissioner, shall be ratified
and confirmed by Us in the fullest manner and extent, and
that We will not suffer them to be violated or counteracted,
either in whole or in part by any person whatsoever. And
We do hereby require and command all Our Officers, Civil
and Military, and all other Our loving Subjects whatsoever,
to be aiding and assisting unto you, the said Richard Oswald,
in the Execution of this Our Commission, and of the Powers
and Authorities herein contained. Provided always, and We

do hereby declare and ordain that the several Offices, Powers, and Authorities hereby granted, shall cease, determine, and become utterly Null and Void, on the First day of July, which shall be in the Year of Our Lord One Thousand seven hundred and eighty-three, although We shall not otherwise in in the meantime have revoked and determined the same. In Witness, &c.

And for so doing this shall be your warrant. Given at our Court at St. James's, the twenty-fifth day of July, One Thousand seven hundred and eighty-two. In the twenty-second year of our reign.

By His Majesty's commands,

"THO. TOWNSHEND.

" To Our Attorney or Solicitor-General."

COPY OF A LETTER TO RICHARD OSWALD, ESQ., FROM MR. TOWNSHEND.

"*July 26th*, 1782.

"SIR,

" I expect to have had the honor to transmit you herewith the King's Commission, authorising you to treat and conclude a Peace, with the American Commissioners at Paris, as well as his Majesty's instructions consequent to it. But, from the length of time necessary to pass the Commission, I have thought it necessary to forward this to you without waiting for it. From the opinion which I have had very good reason to conceive of your ability, I have no doubt but that you will acquit yourself both as to spirit and form, to the satisfaction of his Majesty in this important business.

" As my intention is, and ever will be, in the high office which I have the honor to hold, to conduct my correspondence with the utmost precision and perspicuity, I desire you will, without reserve, communicate to me any doubt that may arise upon your instructions, or any difficulties that may occur in the course of your negociation. Be assured, that you will ever find me ready to pay due attention to your opinions upon the arduous undertaking in which you are engaged, and to communicate to you, his Majesty's pleasure thereupon.

" I think it necessary to acquaint you, that Mr. Fitzherbert, now at Brussels, has orders to join you at Paris, and to replace Mr. Grenville. I have great pleasure in recommending him to your confidence, as he is a person of whose talents and discretion I have the highest opinion, founded on a long acquaintance.

" Of those with whom you are to treat, I have no knowledge of any, except Dr. Franklin. My knowledge of him is of a long standing, though of no great degree of intimacy. I am not vain enough to suppose that any public conduct or principles of mine should have attracted much of his notice; but I believe he knows enough of them to be persuaded that no one has been more averse to the carrying on this unhappy contest, or a more sincere friend to peace and reconciliation than myself. If he does me the justice to believe these sentiments to be sincere, he will be convinced that I shall show myself, in the transaction of this business, an unequivocal and zealous friend to pacification upon the fairest and most liberal terms.

" Though I have not the pleasure of a personal acquaintance with you, Sir, your character is not

unknown to me, and from that I derive great satisfaction in seeing this very important negociation in
your hands.

"When the Commission is made out, you will hear
from me again, and receive at the same time his
Majesty's instructions for the execution of it.

"I have the honor to be, &c.,

"T. TOWNSHEND."

GEORGE III. TO THE KING OF FRANCE.

"Monsieur Mon Frère,

"Ayant fait choix du Sieur Fitzherbert pour
se rendre à votre Cour, en qualité de Mon Ministre,
je vous prie de donner une entière créance à tout ce
qu'il vous dira de ma part, et surtout aux assurances
qu'il vous donnera de mon estime singulière pour
vous, et de mon désir sincère de voir heureusement
rétablir entre nous une amitié ferme et durable.

"Je suis,

"Monsieur Mon Frère,

"Votre bon Frère,

"GEORGE R.

"À. St. James's, ce 27 Juillet, 1782."

INSTRUCTIONS TO MR. OSWALD.

"July 31st, 1782.

(L. S.) George R.

Orders and Instructions to be observed by Our Trusty and
Well-beloved Richard Oswald, of the City of London,
Esquire, whom, by virtue of an Act passed in the present
Sessions of Parliament, entitled An Act to enable His

Majesty to conclude a Peace or a Truce with certain
Colonies in North America therein-mentioned, We have
appointed Our Commissioner for treating and concluding a Peace with any Commissioner or Commissioners named or to be named by the said Colonies
or Plantations or any Part or Parts of them. Given
at Our Court at St. James's this thirty-first day of July,
One Thousand seven hundred and eighty-two. And in
the twenty-second year of Our Reign.

Whereas report has been made to Us, by One of Our Principal Secretaries of State, of Information which he had received
from B. Franklin, Esquire, of Philadelphia, now residing at or
near to Paris, to this effect: — "That he, the said B. Franklin
was commissioned with others (whom he named to be Messrs.
Adams, Laurens, and Jay) to treat of and conclude a Peace;—
that full Powers were given to them for that purpose, and
that Congress promised in good faith to Ratify, Confirm, and
cause to be faithfully observed the Treaty they should make.
But that they could not treat separately from France."

And whereas having received Assurances of His Most
Christian Majesty's sincere disposition towards Peace; and
Paris having been mutually fixed upon, as the most convenient Place, at which all Parties might assemble for the
purpose of entering upon Negociation, We have already sent
Our Trusty and Well-beloved Thomas Grenville, Esquire,
to that Capital, with Full Powers to commence a Negociation
with the Court of France, and the other Belligerent Powers in
Europe; Now in consequence of the Overtures above-men-
tioned on the part of Persons thus stating themselves to be
deputed by the Assembly of Delegates of the Revolted Colonies, and out of Our earnest desire to put an end to the
Calamities of a War, which has so long subsisted; and
because it has also been reported to Us, by one of Our
Principal Secretaries of State, that the said Benjamin
Franklin, Esquire, has expressed a strong desire " Of keep-

ing the Treaties of Peace distinct between the several Parties though going on at the same time;" We have taken these Premises into Our consideration, and have thought fit by Our Commission under Our Great Seal of Great Britain to constitute you, the said Richard Oswald, Our Commissioner for concluding a Peace, and have caused you to be furnished with such Papers and Information as may enable you to interchange Overtures of Peace, giving you at the same time the following instructions for your Conduct in the Execution of the Important Trust We have reposed in you.

1. On the receipt of these Our Instructions, together with Our Commission, you will forthwith enter upon a Conference with the American Commissioners, or as many of them as may be assembled, and you will inform them of Our Purpose in granting you Our Commission with Full Powers, a copy whereof you will deliver to them, at the same time declaring that you shall be ready to produce the Original when desired. You will moreover deliver to them a copy of the Act of Parliament upon which the Powers granted you by Our Commission are founded.

2. You will then express Our Wishes, that the Mutual Powers of Treating and Concluding may be so general and definitive, that matters may thereby be brought to a speedy and determinate Issue. With this View, you will desire to be informed of, and to see the Nature and Extent of the Authority with which the Commissioners are invested by the Congress; and we hereby Authorize you to admit any Persons, with whom you treat, to describe themselves by any Title or Appellation whatsoever, and to represent their Superiors, from whom they state themselves to derive Authority under any denomination whatever.

3. These Preliminaries being settled, You will declare that you are ready and desirous to learn any Ideas and Intentions they (the American Commissioners) may have, for carrying into effect, with most speed and certainty, Our earnest

wishes to restore Peace and Amity between Our Kingdoms,
and the said American Colonies.

4. In case you find the American Commissioners are not
at liberty to treat on any terms short of Independence, You
are to declare to them that you have Our Authority to make
that Concession; Our Earnest Wish for Peace, disposing Us
to purchase it at the price of acceding to the complete Independence of the Thirteen States, namely, New Hampshire, &c.

5. You are moreover empowered to engage Our Promise,
in order to make the Peace, if it should take place, more solid
and durable, to cede to the said Colonies, the Town and
District of New York, and any other Territory, Town, or
Garrison within the Limits of the said Colonies, which may
be in Our possession at the Time of signing the Treaty.

6. The question of Independence thus removed, you will
not fail of course to turn your attention to the consideration
of such Proposals as it is to be hoped they will think it incumbent upon them to make for the purpose of rendering
whatever Terms may be agreed upon, permanent and mutually
satisfactory and beneficial. In the course of this Discussion
you will not fail to pay due attention to the Rights and
Interests of Individuals, and you will particularly press the
speedy Enlargement of such Persons as may be now imprisoned
or confined on account of their attachment to the Government of Great Britain. Under this head You are to consider
and claim as a matter of absolute Justice, all Debts incurred
to the subjects of Great Britain, before 1775, and if, as has
been intimated, you should find the Commissioners unauthorized
to engage for a Specific Redress in this particular, You will
insist on the Justice of these Demands, and that they would
promise and engage for the sincere interposition of Congress
with the several Provinces to procure an ample and full
satisfaction.

7. Whereas many of Our Loyal Subjects having valuable
property in the Colonies in question have, nevertheless, in

these unhappy disputes taken part with Great Britain, and in consequence thereof have been considered as having thereby exposed their Property to Confiscation, Justice as well as Compassion demands that a Restitution or Indemnification should be required on behalf of such sufferers.

On this head you will propose a Restoration of all Rights, as they stood before the Commencement of Hostilities, and a general Amnesty of all Offences committed, or supposed to be committed in the course of them.

8. If you should collect from the answer made to the Representations, that their consent to the preceding article cannot be obtained without some further concessions on Our Part, and the cession before proposed of New York, &c. be not sufficient, you may in that case propose to stipulate for the annexation of a portion of our ungranted Lands to each Province in lieu of what shall be restored to the Refugees and Loyalists, whose estates they have seized and confiscated.

9. In regard to the question of any National Substitution for the Dependent Connection with Great Britain, You must in the first place seek to discover the Dispositions and Intentions of the Colonies, by the Intimations and Propositions of the Commissioners. And if it shall appear to you to be impossible to form with them any Political League of Union or Amity to the exclusion of other European Powers, you will be particularly earnest in your Attention and Arguments to prevent their binding themselves under any Engagement inconsistent with the plan of *Absolute and Universal Independence,* which is the indispensable condition of our acknowledging their Independence on Our Crown and Kingdoms.

10. It were much to be wished, that a foundation for an Amicable Connection could be laid in some mutual Principle of Benefit and Indulgence. In this view We would direct you to propose as a friendly Token of Reconciliation, and of Propensity to those Ties, which are consonant to our mutual Relation, Habits, Language, and Nature, that in future an

unreserved system of Naturalization should be agreed upon between Our Kingdoms and the American Colonies.

11. But notwithstanding you are by Our Commission authorized to conclude, and sign anything that may be agreed upon between You and the American Commissioners, it is Our express Will and Pleasure, that you do not, in virtue of the said Power, proceed to the signature of any Act whatever with the Commissioners for the Colonies, without first having received Our Special Orders for that purpose from one of Our Principal Secretaries of States.

12. Whereas We have at the earnest desire and suggestion of the said Commissioners, as above stated, actually commenced a negociation with the Court of France, which has been extended to other Belligerent Powers, and entrusted as above to Our Trusty and Well-beloved Alleyne Fitzherbert, Esq., with the necessary Powers for that purpose, Our Will and Pleasure is, that you preserve the most constant and intimate Communication from time to time with the said Alleyne Fitzherbert, and in case you shall learn from such Communication, that the Proposals of the Court of France, or of the other Belligerent Powers, without whose concurrence the Court of Versailles will not conclude a Treaty, should be such as We cannot consistently with a due regard for Our own honour, and the Interests of Our Kingdom, accept, and the design of a general Treaty should be thereby frustrated; You will in that event point your whole attention to dispose the American Commissioners towards a separate Negociation, in the hope, that the Concessions you are authorized to make, will appear to them to satisfy the Interests and the Claims of their Constituents, as in that case they can have no justifiable Motive to persist in a War, which, as to them, will have no longer any object, and it is be hoped, will not be inclined to lend themselves to the purposes of French Ambition. At any rate, You will not fail to inform yourself accurately, what will content them and report to Us

accordingly through one of our Principal Secretaries of State waiting for, and expecting further instructions, which shall be sent you with all suitable expedition.

"G. R."

The following letters have been placed in my hands, at my request, by the kindness of the Duke of Portland. There are other letters in the same collection which I have not thought it worth while to publish, on account of the temporary nature of the subjects of which they treat. The arrangements for a contemplated ministry in 1789, seem to have given Mr. Fox much trouble ; the reader will see, perhaps with some surprise, that even at that time it was apparently not intended to place Mr. Burke in the cabinet. With respect to most of the other persons mentioned, all interest respecting their pretensions, and their politics has long passed away.

[*Indorsed*—London, June 29th, 1782. RIGHT HONOURABLE MR. SECRETARY FOX. Received July 4th. Lord Rockingham's Amendment. Cabinet as before.]

" MY DEAR LORD,

" I have only time to tell you that Lord Rockingham is a great deal better indeed. As to other things, just as last night.

" Yours sincerely,

"C. J. FOX.

" RICHMOND HOUSE, *June 29th*, 1782."

[*Indorsed*—London, July 6th, 1782. RIGHT HONOURABLE MR. FOX.
Received 11th.   Reasons for his resignation.]

" MY DEAR LORD,

" The hurry I have been in for some time past
will, I am sure, be a sufficient excuse with your
Grace for not having written to you at this very
interesting moment.   My conduct has been much
blamed, but I have reason to flatter myself that it is
approved by very many, and especially by those
whose opinions I most respect.   I can hardly doubt
but when Richard * explains to you the circumstances
of the case, you will think me in the right.   Possibly
you will hardly wait for an explanation to decide
that it could not be right to remain with Lord
Shelburne as minister.   I shall be very sorry
indeed, if I should have acted contrary to your
Grace's opinion, on many accounts, but among
others, because I really think that all the little
chance that remains of ever doing good depends
upon your taking the lead of us, and animating us
by your firmness and zeal.   After what has passed,
I need not say that my part is completely taken,
and that I hope, whatever other changes may happen,
that the Duke of Devonshire, Lord Fitzwilliam,
your Grace, and I, shall always act together with
the same cordiality that we used to do when we
had other coadjutors; and that we shall always keep
up a standard which all Whigs may repair to when

* Mr. FitzPatrick.

they are so inclined. The defection of the Duke
of Richmond, Lord Temple and others is no doubt
a cruel blow to us, but it is to be hoped (and I am
sanguine in it), that they will soon see their error and
repent. Lord Shelburne says that he did all he
could, at our desire, to persuade H. M. to appoint
your Grace to the Treasury. Therefore I suppose
you will make him your acknowledgments for his
efforts, which though unsuccessful, were undoubtedly
sincere.

> " I am, my dear Lord,
> " Yours ever most sincerely,
> " C. J. FOX.
"London, *July 6th*, 1782."

[*Indorsed* — London, July 12th, 1782. Received 17th. Right
Honourable Mr. Fox.]

" My dear Lord,

" I need not say how much I am obliged to you
for your letter of the 6th, which I have just received.
Nothing could be more flattering to me than your
judging the part I have taken to be right, and your
presuming that I should take it. Richard can much
better explain to you all the circumstances relating
to it than I can do by letter. Your Grace puts it
upon the true point; where there is not confidence,
there must be Power, and Power in this country
must accompany the Treasury. Those who have
thought otherwise will, I am convinced, soon repent
their conduct, and acknowledge that we saw the thing
in the true light. Lord Keppel has declared to the

King his intention of resigning at the end of the campaign. His professional friends prevented his taking the step immediately. I wrote what I knew of the arrangements to Burgoyne last night, so have no news to acquaint you with now. If we had continued, I told the Duke of Rutland that I should have thought it necessary to ask the Garter for you, unless you were to be First Lord of the Treasury, in which case I had no doubt but that you would give it to him. The only thing that vexes me in this business, is, that I am convinced that if we had resigned in a body, Shelburne must have yielded.

" I am, my dear Lord,

" Yours ever sincerely,

"C. J. FOX.

" Grafton Street, *July* 12*th*, 1782."

[*Indorsed*—St. Anne's Hill, January 29th, 1784. 9 a.m. Right Honourable Mr. Fox.]

" My dear Lord,

" I have just received a note from Sheridan, who tells me that Pitt has given an answer, and that you must give one at eleven o'clock, and wish to see me first. It is quite impossible for me to be in town so soon ; but I think our line is quite clear —not to treat with him until he has resigned, and when he has, to adhere to the three preliminaries you mentioned to Marsham formerly. The only doubt can be, whether you should insist upon these being settled previous to your meeting, or at the meeting ; but as I do not understand from Sheridan's note that Pitt has resigned, we are not yet come to that difficulty. I almost flatter myself that you do not want me quite so much as Sheridan says; because I rather think if you had, you would not have trusted to him, but would have sent to me time enough for me to come, and would have let me know what Pitt's answer is, which he has not even hinted. I will be at Devonshire House by two o'clock.

" Yours ever,

" C. J. FOX.

" St. Ann's Hill, Thursday morning, 9 o'clock.
January 29th, 1784."

[*Indorsed*—St. Ann's Hill, February 24th, 1784. 10 p.m. RIGHT HONOURABLE MR. FOX. Received at 15 min. past 1 a.m.]

" MY DEAR LORD,

"It is now near ten, and I have but just received your letter, so that all thoughts of going to town to-night, must of course be out of the question. I will tell you exactly how I understood the matter, by which you will perceive that I do not agree entirely either with Marsham or you. The expedient to which Powis alluded was, as I conceived it, this : that the King should send to you to talk to you upon the subject of a *new* Ministry; that you should mention to the King, the utility of a junction, and take his Majesty's orders to apply to Pitt or any one else upon the subject. I confess I did not mention, nor do I *in this case*, see the necessity of a direct significa-tion to the House of Commons of the end of this ministry. Thus far perhaps I rather lean to

Marsham; but on the other hand, I never could advise you to give into what now appears to be the proposition, viz., that you should go to the King only *pro formâ*, knowing that you are to receive from his Majesty the same proposal in words which you had before in writing, and I think the proposition infinitely the worse for Pitt's being previously a party to it. Marsham and everybody must see that it lies completely open to the old objection of Pitt's being as it were an agent for the King; and I mention this the rather because in every conversation at which I have been present, Powis seemed to feel the whole weight of this difficulty at least as much as myself. I must at the same time say, that Marsham made more light of it. At all events if the King sends you must go, but no man upon reflection, however eager for union, can think it proper, that it should be stipulated and explained beforehand what his Majesty is to say to you. You and not Pitt must be the King's agent, as far as he is supposed to have one, and to this I think you should adhere; but I own I think that part of the difficulty which relates to the honour of the House of Commons will be in a great degree got over whenever the King shall have sent to you to assist *him* (not Pitt) in forming a new administration, because nobody will suppose that *he* takes such a measure but from a sense of the impossibility of maintaining his servants against the House of Commons. I have told you all that occurs to me, but whichever way you decide I shall be perfectly

satisfied.   I will be in town to-morrow morning
certainly.

     " Yours ever sincerely,

               " C. J. FOX.

" St. Ann's Hill, *February 24th*, 1784, 10 *o'clock*."

[*Indorsed*—St. Ann's Hill, July 27th, 1784, half-past 3 p.m. Right
Honourable Mr. Fox.   Received at 8 p.m.]

" My dear Lord,

   " As I happened to be out when your servant
arrived, although he went immediately in search for
me, yet I have but just received your letter, and, consequently, my being in town for any parliamentary
business this day is out of the question. With
respect to the wish you and other friends have of my
attending Parliament, though I little thought I ever
could even demur upon an occasion where you
express yourself so strongly, I must own that my
opinion is so very strong on the other side of the
question, that I cannot do what you desire without
begging you at least to reconsider the subject.   The
propriety of our friends attending as a party without
me I am far from insisting upon ; and, indeed, I was
so very far from supposing such an intention, that I
told Lord John Cavendish that I thought it full as
well he should be out of Parliament for the present,
and have uniformly given it as my opinion to every
individual member who consulted me, that there was
no reason why he should not go out of town.   It is
impossible not to see that the majority is much more
against *us* than *for* the ministry ; and their behaviour

on the India Bill, which had begun to excite much
discontent till I opposed it, is a very sufficient lesson
in my mind that it is not by our interference that we
have the best chance of making them sick of their
folly. At the same time I own that the manner in
which Sheridan and Eden have teazed Pitt, and
shown his ignorance upon so many occasions has had
its use ; but I am convinced that even this advantage would have been less if I had been present, and
given the businesses upon which these skirmishes
have happened, more the appearance of a pitched
battle between ministry and us. With regard, therefore, to the idea of a general attendance in the House,
I must beseech you to reconsider it before I can
adopt it in direct contradiction to my own full conviction. With respect to the Navy Bill business,
whenever it shall be in a shape in which we can
divide against it (I care not with how small numbers),
I will go to town, and enter my protest against what
I conceive to be a breach of public credit. If, therefore, that is to come on to-morrow, and you will let
me know it by a line by the post to-night, or by any
other conveyance which will reach this place before
one o'clock to-morrow, I will go to town immediately. I beg to be understood at the same time
that I do not mean to refuse going up upon other
businesses, too, if *you* should persist in thinking it
desirable ; but I must say it will be as much
against my opinion as my inclination. With
respect to my inclination, I know it ought to give
way ; but yet if any one else had done all I have for

these last eight months, and was as completely tired out with it, body and mind, as I am, I believe he would think he had some right to consult it. I cannot express to you how fatigued I was with the last day's attendance, and how totally unequal I feel myself in point of spirits, to acquit myself as I ought to do, either for the good of the party, or for my own reputation. However, I must submit to your judgment and to theirs if you persist in your opinion. But I am sure you will not repent it, if you will so far trust me as to believe that I know the House of Commons as well, and myself something better than, those who differ from me. I am sure you will do me the justice to believe, that if it were nothing more than caprice or laziness that kept me here, your letter would have produced my immediate attendance in town, instead of this long answer. Great injustice is done me, if I am suspected of any want of zeal for the cause ; but I *know*, that both on my own account, and in consideration of the present state of the House, I can serve it better by lying by for a little while.

　　　" I am, very sincerely, my dear Lord,

　　　　　　　" Yours ever,

　　　　　　　　　　" C. J. FOX.

"ST. ANN's HILL, *Tuesday, half-past* 3."

[*Indorsed*—St. Ann's Hill, August 1, 1784. RIGHT HONOURABLE MR. FOX.]

　　" I shall certainly be in town to-morrow, my dear Lord, as you desire it ; though, as to exposing the absurdity of the plan, there is nobody who has thought of it so little as I,—and who is so unfit for it. I hope, therefore, that others will begin, and that it may be enough for me to support them. I cannot believe in the intention of lowering the national interest. Whenever such a bill comes in I will *divide* against it ; and I hope *division* is intended to-morrow, for I really do hate going to the House of Commons to such a degree, that I wish not to be brought there for nothing.

> " Yours ever sincerely,
>
> " C. J. FOX.

" St. Ann's Hill, *Sunday.*"

[*Indorsed*—January 21st, 1789. Right Honourable Mr. Fox.]

" I send you enclosed a sketch of an arrangement, which, imperfect as it is, may be of some use to you. I believe there are some places, and probably still more claimants wholly omitted in it ; but I have found myself so apt to forget, when I have seen you, some points that I had meant to mention to you, that I thought it best to set down something on paper. I have not taken credit for the Gentlemen Pensioners, as it appears still uncertain whether we shall have them ; and if we have, I think they must be offered to Cholmondeley, whose former place is certainly to be out of our reach.

" If I must have the business of India in my hands (which I confess I do not see any easy way of avoiding), you can scarcely conceive what a relief to me it would be to have Grenville ; but, on the other hand, there are many other uses to be made of the Chief Justiceships, and no other Privy Councillor's place has occurred to me.

" I have seen Adam, and entirely approve stirring without doors as soon as possible, and avoiding, if we can, any more divisions. My health must be so far attended to, as not to appoint for the Westminster Meeting a day likely to follow immediately a long night in the House of Commons.

" I hear the Duke of Northumberland certainly refuses Ireland. If the Ordnance can be kept for Conway, pray do it; and surely if Lord Rawdon is of the Cabinet, *they* ought to be satisfied. I suppose a Commoner cannot be President, otherwise it might be stated to them, that either that office, or the Ordnance, must be kept for Conway. You will think I harp very much upon this part of the arrangement, but I really do feel considerable uneasiness about it. I suppose it will be impossible for you to call here before the House of Lords to-morrow, but I hope we shall meet the day after, and settle finally a great part at least of this troublesome business.

" Yours ever,

" C. J. FOX.

" SOUTH STREET, *Wednesday night.*"

First Lord of the Treasury	Duke of Portland.
Chancellor of Exchequer	Lord J. Cavendish.
Secretary of State (Home)	Lord Stormont.
Ditto, Foreign	Mr. Fox.
First Lord of Admiralty	Lord Fitzwilliam.
President of Council	Lord Carlisle.
Privy Seal	Lord Rawdon.
Chancellor	Lord Loughborough.
Pay Master	Mr. Burke.
Treasurer of Navy	Mr. Sheridan.
Secretary at War	Mr. Fitzpatrick.
Master of Mint	Lord Robert Spencer.

Post Masters . . .	{ Lord Foley. { Lord Cadogan.
Vice-Treasurers . .	{ Lord Sandwich. { Mr. North.
Surveyor of Woods . . .	Lord Charles Spencer.
„ Lands . . .	Mr. J. St. John.
Ranger of Parks . . .	
Treasury	{ Sir G. Cooper. { Sir G. Elliot. { Mr. Windham.
Admiralty	{ Lord Duncannon. { Lord J. Townshend. { Admiral Pigott. { Captain McBride. { Mr. Keene. { Lord Ludlow.
Master-General of Ordnance .	Duke of Northumberland.
Surveyors	{ Mr. Courtney. { Mr. Strachey. { Mr. Kenrick.
Vice Minchin	Colonel Stanhope.
Vice Adam	Mr. Beckford.

" Chief Justice in Eyre, S. of Trent, made up as it was to Lord Grantley, if given to Lord Sandwich, might enable us to keep Lord Mount Edgecombe; if given to Lord Hertford, or Lord Beauchamp, might enable us to keep the Duke of Dorset. Chief Justice N. of Trent, Lord Rochester, or Mr. Thomas Grenville, or Mr. Grey. If I am to be in *effect* the head of the Indian Board, Grenville would be best, as it would be a great satisfaction indeed to me to have him at the Board with me; but, on the other hand, it would enable Grey to be Vice-President to the Board of Trade, which he would like, and would not be unsuitable to him.

" I have left the Parks vacant, but they might be given either to Lord Jersey, Lord Townshend, or Mr.

Charles Townshend; or, if they were made up as before, they might answer one of the purposes for which I have mentioned the Chief Justiceship in Eyre. I have supposed the Duke of Northumberland to have the Ordnance, contrary to my wishes. If he has not, perhaps Sir J. Swinburne must be at the Admiralty, and poor Lord Ludlow give way. Walpole must, I think, in our present distress, be satisfied with his former situation.

India Board	⎧ Mr. Fox.
	⎪ Lord J. Cavendish.
	⎨ Mr. Burke.
	⎪ Lord R. Spencer.
	⎪ Mr. Montagu.
	⎩ Lord Porchester.
Presidency Board of Trade .	Mr. Sheridan.
Vice-President ditto .	Mr. North.

" If Lord Porchester does not take office, Grenville may be in his place, or, if Grey is (Vice-President), North must come to the India Board.

[*Indorsed*—Bath, February 16th, 1789. RIGHT HONOURABLE MR. FOX.]

" MY DEAR LORD,

" I think your observation with respect to what I thought of about our proceedings in Ireland is conclusive against my idea. I am sure you will agree with me that the bulletins, whether good or bad, ought not to make the slightest difference in the conduct of the Prince, or of us. I have written several letters to impress this opinion upon our friends, and I own I am very anxious about it, because I think if we were to alter our conduct, we should tacitly abandon every principle on which we have relied.

" I shall leave this place on Thursday after the

letters arc come in and propose sleeping at Andover, and going Friday to St. Anne's Hill. I mention these particulars of my journey, in order that you may know where to find me if I am wanted. If you wish me to be in town sooner than I intend, which is Monday morning next, I am quite well enough to go at a moment's warning, but should not like to go in less than two days from hence to London.

"Yours ever,

"C. J. FOX.

"Bath, *February* 16*th*."

[*Indorsed*—St. Ann's Hill, July 21st, 1792. Right Honourable Mr. Fox.]

"My dear Lord,

"I am much obliged to you for your letter, and should think I very ill-requited the perfect confidence and openness which you have always used to me, if I hesitated in the least to give you my opinion upon this or any other point of public conduct. I think with you that your acceptance of the Garter at this moment could produce no good effect in any view whatever, and that it might possibly do much mischief; the greatest of all to the public in my judgment, if it should tend (which I confess I do not think impossible) to lessen your weight and influence. I may possibly be too suspicious, but I own I cannot bring myself to think that Pitt has ever meant anything but to make a division among us, or if that could not be done, to give the public the idea of such a division, and by creating jealousies and suspicions (to which some circumstances of the times were but too favourable) to prevent any hearty co-operation against him at a juncture in which he must feel himself so vulnerable. In this view I wished you to see the Duke of Leeds, and am glad you have seen him, because I take for granted, that through him it will be known to the King, that if Pitt has given him any hopes of dividing us, these hopes are delusive. I say this from what I know must have been your conversation with the Duke of Leeds, and from the few words you say, for I have not yet heard from St. John. Rolleston comes to me to-morrow, and will, I suppose, bring me his letter. I agree with you in doubting much the Duke of Leeds's influence anywhere; but for the reason you give, I am very glad you have seen him. Pitt has now made his third offer of the Great Seal to Lord L——, India to Lord North, and the Garter to you. Whether if these things are known they will strengthen him in the opinion of the public, or raise him in that of his party, I much doubt; but that is his business. That we can never with honour or advantage come in *under* him I am convinced, and I deceive myself if I do not ground this opinion much more upon *party* than *personal* reasons and feelings. However, I am sensible that by many it will be, nay it is, attributed to reasonings which are peculiar to *myself;* and I own this idea gives me some uneasiness, though I am sure it is not founded.*

　　　" I am very sincerely,

　　　　　" My dear Lord, yours ever,

　　　　　　　　　　" C. J. FOX.

" St. Ann's Hill, *Saturday night."*

---

* *I. e.* well founded—

　　" Whole as the marble, founded as the rock."—Shakespeare.

[*Indorsed* —July 26th, 1792. Mr. Rolleston.]

"Eaton Street, *Thursday, July 26th,* 1792.

" My Lord,

"I have just returned from St. Anne's Hill, and have the honour to send your Grace the accompanying letter from Mr. Fox, who says he perfectly approves of everything hitherto done respecting the business in question.

"Sir Ralph Woodford, by desire of the Duke of Leeds, he said, told me this morning, that as soon as I forwarded to him your Grace's '*credential*' that he meant to put it in his pocket, and (availing himself of an offer made him by Lord Beaulieu to pass a few days with his lordship in the neighbourhood of Windsor), would take the first favourable opportunity of producing that 'credential' to his Majesty, and of adding everything that he should feel himself authorized to do, in order to bring about that union of parties, which, I understand, he expresses himself not to have less at heart than your Grace, for the benefit of mankind in general, and of this country in particular.

"I shall lose no time in conveying in a proper manner your Grace's letter to the Duke of Leeds, when I am honoured with it for that purpose, and have the honour to be,

"My Lord,

"Your Grace's most devoted and

"most faithful humble servant,

"STEPHEN ROLLESTON.

[*Indorsed*—St. Ann's Hill, July 26th, 1792. RIGHT HONOURABLE MR. FOX.]

" MY DEAR LORD,

" When I read the account you sent to St. John of your conversation with the Duke of Leeds, I was a good deal struck with his apparent backwardness to communicate your sentiments to the King, because I had heard that he had professed on the contrary great readiness for such an employment. Upon enquiry I find that he expected from you a *direct* request that he would make such a communication, and that without such a request he does not think himself authorised to do it. I ventured to say for you, that I was sure you would have no objection to your senti- ments upon the present state of affairs being distinctly known in the closet, but what the Duke of Leeds wants, is an authority from you to this effect. If you see no objection, I am sure I do not, to your writing a few lines to him referring to your conversation and expressing a wish that your sentiments might be known to his Majesty, in order that if the country suffers from the present weakness of Government, the King should know that nothing can be imputed to any backwardness in you or your friends to do their part, and take their share in forming a strong administration. Whether there will be any great use in this, I do not know, but I think there can be no harm ; and if it should be known, would be considered as a measure that would do you credit. And I think too it might be the means of ascertaining whether there is any possibility of our coming in on other terms than those of submission to Pitt. If such a possibility exists, I am as eager for seizing and improving it, as I am, and I believe always shall be, totally averse from acting *under* him. If you think it right to write to the Duke of Leeds, you had better inclose the letter to Rolleston.

" Yours ever sincerly,

" C. J. FOX.

" St. Ann's Hill, *Thursday, July 26th.*"

" I promised Coutts that I would mention to you his being at Cheltenham, not that I suppose that any introduction of him to you is necessary at such a place as Cheltenham ; but I should be sorry he should think I had neglected anything he wished, because I am very much obliged to him.

"I take this opportunity of sending a strange letter, which I have received from Carlisle. I must own I have some difficulty to keep my temper, when I hear of the friends of this Ministry complaining of the weakness of Government, and reflect upon its original formation."

[*Indorsed*—St. Ann's Hill, August 21st, 1792. Right Honourable Mr. Fox.]

" MY DEAR LORD,

" I am sorry you should have had the trouble of writing me an account of what passed, as I had always intended to go to town to-morrow to hear it. I will if you please dine with you to-morrow, and talk

over the present extraordinary state of things, in
which I own that there are some points upon which
I wish for explanation.   Upon what could Dundas
think that he had a right to use any style resembling
complaint towards you, if the old negociation was as
completely at an end as you understood it to be?
Is it possible that *he* understood otherwise?   But we
shall have time to talk over this to-morrow.   You will
do me the justice to say that my nature is not inclined
to suspicion, but I confess if we cannot have a
coalition upon proper terms, of which I despair, I
shall be glad to find the two parties in their old state
of declared hostility again,

" Yours ever,

" C. J. FOX.

" ST. ANN'S HILL, *Tuesday*."

[*Indorsed*—St. Ann's Hill, Half-past six, December 1st, 1792.   RIGHT
HONOURABLE MR. FOX.]

" MY DEAR LORD,

        " I send you enclosed a note I have just re-
ceived from Adam.   If they mention danger of *Insurrec-
tion*, or rather, as they must do to legalise their proceedings, of *Rebellion*, surely the first measure all honest
men ought to take is to impeach them for so wicked
and detestable a falsehood.   I fairly own that, if they
have done this, I shall grow savage, and not think
a French *lanterne* too bad for them.   Surely it is
impossible—if any thing were impossible for such
monsters, who, for the purpose of weakening or
destroying the honorable connection of the Whigs,

U 2

would not scruple to run the risk of a civil war.
I cannot trust myself to write any more, for I confess
I am too much heated.

                    " Yours affectionately,

                                        " C. J. FOX.

" ST. ANN'S HILL, *Saturday, Half past six.*"

[*Inclosure.*]   " W. HALL, *Saturday, Half past two o'clock.*"

" I think it right to send a person on purpose to let
you and the Duke of Portland know, while you are
together, that a Proclamation is to be issued to-day,
calling Parliament to meet the 13th instant. The
ground stated in the Proclamation is, I believe, *Insur-*
rections. The Militia is likewise to be embodied.

" Rolleston tells me this moment that Lord Grenville has sent to the Gazette Office to desire the
Gazettes may not be delivered *out* until farther orders.
He supposes the reason to be that Lord Grenville
thinks it necessary to wait until they hear from
Windsor, whether these measures are sanctioned by
the King, Pitt being gone to the King.

                    " Yours ever,

                              " WILLIAM ADAM."

[*Indorsed*—December 31st, 1792.   RIGHT HONOURABLE MR. FOX.]

" MY DEAR LORD,

          " Though I mean to call upon you in the
course of the morning, yet as it may be uncertain whether I shall have an opportunity for a full conversation
with you, I think I owe it to our long and uninterrupted friendship, to tell you plainly and directly my
thoughts upon the state of this last unpleasant busi-

ness; and especially with respect to what may pass
to-day. That Sir G. E.'s speech was made with the
intention to force you in some way or other to a
declaration which might undo the effect of your
speech in the House of Lords, I have no doubt, and
I certainly suspect that in this project he was the
agent of those who wish, at all events, to widen the
breach, if they can find one, or to make one, if they
cannot find it, between you and me. His indelicacy in
delivering an opinion from you, which, from what has
since passed, I must think you never authorised him
to do in public, and his pertinacity in so doing, when
he knew that Lord Titchfield was to speak, leave me,
I own it, in no doubt of his unfair intentions,—full as
unfair, if not more so, towards you as to me.* I hope
he will not have succeeded in making any breach
between us, but he has in my judgment succeeded in
making it necessary for you, either by yourself or Lord
Titchfield, to declare yourself fully; and it is with
regard to this declaration to be made to-day, as I understand, by Lord Titchfield, that I feel myself incredibly anxious. If it should be in the smallest degree
ambiguous, if it should not be as perspicuous and
explicit as language can make it, the consequences to
me will be very unpleasant indeed, but to *you* much
worse; if after to-day it should remain a question,
whether you are or are not a supporter of the Ministry — whether you still remain the head of that
Opposition which has so long considered you as

---

* See on this subject the Malmesbury Papers. Sir Gilbert Elliot represented at this time the Burke section of the party.

such, I must speak the truth and tell you, that your
name will be bandied about in a manner which
I cannot bear to think of, and possibly it may become necessary for you to make another explanation
and to have the repetition of these scenes, in which,
if I am to judge from myself, you must have felt
much more than is commonly understood by the
words 'anxiety' and 'distress.' My fears upon this
head are the stronger on account of some expressions,
particularly two, which, from what I heard from you
and others who have seen you, I think Lord Titchfield may possibly use. The first is, *relaxing from
the severity of Opposition*. These words when I
heard them first, did not strike me to be so objectionable as they appear to me now upon reflection.
They certainly convey the idea of the system of
opposing more than I understand you to have done ;
because, to what do they apply? Certainly not to
this Bill, and others of a similar complexion, because,
with respect to such measures, you do not relax in
opposition to them, but you actually support them.
They will therefore be not unreasonably applied to
the other measures, or general conduct of Administration, and in fact be considered as tantamount to Mr.
Burke's *dulcification* and *neutralisation*. This sense
I take to be directly repugnant to your speech. You
say you consider the present mischiefs as in part
owing to the misconduct of Ministers. Surely, then,
though it may be necessary to support particular
measures which the safety of the country may require, it is a time with regard to the men rather to

redouble your vigilance and jealousy, than to relax in
your severity. The other expression which I heard
of with alarm, was a hope that we (meaning you and
me) might soon *meet again*. If anything of this sort
is said, it will give great credit to those who give out
with so much industry that we are separated, and
great discredit to me who maintain everywhere the
contrary. I feel the impropriety of suggesting expressions to you, and still more to Lord Titchfield;
but I own I think he ought to be for your sake,
still more than for mine, very distinct and explicit,
and that he ought to declare directly either that he is
a supporter of Ministry, and separated from me, or
the direct contrary,—that he remains in his former
sentiments and conduct with respect to both them
and me. If, as I hope, the last is nearest to his
opinion, I need not say, that the present Bill and
other measures formed upon the ground of the dangers in which you believe, and I do not, may be
made an exception without any inconsistency. To
support individual measures of Administration, while
we act in general opposition to the Ministers, is no
new conduct to us, and though I own that, if such
measures become more important, and are more frequently the subjects of discussion, in such case the
union of those who differ upon them will become
more lax, and the opposition to those with whom we
so often concur more feeble; yet this is an evil
which may arise, but ought not to be anticipated.
Indeed, in the present case, I am the more sanguine,
because I know so few points upon which you and I

do actually differ.   However, this is matter for future consideration, and rather a digression from the immediate object of this letter, which is to press you by every consideration both of friendship for me, and regard for yourself, as well as wish for the preservation of the Whig Party, to think justly of the importance of this day; to see the necessity of being completely explicit.

" Yours most affectionately,

" C. J. FOX.

"SOUTH STREET, *Monday Morning.*"

I now proceed to give the correspondence of Mr. Fox with Mr. Gilbert Wakefield, which was published many years ago.   It turns almost entirely upon literary questions.

MR. FOX TO MR. WAKEFIELD.

"SOUTH STREET, *December 17th*, 1796.

" SIR,

"I received, a few days ago, your obliging letter, together with the very beautiful book which accompanied it.*   The dedication of such an edition of such an author is highly gratifying to me ; and to be mentioned in such a manner by a person so thoroughly attached to the principles of liberty and humanity, as you, Sir, are known to be, is peculiarly flattering to me.

" I am, with great regard,
" Sir,
" Your obedient, humble servant,

" C. J. FOX."

---

* Wakefield's edition of Lucretius, dedicated to Mr. Fox.

SAME TO SAME.

"St. Ann's Hill, *Monday.*

" Sir,

" I received, on Saturday, the second
volume of Lucretius, together with a pamphlet of
yours upon Porson's Hecuba, for which I beg leave
to return you my thanks. I had received, some time
since, your letter, announcing to me the present of
the Lucretius; but delayed answering it till I got
the book, which my servant had not then an opportunity of sending me, lest there might be some
mistake, from your mentioning Park Street, instead
of South Street, for my residence.

" I have read with great pleasure your observations
upon the Hecuba; but not having Euripides here,
there are many points upon which I cannot form a
judgment. One thing near the beginning has very
much puzzled me : I mean the difficulty which you
suppose some persons would find in making a verse
of

$$\phi\iota\lambda\iota\pi\pi\sigma\nu \; \lambda\alpha\sigma\nu \; \epsilon\upsilon\theta\upsilon\nu\omega\nu \; \Delta OPI,$$

which seems to me to be, supposing it to be part
of an Iambic, perfectly regular; though by the word
ΔOPI being put in capitals, I must suppose that
there lies the irregularity. You then quote a verse
of Lucretius, which you call ' *consimilis*,' in which
there is an evident irregularity from the first syllable
in ' *remota*,' which is usually short, being long.

" Now I am writing on a subject of this sort, may I ask the favour of you, who I know have given your attention to Moschus and Bion, to explain three passages to me, which I do not understand ?—

" The first is in the Europa, v. 123, 124 :

$$\text{Οφρα κε νηων, κ. τ. λ.} \text{———}$$

The second is in the Megara, v. 70, 71 :

$$\text{——— επιγνωμων δε τοι ειμι}$$
$$\text{Ασχαλααν, κ. τ. λ.———}$$

no ι subscript to ασχαλααν.
The third is in Bion's Adonis, the end of v. 74.

$$\text{———ποθει και στυγνον Αδωνιν.}$$

" I have no other edition of Moschus and Bion here except Stephens's, in his Greek Poets, without a version and with few notes ; but, in regard to the first passage, I see Casaubon alters it to οφρα μη ῳην, whose annotations upon the Europa I have in Reiske's Theocritus.   This makes it intelligible, but is a violent alteration.

" I feel it to be unpardonable in me to take advantage of your civility in sending me your books, to give you all this trouble ; but I could not refuse myself so fair an opportunity of getting my doubts upon these passages cleared.

" Before I conclude, give me leave to suggest a doubt, whether, in the 38th page of your Diatribe, it should not be ' socios,' instead of ' socii ; ' or, if ' socii ' is what you approve, whether there should

not be a 'sint,' to prevent harshness of construction?"

MR. WAKEFIELD TO MR. FOX.

"HACKNEY, *August* 29*th*, 1797.

" SIR,

          " I am highly gratified by your favourable
acceptance of my Lucretius and Diatribe.   I must
beg of you to correct an oversight or two in the
latter.   At p. 18, ver. 669 of the Hecuba should
not have been referred to; and the Σ', in p. 24, line
7, should be transferred to the beginning of the
line.

"That what I have advanced, in p. 5, should
puzzle you, I must ascribe to an indistinctness in my
representation of the point in discussion.   What I
mean is, that the final ν should never be expressed,
but where a vowel follows; or, in other words, that
this appendage was never employed as a device to
lengthen a short syllable, but merely to prevent the
harshness of an open vowel.   Now, upon this
principle, the difficulty with the generality of
readers would be the proper enunciation of such
verses as that specified by me at the place.   This
difficulty, I maintain, will be none to those accustomed to pronounce Iambics with a suitable tone;
by which I understand a tone similar to that with
which all scholars, I believe, utter Anacreontics; and
which certainly is necessary to all other verses, if
we wish to distinguish them from prose :—

Οὐδ' ω | -λεσε μ | ε Ζεὺς————.

as if λεσεμμ' : and δορι as if δὄρεῖ, with all the emphasis of a long syllable. In short, however, these niceties are scarcely to be conveyed intelligibly but by conversation, where the modes of education have been different, or novelties have been suggested by matured study. Certainly the common mode of reading, with a strange mixture of accent and quantity,

> Arma *virum*que cano——

as long as if it were *vires*, can never be vindicated, and is well ridiculed through the following verses by a late writer :

> *Malo* me Galatea petit——
> Tu ne cede *malis*, sed contra——.

" The passages, which you cite from Bion and Moschus, are considered, whether successfully or not, in my edition, which you will honour me by accepting ; and I will carry a copy of it to your house, when I go to town on Thursday. Ασχαλααν˙ is the Dor. or Æol. form of the infinitive mode for ασχαλαειν, not contracted : otherwise it had been ασχαλᾳν.

" Certainly *socios*, in p. 38 of the Diatribe, would be better.

" Sir ! your apology for taking up my time by these inquiries might well have been spared : occupied as I am, I think it no interruption, but an exquisite pleasure, to comply with any wishes of Mr. Fox : nor could I reap a greater gratification from my studies, than the opportunity of discussing some of these topics in conversation with you ; as it is possible that my elaborate inquiries for some years past might occasionally strike out some new ideas on a subject which is still but imperfectly understood by the best scholars ;—an assertion, which, I believe, my Notes on Lucretius will occasionally confirm.

" I am, Sir,

" With every sentiment of respect,

" Your obedient servant,

"GILBERT WAKEFIELD."

MR. FOX TO MR. WAKEFIELD.

" St. Ann's Hill, *Friday.*

" SIR,

"I received yesterday your very obliging letter, for which I return you many thanks, as well as for the Bion and Moschus, which I will tell my servant to take an early opportunity of sending down to me.

"My puzzle arose from my supposing that, if you meant to refer only to the short syllable at the end of the verse, you would rather have asked, ' How shall we pronounce verses that end with a short vowel ? ' of which there are so many, than have quoted one particular verse out of thousands ; but I now per-fectly understand you, though, I own, I do not think your reasoning quite conclusive. I conceive the reason for adding the final ν is not for the sake of pronunciation, which, in dead languages, is, and always must be, a matter of great uncertainty, but in order to preserve the rules of prosody which appear generally to prevail among the Greek poets. I know

that, in Homer, and in other poets who write hexameters, it is not very unusual to see a short vowel
become long by a particular position, though followed
by a single consonant, and that consonant a mute;
and sometimes even by an aspirated vowel, as φιλε
ἑκυρε and other instances.   But, as far as my limited
and uncertain recollection goes (very limited and
uncertain indeed, since, except four tragedies of
Sophocles last winter, I have not looked into the
Greek tragedians for twenty years and upwards), I
do not think that, in Iambic poetry, any short vowels,
excepting those only where the final ν is used, are ever
put in the place of a long syllable, unless followed by
a ρ, or at least some liquid.   Now, if this be true,
and if those short vowels only, to which the final ν
is occasionally added, do sometimes appear in such
places, one cannot help suspecting that the final ν
may in such cases have been used to lengthen the
syllable, as in other cases it is (as we all agree) used
to prevent the hiatus.   Perhaps, in this inclination of
my opinion, I may be warped by the prejudice of an
Eton education; and, not having ever looked into
any old Greek manuscripts, I do not know how far it
is countenanced by any of them.   I confess, however,
that I should not admit the short vowels at the end,
whether of hexameters or Iambics, to be cases in
point; because it seems to be one of the most universal of those rules to which I before alluded, and
which seem to me to prevail among the ancient poets,
and that the last syllable of a verse may be always
long or short, as is most convenient.

" I am very sorry more encouragement has not been given to your Lucretius ; but I am willing to flatter myself that it is owing to many people not choosing to buy part of a work till the whole is completed. Both the Latin and Greek elegiac verses, in the beginning of the second volume, have given me great satisfaction ; but I should fear the inferior rank which you give to our own country will not generally please ; and certainly, in point of classical studies, or poetry, to which the mention of Apollo naturally carries the mind, we have no reason to place the French above us."

MR. WAKEFIELD TO MR. FOX.

" HACKNEY, *September 2nd,* 1797.

" SIR,

" Excuse this additional trouble, which a desire to explain one point induces me to give you ; and to convey a request, that you will favour me by accepting, with the Bion and Moschus, two or three other books which I have directed my bookseller to send ; and which may possibly amuse you, when nothing more interesting shall be at hand.

" The final syllable of a verse is always long, whatever its real quantity, in consequence both of the pause and tone of voice, which are those of a long syllable ; otherwise the verse would no more appear, and must be wholly vitiated by the reader, attentive only to the quantity of the syllable. That the old MSS. and first editors, who followed their MSS., acknowledge

no final v, in the cases alluded to, is most certain :
some later editors have partly seen, what I apprehend
to be the truth in this respect ; particularly Brunck
and Musgrave ; but, not discerning the true principle
of the fact, fluctuate between the omission and insertion, in their practice, with great capriciousness.
Mr. R. P. Knight, who is a profound and accurate
Greek scholar, assented immediately to my notion,
when I once proposed it to him in a casual conversation at the booksellers' : but I have found no other
person who entered so readily into my conceptions.
Indeed, it is my lot to enjoy the conversation of very
few scholars, on account of the political complexion,
and, let me add, theological complexion, too, of the
times :—

Fœnum habet in cornu : longe fuge !

Will you give me leave, Sir, to say, that you
scarcely appear well founded in your construction of
my Greek verses in the preface ? I think the context and the language alike prove, that my preference
of the French is merely in a political, not in their
literary, character ? And what can be more deeply
sunk in ignominy than we are as a nation, in that
view, at the present moment ?

" Will you excuse me, also, in recommending
Lucretius to your perusal ? I think antiquity has
nothing comparable to his lib. iii. from ver. 842 to
the end of the book : and the whole of his fifth book,
both as a philosophical and poetical effort, is an

admirable composition ; not to mention any other portions of his poem.

"I am, Sir,

"With the highest sentiments of esteem

"and respect,

"Your obliged servant,

"GILBERT WAKEFIELD."

MR. FOX TO MR. WAKEFIELD.

"ST. ANN'S HILL, *Wednesday.*

"SIR,

"I return you many thanks for your letter of the 2d instant; and shall accept with great pleasure the books you propose sending to me.

"I always understood the final syllable of a verse exactly as you do ; but, for the purpose of my argument, it was necessary to mention the effect only, and not the cause, of the rule. Either your authority, or Mr. Knight's, much more both united, would be quite sufficient to convince me, upon a question relative to the Greek language. I only stated to you some arguments which occurred to me on the other side of the question, which, however, must lose all their weight, if the authority of the old manuscripts is any thing like so universally against them as you seem to think. I see Stevens is inconsistent ; but I think he oftener omits than inserts the final *v*, which I had never observed till you started the subject.

"I had no doubt but *political* wisdom and knowledge were what you meant in your epigram ; but I cannot help thinking that Ἐωσφορὸς and Ηελιος lead the mind a little to poetry, or, at least, to knowledge in general; and that Γαὶ Αυσονις and Αθηναι do not contribute to confine the sense to politics: in regard to which, I agree with you in thinking that no nation ever was sunk in more deep ignorance than we seem to be at present; for we are not only in the dark, but have a kind of horror of the light.

" I have deferred reading Lucretius regularly through again, till your edition is completed; but he is a poet with whom I am pretty well acquainted, and whom I have always admired to the greatest degree. The end of the third book is perfectly in my memory, and deserves all you say of it. I do not at present recollect the fifth quite so well.

" I am going, in a few days, into Norfolk, for some weeks; and I shall come back by London, where I will call for the books which you are so good as to intend sending me.

" I am, with great regard,

" Sir,

" Your obedient servant,

" C. J. FOX."

SAME TO SAME.

"St. Ann's Hill, *Tuesday, January* 30*th*, 1798.

" Sir,

" I have received the third volume of your magnificent and beautiful Lucretius, for which I take

the earliest opportunity of returning you my thanks.
I cannot help flattering myself that, now the work is
complete, it will be far more patronized than it has
hitherto been : but it must be allowed, that these
times are not favourable to expensive purchases of any
kind ; and I fear, also, that we may add, that the
political opinions we profess are far from being a
recommendation to general favour, among those, at
least, in whose power it is to patronize a work like
yours.

" I am at present rather engaged in reading Greek ;
as it is my wish to recover, at least, if not to improve,
my former acquaintance (which was but slight) with
that language : but it will not be long before I enter
regularly upon your Lucretius ; and when I do, if I
should find any difficulties which your notes do not
smooth, I shall take the liberty of troubling you for
further information ; presuming upon the obliging
manner in which you satisfied some doubts of mine
upon a former occasion.

" I am, with great regard,

" Sir,

" Your obedient servant,

"C. J. FOX."

[A letter of Mr. Wakefield's, to which the following
is an answer, appears to be wanting.]

SAME TO SAME.

"St. Ann's Hill, *February 2nd*, 1798.

" Sir,

"It is an instance of my forgetfulness, but I really thought I had acknowledged the receipt of the publications which you were so good as to send me. Excepting the Pope, which I have not yet looked into, I read the rest with great pleasure ; and quite agree with you, that Bryant has made no case at all upon the subject of the Trojan war. I cannot refuse myself taking this opportunity of asking your opinion relative to the 24th Iliad, whether or not it is Homer's? If it is, I think the passage about Paris and the Goddesses must be an interpolation; and if it is not, by denying Homer the glory of Priam's expedition from Troy, and interview with Achilles, we take from him the most shining passages, perhaps, in all his works.

"I am, Sir,

"Your obedient humble servant,

"C. J. FOX."

"P. S. Though I have not begun to read Lucretius regularly, yet I have *dipped* in it sufficiently to have no apprehension of quoting the line of Phaedrus. I think the elegiac verses to the poet are very classical and elegant indeed ; and, you know, we Etonians hold ourselves (I do not know whether or not others agree with us) of some authority, in matters of this sort.

MR. WAKEFIELD TO MR. FOX.

[The Note or Introduction to the following Observations, in answer to Mr. Fox's inquiry respecting the 24th Iliad, is supposed to have been mislaid.]

" Ver. 1. The first syllable in Λυτο is made long, in opposition to the practice of Homer in about a dozen places ; and without another instance in the two poems. Homer too, unless two distinct parties are spoken of, uses in these cases ἕκαστος· and so indeed other good writers, in both languages : and on this I have touched somewhere in Lucretius. So that the full construction is : λαοι εσκ. ιεναι επι νηας, ἕκαστος (επι την ιδιαν νηα). There is, indeed, one or two instances of this deviation elsewhere, all tending to confirm my general hypothesis, which I shall hereafter mention. The Scholiast in Villoison, at ver. 6, mentions, that Aristophanes, and others, thought part of this introduction spurious ; viz. verses 6, 7, 8, 9 ; and they may be well spared.

" Ver. 14. επει ζευξειεν is an illegitimate construction. We might read ζευξασκεν· but such an error is not easily accounted for, in so plain a case, from transcribers.

" Ver. 15. The δ' is superfluous and impertinent ; as Schol. Villois. also observes.

" Ver. 28. Macrobius, Saturn. V. 16, beyond the middle, says, that Homer never mentions the Judgment of Paris. The perfect acquaintance of the old

Grammarians with Homer's works indubitably evinces either the spuriousness of this passage, or an abjudication of this book from Homer's writings. The antient critics discarded verr. 20, 21, and from ver. 23—30 inclusive: see Villoison's Scholiast.

"Ver. 44. This verse seems fabricated for the next, which has no pertinency here, and is transferred from Hesiod. Opp. et Dd. 316.

"Ver. 60. No similar instance, perhaps, in the poem, to the lengthening of καὶ so situated; or to that of ΣA in ὁπόσα, ver. 7.

"Verses 71, 72, 73, were rejected by some antient critics.

"Ver. 79. ΜΕΙΛΑΝΙ. He uses this word and its relatives, perhaps, two hundred times; but never thus changes the first syllable.

"Verses 85, 86. Deemed spurious by the Antients.

"Verses 130, 1, 2, were rejected by old critics, for divers weighty and grave reasons.

"Ver. 241. ΟΥΝΕΣΘ'—a word no where else found; as ἐξεσίην, ver. 235, once more only in the Odyssey, though of a signification that might be expected to produce a more frequent usage. Κατηφόνες too, ver. 253, is ἅπαξ λεγόμενον· and three or four others.

"Ver. 293. εὖ only occurs in Il. Ξ. 427, which, in such a word of perpetual demand, is very singular.

"Ver. 307. It is impossible that Homer, or a contemporary using the same language, could employ as a dactyl the three first syllables of εἰσανιδών. The word ἰδω, and all its compounds, had, in that age, another letter prefixed to it—the Æolic digamma, or Ionic Vau, which you please : by the latter name it still keeps its station in the Hebrew alphabet, and others, as the sixth in order ; and its figure, a double Gamma, F, according to the former designation, in the Latin alphabet.   Homer therefore could never be supposed to violate, in *one* instance, a propriety, which he had sacredly observed in 999, and make εισανϝιδων stand in a heroic verse.   As the Æolians and Dorians, who spoke kindred dialects, are known to have been the first Græcian colonists in Italy, hence it is, that the Latin language is mere Æolian Greek engrafted on their indigenous tongue.   On this account, the loss of Ennius, and the first Latin Poets, is more to be regretted, perhaps, than that of any other writers ; because of the light they would have thrown on the Greek and Latin languages. Hence ιδεω, Fideo, i. e. *video ;* ετος, *vetus ;* ιτυλος, *vitulus ;* εντερον, *ventrem ;* ιαχω, *voco ;* ειλω, *volvo ;* and an infinity of others.   The Æolians also, wherever two vowels came together, inserted the digamma : hence ωον, *ovum ; audii* vel *audivi,* &c. ; δια, *diva ;* σκαιος, *scævus ;* νεος, *novus ;* ναυς, *navis,* &c.   Hence, by the common substitution of an *s* for the aspirate, as in εξ, *sex ;* επτα, *septem ;* and ὑλη, *silva ;* παων, *pavo ;* βοος, *bovis ;* and in an infinity of others. Εισανϝιδων, therefore, is the word either of another age, or another province.   This is a curious and copious subject ; and furnishes the true medium of correcting, adjusting, and discerning, Homer's poetry, from the clearest analogy and indisputable premises.

No verse in Homer is genuine where a consonant precedes εποs, ειπω, αναξ, ιδω, and many other words, which began with a digamma. A single page of any edition will show how miserably incorrect we read him. If we had not 'fallen on such evil times and evil tongues,' I should have exerted myself to give editions of all the Greek Poets, from very ample materials now collected, and of the old Lexicographers: but—

> '——aliis post me memoranda relinquo.'

" Ver. 320. Two words with digammas; one right measure, οἱ δε Ϝιδοντεs, i.e. *videntes;* the other wrong, ὑπἐρ Ϝαστεοs. (See verr. 327, 701.) From Ϝαστυ, *a city*, I suppose, came *vastus;* on account of the *size* of such places, and the *large* collection of men. Hence Virgil receives illustration, Æn. V. 119.

> '*Ingentemque* Gyas *ingenti mole* Chimæram,
> *Urbis* opus——.'

"Ver. 325. τετρακυκλον. No similar instance, I believe, of a vowel shortened before those consonants in Homer; by far more chaste in this respect than succeeding Poets.

" Ver. 337. αρ τιs Ϝιδῃ. False quantity: amphimacer for a dactyl: see neighbouring verr. 332, 352, 366, to go no further.

" Ver. 354. φραδεοs νοοῡ Ϝεργα. Bad measure again: verse 213, and others, are right in this respect. Strong presumptions of more than *one finger in this pie.*

"Verse 449. ποιησᾶν Fαvακτι: unquestionably wrong; as αvαξ is universally allowed to have the digamma in Homer's time.   Hence *Phœnix*, φοινικοεις, *puniceus*, a *royal* colour ;　*purpura regum*, *purpurei tyranni*, *regali ostro ;*   Virgil, and Horace, with all others. The error is repeated in verse 452.   There are numerous faults of this kind in the common editions; but they may be corrected by the omission of the paragogic *v :* as verr. 238, 555, 646, 733, and others.

" But to omit a more minute investigation of these niceties, let me give you, in few words, an outline of my theory respecting Homer.

" What is so well known with respect to every male-factor tied up at Newgate ; (most detestable, flagitious practice !) his ' birth, parentage, and education ; life, character, and behaviour ; ' all are utterly unknown of Homer ! We are at liberty, therefore, to frame any hypothesis for the solution of the problem con-cerning his poems, adequate to that effect, without danger of contravening authentic and established history.   Now ὁμηρος is an old Greek word for τυφλος : see Hesych. and Lycophr. ver. 422. I take *Homerus*, then to have originated in the peculiarity of a certain *class* of men (i.e. blindness), and not in that of an *individual*.   That bards were usually blind, is not only probable from the account of Demodocus in the Odyssey, but from the nature of things.   The memory of blind men, because of a less distraction of their senses by external objects, is peculiarly tenacious ; and such people had no means of obtaining a livelihood but by this occupation. All this is exemplified in fiddlers, &c. at this day. Now the Trojan war (the first united achievement of the Greeks) would of course become a favourite theme with this class of men, who are known to have been very numerous. Detached portions of this event, such as the exploits of Diomed, of Agamemnon, the Night Expedition, the Death of Hector, his redemption, &c., would be separately composed and sung, as fitted, by their lengths, for the entertainment of a company at one time : and we find, in fact, that the parts of these poems are now distinguished, by scholiasts, grammarians, and all such writers, by these names, and not by books. These songs, bearing date demonstrably before the use of alphabetic characters in Greece, and when the dialect of the civilized parts of Asia (Ionia and Æolia) was uniform, could never be traced to their respective authors ; and, in reality, we find from Herodotus, the first Greek historian, that no more was known of this *Homer*, nor so much, in his days (2, 3, 4, or 500 years after the event), as in our own. These songs of *blind men* were collected and put together by some skilful men (at the direction of Pisistratus, or some other person), and woven, by interpolations, connecting-verses, and divers modifications, into a whole. Hence ῥαψῳδια. Here we see a reason for so many repetitions: as every detached part, to be sung at an entertainment, required a head and tail piece, as necessary for an intelligible whole: and hence we observe a reason for those unaccountable anomalies of measure, and the neglect of the Æolic digamma, from an ignorance of its power in those later times, whether from new insertions, or from alterations in the transmitted pieces, to effect regularity and consecution. This accounts also for the glaring disparity in some of the pieces : for nothing can be more exquisite than what you so justly admire, the interview of Priam and Achilles : and nothing more contemptible than the whole detail of the death of Hector, and the reconciliation of Agamemnon and Achilles. You are expecting a noble exhibition of generosity and magnanimity on both sides, and you are put off with a miserable tedious ditty about *Atè*.

" It is probable, from various particulars, that, perhaps, as good a poem, if the opportunity had not been lost (and the preservation of the Iliad and Odyssey, under all circumstances, is nearly miraculous), might have been transmitted on the subject of two other events, which equally engaged the notice of the early Greeks,—the Theban war, and the Argonautic expedition. But we have no remains of these exploits, but in the Tragic writers, the spurious Orpheus, and the Roman Epic writers, except the entire poem of Apollonius Rhodius on the latter subject."

MR. FOX TO MR. WAKEFIELD.

"St. Ann's Hill, *February* 16*th*, 1798.

" Sir,

" I should have been exceedingly sorry if, in all the circumstances you mention, you had given yourself the trouble of writing me your thoughts upon Homer's poetry; indeed, in no circumstances, should I have been indiscreet enough to make a request so exorbitant : in the present, I should be concerned if you were to think of attending even to my limited question respecting the authenticity of the 24th Iliad, or to any thing but your own business.

"I am sorry your work is to be prosecuted; because though I have no doubt of a prosecution failing, yet I fear it may be very troublesome to you. If, either by advice or otherwise, I can be of any service to you, it will make me very happy; and I beg you to make no scruple about applying to me : but I do not foresee that I can, in any shape, be of any use, unless it should be in pressing others, whom you may think fit to consult, to give every degree of attention to your cause. I suppose there can be little or no difficulty in removing, as you wish it, the difficulty from the Publisher to yourself; for to prosecute a Printer, who is willing to give up his Author, would be a very unusual and certainly a very odious, measure.

"I have looked at the three passages you mention, and am much pleased with them : I think 'curalium,' in particular, a very happy conjecture; for neither 'cœruleum' nor 'beryllum' can, I think, be right; and there certainly is a tinge of red in the necks of some of the dove species. After all, the Latin words for colours are very puzzling : for, not to mention 'purpura,' which is evidently applied to three different colours at least — scarlet, porphyry, and what we call purple, that is, amethyst, and possibly to many others—the chapter of Aulus Gellius to which you refer has always appeared to me to create many more difficulties than it removes; and most especially that passage which you quote, ‘virides equos.’ I can conceive that a Poet might call a horse ‘viridis,’ though I should think the term rather forced; but Aulus Gellius says, that Virgil gives the appellation of ‘glauci’ rather than ‘cœrulei’ to the *virides equos*, and consequently uses *virides*, not as if it were a poetical or figurative way of describing a certain colour of horses, but as if it were the usual and most generally intelligible term. Now, what colour usual to horses could be called *viridis* is difficult to conceive; and the more so, because there are no other Latin and English words for colours which we have such good grounds for supposing corresponding one to the other as *viridis* and *green*, on account of grass, trees, &c. &c. However, these are points which may be discussed by us, as you say, at leisure, if the system of tyranny should proceed to its maturity. Whether it will or not, I know not; but, if it should, sure I am that to have so cultivated literature as to have laid up a store of consolation and amusement, will be, in such an event, the greatest advantage (next to a good conscience) which one man can have over another. My judgment, as well as my wishes, leads me to think that we shall not experience such dreadful times as you suppose possible; but, if we do not, what has passed in Ireland is a proof, that it is not to the moderation of our governors that we shall be indebted for whatever portion of ease or liberty may be left us.

" I am, Sir,

" Your most obedient servant,

"C. J. FOX."

SAME TO SAME.

"St. Ann's Hill, February 23rd, 1798.

" Sir,

" Nothing, but your stating yourself to be in some degree at leisure now, could justify my troubling you with the long and, perhaps, unintelligible scrawl which I send with this. I most probably have shown much ignorance, and certainly some presumption, in seeming to dispute with you, upon points of which you know so much, and I so little : all I can say in my defence is, that disputing is sometimes a way of learning.

" I have not said anything yet upon the question which you seem to have thought most upon—whether the Iliad is the work of one, or more authors ? I have, for the sake of argument, admitted it ; but yet, I own, I have great doubts, and even lean to an opinion different from yours. I am sure the inequality of excellence is not greater than in ' Paradise Lost,' and many other poems written confessedly by one author. I will own to you, also, that in one, only, of the instances of inequality which you state, I agree with you. Atè is detestable ; but I cannot

think as you do of the death of Hector. There are
parts of that book, and those closely connected with
the death of Hector, which I cannot help thinking
equal to any thing.

"It is well for you that my paper is at an
end, and that I have not the conscience to take a
new sheet.

" Your humble servant,

"C. J. FOX."

[*Inclosed in the above.*]

" Ver. 1. I agree in the objection to λυτο, and
am not satisfied with Clarke's account of it; and,
besides, there is something of a baldness, or of an
affected conciseness, in beginning a narration in
those words, very unlike Homer, or, if you please,
the Ὁμηροι. Ἑκαστοι for ἑκαστος is so small an error
in writing, that it affords little ground for an objection, or even a doubt.

" Verses 6, 7, 8, 9, may be left out, or not, without
affecting the authenticity of the book.

" Ver. 14. I have not skill enough in the language to judge whether your objection to ζευξειεν
be unanswerable; but I know no answer to it.

" Ver. 15. The δ' is easily to be got rid of,
and is one of the most natural mistakes in the
transcribers.

" Ver. 28. Macrobius's authority appears to me
to be decisive, to prove that this passage is an interpolation since his time; and consequently destroys
the argument built upon this passage against the

book itself, upon other parts of which he has commented.

"I do not know why the antient critics discarded verses 20 and 21; nor do I think it material whether they are retained or not.

"Verses 44 and 45, I agree, had better be away; but I know not whether there be any authority for discarding them.

"Verse 60. The lengthening of καὶ in this place does appear to me very awkward; and, *if* there are no similar instances, must be an error: besides, the mythology of this passage is quite new to me: I mean Juno's having nursed Thetis.

"As to the σα in verse 70, I cannot help thinking there are many instances of syllables being lengthened in such situations; and, at any rate, it is one of the verses which you say some critics reject. Probably from want of memory, but I have some doubt about the word ὁπόσα being a Homeric word: it is certainly much oftener ὅσα.

"Verses 71, 72, 73, I had rather were away; but, as I said before, I do not know the authority for leaving them out.

"Verse 79. Μειλανι is indeed a most suspicious word, and I have nothing to say for it.

"Verses 85, 86. I cannot see any objection to them; but, as before, I do not know the authorities or arguments for or against them.

"Verses 130, 131, 132, appear to me to be much in Homer's style; and I should certainly be for keeping them, if there is nothing against them but

Eustathius's saying the passage was rejected by some
of the Antients.

" Ver. 241. Ουνεσθ' always puzzled me; nor do I
know rightly what it means. I do not quite agree
in thinking εξεσιη of such a signification as to make
the rare use of it very surprising. As to εὖ, it is
certainly used once more than you are aware of—
ει πως εὖ πεφιδοιτο, (I believe in the Υ,) and therefore
may possibly be oftener. In the place I quote, it
means *sui*, not *cujus*, as here; and so it means
ejus in the Ξ. 427 : but this, I think, makes no
difference.

" Ver. 307. The three first syllables of εισανιδων,
or, as you write it, εισανϝιδων, cannot (as you say,
and I believe Knight says the same) have been used
by the 'Ομηροι as a dactyl ; and no verse can be a
genuine Homeric verse, where the digamma is (if I
may use such an expression) *slighted* in that manner.
I must be excused, till further informed, from giving
an unqualified assent to this proposition. If the
proportion of instances on one side and the other
were, as you seem to state, nine hundred and ninety-
nine to one, I should not hesitate; but, I confess,
I suspect this to be far from the true state of the
fact. I have not looked into the Iliad since I
received your letter, except to the Ω ; but I recol-
lected immediately four instances—three of them in
one book, the Γ, and one in the Α. In Α, οφρ'
ιλασσωμεθ' ανακτα ; in Γ, ει τις ιδοιτο ; and two in one
line—

Ου τοτε γ' ωδ' Οδυσηος αγ σσαμεθ' ειδος ιδοντες :

besides, ϵργ' ϵιδυια is familiar to my ear, though I do
not know where particularly to look for it.

"In the Odyssey, there are three instances in
the space of fifty lines in the Λ, in the verses 521,
549, 560. The first of these three has, I confess, the air of a spurious line; the second might
be remedied by taking away a δ' but without the
δ' the construction would be hard, and unlike
Homer: but the third cannot well, I think, be
altered; and it is the more remarkable, on account
of the digamma being respected in the same line,
δευρο αναξ ἱν' ϵπος, &c. There is also, in the Odyss. N,
the word προσιδωνται, which, I should conceive, could
hardly be altered to προϊδωνται without changing the
sense. If these which I have mentioned were *all*
the instances, I admit they would not much signify:
but as those from the Iliad have occurred to me
memoriter only, and those from the Odyssey from a
very slight investigation of a very small part of the
poem, I cannot help supposing there may be found
many hundreds of them; so that I can hardly conceive the proportion to be any thing like what you
suppose,—especially as all the cases of the paragogic ν
preceding the digamma make neither for one side nor
the other, but must be thrown out of the question, as
perfectly neutral. I should hardly think you would
(and I am sure Knight would not) consent to take
away from Homer, and give to his collectors, or
joiners, or botchers, the Γ and the Ω of the Iliad,
and the Λ of the Odyssey; and this to make the
cobbler superior to the original artist or artists. Ac-

cording to your system, you may possibly say, that
those parts where the digamma is uniformly respected were written by older poets; those where
it is sometimes slighted, by more modern : but what
if it should appear to be nearly equally respected
and slighted in the different parts of the poem ?
Now my hypothesis, if I dared to form one, would
be this; and (every man loves his own best, — την
αυτου φιλεει και κηδεται) it appears to me more reasonable than any that I have yet heard. I suppose
this digamma, at one period at least, not to have had
the decided sound which belongs in general to consonants; and, consequently, that the poets of that
period, the Ὁμηροι, thought themselves at liberty to
sound it more or less, and consequently to treat it in
the manner most convenient to their verse.   If it
was sounded sometimes more, and sometimes less, it
might naturally happen that, in process of time, one
dialect, viz., the Latin, might erect it into a decided
consonant v; and others, viz., the Attic, &c., might
wholly drop it.   Thus in modern Italian, in the word
uovo, an egg, the *u* is pronounced at Florence in a
manner very difficult to be imitated by foreigners,
and which makes it appear to be something between
a vowel and a consonant ; but in other parts of Italy,
where the language is corrupted, it is in some wholly
dropped, and the word is pronounced *ovo ;* in others,
it is made a complete consonant, and sounded *vovo*.
This may be, and probably is, a fanciful theory of my
own; but, I own, I feel great reluctance to cut the
Iliad and Odyssey to pieces, and to give them, not

only to different authors, but different ages. I do
not know whether Hesiod is, in your opinion, a contemporary with Homer; but, if he is, I think that in
his Εργα και 'Ημεραι there is απ' εργου χειρας ερυκοι:
and εργον is, I suppose, one of the words with the ϝ.

"Ver. 320. I doubt the derivation of *vastus* from
ϝαστυ: though I believe αστυ to have been written
αστυ, because ανα αστυ, ποτι αστυ, are so common:
and surely the comparison of a large vessel to a town
is too natural, when it is meant to exaggerate its size,
to make it necessary to have recourse to any particular derivation.

"Ver. 325. There are certainly some other instances of a vowel short before τρ, though, I believe,
not many. The first syllable of Πατροκλος is short
in more instances than one; but the instance of a
proper name is not, perhaps, quite a fair one; as
Homer might take the same liberty, in such cases,
as the Tragedians did afterwards, which you have
noticed and accounted for, I think, in the best man-
mer. The word προτραποιμην is at the end of a verse
in Odyss. M. ver. 381. Προσηνδα, &c., are often
at the end of lines, and consequently the syllable before
πρ short: but these you may not think cases in point,
because in them the vowel and the consonants are
in separate words; but I do not think the Greeks in
general attended much to that distinction.

"Ver. 337. I have said enough at least upon the ϝ;
I fear too much : but I must just observe, that the
being some times right, and others wrong, does not
prove two fingers in the pie, because they are some-

times right and wrong in the same verse, which probably was all made by one author."

MR. WAKEFIELD TO MR. FOX.

"HACKNEY, February 25th, 1798.

" SIR,

"The best argument against Homer, and
for my hypothesis, appears in my general observations, prefixed to Pope's Odyssey, in the edition
which I prepared for the Booksellers; and of which
I have but one copy for myself, or I should long
since have requested your acceptance of the work.
Certainly, if any thing like your opinion, with respect
to the digamma, could be established, the early
Greek Poets, instead of meriting the encomiums of
all antiquity for their correctness, must be deemed
the most capricious and irregular of all writers; and
emendatory criticism upon them can be modelled by
no rules of analogy whatever : whereas their modes
of expression are so precise and congenial, that the
direct contrary appears to be the truth.

" The detached lamentations of the several characters at the end of Il. Ω. have a very formal appearance ; and much the air of an attempt from different
bards to shew their skill upon the same subject. In
collections of Greek epigrams, and in some works
of the later Sophists, you find compositions introduced with such commas as these : ' What sort of
exclamation Achilles would use on the death of
Patroclus ? ' &c. and then follows a specimen of the
author's talents in that way.

"The Shield of Hercules, in Hesiod, is one of those detached pieces of poetry, such as I suppose the Iliad to be formed of, remaining to us from the highest antiquity; and quite equal to any thing in Homer with which it can properly be compared. His Theogony, too, in versification and language, is perfectly similar to the Iliad; so that their imitation of existing models is almost an inevitable conclusion: and the probability is, that numberless pieces of this kind were existing among the antient bards of Greece, but have been lost, partly from the negligence of succeeding times, and partly from the want of alphabetic characters.

"But before those corrections of Homer, on the principle of the Æolic digamma, could be prosecuted, some general rules must be laid down; as follow:

"I find, suppose, in reading the Theogony of Hesiod, that the digamma is regarded seventy times, and disregarded thirty. (What I am stating is generally the fact, though the numbers may not be perfectly in ratio.) Out of these thirty irregularities, I find ten rectified in the various readings; but I consider that not one MS. in a thousand of Hesiod has come down to our times. I argue, then, for the probability of a rectification of all the thirty, with more MSS., from the general principle of their method and correctness as writers. Again: this circumstance of the digamma has been so unknown to later ages, or at least disregarded by them, that reporters of MSS. it is most certain, have neglected a declaration of those little varieties, which would

settle these controverted passages, from an opinion
of their unimportance. The same ignorance or
inattention would lead the transcribers readily to
fill up these chasms, as violations of measures, or
to leave unnoticed these niceties, as things trivial
and unessential; all which may be shewn, to the
very highest degree of probability, from innumerable
instances: so that, instead of wondering at thirty
anomalies, we must rather be surprised that they
have not been much more plentiful. In short, there
is scarcely an instance of a learned construction, or
a more exquisite peculiarity of numbers, but some
corruption or other may be traced in the various
readings of MSS. or the importunities of modern
editors. Now to your particulars.

" Your instance from Il. A. 444. has been corrected
by Dawes, Misc. Crit. p. 146, from the Florentine
edition, with general approbation, οφρ᾽ ἱλασομεσθα
ανακτα : and all the exceptions that relate to αναξ
are noticed by him, and mostly well and easily
corrected. But all niceties of this kind were so
uniformly obliterated by later scribes and editors,
that in the present wreck of MSS., an emendation,
simple and convincing, is often beyond the reach of
sagacity, and, in many cases, quite impossible. In
Γ. 453. laying aside the digamma, the tenses are
incongruous, and the construction ungrammatical.
What is required, the Scholiast indicates sufficiently :
ει τις ΙΔΟΙΤΟ] ει τις ΕΘΕΑΣΑΤΟ : ʻIf he *had* *seen*
him, he would not have concealed him :ʼ not, ʻIf he
could see him.ʼ Besides, τις is inelegantly repeated.

Now, except other MSS. and the first editions (for
these studies are not to be cultivated duly without
very large libraries at hand) give some further hints,
I see nothing better than the following attempt : for
the verb absolutely requires here *αν* or *κε* :

Ου μεν γαρ φιλοτητι γ' εκευθανον, ει ΚΕ ΙΑΟΝΤΟ :

which will satisfy both measure and construction.

"Ver. 224 can occasion no difficulty, as a most
barbarous and impertinent interpolation ; and I see,
accordingly, a mark of exception prefixed to it by
the antient critics in Villois. Homer. Εργ' ειδυια, and
its parallels, where *α* must be lost, (for *δ'* before the
digamma must be conceded) may be settled by
writing εργα ιδυια· as Il. Υ. 12. ιδυιησι πραπιδεσσι. No
question but we should write προϊδωνται in Od. Ν.
155, *prospicient, See at a distance :* compare ver.
169, Hesiod. Scuti Herc. 385, where one scribe
could not be easy without attempting to substitute
προσιδωνται : otherwise there is an end of all probability in criticism, grounded on the usage and
accuracy of writers.   But, as I said, before some
particular specimens can be acceptable, the reader
must be prepared by general positions, and a detail
of undisputed specimens on good authority : and
this were a work of time and labour.   I have by me
materials for an important, and, as I think, interesting attempt of this nature, not less allied to
philosophy and history, than criticism ; and materials,
indeed, for correcter editions of most of the Greek
and Roman Poets ; but, as I can never pretend to

execute any thing much better than my Lucretius, till the burden of that publication is a good deal more alleviated, my pen never meddles with such subjects again, to the end of my days.

"Sir! my former apologies must serve me for stopping more abruptly than I could wish, and for subscribing myself here, with every sentiment of respect,

"Your obedient servant,

"GILBERT WAKEFIELD."

MR. FOX TO MR. WAKEFIELD.

"ST. ANN'S HILL, *March 16th*, 1798.

"SIR,

"I deferred answering your last Letter, in order to have time to read over attentively some part of Homer, with a view to the digamma. I have read, since I wrote last, ten books of the Odyssey, from Ξ to Ψ inclusive; and find in them eighty-five instances where the digamma is neglected. It is true that, in many of these, the fault, if it be one, is easily corrected; but then the question arises, if the instances are so numerous, What reason have we to think that there is any error or occasion for correction? I will admit, however, that the result of my attention to the subject is, that with the old poet, or poets, whom we call Homer, the natural and common course seems to have been, to consider words beginning with the F like words beginning with a consonant; but then the numerousness of

the instances to the contrary, and, above all, the
circumstance of those instances being spread pretty
equally over those books to which I have attended,
raise great doubts in my mind, whether words
beginning with ϝ were not occasionally considered as
words beginning with a vowel. Nor can I agree
that this supposition would make the old writers so
capricious as you seem to think : for, in fact, it only
supposes them to have treated the digamma as
unquestionably they treated the aspirate '; before
which short vowels are sometimes cut off, sometimes
left standing; long vowels and diphthongs sometimes shortened (though by the way very rarely),
sometimes left long ; and syllables ending with
consonants sometimes retain the shortness natural
to them, at other times not. What you say upon
the three instances I quoted *memoriter* from the
Iliad is very satisfactory, especially as the alteration
to ἱλασόμεσθα is, you say, warranted by an old edition :
and, indeed, the whole of this question must at last
be decided by a reference to such editions and to
manuscripts ; in regard to both which I am un-
commonly ignorant, never having read Homer in
any other editions than the Glasgow and Clarke's.
I have indeed occasionally looked at a very few
passages in H. Stephens's edition of him among
the Greek Poets ; but, with this single exception, I
know nothing of any other text but Clarke's (for the
Glasgow is a transcript from him), nor of any other
Comments or Scholia than those which he has cited.
What you have said has raised in me an ardent

curiosity to look into the old editions ; and I shall
endeavour, in the course of the year, to visit some
libraries where there are collections of them. The
lamentations in the Ω of the Iliad are certainly
rather formal in the manner in which they are introduced, unless one supposes them to be a part of a
sort of funeral ceremony. In regard to the short
syllable before the mute and the ρ, I have found but
one instance (proper names excepted) in the ten
books I have just read ; and in that there seems to
be some error ; the word is δακρυοισι in Od. Σ ver.
172 ; but I recollect, in other parts of Homer to
have read, more than once, ἁδροτητα και ἡβην. ANδρο-
τητα, as I believe it is sometimes written, would only
increase the difficulty. I am sensible that if we
consider the diphthongs οι and αι as short syllables,
the number of instances I have quoted of the neglect
of the   will be something (not greatly) diminished.
Reiske, in his Notes on Theocritus, is positive
these syllables are sometimes short, and were so
used by Homer; and I suspect that all you, who
think the attention to the Ϝ the criterion of authenticity, are of his opinion ; else the famous passage in
Il. Υ. quoted by Longinus for its sublimity, must be
given up, on account of

——— εκ θρονου ἁλτο και Ϝιαχε.———

" I am very much concerned at your Lucretius
meeting with so little encouragement as you say ;
and I feel the more, because I cannot help thinking
that part of the prejudice, which occasions so

unaccountable a neglect, is imputable to the honour
you have done me by the dedication of it—an
honour, I assure you, that I shall always most highly
value.

" I am, Sir,

" Yours ever,

" C. J. FOX."

MR. WAKEFIELD TO MR. FOX.

"HACKNEY, *March* 7*th*,* 1798.

" SIR,

" IT is most certain, that anomalies and inconsistencies of all kinds are much more frequent in
the Odyssey than the Iliad, from a cause which is in
favour of an hypothesis that receives countenance in
proportion to our ability of approximation to antient
sources ; i.e. the fewer transcripts of that poem compared with the Iliad, on account of the less interest
which all ages have taken in its favour; for it is an
acknowledged position, that those authors are most
corrupt of which the fewest MSS. have been preserved.   Now, where old editions and MSS. enable
us to rectify so many of these irregularities without
violence, the presumption is very strong ,in our
favour, from the great antiquity of Homer : for MSS.
five times as old as any now in being, would be
modern in comparison of the oldest MS. of Virgil,
and most other authors.   I have marked in my

---

* Although some mistake appears in the date of this or the preceding
Letter, Mr. Wakefield's is evidently an answer to the preceding of
Mr. Fox. Probably the date of this should be March 17th.

margin all the violations of the theory of the
digamma, but have never numbered them.   I should
suppose that many of your instances would be accom-
modated by an omission of the final ν, or some other
simple process ; remembering always, that the little
words δ' and τ' form no exceptions; and such sounds
were not harsher, I presume, than βδελυρος, γδουπησε,
and some others.   Nor must we forget how all traces
of antiquity, in numerous other instances, have been
so obliterated by the prepossessions and ignorance
of successive transcribers through many ages, as to
leave the truth in some cases absolutely irrecoverable:
of which, even with relation to Latin orthography, I
have given many instances in my Notes on Lucretius.
What you urge upon the variations of quantity from
the influence of the aspirate seems very pertinent :
but I am partly inclined to believe these discordances
to be imaginary, and the offspring of an inaccurate
attention to specific instances.   I do not despair of
pointing out reasons for these variations from general
rules ; but these studies are really in their infancy,
and will continue so, till better forms of government
leave the human race at large more leisure to cultivate their intellects.   Besides, we may well believe,
from numerous deductions, a theory to be legitimate;
though, in the midst of so much darkness and inconvenience, and after so long an interval, no sagacity be
equal to a satisfactory solution of every contradiction ;
but, in truth, nothing can be done with any proper
and adequate nicety in this way without the First
Editions, and a great variety of them; in which

respect I labour under very discouraging impediments ; though, all circumstances considered, I have
but little doubt of being able to claim for myself the
merit of having collected, without gross imprudence
or injustice to my family, from mere personal self-
denial of reasonable indulgences, considering my
income, the best comparative library of any man in
this country. Bentley's note on Callim. Hymn. Jup.
87. has long since set at rest the old controversy on
the quantity of the diphthongs οι and αι, with all those
who do not, like Reiske, bid defiance to all quantity
whatsoever : and yet Primatt, in his book on Accents,
seems never to have met with that note of Bentley.
The instances of syllables short, in Homer, before
two consonants of any kind, I meant to state as
exceedingly few, much fewer than in any author after
him. To the best of my recollection, Dionysius, in
his Periegesis, approaches nearest to Homer's purity
in this peculiarity of smooth versification.

" Most of the specimens of the violated digamma in
ιαχω may be readily and naturally adjusted : your example from Il. Υ. 62. is of a very untractable quality;
and whatever assurance we may feel, in our own
minds, of the general validity of a theory, it were
very unreasonable to expect acquiescence from a
neutral reader in an emendation not recommended by
the utmost facility and probability. What I have
to offer here, is this : the Schol. in Villois. tells us,
that some read ωρτο ; I say, perhaps ωρετο should be
substituted, which is a word of Homer's also : but a
too ready persuasion that it was a variety for ἀλτο

instead of ιαχε would soon turn ωρετο into ωρτο.
Suppose, then,—εκ θρονου ἁλτο και ωρετο— '*leapt* from
his throne in great *bustle* and *perturbation*.' Now
no word whatever could better represent Virgil's
trepident in the parallel passage, than this : whereas
ιαχε has, in the Roman, at present no counterpart.
Further : Eustathius says on the passage, Δεισας δ', εκ
θρονου ἁλτο και ὑπερθορεν η ιαχε. If I were not in quest
of a particular object, I should say, that η and και
must be transposed ; and then the common reading
is right : but you must allow me the advantage of
this variety; from which I have surely as much right
to reason, as another man can have to an arbitrary
correction against the copies. If the copies of Eustathius be correct, it is demonstration that some word
equivalent to ιαχε (which, in that case, from a marginal gloss, has insinuated itself into the text) is
corrected in ὑπερθορεν· which the measure rejects.
Now a word not essentially different from the former
ωρτο and this of Eustathius, either in letters or enunciation, would be most probable. Suppose, then,

————— εκ θρονου ἁλτο και ΩΡΤΕ :

Made a loud bawl. Now the lexicons would make
you believe, that this word is only used of beasts,
dogs, and wolves (See my Notes on Bion, i. 18) ; but
Antip. Sidon. epig. 8, employs it of the roaring of
the *sea ;* and Pindar, Ol. ix. 163, of a *man.*

" Sir, it gives me real concern, that you should
suppose my notice of you in my Lucretius should
have proved injurious to the reception of that work.

Believe me, nothing can be more unnecessary and unsubstantial than your solicitude on this head. My former publications were alone a proof, from *fact*, of what I allege ; which makes me the more decisive in my assertion. I am satisfied, that no man on earth, at all similarly situated, was ever less obnoxious to his political antagonists than you are : and nothing but a persuasion in me, rooted on long and attentive observation, that you had qualities which secured you from the disaffection of every heart tolerably humanised, could have induced me to pay you that trivial token of my respect with such perfect acquiescence ; a token of respect which I shall contemplate, I know, with increasing satisfaction to the end of life. I am glad, however, that I can gratulate you on escaping the inauspicious omen of the Scriptures : " Woe ! unto you, when *all* men speak well of you : " and yet I should not be surprised, if the times mend so much, and such opportunities for a fuller and freer display of yourself present themselves, as actually to excite some *apprehension* and *mistrust* in me in consequence of the *universal* and *unqualified* approbation of the world. When that takes place, perhaps, I may set my wits at work to find out some erratum in the copies of that verse. At present, I must own that such solicitude is not absolutely necessary.

" But the copies of my Lucretius are not numerous ; and I know it must make its way in time against all personal and political opposition, especially when known on the Continent. Mr. Steevens, editor of Shakspeare, who, though a friend of mine, can scarcely endure one of my opinions; an excellent classical scholar, and a most severe censor; who detected, I think, 900 errors in the Heyne's Virgil, lately published in London, and *corrected* by Porson; pronounced, in my hearing, at a bookseller's, last week, my large-paper Lucretius to be the most magnificent and correct work of its kind that had yet appeared. One was ordered for the King's Library last week.

" I remain, Sir,

" Your most obedient servant,

"GILBERT WAKEFIELD."

MR. FOX TO MR. WAKEFIELD.

"ST. ANN'S HILL, *March 1st*, 1799.

" SIR,

" Although I am wholly without any resources, even of advice, and much more of power, to offer you my services upon the present occasion, yet I cannot help troubling you with a few lines, to tell you how very sincerely concerned I am at the event of your trial.

" The liberty of the press I considered as virtually destroyed by the proceedings against Johnson and Jordan; and what has happened to you I cannot but lament therefore the more, as the sufferings of a man whom I esteem, in a cause that is no more.

" I have been reading your Lucretius, and have nearly finished the second volume; it appears to me to be by far the best publication of any classical author: and if it is an objection with some persons,

that the great richness and variety of quotation and
criticism in the Notes takes off, in some degree, the
attention from the Text, I am not one of those who
will ever complain of an editor for giving me too
much instruction and amusement.

"I am, with great regard,

"and all possible good wishes,

"Sir,

"Your most obedient servant,

"C. J. FOX."

MR. WAKEFIELD TO MR. FOX.

"HACKNEY, *March 2nd*, 1799.

"SIR,

"Your kind attention at this time is peculiarly gratifying and consoling; but wholly congenial
to that benevolence of disposition, which is the
brightest jewel in all the accomplishments of
humanity. My defence, though unsuccessful, was,
in the opinion of my best friends, entirely consonant
to my character. Some parts, I am aware, would be
thought, by men of the world, severe and imprudent
to excess; but *such* persecution for *such* things fills
me, I own, with a degree of indignation and sorrow,
to which no words appear to my mind capable of
doing justice. Your approbation of my Lucretius is
also particularly grateful to me.

"I am, Sir,

"with every sentiment of esteem,

"Your obedient servant,

"GILBERT WAKEFIELD."

MR. FOX TO MR. WAKEFIELD.

"St. Ann's Hill, *June 9th,* 1799.

" Sir,

" Nothing could exceed the concern I felt at the extreme severity (for such it appears to me) of the sentence pronounced against you.

" I should be apprehensive, that the distance of Dorchester must add considerably to the difficulties of your situation; but should be very glad to learn from you that it is otherwise.

" If any of your friends can think of any plan for you, by which some of the consequences of your confinement may be in any degree lessened, I should be very happy to be in any way assisting in it. From some words that dropped from you, when I saw you, I rather understood that you did not feel much inclination to apply to your usual studies in your present situation; otherwise it had occurred to me, that some publication, on a less expensive plan than the Lucretius, and by subscription, might be eligible, for the purpose of diverting your mind, and for serving your family; but of this you are the best judge : and all I can say is, that I shall always be happy to show the esteem and regard with which I am,

" Sir,

" Your most obedient servant,

"C. J. FOX.

"Rev. Gilbert Wakefield, *King's Bench Prison.*"

SAME TO SAME.

"St. Ann's Hill, *June* 10*th*, 1799.

" Sir,

" Within a few hours after I wrote to you yesterday, a gentleman called, who informed me that a scheme had been formed for preventing some of the ill consequences of your imprisonment, and upon a much more eligible plan than that which I suggested. Of course, you will not think any more of what I said upon that subject; only that, if you do employ yourself in writing during your confinement, my opinion is, that, in the present state of things, literature is, in every point of view, a preferable occupation to politics.

" I have looked at my Roman Virgil, and find that it is printed from the Medicean MS. as I supposed. The verses regarding Helen, in the second book, are printed in a different character, and stated to be wanting in the MS.

" Yours ever,

" C. J. FOX."

MR. WAKEFIELD TO MR. FOX.

"Κ. Β. παρα Πλουτηϊ: *June* 10*th*, 1799.

" Sir,

" I am very highly gratified by your attention to me, as the attention of one whom I love and reverence.

" In the present distraction of my mind, much

enhanced by the consternation into which I am thrown by hearing this moment of the unexpected sentence on Lord Thanet and Mr. Ferguson, I am scarcely capable of answering your kind inquiries in a proper manner ; and therefore beg leave to inclose a letter, received last night, which I am sure will give pleasure to a heart so interested, not in my welfare only, but in that of all his species : that letter you will be so kind as to return.   What I particularly meditate is a Greek and English Lexicon, at a subscription of a guinea and a-half : but of this plan I shall judge better when I see the place of my destination, whither I expect to be transported in a few days.

" My sentence is not to be ranked among the *calamities* of human life : but it is a very serious *inconvenience* to us on many accounts, and on none more than a separation from a numerous band of the most affectionate and virtuous and disinterested friends, of both sexes, that it ever fell to the lot of any family to possess.

" By the time in which my confinement will expire, I trust a prospect will be opened of calling you from your beloved retirement, to a theatre of more extensive usefulness, alike adapted to the amplitude of your talents, and the benevolence of your disposition.

" I am, Sir,

" with every sentiment of esteem,

" Your obedient servant,

" GILBERT WAKEFIELD."

MR. FOX TO MR. WAKEFIELD.

"St. Ann's Hill, *June* 12*th*, 1799.

" Sir,

" I return you your friend's letter, which gave me great satisfaction. The sentence upon Lord Thanet and Ferguson is, all things considered, most abominable; but the speech accompanying it is, if possible, worse.

I think a Lexicon in Greek and English is a work much wanted; and if you can have patience to execute such a work, I shall consider it a great benefit to the cause of literature. I hope to hear from you that your situation at Dorchester is not worse, at least, than you expected; and when I know you to be in a state of perfect ease of mind (which at this moment could not be expected), I will, with your leave, state to you a few observations, which I just hinted to you when I saw you, upon Porson's Note to his Orestes, regarding the final v.

" I am, with great regard,
" Sir,
" Yours ever,
"C. J. FOX."

MR. WAKEFIELD TO MR. FOX.

"King's Bench, *June* 14*th*, 1799.

" Sir,

" I set out for Dorchester to-morrow or Monday; and shall be glad, at all times and in any place, to receive communications from you, upon

points of criticism, or any other within my sphere.
In the meantime, two of my brothers have been
down to reconnoitre the place; and from their report
I collect, clearly, that this transportation thither was
intended to be nothing less than a Cold-Bath Fields'
business. It so happens, that in the small premises
belonging to the governor, alias keeper, alias gaoler,
a small lodging-room is to be obtained; whether
with or without a fire-place I have hitherto forgotten
to inquire; but with no accommodation for books,
beyond a pocket-full or so: of course every plan of
any laborious undertaking in literature is totally
abandoned, and indeed every object of study beyond
an author such as Homer, who is pretty much con-
centered within himself. The intercourse even with
my family, as far as I understand, will be partial and
restrained; so that if a former occupant had been
equal to that room in the house, nothing but a cell,
in a most detestable building (to my Brothers' fancies),
would have remained for myself. Upon the whole,
considering the great inconveniences of an entire
removal, and dissolution of our former residence, I
am not sure, whether the Bastile, for the same time,
might not have been as eligible. And as I was never
able to pursue any literary object without a comfortable disposition of external circumstances, I must
postpone what projects I had entertained in that way
to a more convenient season, if I should live to see
it; and content myself with the amusements of my
family, and occasional intercourse with my friends by
letter or in person.

" My defence, and other memorials of this prosecution, which I thought it a part of my duty not to
leave unrecorded, will be left for your acceptance,
with a book which Lord Holland lent me.

" I am, Sir, with the truest respect,

" Your obliged servant,

"GILBERT WAKEFIELD."

MR. FOX TO MR. WAKEFIELD.

"St. Ann's Hill, *June 27th,* 1799.

" Sir,

" In consequence of a letter which Lord
Holland showed me, I have written to Lord Shaftesbury and to Lord Ilchester, who are both very
humane men, and would, I should hope, be happy to
do anything that may make your situation less
uneasy.

" I am, Sir,

" Yours ever,

"C. J. FOX."

MR. WAKEFIELD TO MR. FOX.

"Dorchester Gaol, *September 6th,* 1799.

" Sir,

" The courier of this day communicates to
me the very unwelcome intelligence of an injury
received by you, from the bursting of your gun.
Assure yourself, Sir, that your oldest and warmest
friends feel not a more lively interest in all your
pains and pleasures than myself, nor will rejoice more

at your recovery.   And will you do me the justice to
believe, that I would not have taken the trouble of
submitting the following passage of Cicero to your
consideration, but from an absolute conviction of your
magnanimity and benevolence, and love of truth;
and from an entire confidence in your candour, for
assigning no motive to this intrusion, but an ardent
desire of your approximation as nearly as possible to
my own, perhaps visionary and mistaken, notions of
perfection?—'Ego autem, quam diu respublica per
eos gerebatur, quibus se ipsa commiserat, omnes
meas curas cogitationesque in eam conferebam : cùm
autem dominatu unius omnia tenerentur, neque esset
usquam consilio aut auctoritati locus; socios denique
tuendæ reipublicæ, summos viros, amisissem ; nec me
angoribus dedidi, quibus essem confectus, nisi iis
restitissem, nec rursum INDIGNIS HOMINE DOCTO
VOLUPTATIBUS.' *Off.* ii. 1.

   " Am I, Sir, indecently presumptuous and free,
am I guilty of a too dictatorial officiousness, in pro-
nouncing THOSE PLEASURES TO MISBECOME A MAN OF
LETTERS, which consist in mangling, maiming, and
depriving of that invaluable and irretrievable blessing,
its existence, an inoffensive pensioner on the universal
bounties of the common Feeder and Protector of all
his offspring?

" I remain, Sir,

" Your obliged and respectful friend,

"GILBERT WAKEFIELD."

MR. FOX TO MR. WAKEFIELD.

"No. 11, Sackville Street, *September* 14*th*, 1799.

" Sir,

" I assure you I take very kindly your letter, and the quotation in it. I think the question of ' How far field sports are innocent amusements ?' is nearly connected with another, upon which, from the title of one of your intended works, I suspect you entertain opinions rather singular ; for if it is lawful to kill tame animals with whom one has a sort of acquaintance, such as *fowls*, *oxen*, &c., it is still less repugnant to one's feelings to kill wild animals ; but then to make a *pastime* of it—I am aware there is something to be said on this point. On the other hand, if example is allowed to be anything, there is nothing in which all mankind, civilised or savage, have more agreed, than in making some sort of chace (for fishing is of the same nature) part of their business or amusement. However, I admit it to be a very questionable subject : at all events, it is a very pleasant and healthful exercise. My wound goes on, I believe, very well ; and no material injury is apprehended to the hand ; but the cure will be tedious, and I shall be confined in this town for more weeks than I had hoped ever to spend days here. I am much obliged to you for your inquiries, and am,

" Sir,

" Your most obedient servant,

"C. J. FOX."

MR. WAKEFIELD TO MR. FOX.

"DORCHESTER GAOL, *September 20th*, 1799.

" SIR,

" I am unwilling to increase the inconveniences of your present situation, and have therefore not been solicitous of immediately acknowledging your favour; nor do I by any means wish you to incommode yourself, in the least degree, by noticing this, or any other similar intrusion from *me*.

" With your leave, the question of *animal food* (from which the purest philosophers in all ages have abstained, the Pythagoreans, Bramins, Essenes, and others) is no more involved in that of *rural sports*, as commonly pursued, than the question of *racks and tortures* is connected with that of *capital punishments*. I would not now state, ' Is it lawful and expedient to kill animals at all ?' but, ' Is it philosophical and humane to leave numbers of them to perish by pain and hunger, or to occasion the remainder of their lives to be perilous and miserable ?' for such, I presume, are the inevitable consequences of *shooting* in particular. As for hunting ; to see a set of men exulting in the distresses of an inoffensive animal, with such intemperate and wild triumph, is to me the most irrational and degrading spectacle in the world ; and an admirable prolusion to those delectable operations which are transacting in Holland and elsewhere !

" In reading Ovid's Tristia (to my fancy, the first

Poet of all Antiquity) with my children, the other
morning, (who, with my wife, are forbidden by the
justices to come to me more than four days in a
week, from ten o'clock to six,) I thought an error,
not yet discovered, to occupy the introductory lines :—

> Parve, nec invideo, sine me, Liber ! ibis in urbem;
> Hei mihi ! quò domino non licet ire tuo.
> Vade, sed incultus; qualem decet exsulis esse:
> Infelix habitum temporis hujus habe.

By the bye, I have observed, (and mention, I think,
somewhere in Lucretius,) that the Poets never used
nec, but always *neque*, before a word beginning with
a vowel: in the first verse, therefore, it should be
' *neque* invideo.' But is there not something awkward
and obscure, at first, in the construction of the third?
The final *s* is written in MSS. after a manner likely
to occasion errors ; as *incultu*ˢ. I read, therefore,

> Vade; sed *in cultu* qualem decet exsulis esse.

" With my most cordial wishes for your speedy
recovery, and less desolation in that *kingdom*, which
one of my pupils, in construing that noble passage in
the third Georgic,—(from which Gray has borrowed,
in his Elegy,

> ' Nor cast one longing, lingering look behind,') ——
> Et stabula adspectans *regnis* excessit *avitis*,

called *the kingdom of birds.*

" I remain, Sir,
" Your most respectful and obliged friend,
"GILBERT WAKEFIELD."

MR. FOX TO MR. WAKEFIELD.

"St. Ann's Hill, *October 22nd,* 1799.

" Sir,

"I believe I had best not continue the controversy about field sports ; or at least, if I do, I must have recourse, I believe, to authority and precedent, rather than to argument ; and content myself with rather excusing, than justifying them. Cicero says, I believe, somewhere, ' Si quem nihil delectaret nisi quod cum laude et dignitate conjunctum foret, ... huic homini ego fortasse, et pauci, Deos propitios, plerique iratos putarent.' But this is said, I am afraid, in defence of a libertine, whose public principles, when brought to the test, proved to be as unsound, as his private life was irregular. By the way, I know no speech of Cicero's more full of beautiful passages than this is (pro M. Cælio), nor where he is more in his element. Argumentative contention is what he by no means excels in ; and he is never, I think, so happy, as when he has an opportunity of exhibiting a mixture of philosophy and pleasantry ; and especially, when he can interpose anecdotes, and references to the authority of the eminent characters in the history of his country. No man appears, indeed, to have had such real respect for authority as he ; and therefore, when he speaks on that subject, he is always natural, and in earnest ; and not like those among *us,* who are so often declaiming about the wisdom of our ancestors, without know-

ing what they mean, or hardly ever citing any particulars of their conduct, or of their *dicta*.

" I showed your proposed alteration in the Tristia
to a very good judge, who approved of it very much.
I confess, myself, that I like the old reading best,
and think it more in Ovid's manner; but this,
perhaps, is mere fancy. I have always been a great
reader of him, and thought myself the greatest
admirer he had, till you called him the first Poet of
Antiquity, which is going even beyond me. The
grand and spirited style of the Iliad; the true nature
and simplicity of the Odyssey; the poetical language
(far excelling that of all other Poets in the world) of
the Georgics, and the pathetic strokes in the Æneid,
give Homer and Virgil a rank, in my judgment,
clearly above all competitors; but next after them I
should be very apt to class Ovid, to the great scandal,
I believe, of all who pique themselves upon what is
called purity of taste. You have somewhere compared
him to Euripides, I think; and I can fancy I see a
resemblance in them. This resemblance it is, I suppose, which makes one prefer Euripides to Sophocles;
a preference which, if one were writing a dissertation,
it would be very difficult to justify. Euripides leads
one to Porson, who, as I told you, is not content with
putting the final ν as others have put it, before
him, but adopts it even when the following word
begins with a mute and a liquid: and that he
does this merely from a desire to differ as widely
from you as possible, is evident. In his Note
on verse 64 of the Orestes, are the words which I

will copy and inclose. Now the cases of prepositions
in compound words being made long, appear to me
not very *rare*; though *rare* being an indefinite word,
it is difficult to ascertain precisely the force he gives
to it : but of the final vowel being long, of which he
thinks there are *no* instances, there are a great many ;
at least I must suppose so, as I recollect several from
mere memory. But, what is most to the purpose,
there is one in his Hecuba which I must suppose to
be ' indubiæ fidei ;' as he was so far from stating it
as a suspicious passage, that he did not point it out
even as a remarkable one. It is verse 589 :

Ω θυγατερ, ουκ οιδ' εις ὁ, ΤΙ βλεψω κακων·

but he had not then been angered by your observations, and had not, therefore, resolved to support the
use of the *v* in all possible places. You must allow it
is difficult for us unlearned to have a proper confidence in great critics, when they use us in this
manner, and lay down general rules, which they never
thought of before, only for the purpose of making
the difference more wide between them and their
opponents. In the Cyclops, verse 522, there is
ουδενΑ βλαπτει βροτων· in the Electra of Euripides,
verse 1058, there is αρΑ κλυουσα· and, I dare say,
hundreds of more instances against him, as I found
these by mere chance : and it has so happened, that
I have not read any play of Euripides, or Sophocles,
since I read his Note.

" I cannot conceive upon what principle, or indeed
from what motive, they have so restricted the inter-

course between you and your family. My first impulse was, to write to Lord Ilchester to speak to Mr. Frampton; but, as you seem to suspect that former applications have done mischief, I shall do nothing. Your pupil's translation of ' *avitis* ' shows that he has a good notion of the formation of words; and is a very good sign, if he is a young one. Did you, who are such a hater of war, ever read the lines at the beginning of the second book of Cowper's Task ? There are few things in our language superior to them, in my judgment. He is a fine poet, and has, in a great degree, conquered my prejudices against blank verse.

" I am, with great regard,
" Sir,
" Your most obedient servant,
"C. J. FOX."

" My hand is not yet so well as to give me the use of it, though the wound is nearly healed. The surgeon suspects there is more bone to come away.—I have been here something more than a fortnight."

Professor Porson's Note, inclosed in the preceding.

" Orestes, v. 64.

" Παρθενον, εμη τε μητρι παρεδωκεN τρεφειν.

" Erunt fortasse nonnulli, qui minùs necessario hoc factum (that is, the insertion of the final *v*) arbitraturi

sint in παρεδωκεν. Rationes igitur semel exponam,
nunquam posthac moniturus. Quanquam enim sæpe
syllabas naturâ breves positione producunt Tragici,
longè libentius corripiunt; adeo ut tria prope exempla
correptarum invenias, ubi unum modo exstet produc-
tarum : sed hoc genus licentiæ, in verbis scilicet non
compositis, qualia τεκνον, πατρος, ceteris longè fre-
quentius est.   Rarius multo syllaba producitur in
verbo composito, si in ipsam juncturam cadit, ut in
πολυχρυσος, *Andr*. 2.   Eâdem parsimoniâ in augmentis
producendis utuntur, ut in επεκλωσεν, sup. 12. κεκλησθαι,
Sophocl. *Electr*. 366.   Rarior adhuc licentia est, ubi
præpositio verbo jungitur, ut in αποτροποι, *Phœn*. 600.
Sed ubi verbum in brevem vocalem desinit, eamque
duæ consonantes excipiunt, quæ brevem manere
patiantur, vix credo exempla indubiæ fidei inveniri
posse, in quibus syllaba ista producatur.   Ineptus
esset quicunque ad MSS. in tali causâ provocaret,
cum nulla sit eorum auctoritas : id solum deprecor,
ne quis contra hanc regulam eorum testimonio
abutatur ; MSS. enim neque alter alteri consentiunt,
neque idem MS. sibi ipse per omnia constat. Quòd
si ea, quæ disputavi, vera sunt, planum est in fine
vocis addendam esse literam, quam addidi."

MR. WAKEFIELD TO MR. FOX.

"DORCHESTER GAOL, *October 23rd*, 1799.

" SIR,

" I say, also, peace to our controversy !
and I wish that every dispute of every kind could

terminate as amicably, and after such gentle litiga-
tion: the differences of opinion in mankind would
then issue in the general melioration of their tempers,
and the augmentation of mutual esteem; instead of
acrimony, revenge, and bloodshed. Only excuse my
unsolicited freedom of remonstrance.

" On the subject of Cicero, my opinions coincide
with yours: but as the turn of my disposition has
led me to inquiries connected with the history of
human intellect, and human opinions; with the
events of antient times, and the rise and progress
of philosophy; to subjects also more immediately
conversant with philology and criticism, and the
theory of language; my attention and affection have
been fixed on his *philosophical* works, which I exceedingly reverence, rather than on his *orations* and
epistles, the repositories of private incidents, and personal and local manners. But I mean only to state
my propensities, not to extol them, or disparage the
pursuits and predilections of other students.

" What immediately led me to that conjecture in
Ovid, was, an instantaneous repugnance of feeling to
the connection of *qualem* with the participle *incultus :*
and I am very much inclined to think, (for confidence
on these points, of all others, is most inexcusable and
absurd,) that no similar instance will readily be discovered; in which case I should be much more tenacious of the conjecture.

" In appreciating the comparative excellences of
different poets, the first praise seems due to *invention :* and, as I should always omit Homer in these

competitions, from our entire ignorance of the circumstances under which he wrote, and of the assistances which he might receive, no poet of antiquity seems capable of supporting the contest with Ovid. Virgil has produced more perfect poems; but then his obligations for materials are commensurate with the number of his verses; and would be seen still more clearly, if Euphorion and Nicander were now extant, fragments only of whose congenial performances are preserved. Quintilian, with that candour which distinguishes all his judgments, under a strong bias in favour of his countryman, after his admirable comparison of Demosthenes and Cicero, acknowledges that the palm must be yielded in this respect, ' as Demosthenes made Cicero, in a great measure, what he was.' By the bye, I may appear impertinent in recommending to your notice what you know so well: but that chapter of Quintilian, in which the comparison between the Greek and Roman authors is instituted, appears to me one of the most interesting compositions in all antiquity. Horace, I think, has happily comprehended the constituent qualities of a poet in few words :

> Ingenium cui sit, cui mens divinior, atque os
> Magna sonaturum.——

" In the first endowment, fertility of invention and copiousness of thought, Ovid far exceeds his countryman : in the second, a noble enthusiastic fervour of imagination, whose effects are sublimity and pathos, some passages prove Ovid to have no superior among the sons of inspiration : see, in particular, many parts

of his Epistle of Dido to Æneas, Phyllis to Demophoon, and some others; his entire Elegy on the
Death of Tibullus, Metamorph. ii. verses 333 to 344,
vi. 426—433; and the whole story of Pythagoras,
xv. 60, &c., which has no parallel in the monuments
of human wit, to my fancy, among the Antients, (as
at once moral and delightful,) except the conclusion
of Lucretius's third Book, and the adventures of
Ulysses with Alcinous in Homer. Very few readers
have attended more to the peculiarities of elegant
construction and curious phraseology, whether of
figure or combination, than myself; and I find such
exquisite specimens and varieties in no poet, as I find
in Ovid : while, as Quintilian says of Cicero, to the
best of my recollection,—'hæc omnia fluunt illa-
borata; et ea, quâ nihil dulcius esse potest oratio,
præ se fert tamen felicissimam facilitatem.'—As to
the third quality, magnificent language, Virgil has no
rival there.

" I am sorry that you gave yourself the trouble of
transcribing Porson's Note, as his Orestes is one of
the few books which I have got with me. At present,
I am reading some voluminous Greek prose writers,
with a view to my Lexicon incidentally; so that I do
not expect to be able to read through the Tragedians
for some months yet; when I shall pay particular
regard to the points in controversy : in the meantime, I wish not to be positive, but open to conviction. But my persuasions about the final ν are
grounded on this sort of reasoning.

" It is not for us, at this time of day, to lay down

the laws of Greek composition and versification, but to inquire into the actual practice of the Antients. Now it is most certain, that the old editions and old Scholiasts so generally omit the ν, where modern editors interpolate the letter, as to induce a most probable conviction, that it was *universally* omitted by the Antients ; and that the few present exceptions are the officious insertions of transcribers and publishers, who would ' be wise above what was written ;' and modelled the MSS. by their own preconceptions of propriety. Whereas, from the current persuasion, among modern scholars, of the necessity of support to these short syllables by the application of consonants, it is perfectly inconceivable that they should have left the syllables in question unsustained, had they found the ν in their copies. Nay, it cannot be doubted, but modern editors, like Porson, would invariably supply the ν in all those places where early editors were contented to omit it in obedience to their authorities ; and, if the early editions were lost, all traces of the old practice, as it should seem to be, would presently be obliterated beyond recovery.

" I have been furnished with many opportunities of observing PORSON, by a near inspection. He has been at my house several times, and once for an entire summer's day. Our intercourse would have been frequent, but for *three* reasons : 1. His extreme irregularity, and inattention to times and seasons, which did not at all comport with the methodical arrangements of my time and family. 2. His gross addiction to that lowest and least excusable of all

sensualities, immoderate drinking: and 3. The un-
interesting insipidity of his society ; as it is impossible
to engage his mind on any topic of mutual inquiry,
to procure his opinion on any author or on any passage of an author, or to elicit any conversation of any
kind to compensate for the time and attendance of
his company. And as for Homer, Virgil, and Horace,
I never could hear of the least critical effort on them
in his life. He is, in general, devoid of all human
affections ; but such as he has are of a misanthropic
quality : nor do I think that any man exists, for
whom his propensities rise to the lowest pitch of
affection and esteem. He much resembles Proteus
in Lycophron :

$$\text{———— } \tilde{\omega} \; \gamma\epsilon\lambda\omega s \; \alpha\pi\epsilon\chi\theta\epsilon\tau\alpha\iota,$$
$$\text{Και } \delta\alpha\kappa\rho\upsilon\text{———}$$

though, I believe, he has satirical verses in his
treasury for Dr. Bellenden, as he calls him (PARR),
and all his most intimate associates. But, in his
knowledge of the Greek Tragedies, and Aristophanes ;
in his judgment of MSS. and in all that relates to the
metrical proprieties of dramatic and lyric versification,
with whatever is connected with this species of
reading ; none of his contemporaries must pretend to
equal him. His grammatical knowledge also, and his
acquaintance with the antient lexicographers and ety-
mologists, is most accurate and profound : and his
intimacy with Shakspeare, B. Jonson, and other
dramatic writers, is probably unequalled. He is, in
short, a most extraordinary person in every view, but
unamiable ; and has been debarred of a comprehen-

sive intercourse with Greek and Roman authors by his excesses, which have made those acquirements impossible to him, from the want of that *time* which must necessarily be expended in laborious reading, and for which no genius can be made a substitute. No man has ever paid a more voluntary and respectful homage to his talents, at all times, both publicly and privately, in writings and conversation, than myself: and I will be content to forfeit the esteem and affection of all mankind, whenever the least particle of envy and malignity is found to mingle itself with my opinions. My first reverence is to virtue; my second, only to talents and erudition : where both unite, that man is estimable indeed to me, and shall receive the full tribute of honour and affection.—But I am transgressing the rules of decorum, by this immoderate περιαυτολογια, which yet, perhaps, is not unseasonable, and certainly wishes to stand exculpated in your sight.

" I am so wholly immersed in my studies, that my spirits are entirely recovered; and, with the abatement of solitude (which no man ever abhorred more), I never was more comfortable in my life. To this, the most extraordinary solicitude and affection of my friends, some of the most virtuous characters that ever existed, have contributed not a little : and in this confinement, if I live, I shall combat some of that severe and unkindly reading, in authors of less gaiety and elegance, which, in a happier situation, would have been contended with more tardily and reluctantly, if contended with at all. It will give you pleasure to be informed, that a former pupil sent me, about a month ago, from Jamaica, 1000*l.*

" I have occasionally looked in Cowper, though I possess him not. He appeared to me too frequently on the verge of the ludicrous and burlesque; but he deserves, I dare say, the character which you give him. Whilst I am in health, and able to endure fatigue, I mortify myself by keeping to my main pursuits,

——senex ut in otia tuta recedam:

hoping, if I live to grow old, that I may then indulge myself more freely in gayer literature. But surely Milton might have reconciled you to blank verse, without the aid of Cowper !

" I rejoiced to observe your Letter dated from your beloved retirement in the country ; but your in- formation respecting the amendment of your hand communicates but a mixed pleasure, if the gradual extrication of other fragments of the bones must be expected ; a process, I fear, attended with inflamma- tion and torture, in most cases of the kind. My best wishes attend you on all occasions ; and excuse me, if, in the French style, which appears to me most manly and becoming, even for the sake of variety itself, I conclude myself,

" Ever yours, with health and respect!
                    "GILBERT WAKEFIELD."

[The second of the two Letters from Mr. Wake- field, which the following of Mr. Fox shows to have intervened, is wanting.]

MR. FOX TO MR. WAKEFIELD.

"Sir,　　　　　"St. Ann's Hill, *November 22nd*, 1799.

"I am much obliged to you for your two Letters, and am very happy to find that your situation is become more easy than I had apprehended it was. If I should have an opportunity of getting you the use of any manuscripts from the persons you mention, or from any others, you may depend upon my attention to it. I know that Mr. Coke has some ; and I will write to a friend who goes often to Holkham, to inquire whether there are any worth your notice. I have looked at the quotation in Diodorus, which certainly, as far as it goes, makes much for your system ; but it is to be remarked, that some other parts of it stand in need of emendation ; and therefore the whole may be supposed not to have been very accurately transcribed. Since I wrote last to you, I have read three plays of Euripides ; and in them I find no less than five instances of that description, of which Porson, in his Note on the Orestes, supposes that there are none ' *indubiæ fidei.*' They are as follow : Medea, verses 246, 582. Troades, verse 628. Heraclidæ, verses, 391, 1044 ; and I have little doubt but in the rest of his works, and probably in those of the other Tragedians, instances would occur in nearly a similar proportion. Porson's assertion, therefore, appears to me so outrageous a neglect of fact, that he ought to be told of it. In his Notes upon the Hecuba, verses 347 and 734, he makes two very singular remarks, in

regard to metre, which (singular as they appear) are
nevertheless, as far as my observation goes, just : but
these were probably made upon much examination
and consideration, and not for a particular purpose of
supporting a new system, that had occurred to him,
of inserting the final v, where nobody else had done
it : to which he could be tempted by no other motive
than that of differing *toto cœlo* from you ; and saying,
' So far from listening to your advice of omitting the
v where others insert it, I will now insert it where
nobody ever thought of it.'   This is abominable.—In
regard to the *general* question of the final v, I agree
with you that it must depend, in a great measure, upon
MSS. ; and in so far as it does I am no judge of it,
never having seen any of the Tragedians, nor indeed
scarcely of any other Greek Poets : but, upon general
reasoning, I own I am inclined to preserve it, because
I think there is much in this argument.   Vowels of
a certain description are uniformly short in certain
given positions, with the exception of such of those
vowels only as occasionally admit the final v (for the
purpose of preventing the hiatus, &c.).   Is it not,
therefore, a fair conjecture, at least; and, if supported
by any one old MS., almost a certain one, that, in
such exceptions, the final v, which they, and they
alone, were capable of admitting, was added ?   Porson
uses this argument; but then he is not, as I have
shown you, supported by the fact.   I have read over,
possibly for the hundredth time, the portion of the
Metamorphoses about Pythagoras ; and I think you
cannot praise it too highly.   I always considered it

as the finest part of the whole poem ; and, possibly,
the Death of Hercules as the next to it. I think
your proposed alteration of ' pendet' to ' pandit,' is
a very fair one, if any is wanted ; but upon looking
into Ainsworth, the only Latin Dictionary I have, I
find that Pliny uses ' aranea' for the *down* that
appears on some parts of willow : now I think he
never could do this, unless ' aranea' meant the web
of a spider, as well as the animal itself. The Dictionary gives ' *spider's web* ' too, as one of the senses of
' aranea ; ' but then it cites only the very passage we
are upon, and is therefore nothing to the purpose.

"I own, I do not see why, in the passage of the
Fasti, ' defensæ ' should be certainly erroneous.
' Frondes defensæ arboribus,' instead of ' arbores
defensæ frondibus,' seems not unlike the poetical
diction of the Latin Poets in general ; but, if that is
wrong, at any rate the other old reading of ' excussæ ' is unexceptionable ; or, perhaps, a reading
compounded of the two might do, such as ' de-
cussæ.' The change of the punctuation in Juvenal is
clearly, I think, an amendment. I have read again
(what I had often read before) the chapter you
refer to of Quintilian, and a most pleasing one it is ;
but I think he seems not to have an opinion quite
high enough of our favourite Ovid ; and, in his
laboured comparison between Demosthenes and
Cicero, he appears to me to have thought them more
alike, in their manner and respective excellences,
than they seem to me. It is of them, I think, that
he might most justly have said, ' Magis pares quàm

similes.' I have no Apollonius Rhodius, and have
never read of him more than what there is in our
Eton *Poetæ Græci,* and the Edinburgh *Collectanea:*
but, from what I have read, he seems to be held far
too low by Quintilian; nor can I think the ' æqualis
mediocritas' to be his character. The parts extracted
in the above collections are as fine as poetry can be;
and, I believe, are generally allowed to have been
the model of what is certainly not the least admired
part of the Æneid: if he is in other parts *equal* to
these, he ought not to be characterised by *mediocrity.*
I wish to read the rest of his poem, partly for the
sake of the poem itself, and partly to ascertain how
much Virgil has taken from him: but I have not
got it, and do not know what edition of it I ought
to get: I should be much obliged to you if you
would tell me. Shaw's is one of the latest; but I
think I have heard it ill spoken of. If, at the same
time, you would advise me in regard to the Greek
Poets in general (of the second and third order,
I mean), which are best worth reading, and in
what editions, you would do me a great service.
Of Aratus, Nicander, Dionysius, Oppian, Nonnius,
Lycophron, I have never read a word, except what
has occurred in notes on other authors; nor do I
know what poems those are which Barnes often
alludes to, calling them *Troïca.* Against Lycophron,
I own, I am somewhat prepossessed, from hearing
from all quarters of the difficulty of understanding
him. The Argonautics, that go under the name of
Orpheus, I have read, and think that there are some

very beautiful passages in them, particularly the description of Chiron, &c. I have read, too, Theognis; and observed four verses in him that are full as applicable to other countries, as ever they could be to any city in Greece:

Λαξ επιβα δημω κενεοφρονι· τυπτε δε κεντρω
Οξεῖ, και ζευγλην δυσλοφον αμφιτιθει.
Ου γαρ εθ' εὑρησεις λαον φιλοδεσποτον ὡδε
Ανθρωπων, ὁποσους ηελιος καθορᾳ.

" I wish to read some more, if not all, of the Greek Poets, before I begin with those Latin ones that you recommend; especially as I take for granted that Valerius Flaccus (one of them) is in some degree an imitator of Apollonius Rhodius. Of him, or Silius Italicus, I never read any; and of Statius but little. Indeed, as, during far the greater part of my life, the reading of the Classics has been only an amusement, and not a study, I know but little of them, beyond the works of those who are generally placed in the first rank; to which I have always more or less attended, and with which I have always been as well acquainted as most idle men, if not better. My practice has generally been ' multum potius quàm multos legere.' Of late years, it is true that I have read with more critical attention, and made it more of a study; but my attention has been chiefly directed to the Greek language, and its writers; so that in the Latin I have a great deal still to read: and I find that it is a pleasure which grows upon me every day. Milton, you say, might have reconciled me to blank verse. I certainly, in common with all the world, admire the grand and stupendous passages of the Paradise Lost ; but yet, with all his study of harmony, he had not reconciled me to blank verse. There is a want of flow, of ease, of what the painters call a free pencil, even in *his* blank verse, which is a defect in poetry that offends me more perhaps than it ought : and I confess, perhaps to my shame, that I read the Fairy Queen with more delight than the Paradise Lost : this may be owing, in some degree, perhaps, to my great partiality to the Italian Poets.

" I have no doubt but your Dictionary will be a very interesting work, to those who love the Greek language ; but 20,000 new words seem impossible ; unless you mean, by new words, new significations of old words. I have some notions upon the subject of a Greek Dictionary that are perhaps impracticable, but, if they could be executed, would, I think, be incredibly useful : but this Letter is too unconscionably long to make me think of lengthening it by detailing them.

" My hand mends slowly, but regularly ; and I do not now think there will be any exfoliation of the bone, though that is not certain. I am very glad to hear your Jamaica pupil, whoever he be, has done both you and himself so much honour. I say nothing of the late surprising events : the ends may be good, but the means seem very odious.*   I shall think the degree of liberty they allow to the press the great criterion of their intentions.

" Yours ever,

" C. J. FOX."

* Mr Fox no doubt alludes to the 18th Brumaire, or 9th of November, 1799.

MR. WAKEFIELD TO MR. FOX.

"DORCHESTER GAOL, *November 27th,* 1799.

" SIR,

        " Our want of accord on the final *ν* and
critical emendations proves to me the necessity of a
work (of which all the materials are ready on my
papers) on the rationale of criticism, as founded on
philosophical principles, corroborated and ascertained
by the real practice of transcribers and indubitable
specimens from authors ; otherwise, no assent can
be expected in the majority of cases.   My argument
for the perpetual omission of the *ν* stands thus :   It
is universally allowed, that the early editors adhered
more closely to their MSS.   In their editions, the
final *ν* is *commonly* omitted.   In such works as Scholia,
of which few copies were circulated, that *ν* is *always*
omitted.   Good reasons may be assigned for the
occasional insertion, but none possibly for the omission.
Owners of MSS. have perpetually corrected them, as
we see at this day, according to their own fancy ;
and if Porson, for example, had them all, in time he
would put in the *ν* throughout ; and these MSS. might
go down as vouchers for the practice of antiquity.
Very little learning would suffice, to induce men to
insert *ν*, from an opinion of vicious quantity ; so that
a very old MS. now might abound in that insertion,
though its prototype were without it ; and so on.
But the acknowledged omission in innumerable
instances even now, and that obvious reason for its

insertion in the rest, when no possible solution can be given for the regular omission, induce, to my apprehension, a probability of the highest kind, that the Antients never used it at all.—More might be said; but this is the substance of the argument.

" In Ovid, Fast. iii. 537, the case stands thus: I find in books of authority two very different readings, *detonsæ* and *excussæ*. Whether either of these words will do, is by no means the first consideration. I want some probable account of this strange variation, which, like all other facts, must have a cause; and before the passage can be mended, a probable cause must be alleged. There is no resemblance in the letters; therefore we cannot satisfactorily suppose one word to have been mistaken for the other, by the transcriber's eye. I think, therefore, that Ovid gave *exustæ*. Why? 1. Because it resembles *excussæ* in its characters, and most likely in its pronunciation; so as to be confounded, either through eye-sight, or through dictation. 2. Because either *detonsæ* or *excussæ* may be reasonably supposed a marginal gloss, or interlineary interpretation of the word proposed; of which MSS. are full. 3. *Exustæ*, being an elegant word, and a word which implies some reading and taste to relish and understand it, would be readily superseded in the hands of a sciolist (whether transcriber, or owner of a MS.), by one more suited to his fancy; such as the other readings. These are my reasons; none of which can be assigned for the other two words. If now it should be said, that either of the other will do, I say, No: 1. Because no man, I dare say, can bring me any passage, from all antiquity, in which frost or cold is said ' *tondere* folia,' or any thing like it. 2. Because *excussæ* and its kindred are words of *violence*, and, I will venture to affirm, are never applied to the gentle and gradual operation of a *frost*. (Excuse me, if I appear positive : it is only in the expression, which one acquires from the study of mathematics ; where, after constructing the figure, it is usual to add, ' *I say*, the triangle so and so is the triangle required.') And with respect to phrases, I have noted their peculiarities so copiously in my own Dictionary, that I speak with some confidence, on that account merely, with respect to them.

"Apollonius Rhodius was a great grammarian, as well as a poet ; and therefore you should by all means have an edition with the Scholia. Shaw's, though of no value as a critical work, is prettily printed, has the Scholia, and a most excellent Index ; and is therefore a very commodious book for use. You should get the last 8vo edition. Brunck, however, it is impossible to do without, on account of his accuracy, and his MSS. It is a 12mo, not very easily got : there was one at Lackington's the beginning of this year. Stiffness, and want of perspicuity and simplicity, appear to me the failings of Apollonius Rhodius.

"Aratus, as a versifier, is much in the same style ; and in language harsh and difficult, partly from his subject. His *Phænomena* will hardly be relished, but by the lovers of astronomy ; but his other work, on the Signs of the Weather, must be read, as it has

been translated nearly by Virgil, in Geo. i. The
small Oxford edition is the best I know : it is become scarce and dear. I rather think they are
republishing this poet in Germany. You would
know by inquiring at Elmsley's. This poet has been
little read, and seldom published.

" Nicander you will never have patience to read,
I think ; otherwise, he was also a great linguist, but
as obscure at least as Lycophron ; though his (Nicander's) obscurity is in the quaint and learned phrase,
not in the meaning. His first poem, of about six
hundred verses, treats of vegetable, mineral, and
animal poisons, and their remedies : his second, of
about a thousand verses, of noxious animals, their
bites and stings, and remedies. They are good for
me, as a Lexicon compiler, and a scholar by pro-
fession ; but I cannot recommend them to you.

" Dionysius Periegetes is, to my mind, the sweetest
and simplest writer, both for verse and diction, of all
the Greeks, far and wide, after Homer. The best
and pleasantest edition, to my knowledge, is Stephens's, or the Oxford, which may easily be procured. They are very numerous. There are also
some London editions ; but beware of Wells's mutilated and interpolated edition, for the use of Westminster School.

" Oppian is very puerile, and writes in a false
taste ; but his descriptions are entertaining and
exact. He alone, of all the Antients, delineates the
camelopard very accurately, and from nature. He
will recompense the trouble of perusal. The best

edition is Schneider's. Ballu, a Frenchman, began a very pretty edition; but the *Halieutics*, by him, have not yet appeared. Rittershusius' also is not amiss.

"Nonnus was a Christian poet of much later date than the former; of a most puerile and romantic cast: wrote a poem as long as all Homer: difficult to be procured, and not likely to approve himself to you. He versified also, pleasantly enough, John's Gospel.

"Lycophron by all means read, in Potter's later edition. A spirit of melancholy breathes through his poem, which makes him, with his multitude of events, as delightful to me as any of the Antients. I have read him very often, and always with additional gratification. His poem is delivered in the form of a *prophecy;* and therefore affects an ænigmatical obscurity, by enveloping the sentiment in imagery, mythological allusions, and a most learned and elaborate phraseology. Most obscure in himself, he is rendered perfectly plain and easy by his scholiast, Tzetzes, who was a Jew. No man equal to him in the purity of his iambics; so that anapæst, tribrachys, and dactyl, are extremely rare in him. His narrative of the adventures of the Grecian chiefs, particularly Ulysses, after the fall of Troy, is infinitely interesting; and his prospect of Xerxes' expedition into Greece, the devastation of his army, &c., is nobly executed. You cannot fail, I think, after the first difficulties are surmounted, to like him much.

"No resemblance, but in the name of the poem, between Apollonius Rhodius and Valerius Flaccus.

He and Statius have ideas and expressions frequently beyond Virgil. Varro wrote an Argonautic Expedition, which Valerius Flaccus may possibly have imitated.

"The Classics have been your *amusement*, not your *study*. Alas! the reverse has been the case very much with me. I have always reckoned upon amusing myself, if I live to grow old; and have been therefore resolutely *labouring*, under almost every species of disadvantage, in my youth. On this account I never purchased Cowper : I have met with him occasionally. He appears to me a man of fine genius; but his *Task* borders too much on the burlesque for a fine poem. My revisal of Pope's Homer led me to read his translation of the Greek; and of all the miserable versification in blank verse, that is the most miserable I have yet seen. I have scarcely any books here; but I remember the beginning of Odyssey X. to be the most calamitous specimen of want of ear that ever came under my notice. It would be rash in me to give an opinion of his versification elsewhere; but between *his* versification in Homer, and that of Milton's *Paradise Lost*, there is, to my sense, as great a difference as can exist between two things that admit comparison at all. The *Faery Queen* stanza was always tiresome to me.

"You would cease to wonder at my twenty thousand words, if you saw my Lexicons; words good and true. You may cease also, when I mention that there are at least as many words of Nicander as that poet has verses, in no common Lexicon; two

or three hundred in Oppian, as many thousand in
Nonnus; and when I mention further, that in a day,
one day with another, when I am occupied in this
work, I at least add twenty from my reading, for
months together; some, original words; the generality compounds.   What think you of five hundred
solid and nervous words on the margin of my Johnson, not found in him, from *Milton* only; and perhaps two hundred from the same source, which Johnson gives, but without authority?

"I am very glad to hear so good an account of
your hand.

"I am, Sir,

"Your obliged friend,

"GILBERT WAKEFIELD."

TO THE SAME.

"DORCHESTER GAOL, *March*, 1800.

"SIR,

"I trouble you with the Proposals for my
Lexicon; an enterprise of such magnitude, and such
ungrateful labour, as almost overpowers my mind in
the prospect of it.   Had some of our most opulent
countrymen your taste and zeal for antient literature,
a small portion of your superfluous wealth would be
readily applied to a much more complete performance,
which would not reach above two good volumes in
folio; and the civilisation of our present barbarous
manners would be essentially promoted, I think, by
the promotion of useful letters.   In general, I have
been always desirous of considering sound learning

and virtuous manners as convertible terms,—generally, I say, not universally; and would willingly
subscribe to the truth of one of the noblest passages
in antient poetry :

$$\text{————— } ουτε \ γαρ \ ὕπνος,$$
$$Ουτ' \ εαρ \ εξαπινας \ γλυκερωτερον, \ ουτε \ μελισσαις$$
$$Ανθεα, \ ὅσσον \ εμιν \ Μωσαι \ φιλαι· \ οὑς \ γαρ \ ὁρευντι$$
$$Γαθευσαι, \ τως \ ου \ τι \ ποτῳ \ δαλησατο \ Κιρκα.$$

                    " I am, Sir,
                        " Your obliged servant,
                            "GILBERT WAKEFIELD."

                MR. FOX TO MR. WAKEFIELD.

                        "St. Ann's Hill, *March* 12*th*, 1800.
    " Sir,
            " I received yesterday your Letter, with
the Proposals for the Lexicon. I see innumerable
advantages in an English interpretation; to which
the only objection is, that it will confine the sale to
this country: and, how far it may be possible to get
two thousand subscriptions for a work useful only
to English readers of Greek, I am afraid is doubtful.
If Schools and Colleges are excepted, the number of
those who ever even look at a Greek book in this
country is very small: and you know enough of
Schools, no doubt, to suspect that partiality to old
methods is very likely to make them adhere to Latin
interpretations, notwithstanding the clear advantage
of using for interpretation the language we best
understand. My endeavours to promote the work
shall not be wanting, and you will of course set me

down as a subscriber. My idea with regard to a
Greek Dictionary, which I hinted at in a former
Letter, was suggested by a plan of a French Dictionary, mentioned by Condorcet in his Life of Voltaire.
It is this : That a chronological catalogue should be
made of all the authors who are cited in the work ;
and that the sense of every word should be given,
first, from the oldest author who has used it ; and
then should follow, in regular chronological order,
the senses in which it was afterwards used by more
modern authors. Where the sense has not altered,
it should be observed in this manner : ' Θεος, *a God.
Homer : and is used in the same manner by the other
authors.*' Thus we should have a history of every
word, which would certainly be very useful ; but
perhaps it would require a greater degree of labour
than any one man could perform. Condorcet says,
that Voltaire had offered to do one letter of a Dictionary upon a principle something like this : but, even
if he would have kept his word, one letter of a *French*
Dictionary, upon this plan, would not be a hundredth
part of a Greek one ; for, besides the much greater
copiousness of the Greek, the great distance of time
between the early and the late writers must make a
Dictionary upon this principle more bulky when
applied to that language, (but, for the same reason,
more desirable,) than it would be in any other.

" Soon after I wrote to you last, I read Apollonius
(in Shaw's edition, for I have not been able to get
Brunck's); and upon the whole had great satisfaction
from him. His language is sometimes hard, and

very often, I think, prosaïcal; and there is too much
narration : but there are passages quite delightful to
me, and I think his reputation has been below his
merit.   Both Ovid and Virgil have taken much from
him; but the latter less, as appears to me, than has
been commonly said.   Dido is, in very few instances,
a copy of Medea; whereas I had been led to suppose
that she was almost wholly so: and of Hypsipyle,
whose situation is most like Dido's, Apollonius has
made little or nothing.   I have lately read Lycophron,
and am much obliged to you for recommending it to
me to do so : besides there being some very charming
poetry in him, the variety of stories is very entertaining.   Without Tzetzes I should not have understood,
however, a tenth part of him; nor would they,
perhaps, who treat this poor Scholiast with so much
contempt, have understood much more.   There
remain, after all, some few difficulties, which if you
can clear up to me, I shall be much obliged to you;
and upon which neither Canterus, Meursius, nor
Potter, give me any help.   The most important of
these is, that which belongs to the part where he
speaks of the Romans in a manner that could not be
possible for one who lived in the time of Ptolemy
Philadelphus, that is, even before the first Punic war.
Tzetzes speaks, it is true, of such an observation
having been made; but remarks only upon the absurd
way in which it has been expressed, without answering
the observation itself: and the other commentators
above mentioned are silent upon it.   I see no remedy
but leaving out verse 1226, and all the following

verses down to v. 1281; and in favour of doing this,
it is to be observed, that 1281 and 1282 have a much
more correct sense if they follow verse 1225, than
placed as they now are: for οἱ τὴν ἐμὴν μελλοντες
αιστωσαι πατραν cannot well apply to Æneas or the
Romans; and τοσαυτα, in v. 1286, naturally applies to
the *last-mentioned* calamities.   If these verses are to
stand, I think it must be admitted, that the poem is
not so antient as is supposed, and that, if the
author's name was Lycophron, it was not at least that
Lycophron who lived in Philadelphus's time.   If this
hypothesis is admitted, then Tzetzes' interpretation
of v. 1446 and the following verses is not so absurd
as the other commentators state it to be; and they
may very well relate to the first of the Ptolemies who
was in alliance with Rome (I forget his surname);
or still better to Philip of Macedon, if the poem was
written soon after his peace with Rome, and prior to
the Roman war with his son Perseus.   As the matter
now stands, the allusion is given up as desperate.
My next difficulty is in line 808, in regard to the
word ποσις, which, how it can describe Telemachus
(as is supposed) I cannot conceive.   The husband of
whom? of nobody mentioned before: certainly not
of the δαμαρτος, whom he killed: and if of her who
is mentioned after, she is called *sister*, and therefore
the word husband does not naturally refer to her; for
though she is supposed to be both sister and wife,
yet when you say 'the husband was killed by his
sister,' it cannot mean a sister that was wife too.
Scaliger, in his translation, has it 'frater:' and κασις

would do for the verse ; but even then the construction
is very hard, as the κασις must refer to the αδελφη
mentioned two lines after. As it now stands, I think
it must allude to some lost story, in which Telemachus,
or some son of Ulysses, is supposed to have killed his
own wife, and to have been killed in revenge by that
wife's sister, or his own. The difficulty does not
seem to be felt, at least it is not explained by the
commentators. I could not at first understand
ver. 407 ; but I thought I remembered something of
yours upon the subject; and, upon looking into your
notes upon Ion, I found it perfectly explained ; only
I cannot find in my Lexicons (I have only Stephens's
Thesaurus and Morell's Hederic) that πονη ever
signifies the string of a bow. In v. 1159, I find the
word εφθιτωμενης, from some such word as φθιτοω,
which I cannot find any where. Of this the commentators take no notice. In v. 869, I think πηδημα
is an incomprehensible expression, if the sense is as
is supposed (for I do not take it to have the double
meaning of the Latin word ' saltus ') ; and I understood it, before I looked at the comment, to be a
description of Venus herself, according to one of the
mythological accounts of her birth ; nor am I quite
sure I was wrong. The omission of the particle γε
after κογχειας, in the same line in one MS, would
rather favour my interpretation. If you have a
Lycophron with you, and much leisure, I shall be
obliged to you for your opinion upon some of the
above passages ; for, excepting these, I do not think
there are any about which I have much difficulty ;

though I may have forgot some, as I did not note down any whilst I was reading him : and there are, besides, many words new to me ; but where the commentators have taken notice of them, and so explained them that I can acquiesce in their explanation, I do not trouble you with them.   The passage you quote from Theocritus is most beautiful : I suppose Horace took his idea of his

Quem tu, Melpomene, semel——

from it ; for, besides the general resemblance of the sentiment, the shape in which it is put seems exactly the same ;

Ους γαρ ὁρητε, τως ουκ, &c.
Quem tu videris, illum non, &c.

I have written it ὁρητε, because I understand, from my edition, that is the oldest reading; and if so, I think the change of Porson rather an elegance than a defect: not that I should think it worth while to alter it, which ever way it stood.   At any rate, I like ὁρευντι γαθευσαι, as you write it, better than ὁρωσαι γαθεωσι, which is in the text of my edition.

" You have heard from the newspapers, of course, of my going to the House of Commons last month. I did it more in consequence of the opinion of others, than from my own ; and when I came back, and read the lines 1451, 2, 3 of Lycophron,

Τι μακρα τλημων εις ανηκοους πετρας,
Εις κυμα κωφον, εις ναπας δυσπλητιδας
Βαζω, κενον ψαλλουσα μαστακος κροτον ;

I thought them very apposite to what I had been

about. In the last of the three, particularly, there is something of comic, that diverted me, at my own expense, very much. I mean

Βαζω, κενον ψαλλουσα μαστακος κροτον.

" I believe I ought to make you some apology for this long and tedious Letter; but trusting to your goodness, I shall make none, except that it is, in part, the consequence of that zeal for literature, which you suppose (and I hope, in general, truly—universally certainly *not*) leads to better things.

" Yours ever truly,

"C. J. FOX."

MR. WAKEFIELD TO MR. FOX.

"DORCHESTER GAOL, *March* 13*th*, 1800.

" SIR,

" I am very glad that you like Lycophron. The only exception to him is, that quaintness of phraseology which borders on burlesque : but I suppose the necessity of correspondence with the oracular style of antiquity produced this singularity, for the old oracles are altogether in this strain. Some time ago I sent for my Oxford Lycophron, — but great inconvenience attends the search of my books, —and an old copy of another edition came in its stead, which I cannot use commodiously. I expect the right book by the first convenient opportunity of conveyance; when I mean to read him again very attentively, and will keep in view your difficulties and doubts. In truth, I am very careful about this

migration of my library; because all my notes are
on the margins, and I am not fond of hazarding in-
considerately the labours of my life. These little
things are great to little men. The disadvantages
and vexations which this confinement has occasioned,
in this way, cannot easily be enumerated, and are
very irksome to my feelings.

"That disadvantage of an English interpretation
to the Lexicon was foreseen, and, on a general estimate, disregarded. I am not very solicitous for its
success; and shall abandon the project without reluctance, if the country does not furnish' encouragement sufficient for it. No word, properly speaking,
can have more than two senses: its primary *picture*
sense, derived from external objects and operations;
and its secondary and consequential: a rule which
would make short work, but very proper work, with
most Dictionaries; and reduce Johnson's strange
ramifications of meaning into twenty or thirty shoots,
to one *original* sense, and two or three shades of
inferential.

"What I once said of my number of additional
words, surprised you. I am reading Manetho, an
old astrologer, whom I have read before, but not
with this particular view; and one who probably
never came in your way. He is a good writer of
his class, and a most correct versifier; but deals very
largely in new words. Before your letter came, for
the gratification of my own curiosity, I had noted
all the words, not inserted in Hederic, which I had
met with since the morning. They amount to

seventy-two; and not so much as *two-thirds* of my day's work is yet finished.

" I should have thought that you might have got a Brunck's Apollonius Rhodius at Lackington's. They had several before my departure from the world. I shall begin him in a few days; and may perhaps trouble you with a few conjectures, though my principal copy is not here.

" To my mind, nothing was ever more soothing, in the melancholy strain, than many passages in Lycophron; but, as you justly observe, he would be absolutely unintelligible, in most parts, without his Scholiast, to whom more obligations are due, on that account, than to the Scholiast of any other author whatever.

" I never met with that reading, ὀρῆτε, in the second person, in that passage of Theocritus. I should except to it, because not in his way, as his poetry does not furnish a beauty of that kind. Milton very finely adopted it from Virgil, in his Evening Hymn :

> ———— Thou also mad'st the night,
> Maker omnipotent ! &c.

" In the next page but one of my Silv. Critica, (vol. i. p. 22,) where I have illustrated the verses of Theocritus by some very beautiful parallels, p. 23, are some excellent exemplifications of that sudden conversion to *address* from *narrative :* to which add Acts of the Apostles, xiii. 22, xiv. 22 ; for no writer has been more successful in this respect than Luke : see, too, Polybius, i. 344, Ernesti's edition.

"Your absentation from the House is a measure which always had my most entire concurrence; nor do I less approve your late appearance there : not that I expected any immediate benefit from your exertions; but because I think your friends and the public expected that effort from you. My opinion was, I own, (but I venture a dissent from you on any subject, and most of all on this, with extreme diffidence,) that you should have absented yourself sooner; and for this plain reason : Such discussion and debate, in opposition to Ministers, contributed to encourage a delusion through the country, that measures were to be carried in that House by argument and the force of truth, when they certainly were not to be carried by such influence.

"There is another author, Tryphiodorus, who is short, and therefore not very troublesome in that respect, whom you might wish to read : Merrick published an edition of him, with an excellent English translation : an edition has been given also by a pupil of mine, Mr. Northmore : either are easily procurable, and you would not regret the bestowal of two or three hours upon him.

"No apology is necessary for any application to me on these subjects. I shall be abundantly recompensed, if my superior assiduity may enable me to contribute any particle of gratification to your studies.

"I remain, Sir,

"Your obliged friend,

"GILBERT WAKEFIELD."

MR. FOX TO MR. WAKEFIELD.

"St. Ann's Hill, *March 14th*, 1800.

" Sir,

"I have received your letter, and will
certainly write to Lord Ilchester, and apply, through
some channel that may be proper, to the persons you
mention; or take such other measures as, upon consultation with my nephew, may be thought advisable.
In regard to the question of submitting to extreme
extortion, if it should come to that, I confess myself
not to be of the stout side, unless it should be necessary upon a prudential principle, which I hope it is
not.   A person in your situation is not called upon
for any voluntary sacrifices to public considerations,
for which he already suffers quite sufficiently.

" Yours ever,
"C. J. FOX."

TO THE SAME.

"St. Ann's Hill, *March 19th*, 1800.

" Sir,

"My nephew writes me word that he is to
see Mr. Moreton Pitt, who, I believe, has more influence, in regard to the prison, than any of the other
magistrates.   When I mentioned *prudential* reasons,
it was not with a view to discourage them, but on
the contrary.   But with regard to the effects of an
ill example, I am clearly of opinion that your situation
dispenses with your making any sacrifice to such a

consideration, when put in competition with your ease and convenience.

" I am much obliged to you for what you mention in regard to the Anthologia, which I shall attend to, as well as to your recommendation of Hales of Eton. I thought the principal beauties of the Anthologia would be in Brunck's Analecta; a book which I have not yet got, though it is a year since I commissioned my bookseller to get it for me. I believe the next Greek author I shall read will be Diogenes Laertius.

" Yours ever,
" C. J. FOX."

" P. S. Till I know the result of Lord Holland's application to Mr. Pitt, I think it best to delay any other application ; but, you may depend upon it, whatever my nephew and I can do, shall be done."

MR. WAKEFIELD TO MR. FOX.

"DORCHESTER GAOL, *March 20th*, 1800.

" SIR,

" It is well that you have not obtained Brunck's Analecta; because Jacobs' is a republication of the very book, with infinite improvement ; and may be had, except the last volume, at any time, I should think, of Elmsley, if not of your own bookseller.

" Another book I forgot to mention, as worthy of

your notice—the edition of *Orpheus de Lapidibus*, by that very modest and most ingenious person, the late Mr. Tyrwhitt : but take care that his Dissertation on Babrius, with the exquisite fragments of that neat and simple writer, be annexed. Scarcely any loss is more to be regretted than that of Babrius, as you will judge from his remains ; which I think it probable that you may not have seen collected.

" When you are at a loss, Quintus Calaber would amuse you, from the light which his long poem throws on the Trojan war : and his connection, in these respects, with the nobler poets confers an indirect and incidental value on his rambling, and, in general, puerile performance.

" It is singular, and probably you might observe it, that all the words quoted from Lycophron, in Morell's Hederic, are stated as being found in Lycurgus : ' *Lycurg.*' at least in my 4to edition of 1790. And, on the subject of mistakes, Is it not also extraordinary, that the verses from Shakspeare, which are put at the head of the daily occurrences in the *Morning Chronicle*, have been wrongly arranged to this day, through the last ten years, the term of my acquaintance with the paper?

" I am sorry that you do not readily procure Brunck's Apollonius Rhodius. The text is wonderfully improved from his MSS. ; and my doctrine of the final *v* evinced beyond all dispute. Brunck, however, did not see, or would not acknowledge, the omission to that extent in which I maintain it ; and, you will perceive, involves himself accordingly in numerous embarrassments and self-contradictions, both in that edition, and his edition of the Tragedians.

" I remain, Sir,

" Your obliged friend,

"GILBERT WAKEFIELD."

SAME TO SAME.

" DORCHESTER GAOL, *April 8th,* 1800.

" SIR,

" As Mr. M. Pitt is going to town to-morrow, and the Duke of Grafton and Lord Holland have promised to see him, an application at the same time to Mr. Frampton could not fail of a beneficial effect; who, during Mr. Pitt's absence in Ireland, has interested himself much in the affairs of this place.

" It should be understood that I want no interference with A. in the management of his own family, or the disposal of his house; but merely a provision, by the Magistrates, of a place where I shall not perish with the inclemency of winter, if A. will not continue me under his roof at the expiration of this year. Mr. F. will receive another application, through his tutor, Dr. Huntingford, warden of Winchester College, with whom I have occasionally communicated by letter in former days.

" You will find in the Life of Diogenes, in Diogenes Laertius, whom you spoke of as your next author to be perused, many diverting applications of Homer's verses; and if you have Casau-

bon's Athenæus, the Index prefixed will point out
a most ludicrous appropriation of the initial verses
of Sophocles' Electra, by a celebrated courtesan.
If you should not discover the place, or not have
an Athenæus at hand, I will relate the circumstance for your entertainment, when less incommoded
by the pressure of those inconveniences which
attend these sudden movements at this place; for
I learn but this moment, Mr. Pitt's intention to visit
London before the Sessions.

" I am, Sir,

" Your obliged friend,

"GILBERT WAKEFIELD."

MR. FOX TO MR. WAKEFIELD.

"St. Ann's Hill, *April* 13*th*, 1800.

" Sir,

          " I have not yet begun Diogenes Laertius,
having been a good deal occupied of late.   The little
Greek I have been reading lately has been in Pindar,
where I confess I find some difficulties; nor have I
yet met with any passages equal in beauty to those
odes of his which are in the Eton Extracts.

" I have Casaubon's Athenæus, but (owing perhaps
to my not knowing how to search them) I cannot
find, in any of the Indexes, the appropriation of the
beginning of Sophocles' Electra, which you mention.
In the list of plays quoted under the head of
Sophocles' Electra, it does not appear; nor can I

find it from the Index at the end, under the heads
of Phryne, Thaïs, or Laïs.

" I am, dear Sir.

" Yours ever,

"C. J. FOX."

SAME TO SAME.

"St. Ann's Hill, April 20th, 1800.

" Sir,

  " I have received a letter from Lord Ilchester, who promises to speak to Mr. Frampton.
My nephew has spoken to Mr. M. Pitt, who seems to
be very willing to do what is right, and says he will
speak with you concerning the business. A room at
the gaoler's, if it can be had on moderate terms, I
should think most eligible; and of your obtaining
that, either by Mr. M. Pitt's interference, or otherwise, I should hope there is little doubt.

" Pindar's Pythics appear to me much superior, in
general, to his Olympics : I do not know whether
this is a general opinion : however, the second
Olympic is still my favourite.

" I am, Sir,

" Yours ever most truly,

"C. J. FOX."

MR. WAKEFIELD TO MR. FOX.

"Dorchester Gaol, May 27th, 1800.

" Sir,

  " I received my Lycophron a little time

since; and have been reading him again. I have neither the proper books here, nor chronological memory, sufficient to judge of your objection to the authenticity of the passage from ver. 1226 to 1281, from the progress of the Roman conquests at that time: but a general objection arises to the latter parts of the poem, from the awkward poetical salvo in ver. 1373, which one aware of the prophetic character was not likely to have introduced. But is it incredible, that an attentive observer of the times, and the rising greatness of the Romans, might venture to predict the extent of their future sway in the general terms of ver. 1229, especially with Homer's example before him, Il. Υ. 307, 308? Just as that remarkable prophecy also of Seneca,

——————— venient annis
Secula seris, &c.

might readily force itself on the mind of a philosopher at all acquainted with the figure of the globe, and the disproportion of the terrestrial parts, then known, to the seas and ocean. The absence of my books disables me from specifying the tragedy and verse: but you will probably recollect the passage. The greatest singularity of this nature, which recurs to my memory, is an anticipated description of the Jesuits before the establishment of that fraternity; which is quoted, somewhere about the time of their origin, in the Notes to Mosheim's Ecclesiastical History—Maclean's translation.

"At ver. 807—812, I perceive no difficulty, but

one, occasioned by the word ποσις, rendered obscure
by its nearness to δαμαρτος, to which it does not refer.
I render thus, and understand: 'When he (Ulysses)
shall breathe out his life, lamenting the calamities of
his son and wife; which wife (Circe), *a* husband, or
married man, (namely, of Cassiphone the daughter,)
having slain, will himself go in the next place to the
grave, *killed off* by his sister (his relation), who was
the relation of Glaucon, &c.'

"The difficulty is increased by the expression of
ver. 809, which naturally carries you to Ulysses,
and his descent into the infernal regions; but may
easily mean, that she (the wife) went the πρωτην
οδον, for πρωτη *first;* and Telemachus went the
δευτεραν, or *after her:* which are common variations
of phrase.

"As to ver. 407, Παγην, or παγιν var. lect.
means a *snare;* and so, by inference, a *string,*
or *nervum;* as *bird-snares* were made of *nerves* or
strings.

"Your interpretation of ver. 869 is exceedingly
ingenious and just. Ἀρπη is used by Nicander for
any *pointed instrument* in general, as a *tooth,* &c.;
and στορθυγξ, στοινξ, and equivalent words, are used
in the Anthologia, and elsewhere, for that far-famed
implement in question; for which αρπη is a proper
term of disguise, in such a composition as the Cassan-
dra. Observe, also, how the congenial word θορος,
from θορω *salio,* agrees with πηδημα: and the θ' may
either be omitted, or remain, as the exordium of an
aggregate: ' doubling *both* the water, &c.' So that

your conception of the verse seems every way unexceptionable and appropriate.

" For myself, I seem arrived nearly at the end of my reading in this place, with my present stock of books; and my appetite is apt to flag with the hilarity of the season, and the tempting appearances of nature : so that I should not much object to a liberation at this time, with Lord Thanet and Mr. Ferguson : but

> Truditur dies die,
> Novæque pergunt interire Lunæ;

and will soon accomplish my desires, if not anticipated by a more arbitrary and speedy summons from this terrestrial existence.

" I remain, Sir,

" Your obliged friend,

" GILBERT WAKEFIELD."

MR. FOX TO MR. WAKEFIELD.

"St. Ann's Hill, *June* 20*th*, 1800.

" Sir,

" I have been a good deal occupied of late, which has prevented me thanking you sooner for your letter, in which you clear some of my doubts about Lycophron. I am very glad you approve of my conjecture about ἁρπη; but it is not even necessary to it that ἁρπη should bear the figurative sense you men-

tion. It may mean the instrument with which Saturn
mutilated his father Cœlus. I was aware the θ' or $\tau\epsilon$
was very consistent with my interpretation; but to
the common one it is absolutely necessary; and therefore its being absent from some of the old copies
makes in favour of my guess; for, in my supposition,
it may be there or not. I confess I cannot think it
possible, that Lycophron, writing before the first
Punic war, could speak of the Romans as he does:
besides, there is a passage, which I cannot immediately lay my finger upon, foretelling an alliance between the Romans (or at least the descendants of the
Trojans) and the Macedonians; which may allude
either to that between the Romans and Philip, or to
that between them and Ptolemy, but which, as a
particular fact, could never be guessed at so long
before it took place. The prophecy in Seneca's Medea
is very curious indeed. I once saw one relating to
the Jesuits in some history of Ireland (not certainly
Leland's) which may perhaps be the same to which
you allude. It appeared to me to be the most extraordinary thing of the kind I had ever met with; so
much so, that I am very sorry I did not take a
note of the book and page. I will endeavour to
recover it. Homer's I do not think much of, as
it is easily explained by the supposition that in
his time Æneas's posterity were in power somewhere: whether in Asia, or in Europe, the words
are equally applicable.

"In one of your Letters, long since, you men-
tioned that Dawes said, that instead of $\iota\lambda\alpha\sigma\sigma\omega\mu\epsilon\theta$'

ανακτος, it was in the Florentine edition ἱλασομεσθα, so that the digamma was respected. I have lately been extravagant enough to purchase the Florentine edition; and find that it has ἱλασσωμεθ', like the other editions: the line is in the A. 444.

" I am truly glad that you have settled your own business. I never supposed I could have any influence with Mr. Frampton. His father-in-law, I think, would be glad to oblige me, and, even independently of such a wish, would be of the good-natured side of any question.

" I like parts of the imitation of Juvenal very much : it is full of spirit. You do not say by whom it is.

" Yours ever,

"C. J. FOX."

MR. WAKEFIELD TO MR. FOX.

"Dorchester Gaol, June 21st, 1800.

" Sir,

" No apology for any interval of time in noticing my Letters is at all necessary. I usually send answers immediately, partly from regular practice, and partly from want of room in this place; so that what once is dismissed from my sight on the table, is in danger of being totally forgotten. But I make no requisitions of any one.

" I cannot now recollect what I said about Homer, Il. A. 444; but I probably misrepresented what

Dawes asserted, from defect of memory. Common editions have ἱλασσωμεθ᾽ ανακτα. My Florentine, which is now open before me, has ἱλασσωμεσθα ανακτα, which you see is removed from what is apprehended to be the truth, ἱλασομεσθα, by only very common and accountable variations, the doubling of σ, and long for short ο. If it be in yours, as you state, ἱλασσωμεθ᾽, it is very strange. I collated the Florentine soon after I came hither, and found it less serviceable than I expected. A good deal of suffrage in the final ν; but as much in the Etymologicon Magnum. See Od. Γ. 419. Some small confirmation of the proposed correction for Il. A. 444, exists in Etymologicon Magnum, p. 97, in as far as ο for ω; for the author, though the passage is most corrupt, very evidently refers to the verse in question.

" I am, Sir,

" Your most obliged friend,

"GILBERT WAKEFIELD."

MR. FOX TO MR. WAKEFIELD.

"St. Ann's Hill, *June 26th*, 1800.

" Sir,

" It is very extraordinary, that our copies of the Florentine Homer should be so different. In mine, the dedication to which (to Peter of Medicis, the son of Lawrence) is dated 1488, it is most distinctly, as I stated, ἱλασσωμεθ᾽. Observe, that the ι is marked with the *lenis*, instead of the aspirate.

As my eyes are very indifferent, I at first thought it might be a mistake of mine, and that there was a thickness at the bottom of the θ, which might stand for a σ; but I observe it is quite the same letter as in Φοίβῳ θ' ἱερην ἑκατομβην, in the preceding line; and the mark of elision at the end, instead of the a is quite clear. Its being ἱλασσωμεσθα in your copy, is a clear justification of the reading ἱλασομεσθα, if that use of the future is common in Homer, which upon mere recollection, I cannot say. This variation between our copies is a very singular circumstance.

"You see the turn affairs have taken in Italy. God send it may lead to a peace !

"Yours ever,

"C. J. FOX."

MR. WAKEFIELD TO MR. FOX.

"Dorchester Gaol, *June* 28*th*, 1800.

" Sir,

"When Heath recommended a reading in Sophocles on the authority of the second Justine edition, Brunck, who had never seen that edition, nor knew indeed of its existence, made himself merry at the expense, as he supposed of our countryman, ' as if he had got an impression of Sophocles made on purpose for himself.' I did not entertain so high an opinion of you, as to suppose the Fates to have gifted the Italian typographers with a prophetic impulse for a provisionary accommodation of a

Florentine Homer to your future purposes, in exclusion of all other admirers of that poet: but rather concluded, from your accuracy on these occasions, that two different impressions of this work, much at the same time, must have gone abroad, as the product of the same operation; as we know of two Aldine Demosthenes, and two Baskerville's Virgils, only distinguishable by the more knowing dealers in these articles.

"The verse in question is most distinctly and unambiguously written at length in my copy, and stands the second in the right-hand page; perfectly conformable to my former representation of it. I suspect yours to be some spurious and managed copy: of the legitimacy of my own, its pedigree will not suffer me to doubt. Its original owner, of late years, was Mr. Cracherode: it is a very fine copy; but when its curious possessor procured a finer, it past over to the library of Lord Spencer; and he, on procuring one more suited to his taste, transferred it to Edwards the bookseller, who conveyed it to my hands for a large-paper Lucretius: so that it exhibits a genealogy almost comparable to that of Agamemnon's sceptre, or Belinda's bodkin. The knowing ones, who must occasionally come in your way, will be able, I dare say, to solve your doubts, and clear up the difficulty. If a surreptitious copy has been foisted on you, it will be prudently returned to its late owner; who, if a craftsman, might be aware of its illegitimacy. But I speak merely from conjecture, founded on the facts, which our respective copies unquestionably would furnish in greater numbers, from more minute comparison of passages.

" With reference to the conclusion of your favour : in other circumstances, I might say, that I was so affected, as not to know whether my head or heels were uppermost. In my present situation, I shall employ language more significant and appropriate, if I say, that I scarcely know whether I am in a prison, or without. For that man (whom I have long revered), and for every son of peace and mercy, my aspiration is, what is inscribed on the entrance of our cloisters in Jesus College : PROSPERUM ITER FACIAS !—My spirit is with him and them.

" It amazes me, that any man can pretend to believe in Revelation, (and these pretenders are very numerous,) and not see, if he read but a page of Christ's lectures in the Gospel, that his religion, and every hostile propensity, much more actual and offensive war, are not only incompatible with each other, but the most unequivocal contradiction in terms.

" I remain, Sir,

" Your obliged friend,

"GILBERT WAKEFIELD."

" Οφρα, which I omitted to mention, is very variously employed in Homer : a similar government and power of the word may be seen in verse 147 of the same book."

MR. FOX TO MR. WAKEFIELD.

"ST. ANN'S HILL, *October 17th*, 1800.

" SIR,

" You mentioned to me, some time since, a wish to have the perusal of some MSS. of the Classics that may be in private libraries. I shall go to Mr. Coke's, at Holkham, the beginning of next month; who has, as I understand, several, which I will look at : but if there are any particular authors of more consequence to you than others, I wish you would give me a hint, and I will endeavour to get the loan of them for you. I have not been able yet to account for the difference between my copy of the Florence Homer and yours ; but have desired an intelligent person to examine such other copies as may fall in his way.

" I am, Sir,

" Your friend and servant,

"C. J. FOX."

MR. WAKEFIELD TO MR. FOX.

"DORCHESTER GAOL, *October 18th*, 1800.

" SIR,

" I thank you for this recollection of my request. The loan of any Greek MS., prior in date to the invention of printing, will be acceptable, of any poet, except Aristophanes ; and of prose writers, Clemens Alexandrinus and Philo Judæus. Of the Latin poets, Silius Italicus, Valerius Flaccus ; and Virgil, if very antient and uncollated, otherwise a MS. of him cannot be presumed of much utility.

" Suffer me to employ this opportunity of thanking you for your Address to your Electors : it was seasonable, spirited, and judicious. I know no men, who pour out such an abundance of practical good sense on all subjects, intelligibly to the meanest capacities and instructively to the best, as Dr. Paley (I wish that he did not sophisticate too frequently against his convictions, in vindication of his craft), Dr. Priestley, and the man who is now addressed

" By his obliged servant,

"GILBERT WAKEFIELD."

MR. FOX TO MR. WAKEFIELD.

"St. Ann's Hill, *January 26th,* 1801.

" Sir,

" I was at Holkham this year a much shorter time than usual; and I am ashamed to say, that I could not find time to do what I certainly had voluntarily engaged to do, by searching the library. Partly a *malus pudor,* and partly an expectation of hearing from Mr. Wilbraham that he had repaired my omission, have prevented me hitherto from giving you this account : but it is the true one, nor will I attempt at any palliation. Clemens Alexandrinus, if I remember right, was the author you particularly mentioned, as a manuscript you most desired.

" I am much afraid that it will be much longer than you seem to think, before Europe will be delivered from the horrors of war ; if that be the delivery to which you look. If you mean only a deliverance from the odious projects of our Ministers and their allies, I consider that as already in effect accomplished.

" I am at present engaged in an attempt to write a History of the times immediately preceding and following the Revolution of 1688. Whether my attempt will ever come to any thing, I know not ; but, whether it does or not, I shall grudge very much the time it takes away from my attention to poetry and antient literature, which are studies far more suitable to my taste. However, though these studies are a good deal interrupted, they have not wholly ceased ; and therefore I should be obliged to you, if you would tell me your opinion concerning the best edition of Æschylus. I see, in a Catalogue now before me, that I can have Pauw's for four guineas, which, if it be the best, I do not think much. I have no edition of this poet at all ; and, consequently, have not of late years read any of his plays, except the Eumenides in your collection. Some passages are grand indeed ; but there is a hardness of style, and too continual an aim at grandeur, to be quite to my taste. I think I have heard that there are detached editions of some of his plays that are worth having. Now I am troubling you upon these subjects, If I have time only to read one or two of Aristophanes' plays, which would you recommend me? I never read any of them.

"I suppose Porson's parenthesis, in his Note on the Phœnissæ, ver. 1230, is meant to apply to the Tragedians exclusively. Whether, even so applied, it be true, I doubt; but if applied generally, it is ridiculous. The parenthesis is, "Neque enim diphthongus ante brevem vocalem elidi potest."

"The more I consider the passage I once before mentioned to you in Lycophron, the more I am convinced that it is morally impossible that a man living in the time of Ptolemy Philadelphus (that is, before the first Punic war) could have written the verses concerning Rome, beginning at ver. 1226; still less those beginning at 1446: and yet I believe nothing of the sort is more generally believed than that Lycophron did live in the time of Ptolemy Philadelphus. Tzetzes takes notice of the objection; but only cavils at the manner in which it is stated, without answering the substance of it. The other Commentators say nothing about it; only, as to ver. 1446, one of them is satisfied with saying that he does not know what it alludes to.

"I have to return you thanks for the Dio Chrysostom, which, however, I have not yet looked into.

"I am very truly, Sir,

"Your obliged servant,

"C. J. FOX.

" P.S. I cannot clear up the mystery of my Florence edition of Homer, differing from yours in the word ἱλασσωμεθ'. I begin to be afraid that mine must be a spurious copy ; but it has not the appearance of it. I have not seen any other Florence Homer lately, to compare it with ; but I have commissioned a friend to examine one."

MR. WAKEFIELD TO MR. FOX.

" DORCHESTER GAOL, *January 27th*, 1801.

" SIR,

"MSS., I know, are so scarce in this country, even in public libraries, that I had formed no flattering expectations from your researches at Mr. Coke's ; and, of course, shall feel but little disappointment at an unpropitious issue.

" Several visitors to me at this place had mentioned your engagement on that part of our political history which your letter specifies ; and I cannot but lament that you express yourself with any uncertainty respecting its accomplishment ; a failure which would occasion lasting regret to your friends in particular, and your contemporaries at large : nor do I learn with pleasure that your affections are not so cordially in unison with this important and interesting occupation, as with other studies, poetry and ancient literature.

" You will do well to purchase that edition of Pauw's Æschylus, unless it be a very inferior copy : four guineas, as times go, is a moderate price. Pauw contains the whole of Stanley, who was a very modest and learned man, of the Derby family; and the same who wrote the Lives of the Philosophers. Pauw's own Notes are of little worth: he was a noisy, boastful, and injudicious critic. The book is very neatly printed, and pleasant to the eye. Æschylus is pompous, but frequently sublime: his principal defect, as a dramatic writer, seems want of action. His Prometheus is interesting, as a collection of ancient mythology and history, not so distinctly preserved elsewhere: and Milton's Satan was most evidently formed on that character. The Septem ad Thebas is a fine delineation of heroic manners, but is made up, almost wholly, of descriptive speeches. His Persæ is not very interesting, and may be considered as a mere sacrifice to Grecian vanity. In the Agamemnon are some very sublime passages: part of a chorus in dialogue, verses 1560-1569, contains the bitterest irony, the most cutting insult, that ever was written, I think, by man. One feels more respect for the poet, from his distinction as a citizen, and his gallantry at the battle of Marathon.

"Schutz has published Æschylus: three volumes had come out before my arrival hither; and two more are expected, containing the last play, index, &c. They are become, I believe, enormously dear, and very scarce. I would not advise you to look after them, except you feel your thirst increase for a more elaborate perusal, after reading Stanley. The text of Æschylus is in a much less correct state than that of the other tragedians.

" The two most popular and most approved, plays
of Aristophanes, are the Ranæ and Plutus: but, to
say the truth, Plato and Aristophanes are the only
two celebrated authors of antiquity whom I never
could read through. Often have I determined to
surmount my disinclination ; and as often recoiled, in
the middle of my enterprise :—

—————— ter saxea tentat
Limina nequicquam ; ter fessus valle resedit.

" If a man loves nastiness and bawdry, he may
find both to satiety, *usque ad delicias votorum*, in his
Lysistratus, and other plays. I do not profess much
squeamishness and prudery on these points, as a
student : but an author whose object is principally
pleasure, and not utility, must bring with him either
sublime sentiment, magnificent language, or sonorous
verse, to rivet my affection ;—and there is nothing of
these in Aristophanes. Pure diction, easy versification, and coarse wit, are his excellences. But the
principal obstacle is that obscurity which attends all
writers whose chief object has been the delineation of
vulgar manners, and the transitory peculiarities of
the day. Brunck's edition is the most correct; but
you would scarcely understand him without the
Scholia, which are not in him, but may be read to
most advantage in Kuster. Perhaps you will prefer
procuring the common London edition, of the beginning of this century, which is easily procured, and
contains the *Nubes* and *Plutus*, with the Scholia.

" At the desire of the editor, I have reviewed,

in the Critical Review, two months ago, Porson's *Hecuba* and his *Orestes*, for the coming month. Porson will know the author; but I never yet did anything in this way which I wished to be concealed, though not ambitious to divulge it; nor am I at all fond of the reviewer's employment, nor engage in it but on particular solicitation.

" If I live to see London again, I shall take great pleasure in mentioning your difficulty on Lycophron to a gentleman, who has studied him more than any man living, I suppose. He is vicar or rector of some parish in Bread Street: his name is Meek; and he is rightly so called; for a more pacific, gentle, unassuming, human creature never did exist. He was somewhat senior to me at Cambridge.

" Some of my friends have very much urged me to give Lectures on the Classics; and, on a mature consideration of the project, I mean to make the attempt, by beginning with the second Æneid, when I leave this place. I shall not wish it to be regarded as a benevolent scheme, in the least degree; but as one, in which those on the spot, and interested in such pursuits, may expect to receive something like an equivalent for their money. When my proposals are digested and printed, I shall take the liberty of sending you one; more as a token of respect for your judgment, than with any desire of troubling your services on this occasion.

" I remain, Sir,

" Your respectful friend,

"GILBERT WAKEFIELD."

SAME TO SAME.

"Dorchester Gaol, *April 2nd*, 1801.

" Sir,

" I once mentioned, if I rightly recollect, my intention of troubling you with the enclosed plan ; supposing it probable that you might meet with an opportunity of speaking on the subject, if you should be in town.

" My printer, I expect, will have conveyed to you a small performance on the versification of the Greek epic writers. This trifle, which I could have printed in this country, since my commencement of authorship, for six pounds, and could now print in Paris for less than four pounds, has cost now no less than seventeen pounds. I congratulate myself more and more on abandoning my Lexicon, as the full list of subscribers would not have defrayed the bills of the stationer and printer. Indeed, all private adventure in the classical way, to any extent, is become utterly impracticable in this island ; and must benumb the activity, and destroy the engagements, of those who reposed the future comfort of their lives, in some measure, on these pursuits.

" Our joy on the near approach of liberation has been tempered by a severe affliction—the loss of our youngest child, on Sunday last. To express the miseries which my absence has occasioned to my wife and family, during an agonising illness, of alternate hope and despair, would look like an ostentation of sorrow, to all, but those who have been exercised in similar circumstances by a similar calamity.

"I remain, Sir,

"Your respectful friend,

"GILBERT WAKEFIELD."

MR. FOX TO MR. WAKEFIELD.

"St. Anne's Hill, *April 5th*, 1801.

"Sir,

"I am exceedingly concerned to hear of the loss you have sustained, as well as of the additional suffering which your family has experienced (as of course they must), from your separation from them during so trying a calamity.

"You mentioned to me before, your notion of reading Lectures upon the Classics, but not as a point upon which you had fully determined. If I can be of any use in promoting your views, I will not fail to do so: for in proportion as classical studies are an enjoyment to myself (and they are certainly a very great one), I wish them to be diffused as widely as possible.

"I have run over, with great pleasure, your dissertation upon the metre of the writers of Greek hexameters. There are one or two things that I am not quite sure that I understand, but upon which I have not time, just now, to trouble you with my doubts. The observations upon verses of the following form,

Εγνως, Εννοσιγαιε—εμην εν στηθεσι βουλην·

and on the aspirate in the pronouns οἶ, ὅς, ἕος, always
telling as a consonant, appear to me to be quite new,
and very striking.　I had myself observed how
sparing Homer is in leaving a vowel short between
two consonants, though one of them be a liquid; but
it seems strange, that the author of the Argonautics,
which go by the name of Orpheus, should have been
less scrupulous in this licence than poets of a period
more distant from Homer.　That poem is supposed
(is it not?) to have been written as early as the
age of Pisistratus.

" Yours ever,

" C. J. FOX."

MR. WAKEFIELD TO MR. FOX.

" DORCHESTER GAOL, *April 6th,* 1801.

" SIR,

　　" The project of my Lectures is a very
important event in my future life; but one, whose
success appears, I own, extremely doubtful to myself.

" The principal points of my metrical dissertation
seem tolerably well ascertained.　Some difficulties will
arise of impossible solution, partly from inexplicable
corruptions, and partly, perhaps, from the inconsistency and incorrectness of the writers themselves.
That hiatus in the middle of the third foot I once
mentioned to Dr. Parr, and desired his opinion on
it; but, as he revolted at the very mention of it,
and condemned it as a peculiarity unheard of, and

inadmissible, I made no reply, but concluded it to have been unobserved by all readers but myself.

"You quote me as speaking of οἱ, ὅς, and ἑος: whereas, my rule is not true of this last, nor of ἑοι, the substantive in the dative case. I suspect, that, in many cases, the aspirate has passed into a letter ; and that ἑοι, by the rule of dactyls, should frequently be substituted for οἱ. In antient inscriptions, the aspirate is found expressed by half the **H**, thus **⊢**, which, from quick writing, might easily pass into an ε, by the loss of two angles; as the present aspirate ' is exhibited in the Apollonius Rhodius with capital letters, and other books, in its primitive shape ⊦.

The author of the Argonautic Expedition, under the name of Orpheus, probably interwove in his poem verses from pure authors, who had previously treated this subject; of whose works various copies once existed, as appears from fragments in Suidas, and from other testimonies : but the present poem was evidently put into the form now extant by a writer of very late date, and probably some centuries posterior to the Christian æra.

" I remain, Sir,

" Your respectful friend,

" GILBERT WAKEFIELD."

[A letter from Mr. Wakefield to Mr. Fox seems to be wanting here.]

MR. FOX TO MR. WAKEFIELD.

" St. Anne's Hill, *April* 13*th*, 1801.

" Sir,

" Your story of Theseus is excellent, as applicable to our present Rulers ; if you could point out to me where I could find it, I should be much obliged to you. The Scholiast on Aristophanes is too wide a description.*

" The whole affair relating to the late changes is as unintelligible to me as to you. That there is some sort of juggle in the business, appears to me certain ; but to what degree is difficult to ascertain.

" I think, as you do, the success of your proposed Lectures doubtful ; but am rather inclined to be sanguine ; if I can do anything to promote it, you may depend upon me. The second book, upon which you propose to begin, is a delightful composition. If the lines omitted in the Medici Manuscript are spurious, they are, I think, the happiest imitation of Virgil's manner that I ever saw. I am indeed so unwilling to believe them any other than genuine, that rather than I would consent to such an opinion, I should be inclined to think that Virgil himself had written, and afterwards erased them, on account of their inconsistency with the account he gives of Helen, in the sixth book.

---

* The story of Theseus, as applicable to Mr. Addington, was quoted by Mr. Sheridan in the House of Commons. It came from Mr. Wakefield.

" I certainly quoted you erroneously, about ἑος, ἑοι, &c.; and I perfectly understand your observation to apply only to ἑο, οἱ, ἑ, ὁς, when in the possessive sense; and I suppose to εὑ, when used for ἑο, οὑ, for ἑο is not, I believe, used in Homer: οὑ, for οἱο, follows of course, I suppose, the rule of ὁς. I do not know whether you have remarked how very rarely in the Iliad the final iota of the dative plural is omitted before a consonant; and even, of the few instances that do appear, there are several in which there are various readings. In the one, therefore, which you mention on another account, it is an additional reason for preferring your reading;

Χειρεσιν αμφοτερῃσιν ανηρ φεροι·

because in the other, αμφοτερης φεροι ανηρ, the final iota is omitted. The preference of dactyls in the Greek hexameter Poets is certainly pretty general; but more remarkable, I think, in Apollonius, than in any other, except, perhaps, the Doric Poets. In Homer there appears to me to be more variety in this respect; and his versification is therefore, to my ear, the most agreeable: but there may be, and I suspect there is a great deal of fancy in this, on our part, who are so ignorant of the true antient mode of pronunciation. Virgil is, I believe, the most spondaïc amongst the Latin Poets; and sometimes evidently with a view to a particular expression, in which he is often very successful. I believe the following lines are in the third book of the Æneid, but I am not sure:

——————— Secretæ Troades actâ
Amissum Anchisen flebant, cunctæque profundum
Pontum aspectabant flentes ; heu! tot vada fessis, &c.

Every foot is here a spondee, except those in the fifth place ; and it seems to me to have a wonderful effect. There are two lines in the Iliad, one in the Λ. 130 ; the other in Ψ ; which, as they are now written, consist of six spondees each ; but I suppose they should be written,

ΑτρΕΙδης· τω δ’ αυτ’ εκ διφρΟΟ (or διφροϜο)—,

and

Ψυχην κικλησκων ΠατροκλΕΕος δΕΕλοιο.

"I remain, Sir,

"Yours ever,

"C. J. FOX."

MR. WAKEFIELD TO MR. FOX.

"Dorchester Gaol, *April* 14th, 1801.

" Sir,

" My Aristophanes with the Scholia is not here. If I am right in my recollection, the story probably occurs in the Scholia on the Frogs, and would soon be found by reference to the name of Theseus in Kuster's Index. Nor is my Burman's Virgil with me, whose margin contains my references: there I should probably have found the desired passage at Æn. vi. 617 ; and there, I doubt not, you will find references in Heyne's Virgil, which will conduct you to other authors of the story, Apollodorus and Pausanias, or their commentators. Heyne, you will see, mentions the fable without its jocular appendage ; not foreseeing your wishes on this occasion.

" Your supposition, that the verses in Æn. ii. were Virgil's own, and omitted by him, with the reason for that omission, pleases me entirely.

" Your opinion of a versification more dactylic in Apollonius Rhodius than Homer will scarcely continue with you, I think, after another trial or two. Where Homer appears spondaic, the cause is assignable often to a modern orthography, agreeably to a just remark of your own at the conclusion of your letter. It will scarcely be disputed, I believe, that the former verse, which you cite, Il. Λ. 130, should be thus written, as far as the present point is concerned:

$$Ατρε Fιδης· τοο δ' αυτ' εκ διφρο' εγουναζεσθην·$$

which makes great alteration of celerity.

" Your passage of Virgil is not in Æn. iii. but Æn. v. 613, where you should observe the sluggishness of the spondaïc measures to be relieved by two elisions, which, with a suitable rapidity of enunciation, become equivalent to dactyls. Have you never remarked also, in that same book, a stroke of nature and pathos nowhere surpassed, and, as far as is known, unborrowed from the Greeks ? What strains of immortality from verse 765 to 772 ! Heyne miserably mars the passage, by putting *nomen* for *numen* (the beauty of which he did not discover), into the text. *Numen* is the δαιμων, the EXISTING CIRCUMSTANCES, chiefly of a *melancholy complexion* (as those of our time and country), which influences or governs the man and his life at that crisis ; and the verse may be well compared with Æn. iii. 372, where also Heyne appears to be inaccurate.

" Your remark on the unfrequency of the termination ης in Homer, compared with succeeding Ionic writers, is entirely just.

" My reason for beginning my Lectures with the second Æneid was its superior importance to the first, and its priority in order to the other important books; which to me are, iii. v. vi. vii. and viii.

" I remain, Sir,

" Your respectful friend,

" GILBERT WAKEFIELD."

MR. FOX TO MR. WAKEFIELD.

" St. Anne's Hill, *April* 13*th*, 1801.

" Sir,

" I am much obliged to you for your letter; and found immediately, from Kuster's Index, the passage in question. It is in a note upon Ἱππεῖς, ver. 1365. The verses you refer to in the fifth Æneid are indeed delightful; indeed I think that sort of pathetic is Virgil's great excellence in the Æneid, and that in that way he surpasses all other poets of every age and nation, except, perhaps (and only perhaps), Shakspeare. It is on that account that I rank him so very high; for surely to excel in that style which speaks to the heart is the greatest of all excellence. I am glad you mention the eighth book as one of those you most admire. It has always been a peculiar favourite with me. Evander's speech upon parting with his son is, I think, the most beautiful

thing in the whole, especially the part from ver. 574;
and is, as far as I know, wholly unborrowed. What
is more remarkable is, that it has not, I believe, been
often attempted to be imitated. It is so indeed in
Valerius Flaccus, lib. i., v. 323, but not, I think,
very successfully.

Dum metus est, nec adhuc dolor——

goes too minutely into the philosophical reason to
make with propriety a part of the speech. It might
have done better as an observation of the poet's, in
his own person; or still better, perhaps, it would
have been, to have left it to the reader. The passage
in Virgil is, I think, beyond any thing.

Sin aliquem infandum casum——

is nature itself. And then the tenderness in turning
towards Pallas,

Dum te, care puer! &c.

In short, it has always appeared to me divine. On
the other hand, I am sorry and surprised, that, among
the capital books, you should omit the fourth. All
that part of Dido's speech that follows,

Num fletu ingemuit nostro?——

is surely of the highest style of excellence, as well as
the description of her last impotent efforts to retain
Æneas, and of the dreariness of her situation after his
departure.

"I know it is the fashion to say Virgil has taken a
great deal in this book from Apollonius; and it is
true that he has taken some things, but not nearly so

much as I had been taught to expect, before I read
Apollonius.   I think Medea's speech, in the fourth
Argonaut. ver. 356, is the part he has made most use
of.   There are some very peculiar *breaks* there, which
Virgil has imitated certainly, and which I think are
very beautiful and expressive : I mean, particularly,
ver. 382 in Apollonius, and ver. 380 in Virgil.   To
be sure, the application is different, but the manner
is the same : and that Virgil had the passage before
him at the time, is evident from what follows :

> ————— Μνησαιο δε και ποτ᾽ εμοιο,
> στρευγομενος καματοισι,———

compared with

> Supplicia hausurum scopulis et nomine Dido
> Sæpe vocaturum.———

It appears to me, upon the whole, that Ovid has taken
more from Apollonius than Virgil.

" I was interrupted as I was writing this on
Sunday; and have been prevented since, by company,
from going on.   There is another passage in Apollonius, lib. iii. 453, which Virgil has imitated too, very
closely, lib. iv. 4, &c., and in which I confess that he
has fallen very short of the original.   Before I leave
Apollonius, let me ask you, whether in Medea's
speech, in the fourth book, to which I have before
alluded in ver. 381, the insertion of *ov* in the manner
it is there, or at least the collocation of it, is not very
unusual and awkward ?   With respect to the comparison between Homer and him, in point of dactyls,
I cannot help being a little obstinate in my former

opinion. I think I would even venture to put it
to this trial : Let all the long vowels and dipthongs
in Homer be resolved into two vowels, that can be
so, consistently with the metre ; and leave those
in Apollonius as we find them ; and, I say, the
spondees in Homer would still exceed those in Apollonius. If you change εν into ενι, and ελθειν into ελθεμεν,
&c., in one, it would be fair to do the same, of course,
in the other. My remark, with respect to the datives
plural in Homer, is not confined to those in ῃσι ; but
extends also to those in οισι : the final iota is very
rarely omitted in either of them, except, of course,
where it is elided by a subsequent vowel. Heyne's
substitution of *nomen* for *numen*, in the lines of the
fifth Æneid, appears to me, as to you, very absurd :
but it is fair to say, that in my Roman edition of
Virgil, in which the text is taken from the Medici
MS., notice is taken of various readings, viz. *cœlum* in
the Vatican, and *nomen* in the Leyden : and then it is
added, ' *In codice olim erat* NOMEN.' By the *codice*
without any addition, I presume is meant the Medici ;
from which, as I said, the text is uniformly professed
to be taken. What difficulty Heyne can find in
regard to *numen*, Æn. iii. ver. 372, is still more
incomprehensible ; but I have not his edition, nor ever
had an opportunity of looking much into it.

" Here let me finish this unconscionable Letter :
but I have dwelt the longer upon Virgil's pathetic,
because his wonderful excellence in that particular
has not, in my opinion, been in general sufficiently
noticed. The other beauties of the eighth Æneid,

such as the Rites of Hercules, and the apostrophe to him, both of which Ovid has so successfully imitated in the beginning of the fourth Metamorphosis; the story of Cacus; the shield; and, above all, the description of Evander's town, and of the infancy of Rome, which appears to me, in its way, to be all but equal to the account of Alcinoüs, in the Odyssey, have been, I believe, pretty generally celebrated; and yet I do not recollect to have seen the eighth book classed with the second, fourth, and sixth, which are the general favourites.

> " I am, with great regard, Sir,
> " Yours ever,
> "C. J. FOX."

MR. WAKEFIELD TO MR. FOX.

" DORCHESTER GAOL, *April 22nd*, 1801.

" SIR,

" My reason for omitting Æn. iv. in the list of those on which I proposed to give Lectures, was not a disparaging opinion of its worth; for, if the delineation of human passions, in their most operative and interesting circumstances, be meritorious, Virgil's success in that book has attained to merit of the highest kind; but because it contains passages (such particularly as ver. 318, less delicate, perhaps, than its parallel, Soph. Aj. 521) which would lead to a discomposure of decorum in a miscellaneous assembly; and because the *dramatic* appears to me less calculated for public exposition than *narration* and *description;* in both which Virgil supereminently excels. As to the second book, with which I commence (if I do commence), the whole imposture of Sinon, the catastrophe of Laocoön, and all connected with them, are, and always were to me, the most unpalatable parts of Virgil, and through which I always work my way with weariness and impatience.

" That intermixture of antient history and primæval manners in Æn. viii. very much recommends that book to my fancy ; as the enumeration of the warriors is the capital excellence of the seventh ; and, in my mind, as it exceeds everything of the same kind in Homer, has nothing comparable to it within the same compass in Greek and Roman poetry. Apollonius deserves great praise on that article ; but then, exclusive of the sentiment, the dignity of Virgilian language, the magnificence and pomp of his versification, who has equalled of antient or modern artists ? Evander's farewell speech to Pallas justly merits your applauses. I suppose that I may have repeated to myself the twelve last verses of it once a month for these twenty-seven years last past, upon a moderate average computation. The epilogue to the same subject, Æn. xii. ver. 139—182, is little, if at all, inferior. The part of Evander's speech, which you quote, has something heavy and unfinished in the monotonous terminations of the adjoining words : which the poet, I am inclined to think, would have corrected on revisal :

Sin ali*quem* infan*dum* ca*sum*——.

" Æn. iv. 457—469, is finely imagined, and imi-

tated with great success by Ovid, and Pope in his
Eloïsa.

" As for Virgil's imitations of Apollonius Rhodius,
they detract very little from his sum of excellence.
The characteristic merit of a poet is founded on his
general delineation of human character, with the
main conformation of his poem, and the concatenation
and correspondence of its parts; not on a few incidental obligations to his predecessors. On the
whole, I read Virgil's Dido with more pleasure than
the Medea of his original : one appears to me somewhat artificial and indistinct; the other, all perspicuity
and nature.

" Your hesitation at Apollonius Rhodius, iv. 381,
and mention of the difficulty in your Letter, furnishes
me with an additional proof, to the many which I
have before experienced, how important the sugges-
tions and communications of another are found, even
with respect to passages the most familiar, and to a
superficial view the most unexceptionable. I perceived instantaneously, on turning to it at your suggestion, what never else, in all probability, would
have presented itself to my mind—that a slight error,
which I think you will acknowledge, occasions the
awkwardness in question. We should read, I am
persuaded:

$$\text{Ηε μαλ' ευκλειης; Τινα δ' ΑΥ τισιν ηε βαρειαν}$$
$$\text{Ατην ου σμυγερως, κ. τ. λ.}$$

' *Nay, rather, on the other hand*—:' which is perfectly
consonant, in my opinion, both to the power of the
particle, and the exigence of the context. But is the

passage unexceptionable yet ?   I think not.   Brunck
perceived a difficulty, it is plain, though he says
nothing ; and he has accordingly attempted to remove
it by an interrogation at ευκλειης.   But does ηε ever
introduce a question, unless another ηε, or η, precedes ?
I believe not : and, without an interrogation, it is
made in Shaw and others equivalent to η *certe*, or
δη ; which is inadmissible again ; for ηε never has
any such power.   I read, therefore, and the reasons
for corruption are obvious and probable,

Η μαλ' εὔκλειης·————

' *Certainly, very honourable !*' sarcastically and ironi-
cally ; which seems quite in character, and escapes all
embarrassment and exception of phraseology.

"You have a right, I believe, from an experimental
comparison of a few passages, not to be, as you
candidly express yourself, a *little obstinate* in your
opinion respecting the superior frequency of dactyls
in Apoll. Rhodius to Homer, but *greatly persevering*
in that opinion.   Homer's deficiency, however, seems
ascribable to the more frequent recurrence and greater
number of his *proper* names ; many of which are spondaïc in their syllables : Αιας, Ατρειδης, Ηρη, Αθηναιη,
Κιρκη, Ποσειδαων, Νεστωρ, Ἑκτωρ, Αχαιοι, Οδυσσευς,
Πηλειδης, Αχιλλευς, Καλυψω, Απολλων, Ἑρμης, Ἑρμειας,
Αφροδιτη, φιλομμειδης, &c., perpetually recurring.

"I did not censure Heyne, or did not mean to
censure him, at Æn. ver. 768, for preferring *nomen*
as his own conjecture, but for accepting this reading
of the MSS., to the exclusion of the other.   You
surprise me exceedingly by saying that you have not

Heyne. I know it has been fashionable, of late, with many, to undervalue his exertions on Virgil, and particularly with the Eton men, who *primi rerum omnium esse volunt* ; but I would not want his edition, and Burman's, on any consideration : they are absolutely essential, in my judgment, not only to a *critical perusal*, but to an *elegant perception* of this most accomplished and delightful author.

" My Lectures are, with me, an object of great importance : for, without the assistance of this project, all my schemes of future editions must be frustrated, under the present conditions of this country,—the monstrous price of printing in the dead languages, and the enormous rise on paper, such as to be doubled since my sepulture in this *delectable* abode. Should this attempt on Virgil meet with tolerable countenance, I had meditated a similar experiment on a Greek Poet, in the winter.

" A thought comes into my head, which I do not recollect to have imparted to you before. A very imperfect notion is entertained in general of the copiousness of the Latin language, by those who con- fine themselves to what are styled the Augustan writers. The old Comedians and Tragedians, with Ennius and Lucilius, were the great repositories of learned and vigorous expression : and their language, with the diction of Lucretius and Virgil, is, to a cer- tainty, largely preserved to us in some writers, little read, but to me, I own, the sources of much amuse- ment, and more information ; several of them at the same time characterised by a truly masculine and

original eloquence : Tertullian, Arnobius, Apuleius,
A. Gellius, and Ammianus Marcellinus. Their words
are usually marked in Dictionaries as inelegant and
of suspicious authority ; when they are, in reality, the
most genuine remains of pure Roman composition. I
have ever regarded the loss of the old Roman poets,
particularly Ennius and Lucilius, from the light which
they would have thrown on the formations of the
Latin language, and its derivation from the Æolian
Greek, as the severest calamity ever sustained by
philological learning.

" Another thought also, of a different complexion,
recurs to memory. I often wonder, that your highly
respectable friends in the House of Commons, who
are tossing their words with such wonderful per-
severance, day after day, to every wind that blows,
when the objection of no petitions coming against the
suspension of the Habeas-Corpus Act, &c., is urged
upon them by Ministry, do not reply, by stating the
inefficacy of petitions in one very singular and apposite example,—the case of the Slave Trade ; on which
occasion few counties and towns in England, to the
best of my recollection, were wanting in this effort :
with what success I need not mention.

" The stations of no men in this kingdom do I ever
feel myself inclined to regard with an eye of envy,
except those of the masters and tutors of colleges in
Oxford and Cambridge ; who are possessed of all
possible implements and opportunities to pursue and
encourage literature, and continue sleeping

——— μαλα μακρον
ατερμονα νηγρετον ὑπνον,

over their desirable appointments. The masters, also, of our great public schools are placed, to my apprehension, in enviable situations. In short, education is of such incomparable value, in my opinion, that I cannot help coveting the condition of every man who is rendered capable of conducting it with efficiency and extent.

"I remain, Sir,

"Your obedient servant,

"GILBERT WAKEFIELD."

MR. FOX TO MR. WAKEFIELD.

"ST. ANN'S HILL, *April* 28*th*, 1801.

"SIR,

"I am much obliged to you for your caution about Heyne's Virgil; and if I purchase it at all, I will wait for the new edition. When I was a book buyer, in my younger days, it was not in existence; and lately I have bought but few classical books, except Greek ones; and some Latin authors, of whom I had before *no* edition. I had once a good many editions of Virgil; but having had frequent occasions to make presents, and Virgil being always a proper book for that purpose, I have now only the fine Roman one, in three volumes folio; a school Delphin; a Variorum; and Martyn's Georgics. I am glad to find that you are not the heretic about the fourth book that I suspected you to be. Your reason for omitting it may be a very good one. I think the coarsest thing in the whole book (not indeed in point of indecency, but in want of

sentiment) is ver. 502, '*She thought she would
take it as she did the last time,*' is surely vulgar
and gross to the last degree. How very strange
it appears to me, that that character of perfection
or faultlessness, which so justly belongs to the
Georgics, should have been so frequently applied
to the Æneid! and yet even in Quintilian there is
the expression of ' Quanto eminentioribus vincimur,
æqualitate pensamus,' or something like it, which,
according to the common interpretation of the words,
seems to justify such an opinion, as far as his authority
goes. I am much obliged to you for referring me to
the passage in the Ajax, which is exceedingly beautiful, and certainly more delicate than Virgil's; and
yet, I own, I should never have thought there was
much indelicacy in *si quid dulce meum ;* but perhaps
I am not so nice upon such subjects as others are.
By the way, in the Ajax, v. 514, there is ὅ τι βλέπω,
another instance in refutation of Porson's absurd
assertion in the Note upon the Orestes, ver. 64, ' ubi
verbum in brevem vocalem desinit,' &c. Is not τι a
short syllable? and is it not followed by βλ, two consonants ' quæ brevem esse paterentur ? ' In short, I
doubt whether, except the play he was actually publishing, and the Phœnissæ, he could have found
another wherein there was not a contradiction to his
position. The epilogue, as you call it, to the story of
Pallas, and which you erroneously quote as being in
Æneid xii. (it is in Æneid xi.), is indeed capital, but
not equal, in my opinion, to the parting speech; but
then, *I* think that nothing *is.* There appears to me

something harsh and difficult in the construction
in the last lines of the epilogue. It may, perhaps,
be owing to the habit we are in of comparing him
to Homer, the most perspicuous of all poets ; but, to
say the truth, perspicuity does not appear to me to
be among Virgil's chief excellences. As we are upon
the subject of Pallas (in which the poet is always
peculiarly happy), I hope you admire the two lines,
Æn. x. 515, 516. I quite agree with you as to
Sinon and Laocoön ; though some of those passages,
which are become so trite as quotations, are in themselves very good ; such as ' Timeo Danaos,' ' Hoc
Ithacus velit,' &c. ; but if Sinon and Laocoön are
cold and forced, the Death of Priam, the Apparition
of Hector, &c., amply compensate. Your notion, in
respect to poets borrowing from each other, seems
almost to come up to mine, who have often been
laughed at by my friends as a systematic defender of
plagiarism : indeed, I got Lord Holland, when a
school-boy, to write some verses in praise of it ; and,
in truth, it appears to me, that the greatest poets
have been most guilty, if guilt there be, in these
matters. Dido is surely far superior to Medea in
general ; but there are some parts of Apollonius,
such as lib. iii. from 453 to 463, and from 807 to
816, that appear to me unrivalled. Your correction
in Arg. iv. 380, from ov to av, must please me ; for I
had thought myself of changing the other ov, in the
following line, to av ; but I dare say your collocation is
better. The difficulty also of $\eta\epsilon$ for η or $\delta\eta$ had struck
me ; but seeing no notice taken of it by the editor, I

was too diffident of my own knowledge of the language to pronounce it to be wrong. In my edition (Shaw's octavo), it is without the note of interrogation; and I think such a note would take off greatly from the spirit of the passage; besides the impropriety, which you suggest, of the use of ηε, even in that case. If it is a question, it should be, I suppose, either ηρα or ἆρα. Your emendation, η μαλ' εὐκλειης, seems to take away all difficulty, and is quite simple. By the way, a few lines below, the pronoun σε is repeated without any apparent cause; or any elegance, that I can see, in the repetition. I suppose the second σ may be omitted, and that εμα may stand in that part of the verse without it; or if not, should the first ε be changed into τε, "εκ δε ΤΕ πατρης"? Your observation on the utility of communications upon these subjects may possibly be the cause of my making many trifling ones upon them. There is a strong instance of Apollonius's delight in dactyls, in one of the passages quoted, lib. iii. ver. 813, where he changes Homer's ὁμηλικιης ερατεινης into περιγηθεος. The loss of the older Roman writers is certainly the greatest that could have happened to philology; and probably, too, on account of their own merit, is in every view a considerable one. Of the more modern writers whom you mention, I have never read any but A. Gellius. I bought Apuleius last year, with an intention to read him, but something or other has always prevented me. I never saw one quotation from Tertullian that did not appear to me full of eloquence of the best sort; and have often thought, on that account, of buying an edition of him ; but have been rather discouraged, from supposing that it might be necessary to know more than I do of the controversies in which he was engaged, to relish him properly.

" With respect to your Lectures, I should think that Latin would succeed better than Greek authors ; but this is very uncertain. From the audience, however, which you may have upon the first, it will not be difficult to collect what probability there is of getting as good, or a better one, to the second.

" It would be very good in argument, to state the inefficacy of the petitions on the Slave Trade, in the way you mention ; and I do believe that, in fact, the supposed inefficacy of petitions has been one of the great causes of the supineness, or rather lethargy, of the country: but it is not true, that petitions, though they have been ultimately unsuccessful, have been therefore wholly inefficacious. The petitions in 1797 produced, as Mr. Pitt says (and I suspect he says truly), the negotiation at Lisle : no great good, you will say ; but still they were not wholly inefficacious. And even with regard to the Slave Trade, I conceive the great numbers which have voted with us, sometimes amounting to a majority, have been principally owing to petitions. Even now, in this last stage of degradation, I am not sure that if the people were to petition generally (but it must be very generally) that it would be without effect.

" Your attention to the unfortunate wretches you

speak of must do you the highest honour, in the eyes of all men, even of Tory justices; and that is saying θαρσαλεον επος.

"Yours ever,

"C. J. FOX.

"P. S. According to your maxim of not allowing the valuable article of paper to go unemployed, I will trouble you with one more question, relative to Ajax, ver. 511, and that is, how do you construe διοισεται there? Stevens says 'διοισεται, apud Sophoclem, "*deportabitur*,"' as if it were a peculiar use of the word by that poet. But I do not think *deportabitur* will do in this place well. The Latin version in my edition, that is, Johnson's, printed at Eton, says *deseretur;* but how διοισεται, which I suppose to be the future middle of διαφερεσθαι, is to mean *deseretur*, I do not conceive.

"C. J. F."

MR. WAKEFIELD TO MR. FOX.

Dorchester Gaol, *April 29th*, 1801.

"Sir,

"Your Variorum Virgil, if Emmenesius's, is a good book, and contains Servius's Exposition; without which every Virgil is defective, on account of that grammarian's antiquity and real merit. There is, in the British Museum, an unpublished MS. of the same grammarian's, a Vocabulary of Synonymes:

and everything of this kind, which will soon perish for ever, and which abounds everywhere, should be published: and these helps to literature, if a national concern, would not all amount to one's day's expenditure by frensy and corruption.

" Æn. iv. 502, is a very difficult passage, and unintelligible, I own, to me. If *quam* be genuine, the construction must be, *quam evenit in morte Sychæi;* but where can such another construction with the comparative be found? Your acceptation, in that case must be admitted. I had conjectured, I see, *jam* for *quam :* and I conceived the general sentiment to be this: 'As Dido had endured that great calamity, under lamentable circumstances (the death of Sychæus by her own *brother*, Pygmalion), without such an act of desperation as suicide; her sister had not anticipated this catastrophe now, nor prepared her mind for it.' See vi. 104, 105, which seems not much amiss: but I have referred, with approbation, to Koen on Corinthus upon Dialects ; and that book I sent home, to my house in the town, a few days ago.

"The imperfect state of the Æneid is sufficiently clear from the hemistichs, little inconsistencies and inaccuracies which the author would certainly have corrected; but this imperfection might have been indubitably inferred from his own dying directions for its destruction ; a piece of history, which never admitted, to my recollection, of any controversy. Quintilian, I presume, by his *æqualitate pensamus*, means to intimate, that Virgil, if he have not taken such lofty flights as Homer, never approaches so near the ground, nor degrades himself by the puerilities and coarsenesses of his master.

"I have no Virgil here, which contains Servius; but you may consult him on the *quid dulce meum*, and see what the Antients collected from that expression.

"As to your passage from Sophocles, τῦ βλεπω, βλ are *not* those consonants before which the Tragedians *shorten* syllables.

"I call the part of Æn. xi., which finishes the story of Pallas, the *epilogue*, in the rhetorical meaning of the term; for the *lamentable* termination of his warfare. The ἐπιλογος was that portion of the oration which was devoted to *commiseration* only; and as this was the *conclusion*, the term gained the secondary sense, afterwards, of *conclusion* in general. A beautiful passage in Longinus owes its excellence to this primary and proper use of the word, perceived by no editor before Toup: where Longinus, in speaking of those parts in the Odyssey which relate the death of Antilochus and the other Grecian chiefs, in allusion also to the νεκυομαντεια, calls that poem the *epilogue* of the Iliad; i. e. the *funeral oration*, as it were, of those heroes whose *living adventures* had been celebrated in the former poem.

"Certainly Æn. x. 515, 516, are highly spirited; and the vivacity of the conceptions is well delineated by the rapidity of the composition, unfettered by copulatives, and unretarded by epithets. The second Æneid, abating those exceptions of Sinon and Laocoön, is incomparable. The exordium is most

dignified and solemn, as well as natural and pathetic
to perfection ; and what follows the introduction to the
havoc of the Greeks, after issuing from their retreat,
exhibits, to my fancy—in an adequate display of
events, the most awful and affecting, of the most
turbulent and soft emotions — all the capacities of
human genius.

" With respect to imitation, much may be said on
so copious a subject. The uniformity of Nature sup-
plies, of course, those thoughts which inevitably suggest themselves to every contemplator, but which
become the *property* of the *first occupant ;* so that
sameness and similarity often subsist without imitation in reality. Then, as few poets have written
without some excellences, these catch the peculiar
attention of every succeeding genius, and are often
imperceptibly assimilated with his own ideas, and
often borrowed for the purpose of different application or improvement. Virgil's Georgics arose probably from the works of Hesiod and Nicander ; but
how much superior to one, and probably to the other ?
The same of Pope's Rape of the Lock, and many
other poems, which would be but ill exchanged for
their originals. There is scarcely a verse in Virgil,
Milton, and Pope, that does not savour of their predecessors ; and yet they will ever be acknowledged
as prime artists in Parnassus.

"As to Apoll. Rhod. iv. 386, it is rather observable,
that Brunck has put into the text his conjecture,
which is also yours, εκ δε ΤΕ πατρης· and that I, from
observing (as fully shown in my *Noctes Carcerariæ*)

how ΓΕ follows the pronouns, had conjectured on my
margin, Αυτικ᾽ εμαι Γ᾽ ελασειαν; and this is confirmed
by two Paris MSS.

" One reads Tertullian purely for his style and con-
ceptions, not for the pertinency of his argumentation.
They were miserable advocates of their own system.
Apuleius is to Cicero, and such writers, what Burke,
in his most glorious extravagances, is to Addison or
Swift, as to composition.

" As to petitions to Parliament, many powerful
impediments stand in their way. 1. The political
acrimony of the times, which terrifies *some* of independent conditions; and *many*, who subsist by their
superiors. 2. The general and constitutional indifference of the *majority* in all societies, who prefer
indolence with suffering, to the chance of redress
from exertion and activity. 3. The more extended
speculations of some, who cannot acquiesce in those
formalities of language, respecting Royalty and
Parliaments, which commonly enter into these petitions. 4. The expense, more or less, of such efforts,
which usually falls on a few; and on whom the
demands of all sorts, for money, have been pressing
and frequent during the war, in consequence of
their principles. My experience and connections
have led me to some knowledge of these matters.
I have a brother at Nottingham, who is a prime
mover in all business of a public nature, whether
political or benevolent, to an extent, and with an
estimation among his townsmen, with which, I
believe, no private individual in this country can

compare; and my own actual observation agrees
with his reports.   5. The tricks in countcracting,
and counter-petitioning, are innumerable, and too
successful.

"As to the prisoners here, not a man among them
but would be reformed to a certainty, by good instruction from those who proved themselves kindly
interested in their welfare by their actions; and it is
most afflicting to see them sentenced by the justices
to one, two, &c., to *seven* years, for the veriest trifles,
if all the circumstances of their condition be considered.   Time, and the necessity of endurance, will
blunt the acutest sensations of the heart; but the
miseries sustained by these unhappy people, without
one effort of instruction and reformation, in the
midst of keen hunger (which the prison allowance
leaves in painful exertion unremittingly), when I first
came among them, prest down my spirit to the
earth :

Κλαιον ενι λεχεεσσι καθημενος, ουδε νυ μοι κηρ
Ηθελ' ετι ζωειν, και ὁρᾳν φαος ηελιοιο.

"As to διοισεται in Soph. Aj. 511, I see, from my
margin, that Suidas touches on the word; but I
have no Suidas here, nor any Sophocles with Notes
or Scholia.   The sense of the word, however, if you
do not look too far, but consider only its simple
energy, is most satisfactory and evident.   Διαφερω
is essentially and literally *to carry through*; and, in
the middle voice, *to carry one's self through.*   'How
then, when forsaken by you, will he carry himself

through (*get himself through—go through*, i. e. life),
under guardians of unkindly manners and affections ? '

" I remain, Sir,

" Yours respectfully,

" GILBERT WAKEFIELD."

MR. FOX TO MR. WAKEFIELD.

"St. Ann's Hill, *June 5th*, 1801.

" Sir,

" I was called to town upon business just
after the receipt of your last Letter ; and partly by
going backwards and forwards, partly by company
here, I have been so taken up, that I have had little
time to myself.   But if I do not write now, I think,
by my computation, that I shall scarcely have an
opportunity of directing another Letter to Dorchester
Gaol.   I am much obliged for the great quantity of
information which your latter Letters have given me ;
but at this moment have only time to notice one or
two points.   βλ, you tell me (and I doubt not but
you are right), are not two letters before which the
Tragedians make vowels short.   I was led to suppose
they were, from τλ, κλ, πλ, θλ, χλ, φλ, being undoubtedly
of that description.   Your information diminishes
considerably the number of instances which had
occurred to me, against Porson's dictum, in his Note
upon Orestes, ver. 64.   If γλ and γν are taken from
me, it will be diminished still more : but even then
I have some instances remaining ; and have no

doubt, upon reading with that view, of finding many more, as those I had collected were entirely by chance. For the present, take two : Medea, 246, and Euripides' Electra, 1058. Upon looking again at Medea's speech, in the fourth book of Apollonius, I doubt whether ηε be not used, ver. 357, in nearly the same way as Brunck, when he puts the note of interrogation, supposes it to be, ver. 380 ; and yet I can conceive *or*, by an ellipsis of *the sense*, to have a meaning in ver. 357 which it cannot have in ver. 380.

" I sincerely congratulate you, upon your being arrived so near to the end of a confinement which I shall ever consider to have been as disgraceful to the government of the country, as it has been honourable to you.

" Your obedient servant,

" C. J. FOX."

SAME TO SAME.

" St. Ann's Hill, *June 17th*, 1801.

" Dear Sir,

" Fenton, in a sort of note prefixed to his translation of Sappho to Phaon, says, that we learn from the Antients that Phaon was an old mariner, restored to youth by Venus. In Burman's Ovid there is a note from Egnatius, referring to some other work of his (Egnatius's) upon the subject; and there is some reference too, in my Variorum Ovid, to Ælian's Various History, which I have not.

This is not a very important subject of inquiry; but I own I have a sort of curiosity concerning this history of Phaon, which if you can instruct me how to gratify you will much oblige me.

" I sincerely hope you are better satisfied with the state of your son's health than you seemed to be when you were here. If accident (I hope not of the same sort as the last) should bring you again this way, I flatter myself you will make me a longer visit.

" I am, dear Sir,

" Yours ever,

" C. J. FOX."

MR. WAKEFIELD TO MR. FOX.

" HACKNEY, *August* 12*th*, 1801.

" DEAR SIR,

" I hope, in no long time, to be able to consult my books, with a view of answering the queries in your last favour, as I have taken a house in Charter House Square, to which I expect to remove by the latter end of next week.

" There is, at a bookseller's in Oxford Street, a large-paper Brunck's Apollonius Rhodius, price eighteen shillings. The book is become so scarce as not be procured in common paper; but I could not determine whether you would choose a finer copy, or I would have secured it for you.

" I am, Sir,

" Your respectful and obliged friend,

" GILBERT WAKEFIELD."

MR. FOX TO MR. WAKEFIELD.

"St. Ann's Hill, *August* 21*st*, 1801.

"Dear Sir,

"On my return hither yesterday, from a short excursion, I found your Letter, with its inclosure, which I return. It is a piece of *news* to me (that would be very agreeable, if it were true), that I have *finished* an historical work. That I have begun one, is true; and that I have had numerous applications relative to the publishing, is equally so: and I should be obliged to you, if you would give the same answer to Mr. Phillips that I have given to other applicants; which is, that I do not mean to decide on the mode of publication, much less upon the bookseller to be employed, till the work is nearly finished; and till that time I wish to remain entirely unfettered by any promise or engagement. The hard usage Mr. P. experienced at Leicester would certainly incline me at any time to do him a good office, if it were in my power.

"I should be very glad to have the copy you mention of Brunck's Apollonius; and if you had mentioned the name of the bookseller in Oxford Street where it is, I would have written to him. If you have an opportunity, I will trouble you to bid him send it me by the stage, and I will remit him the price.

"I have found, since I wrote to you, a great deal about Phaon, by looking into Bayle, who referred me to Lucian ; a note in Heyne's Virgil, which I found at Woburn, and Palæphatus, which I have not seen, but from whom there are extracts, in some of the books I have looked into, containing, as I suppose, all he says upon the subject.

"I observe in Brunck's Analecta, which I have lately purchased, that he takes no notice of the doubts concerning the authenticity of the Remains of Anacreon. I have always supposed them modern ; but I understand there has been discovered a Manuscript which proves them to be of a certain degree of antiquity, or at least not a forgery of H. Stephens. The style of them appears to me *very* modern ; but yet that preserved in A. Gellius bears a strong resemblance to some of the others. As to their being really Anacreon's, I should require very strong evidence to satisfy me.

" Yours ever,

"C. J. FOX."

LETTERS FROM MR. FOX TO MR. TROTTER.

LETTER I.

"St. Ann's Hill, *February* 21st, 1799.

" My dear Sir,

"I do assure you, your letter of the 28th ultimo, gave both Mrs. F. and myself the highest satisfaction, as it was a long time since we had heard from you, and had learned from Bob that you had been very ill. He is not now here, but the next time

I see him, I will tell him how shabby it is of him not to write to you.

" I am sorry to hear your account of the people of the North, and I think they are bad politicians not to see that the support of the Anti-unionists would infallibly lead to the procuring of the substance, instead of the name, of a parliament. The Anti-unionists must feel (and this was my opinion before their defeat on Lord Corry's motion) that they are far too weak to struggle against our minister, without the assistance of the people; and, consequently, they must accede to Reform of Parliament, Catholic Emancipation, and, in one word, to a real and substantial representation of the people, which must produce a government as popular and democratic as any government ought to be. As things are, I am afraid they will fail for want of support, and that even the Union itself may be forced upon you; and then the consequences, either way, will be dreadful indeed.

" We are very glad you think of being in England in April, when I hope you will come and hear our nightingales. We have had a great deal of bad weather, but it is growing better, and the crocuses, snowdrops, &c., are giving us, every day, beautiful indications of approaching spring. Mrs. F. desires to be kindly remembered to you.

" I am, my dear Sir,

" Yours ever,

"C. J. FOX."

" JOHN B. TROTTER, ESQ., *Vianstown,*
    near Downpatrick, Ireland."

LETTER II.

"St. Ann's Hill, *Thursday.*

" Dear Sir,

" I received by Tuesday's coach your pamphlet upon the Union, and your verses, for which Mrs. F. particularly desires me to thank you; we both like them very much. I think you put your objections to the Union entirely upon the right grounds; whether there is spirit in Ireland to act up to your principles, is another question. I do not know whether you ever heard that it is a common observation, that Irish orators are generally too figurative in their language for the English taste; perhaps I think parts of your pamphlet no exception to this observation; but this is a fault (if it be a fault) easily mended.

" As to Italian, I am sure, from what you said, that you are quite far advanced enough, to make a master an unnecessary trouble and expense; and therefore it is no excuse for your not coming, especially, as it is a study in which I can give you, and would certainly give you with pleasure, any assistance you could wish. In German, the case is, to be sure, quite different, as I do not know a word of it, nor have any German books; of Italian, you know we have plenty.

" I am sure I need not tell you, that whenever you do come, you will be welcome.

" Yours ever,
"C. J. FOX."

LETTER III.

" I KNOW of no better, nor, indeed, scarce of any
other life of Cicero, than Middleton's. He is certainly
very partial to him, but, upon the whole, I think
Cicero was a good man. The salutary effect of the
burning of his houses, which you mention, is, indeed,
too evident; I do not think quite so ill of his poem
upon Cæsar as you do; because I presume he only
flattered him upon the points where he really deserved
praise; and as to his flatteries of him after he was
dictator, in his speeches for Ligarius and Marcellus, I
not only excuse, but justify, and even commend
them, as they were employed for the best of purposes,
in favour of old friends, both to himself and the
republic. Nay, I even think that his manner of
recommending to Cæsar (in the pro Marcello) the
restoration of the republic, is even bold and spirited.
—After all, he certainly was a man liable to be
warped from what was right either by fear or vanity;
but his faults seem so clearly to have been infirmi-
ties, rather than bad principles or bad passions,
that I cannot but like him, and, in a great measure,
esteem him too. The openness with which, in his
private letters, he confesses himself to be ashamed
of part of his conduct, has been taken great advantage
of by detractors, as an aggravation, whereas I think
it a great extenuation of his faults. I ought to
caution against trusting to the translations in Middleton; they are all vile, and many of them unfaithful.

" If your sister does not understand Latin, you
should translate them for her yourself. I do assure
you, my dear Sir, it always gives Mrs. F. and me
great pleasure to hear from you, and especially when
it is to inform us that you are well and happy.

" Yours ever,
"C. J. FOX."

LETTER IV.

" St. Ann's Hill, Monday.

" I was much gratified, my dear Sir, with your
letter, as your taste seems so exactly to agree with
mine; and am, very glad, for your sake, that you
have taken to Greek, as it will now be very easy to
you, and if I may judge from myself, will be one of
the greatest sources of amusement to you. Homer
and Ariosto have always been my favourites, there is
something so delightful in their wonderful facility,
and the apparent absence of all study, in their expression, which is almost peculiar to them. I think you
must be very partial, however, to find but two faults
in the twelve books of the Iliad. The passage in the
ninth book, about Λαιτι, appears to me, as it does to
you, both poor and forced; but I have no great objection to that about the wall in the twelfth, though, to
be sure, it is not very necessary. The tenth book
has always been a particular favourite with me, not
so much on account of Diomede's and Ulysses's
exploits (though that part is excellent too), as on
account of the beginning, which describes so forcibly
the anxious state of the generals, with an enemy so

near, and having had rather the worst of the former
day. I do not know any description any where that
sets the thing so clearly before one; and then the
brotherly feelings of Agamemnon towards Menelaus,
and the modesty and amiableness of Menelaus's character (whom Homer, by the way, seems to be particularly fond of) are very affecting. Ariosto has
certainly taken his night expedition either from
Homer's or from Virgil's Nisus and Euryalus. I
scarcely know which I prefer of the three; I rather
think Virgil's; but Ariosto has one merit beyond the
others, from the important consequences which arise
from it to the story. Tasso (for he, too, must have
whatever is in the Iliad or Æneid) is a very poor
imitation, as far as I recollect.

" I suppose, as soon as you have done the Iliad,
you will read the Odyssey; which, though certainly
not so fine a poem, is, to my taste, still pleasanter to
read. Pray let me know what parts of it strike you
most, and believe me you cannot oblige me more
than by corresponding on such subjects. Of the
other Greek poets, Hesiod, Pindar, Eschylus, Sophocles, Euripides, Apollonius Rhodius, and Theocritus,
are the most worth reading. Of the Tragedians, I
like Euripides the best; but Sophocles is, I believe,
more generally preferred, and is certainly more
finished, and has fewer gross faults. Theocritus, in
his way, is perfect;—the two first Idylls, particularly,
are excellent. I suppose the ode you like is Αδωνιν ἀ
Κυθηρη, which is pretty enough, but not such as to
give you any adequate idea of Theocritus. There is

an elegy upon Adonis, by Bion, which is in parts very beautiful, and particularly some lines of it upon the common-place of Death, which have been imitated over and over again, but have never been equalled. In Hesiod, the account of Pandora, of the Golden Age, &c., and some other parts, are very good; but there is much that is tiresome. Perhaps the work, which is most generally considered as not his, I mean the Ασπις, is the one that has most poetry in it. It is very good, and to say that it is inferior to Homer's and Virgil's shields, is not saying much against it. Pindar is too often obscure, and sometimes much more spun out and wordy than suits my taste; but there are passages in him quite divine. I have not read above half his works. Apollonius Rhodius is, I think, very well worth reading. The beginning of Medæa's love is, I believe, original, and though often copied since, never equalled. There are many other fine parts in his poem, besides some which Virgil has improved, others scarce equalled. There is, however, in the greater part of the poem an appearance of labour, and a hardness, that makes it tiresome. He seems to me to be an author of about the same degree of genius with Tasso; and if there is more in the latter to be liked, there is nothing, I think, to be liked in him so well as the parts of Apollonius to which I have alluded. I have said nothing of Aristophanes, because I never read him. Callimachus and Moschus are worth reading; but there is little of them. By the way, I now recollect that the passage about death, which I said was in Bion's elegy upon Adonis, is in Moschus's upon Bion.　Now you have all my knowledge about Greek poetry.　I am quite pleased at your liking Ariosto so much ; though indeed I foresaw you would, from the great delight you expressed at Spenser, who is certainly inferior to him, though very excellent too.　Tasso, I think below both of them, but many count him the first among those three ; and even Metastasio, who ought to be a better judge of Italian poetry than you or I, gives him upon the whole the preference to Ariosto.

" You will, of course, have been rejoiced at the peace, as we all are.　Mrs. F. desires to be remembered to you kindly.　She is very busy just now, but will write to you soon.　I think this place has looked more beautiful than ever this year, both in spring and summer, and so it does now in autumn.　I have been very idle about my History, but I will make up for it by and bye ; though I believe I must go to Paris, to look at some papers there, before I can finish the first volume.　I think in the last half of the Iliad you will admire the 16th, 20th, 22d, and 24th books particularly.　I believe the general opinion is, that Homer did write near the shore, and he certainly does, as you observe, particularly delight in illustrations taken from the sea,—waves, &c.　Perhaps a *lion* is rather too frequent a simile with him.　I dare say you were delighted with Helen and Priam on the walls in the 3d book ; and I suspect you will be proportionably disgusted with Tasso's servile and ill-placed imitation of it.　Do not imagine, however, that I am not sensible to many beauties in Tasso, especially the parts imitated by Spenser, Erminia's flight and adventure, the description of the pestilence, and many others.

> " I am, dear Sir,
>> " Most truly,
>>> " Yours ever,
>>>> " C. J. FOX."

(*Post-mark, October* 20*th*, 1801.)

LETTER V.

" My dear Sir,

" I am quite scandalized at having so long delayed answering your letters, but I put it off, as I am apt to do everything, from day to day, till Christmas: and on that day, Mrs. F. was taken very seriously ill with a fever, and sore throat of the inflammatory kind. The violence of the disorder was over this day se'nnight, but though she has been mending ever since, she is still weak. However, she may now be called, comparatively speaking, quite well; and I did not like to write till I could tell you that she was so. I hope you go on with your Greek, and long to know whether you are as fond of the Odyssey as I am, as also what progress you have made in the other poets. The *Plutarchus*, whom you ask after, is, I believe, the same Plutarch who wrote the lives, and who certainly was of Chæronea. At least, I never heard of any other author of that name, and he wrote many philosophical works. I think when you

say you *despise* Tasso, you go further than I can do,
and though there is servility in his *manner* of imitation, which is disgusting, yet it is hardly fair to be
angry with him for translating a simile of Homer's, a
plunder, if it be one, of which nearly every poet has
been guilty.   If there be one who has not, I suspect
it is he whom you say you are going to read, I mean
Dante.   I have only read part of Dante, and admire
him very much.   I think the brilliant passages are
thicker set in his works, than in those of almost any
other poet ; but the want of connection and interest
makes him heavy ; and besides the difficulty of his
language, which I do not think much of, the obscurity
of that part of history to which he refers is much
against him.   His *allusions,* in which he deals not a
little, are, in consequence, most of them lost.

" I agree in liking Armida, but cannot help thinking Rinaldo's detention in her gardens very inferior to
Ruggiero's.

> " Or fino agli occhi ben nuota nel golfo
> Delle delizie e delle cose belle,"

may seem to some an expression rather too familiar,
and nearly foolish ; but it is much better for describing the sort of situation in which the two heroes
are supposed to be, than the *Romito Amante* of Tasso ;
not to mention the garden of Armida being all on the
inside of the palace, and walled round by it, instead
of the beautiful country described by Ariosto.   Do
you not think, too, that Spenser has much improved
upon Tasso, by giving the song in praise of pleasure

to a nymph rather than to a parrot? Pray, if you
want any information about Greek poets or others,
that I can give you, do not spare me, for it is a great
delight to me to be employed upon such subjects,
with one who has a true relish for them.

" I do not wonder at your passionate admiration
of the Iliad, and agree with you as to the peculiar
beauty of most of the parts you mention. The interview of Priam and Achilles is, I think, the finest of
all. I rather think, that in Andromache's first lamen-
tation, she dwells too much upon her child, and too
little upon Hector, but may be I am wrong. By
your referring to the 4th book only for Agamemnon's
brotherly kindness, I should almost suspect that you
had not sufficiently noticed the extreme delicacy and
kindness with which he speaks of him in the 10th,
ver. 120, &c.

" We have not at all fixed our time for going to
Paris yet. Mrs. F. desires to be most kindly remembered to you.

           " I am very truly,
                 " My dear Sir, yours ever,
                          " C. J. FOX.

" I do not know which is the best translation of
Don Quixote; I have only read Jarvis's, which I
think very indifferent. I liked Feijoo very much
when I read him, but I have not his works."

LETTER VI.

"St. Ann's Hill, *Thursday.*

" My dear Sir,

"You made Mrs. F. and me very happy,
by letting us know you had had so pleasant a tour,
and that your sister and yourself were so well after
your fatigues; though we both think your walks on
some days must have been too long. I am not sorry
t hat Mrs. F., who is very busy to-day, has commissioned me to answer your letter for her, as it gives
me an opportunity of mentioning something to you
which I have had in my head some time. We are,
as you know, going abroad soon, chiefly on account
of some state papers which are at Paris, and which it
is necessary for me, with a view to my History, to
inspect carefully; but we also think of taking in our
way a tour through Flanders to Spa. It has sometimes occurred to me, that this would not be a bad
opportunity for you to gratify a curiosity, which you
can scarcely be without, of seeing something on the
continent, and Paris particularly. We have a place
in our carriage, and of course you would be our guest
when at Spa, Paris, &c. I am sure it will be an
additional motive with you to know that, besides the
pleasure of your company, your assistance in examin-
ing and extracting from the papers at Paris, would
be materially useful to me; but I would by no means
have this consideration weigh with you, unless the
plan is otherwise suitable and agreeable to you. I

cannot yet determine our precise time of setting out,
as it depends upon some business not altogether in
my own power ; but I should think, not sooner than
the 15th, nor later than the 30th of next month,
and I hope to be back about Michaelmas. I need
not say that, if you do think of coming with us, with
respect to a week or two we would adapt our time to
yours ; only it is so great an object with me to be
at home very early in October, if not in September,
that I cannot put off our departure long.

" If I hear anything within these few days (which
is not unlikely) which may make me more able to fix
what time will be most convenient to me, I will let
you know without waiting for your answer. I think
you were in great luck to have had fine weather on
your journeys, for we have had a great deal of bad
here, though not very lately. You never told me how
you liked the last half of the Odyssey ; I think the
simplicity of all the part with the Swine Herd, &c., is
delightful, though some persons account it too low.—
Did you observe in one passage, that the suitors have
exactly the *Scotch second sight ?*

" Yours ever,

" C. J. FOX."

(*Post-mark, July 5th,* 1802.)

LETTER VII.

" St. Ann's Hill, *4th July.*

" MY DEAR SIR,

        " I received yesterday your letter of the
28th, which seems to have been a good while upon

the road. We are very happy at the thoughts of your accompanying us, and I make no doubt but we shall have a pleasant tour. Do not by any means hurry yourself, as I think the 18th or 19th of the month will be the earliest day on which we possibly can set out, but I will write again on Tuesday (the day of my election) from London, by which time I may be able to tell you something more certain, and at any rate you will not be too late by waiting for that letter. Mrs. F. desires to be kindly remembered.

" Yours ever,

" C. J. FOX."

LETTER VIII.

" SHAKESPEARE TAVERN, COVENT GARDEN, 7th July.

" MY DEAR SIR,

" I had intended to write yesterday, thinking I should have no opposition here, and that of course I could tell you, with some certainty, the day of our setting out ; but there is an opposition, which, though foolish and contemptible to the last degree, may occasion the poll to be protracted, which leaves me in great uncertainty. At all events, the 21st is the earliest day I can think of, even upon the supposition that this business is over this week ; if it lasts, our journey cannot take place till the 29th or 30th ; however, I will write to you again tomorrow, or next day. Write a line, directed to St. Ann's Hill ; or set out, and make up your mind to the chance of being kept some days in this vile place; at St. Ann's, I know you would not mind it.

" Yours ever,

"C. J. FOX.

" NUMBERS :—

Fox	.	.	.	.	.	504
Gardner	.	.	.	.	.	401
Graham .	.	.	.	.	.	193 "

LETTER IX.

" Shakespeare, Covent Garden, 9th July.

" My dear Sir,

" Though this vile election is not over, nor will be, I believe, for some time, yet I can now fix the time of our departure, with a reasonable certainty, for the 23rd or 24th of this month. I have no time to write more.

" Yours ever,

" C. J. FOX.

" NUMBERS :—

Fox	.	.	.	.	.	1194
Gardner	.	.	.	.	.	1081
Graham	.	.	.	.	.	533 "

" I shall go to St. Ann's Hill to-morrow, and only come here occasionally, next week."

LETTER X.

" Paris, October 27th.

" My dear Sir,

" Mrs. Fox has had two letters from you, one from Dover, which was longer coming than any letter ever was, and one from Chester, and desires me to thank you for her, though she has no excuse, that I know of, except idleness, for not doing so herself. She has had another bad cold, with rheumatism, but is, thank God, nearly well. We do not wonder at your finding the difference between French and English manners, in casual acquaintance, very great; and I doubt much, whether we have any great superiority in more intimate connections, to compensate our inferiority in this respect; you remember, no doubt, Cowper's character of us in the Task; it is excellent.

"I do not think we have seen any thing worth mentioning since you went, or rather since Mrs. F. wrote to you after her presentation; only we were one day at Raincy, formerly the Duke of Orleans's, which, though in a state of neglect, is still very beautiful. We have seen Madame Duchesnois again, in Roxane, in Bajazet, and either the part suited her better than the others, or she is very much improved. My work is finished, and we stay now only in expectation of my brother, who writes word that he will be here the 2nd of November; we shall, of course, stay some days with him, and set out, I think, the 7th. I have made visits to your friends the consuls, and dined with Le Brun; he seems heavy, but if he is the author, as they say he is, of the Chancellor Maupeoux's addresses to the parliament at the end of Louis XVIth's reign, it must be his situation that has stupified him, for they are very good indeed. As you had a curiosity about an over-turn, it is very well it was satisfied at so cheap a rate. We shall be very glad to hear that your mode of travelling has been attended with no worse consequences.

"I suppose you will now go in earnest to *law.*—I do not know much of the matter, but I suspect that a regular attendance (and with attention) to the courts, is still more important than any reading whatever; you, of course, read Blackstone over and over again; and if so, pray tell me whether you agree with me in thinking his style of English the very best among our modern writers; always easy and intelligible; far more correct than Hume, and less studied and made up than Robertson. It is a pity you did not see, while you were here, Villoison, the great Grecian, if it were only for the purpose of knowing how fast it is possible for the human voice to go without indistinctness. I believe he could recite the whole Iliad in four hours. He has a great deal of knowledge of all kinds, and it is well he has, for, at his rate, he would run out a moderate stock in half an hour. I hope soon to hear you are got safe to Dublin; direct your next to St. Ann's Hill, where we hope to be by the 13th of next month. I find the baronet and Grattan are both in England, so I have no message to send to your country. We have just begun the Roman Comique, and have already found the originals of several of Fielding's bloody noses, &c. which made you so angry. We are just going to pay a visit to the museum.

"Your affectionate friends,

"C. J. FOX.

"HOTEL DE RICHELIEU, 28*th October.*   "E. FOX."

LETTER XIII.

" My dear Sir,

" Pray do not think you trouble me, but quite the contrary, by writing to me, and especially on the subject of your poetical studies. What I do not like in your letter is, your account of yourself; and I am afraid a winter in Dublin, which may be so useful to you in other respects, may not be quite so well for your health; which, after all, is the grand article. Mrs. F. has not written lately, because you had not told her how to direct; and as she had not heard of your receiving the last letter she directed to Glasnevin, she feared that might not do. She desires me to say every thing that is kind to you.

"I am very glad you prefer Euripides to Sophocles, because it is my taste; though I am not sure that it is not thought a heresy.—He (Eur.) appears to me to have much more of facility and nature in his way of writing than the other. The speech you mention of Electra is, indeed, beautiful; but when you have read some more of Euripides, perhaps you will not think it quite unrivalled. Of all Sophocles's plays, I like Electra clearly the best, and I think your epithet to Œd. Tyr. a very just one; it is really to me a *disagreeable* play; and yet there are many who not only prefer it to Electra, but reckon it the finest specimen of the Greek theatre. I like his other two plays upon the Theban story both better, *i. e.* the

Œd. Col. and the Antigone. In the latter there is a passage in her answer to Creon that is, perhaps, the sublimest in the world; and, in many parts of the play there is a spirit almost miraculous, if, as it is said, Sophocles was past eighty when he composed it. Cicero has made great use of the passage I allude to, in his oration for Milo. I suppose you selected Hipp. and Iph. in Aulis, on account of Racine; and I hope you have observed with what extreme judgment he has imitated them. In the character of Hipp. only, I think he has fallen short of his original. The scene of Phædra's discovery of her love to her nurse, he has imitated pretty closely; and if he has not surpassed it, it is only because that was impossible. His Clytemnestra, too, is excellent, but would have been better if he had ventured to bring on the young Orestes as Eur. does. The change which you mention in the Greek Iphigenia, I like extremely; but it is censured by Aristotle as a change of character,—not, I think, justly. Perhaps the sudden change in Menelaus, which he also censures, is less defensible. Now, though the two plays of Eur. which you have read, are undoubtedly *among* his best, I will venture to assure you, that there are four others you will like full as well; Medea, Phœnissæ, Heraclidæ, and Alcestis; with the last of which, if I know any thing of your taste, you will be enchanted. Many faults are found with it, but those faults lead to the greatest beauties. For instance, if Hercules's levity is a little improper in a tragedy, his shame afterwards, and the immediate consequence of that shame being a more than human exertion, afford the finest picture of an heroic mind that exists. The speech beginning ω πολλα τλασα καρδια, &c. is divine. Besides the two you have read, and the four I have recommended, Hercules Furens, Iph. in Tauris, Hecuba, Bacchæ, and Troades, are all very excellent. Then come Ion, Supplices, Electra and Helena; Orestes and Andromache are, in my judgment, the worst. I have not mentioned Rhesus and Cyclops, because the former is not thought to be really Euripides's, and the latter is entirely comic, or rather a very coarse farce; excellent, however, in its way, and the conception of the characters not unlike that of Shakespeare in Caliban. I should never finish, if I were to let myself go upon Euripides. In two very material points, however, he is certainly far excelled by Sophocles: 1st, in the introduction of proper subjects in the songs of the chorus; and, 2dly, in the management of his plot. The extreme absurdity of the chorus in Medea suffering her to kill her children, and of that in Phædra letting her hang herself, without the least attempt to prevent it, has been often and justly ridiculed; but what signify faults, where there are such excessive beauties? Pray write soon, and let me know, if you have read more of these plays, what you think of them.

"If you do not go to Dublin before my brother returns, you had better commission somebody to call at the Royal Hospital, for some books of which Mrs. H. Fox took the charge for you, but which, as she writes, she does not know where to send. I think my brother's return a very bad symptom of the intentions of government with regard to poor Ireland ; but that is a subject as fruitful, though not so pleasant, as that of Euripides.

" Yours, ever most truly,

"C. J. FOX.

" P.S. When you have read the two farewell speeches of Medea and Alcestis to their children, I do not think you will say that Electra's is quite unrivalled, though most excellent undoubtedly it is."

LETTER XIV.

"St. Ann's Hill, Monday.

" My dear Sir,

" I enclose you a letter for Mr. G. Ponsonby, to whom also I mentioned you in a letter I wrote him a few days since, upon another subject. We are very happy, indeed, to hear so much better account of your health, than that which you gave in your former letters. Now that you are settled in Dublin, and <i>hard at it</i> with the law, I ought not, according to common notions, to answer your questions about Æschylus, &c., but I am of opinion, that the study of good authors, and especially poets, ought never to be intermitted by any man who is to speak or write for the public, or, indeed, who has any occasion to tax his imagination, whether it be for argument, for illustration, for ornament, for sentiment, or any other purpose. I said nothing of Æschylus,

because I know but little of him; I read two of his
plays, the Septem apud Thebas, and the Prometheus,
at Oxford; of which I do not remember much, except that I liked the last far the best. I have since
read the Eumenides, in which there are, no doubt,
most sublime passages; but in general the figures
are too forced and hard for my taste; and then there
is too much of the grand and terrific, and gigantic,
without a mixture of anything, either tender or pleasant, or elegant which keeps the mind too much on
the stretch. This never suits my taste; and I feel
the same objection to most parts of the Paradise Lost,
though in that poem there are most splendid exceptions, Eve, Paradise, &c. I have heard that the
Agamemnon, if you can conquer its obscurity, is the
finest of all Æschylus's plays, and I will attempt it
when I have a little time. I quite long to hear how
you are captivated with Alcestis, for captivated I am
sure you will be.

" Mrs. Fox desires to be remembered kindly; we
have been a great deal from home these last two
months, twice at Lord Robert's, and at Woburn, and
Mr. Whitbread's; we are now here, as I hope, to
stay with little interruption; and very happy we are
to be here quietly again, though our parties were very
pleasant; and I think change of air at this time of
the year is always good for the colds to which Mrs.
Fox is so subject.

" I was just going to end without noticing *Pindar*;
I dare say the obscurities are chiefly owing to our
want of means of making out the allusions; his style

is more full of allusions than that of any other poet,
except, perhaps, Dante, who is on that account so
difficult, and as I think on that account only. The
fine passages in Pindar are equal to, if not beyond,
anything; but the want of interest in the subjects,
and, if it is not blasphemy to say so, the excessive
profusion of words, make him something bordering
upon *tedious*. There is a fire in the celebrated passage
in the 2nd Olympic, which begins σοφος ὁ πολλα ειδως
φυᾳ, that is quite unequalled in any poem whatever;
and the sweetness in the preceding part, describing
the happy islands, is in its way almost as good. Pray
let us hear from you soon, that you are well, and
happy; if you read the Heraclidæ of Euripides, pray
tell me if you are particularly struck by one passage
in Demophoon's part; if you miss it, I will point it
out to you.

"Yours sincerely,

"C. J. FOX.

"P. S. Woodlarks are said to be very common in
the West of England; here we have a few, and but
few. The books which you left were sent by my
brother, but he not being able to find your direction,
brought them back."

LETTER XV.

"St. Ann's Hill, *Tuesday*.

"My dear Sir,

"I heard yesterday, for the first time, a
report that you had been very unwell; pray lose no
time in writing me a line, either to contradict the

report, or to say that you are recovered. I know you will excuse my having been so long without writing, on the score of the constant business which I had in London, and which you know me enough to know is not very agreeable to my nature.

" I have now been here a little more than three weeks, and hope soon to get again to my Greek, and my History, but hitherto have had too many visit-ants to have much leisure. I have read Iphigenia in Aulis since I last wrote, and think much more highly of it than I did on the first reading. The scene where the quarrel and reconciliation between the brothers is, has always been blamed, on account of the too quick change of mind in Menelaus; but I like it very much, and there is something in the man-ner of it that puts me in mind of Brutus and Cassius, in Shakespeare. We have had no very good weather; but this place has been in great beauty, greater, if possible, than ever. Is there any chance of your coming to England? If there is, you know we expect and insist that you come directly hither. I hope that, with the exception of a few occasional visits of two or three days, I shall be here with little interruption, till the meeting of Parliament. Mrs. Fox desires me to say everything that is kind for her. She, too, says she has been too busy to write; and the truth is, that the company we have had here has entirely taken up her time. Pray lose no time in writing.

" Yours, ever affectionately,

" C. J. FOX.

"P.S. I am sure it will give you pleasure to hear that Grattan's success in the H. of C. was complete and acknowledged, even by those who had entertained great hopes of his failure.

"I do not know what interest your relations have in the county of Down, nor what you have with them; but if their interest could be got in favour of Mr. Meade, I should be very happy; if you should hear how the election is going on, I should be obliged to you if you would mention it."

LETTER XVI.

"St. Ann's Hill, *Wednesday.*

"My dear Sir,

"It gives Mrs. F. and me great pleasure to hear that you think you are getting better, and that, too, in spite of the weather, which, if it has been with you as with us, has been by no means favourable to such a complaint as yours. The sooner you can come the better; and I cannot help hoping that this air will do you good. Parts of the 1st, and still more of the 2nd book of the Æneid, are capital indeed; the description of the night sack of a town, being a subject not touched by Homer, hinders it from having that appearance of too close imitation which Virgil's other battles have; and the details, Priam's death, Helen's appearance, Hector's in the dream, and many others, are enchanting. The Proëm, too, to Æneas's narration is perfection itself. The part about Sinon and Laocöon does not so much please me, though I have nothing to say against it. Perhaps it is too long, but whatever be the cause, I feel it to be rather cold. As to your friend's heresy, I cannot much wonder at, or blame it, since I used to be of the same opinion myself; but I am now a convert; and my chief reason is, that, though the detached parts of the Æneid appear to me to be equal to anything, the story and characters appear more faulty every time I read it. My chief objection (I mean that to the character of *Æneas*) is, of course, not so much felt in the three first books; but, afterwards, he is always either insipid or odious, sometimes excites interest *against* him, and never for him.

" The events of the war, too, are not striking; and Pallas and Lausus, who most interest you, are in effect exactly alike. But, in parts, I admire Virgil more and more every day, such as those I have alluded to in the 2nd book; the finding of Andromache in the third, every thing relating to Dido; the 6th book; the visit to Evander, in the 8th; Nisus and Euryalus, Mezentius's death, and many others. In point of passion I think Dido equal, if not superior, to any thing in Homer, or Shakespeare, or Euripides; for me, that is saying every thing.

" One thing which delights me in the Iliad and Odyssey, and of which there is nothing in Virgil, is the picture of manners, which seem to be so truly delineated. The times in which Homer lived undoubtedly gave him a great advantage in this respect;

since, from his nearness to the times of which he
writes, what we always see to be invention in Virgil,
appears like the plain truth in Homer. Upon this
principle a friend of mine observed, that the characters in Shakespeare's historical plays always
appear more real than those in his others. But,
exclusive of this advantage, Homer certainly attends
to *character* more than his imitator. I hope your
friend, with all his partiality, will not maintain
that. the simile in the 1st Æneid, comparing Dido
to Diana, is equal to that in the Odyssey, comparing
Nausicaa to her, either in propriety of application,
or in beauty of description. If there is an Apollonius Rhodius where you are, pray look at Medea's
speech, lib. iv. ver. 365, and you will perceive,
that even in Dido's finest speech, *nec tibi diva
parens, &c.* he has imitated a good deal, and especially those expressive and sudden turns, *neque te
teneo, &c.;* but then he has made wonderful im-
provements, and, on the whole, it is perhaps the
finest thing in all poetry.

Now, if you are not tired of all this criticism,
it is not my fault. The bad weather has preserved
a verdure here, which makes it more beautiful than
ever; and Mrs. F. is in nice good health, and so
every thing goes well with me, which I am sure
you will like to hear; but I have not yet had a
moment for history. I sent you, some weeks ago,
though I forgot to mention it in my letter, some
books you had left in England, by a gentleman
whose name, I think, is Croker. It was Rolleston

who undertook to give them him, directed to you in Capel-street. I added to them a duplicate I had of Miller, on the English Constitution; a book dedicated to me, and which is written on the best and soundest principles; but I fear it is more instructive than amusing, as, though a very sensible man, he was not a lively one.

" Yours very affectionately,
"C. J. FOX.

" P.S. Even in the 1st book, Æneas says, ' *Sum pius Æneas, famá super æthera notus.*' Can you bear this ? "

I have not inserted as I had intended the letters of M. de Talleyrand and Mr. Fox, as they are given in the Parliamentary Debates of 1806. On further reflection, I thought it was unnecessary to copy papers, which were so easily accessible. The perusal of the letter marked No. 3, " Extract of M. Talleyrand's," of March 5, 1806, will convince any one that the first overture for negotiations came from the French government.

The reader who has thus far followed the private Letters of Mr. Fox, may feel a melancholy interest in the account of his last illness, given by his nephew Lord Holland. I therefore transcribe the narrative from the " Memoirs of the Whig Party " published by his son, the present Lord Holland.

" I had been struck, on my return to England, with the change in Mr. Fox's countenance. The cheerfulness of his spirits, and the charms of his conversation, soon wore out the impression. He was, however, more liable to slight indispositions than he had been ; and, at the funeral of Lord Nelson, which I attended with him, I observed that the length of the ceremony, and coldness of the cathedral, overpowered him in a way that no fatigue which I had ever known him undergo had done heretofore. I attributed, however, these slight illnesses to accidental causes, combined with habits of indulgence, which long and uninterrupted health had given him. I little suspected that in his frame were lurking the seeds of a disorder which, in one short year, was to deprive our country and (is it an exaggeration to add ?) mankind of its best hope and brightest ornament. The debates during the Session had much fatigued him. He had, once or twice, had recourse to medicine at the suggestion of his friends and of his physician, Dr. Moseley. But none of them, I believe, apprehended (certainly I did not) any fatal disease, till Lord Lauderdale, who was well acquainted with the symptoms of dropsy, from having attended his own father, who died of that disorder, called our attention to the swelling of his legs, and the falling away about the neck and chest. From this time, though naturally sanguine, I was more observant. Mr. Fox's vigour, appetite, and even spirits, were sensibly impaired.

Having discovered that he was vexed with another complaint * comparatively of slight consequence, I was willing to ascribe the unusual thoughtfulness and dejection of his countenance to a combination of fatigue and meditation on the nature of a troublesome disorder, of the remedy necessary to remove it, and of the postponement of that remedy which was equally necessary to a perfect cure.

" Early in June I dined and spent the day with him, at the request of Mrs. Fox. He had been attacked by rheumatism in the thighs, and by a very unusual dejection of spirits. In consequence of my observations on his appearance that day, I concurred earnestly with Mrs. Fox in pressing him to consult some other physician as well as Dr. Moseley, who, though full of attachment to him, and not perhaps devoid of skill, was far from enjoying a high reputation. Sir Henry Halford, then Dr. Vaughan, had indeed seen him once ; he had urged, very strongly, the necessity of care, attention, and quiet ; but he had advised no material alteration of medicines, and did not seem, to me, to apprehend any immediate danger of dropsy. In the meanwhile, Mr. Fox had gone up to the House of Commons. His earnestness about the abolition of the Slave Trade induced him to continue his attendances longer than the advice of his friends or his own judgment approved ; but even after he absented himself from Parliament, he wrote his despatches with his usual perspicuity and ease, and talked occasionally on public as well as private

* Hydrocele.

matters, with as much vivacity, earnestness, and wisdom as ever. When, however, he gave Lord Henry Petty and myself directions to draw out the sketch of a treaty with Sicily, about which he was particularly earnest, the exertion of attending to the detail of the articles fatigued and oppressed him exceedingly. That was the last business which he could strictly be said to transact ; his exertions henceforward were limited to signatures, occasional conversations with his colleagues, a few letters, which he wrote himself, and others which he dictated. The latter practice was to him entirely new. ' I thought it ' (said he) ' very difficult ; but I soon found I could do it well enough, and it is a great relief.'

" At a very early period of the Administration, he had told me that he looked forward some time or other to retire from the office which he held ; that, in the event of peace, the tiresome and unimportant duties annexed to it would increase, that he would then take some less active situation, or remain in Cabinet without any, and give me the seals of the Foreign Office, as he could, in that case, without indelicacy, superintend all matters of importance, and make opportunities of talking them over, when he was so inclined, or avoid them, when he had a fancy for literature or any other pursuit. This scheme, he observed, would inure me to business ; and with that contented tone of voice which always accompanied his kindness, he added : ' It will be nice too, for it will secure my seeing you at St. Ann's when I am there.' Of these projects, though made for some

distant time, he had probably spoken to others; for
when his disorder assumed a more alarming appearance, his colleagues offered some arrangement of the
sort.　Lord Howick (Grey) came to him with a
proposal, which included a Peerage, if he liked it, to
save him from the yet more laborious duty of the
House of Commons.　Mrs. Fox was in the room
when this suggestion was made.　At the mention of
the Peerage, he looked at her significantly, with a
reference to his secret but early determination never
to be created a Peer; and, after a short pause, he
said : ' No, not yet, I think not yet.'　On the same
evening, as I sat by his bedside, he said to me : ' If
this continues (and though I don't fear any immediate
danger, I begin to see it is a longer and more serious
business than I apprehended), I must have more quiet
than with my place I ought to have, and put the plan
I spoke to you about, sooner in execution than I
intended.　But don't think me selfish, young one.
The Slave Trade and Peace are two such glorious
things, I can't give them up, even to you.　If I can
manage *them*, I will then retire.'　He then talked
over some arrangements connected with that scheme,
and his own situation in the Cabinet without office,
and added : 'The peerage, to be sure, seems the natural
way, but that cannot be.　I have an oath in Heaven
against it; I will not close my politics in that foolish
way, as so many have done before me.'

" His disorder was pronounced to be dropsy, when
Sir Henry Halford (Vaughan) was called in for the
second time, and allowed to examine him more

strictly than he had hitherto permitted him or any
other physician to do.   Though neither impatient
nor desponding in sickness, Mr. Fox had little confidence in medical skill, and less curiosity even, on
subjects connected with the health and management
of the human body, than on any other.   He was,
consequently, very averse to relate symptoms which
put him to no immediate inconvenience.   He would
not have been easily prevailed upon to take any
strong drugs, or to submit to any regimen or discipline,
upon the apprehension of remote danger ; for whoever
had been his medical attendant would have found it
difficult to obtain credit with him for much foresight
on such subjects.   I mention this, because it afterwards appeared that the seeds of his disorder had
been laid full two years before.   A severe pain in his
side, which attacked him at Cheltenham in 1804,
proceeded, no doubt, from that affection in the liver
which ultimately brought him to the grave.   It
would, however, have required great sagacity in any
physician, even with a willing and confiding patient,
which Mr. Fox never was, to detect the latent cause
of his illness at that period ; and it would even then
have been still more difficult to persuade Mr. Fox of
his sagacity, and of the truth of his apprehensions,
and of the necessity of submitting to severe discipline
to remove a complaint, the existence of which was
conjectured by his physician, but not proved by his
own sensations.   The details of the progress and
management of Mr. Fox's disease cannot, I am aware,
be very interesting to the world ; but I have

mentioned these circumstances in justice to his friends
and his physicians, lest the rumours circulated at the
time should lead any future biographer or historian
to imagine that his death was occasioned by neglect
or mismanagement. If there were any neglect in the
commencement of his disorder, it arose from his
habits, opinions, and character, and was entirely his
own : if there were any mismanagement, it was of a
kind that the eminent physicians latterly called in,
Sir Henry Halford, and Dr. Pitcairn, and his friend
Mr. Hawkins the surgeon, never discovered nor
corrected.

" Soon after the serious nature of his disorder had
been ascertained, Lord Yarmouth abruptly and
unadvisedly produced his full powers at Paris ; the
Cabinet, in consequence, named Lord Lauderdale to
conduct the negotiation. My uncle's intention had,
at one time, been to send me or General Fitz Patrick.
In his then state of health, I should certainly have
declined it ; but I own that I was weak enough to
feel two minutes' mortification, on Lord Howick's
(Lord Grey) not giving me the option. I felt this
more sensibly when, on approaching my uncle's
bedside after he had heard of, and sanctioned, Lord
Lauderdale's appointment, he said, with a melancholy
smile of affection that I can never forget—' So you
would not leave me, young one, to go to Paris, but
liked staying with me better—there's a kind boy.'
He thus gave me credit for refusing what had never
been offered to me, and I did not like to explain the
circumstances for fear he might misinterpret my

explanation into an expression of disappointment at not going. I answered: ' Why, I hope I may be useful to you here ; and I am sure, if you like my being here, it would be very odd if I did not prefer staying.'

" From this period, in addition to frequent calls in the morning, I regularly attended his bedside for an hour or two every night after his visitors and secretaries had retired. Mr. Trotter, Mrs. Fox, or my sister, generally read to him during the day. The books he chose were chiefly novels. When he wished to hear anything else, he expressed that wish while it was my sister's turn, with whose reading he was very naturally delighted, or he reserved it till the evening for me. ' For ' (said he) ' I like your reading, young one, but I liked it better before I had heard your sister's. That is better than yours I can tell you.' I noticed that he was growing to love his niece more and more every day. Various accidents had prevented his seeing much of her till the year 1803. All her excellent qualities, both of head and heart, came upon him at once, and endeared her, as well they might, most sincerely to her uncle.

" I read the whole of Crabbe's ' Parish Register ' over to him in MS. Some parts he made me read twice ; he remarked several passages as exquisitely beautiful, and objected to some few, which I mentioned to the author, and which he, in almost every instance, altered before publication. Mr. Fox repeated, once or twice, that it was a very pretty poem ; that Crabbe's condition in the world had improved since he wrote the 'Village,' and his view of life and of mankind had improved likewise. The 'Parish Register' bore marks of some little more indulgence to our species; though not so many as he could have wished, especially as the few touches of that nature are beautiful in the extreme. He was particularly struck with the description of the substantial happiness of a farmer's wife. He did not, however, observe, what was nevertheless quite true, that the improvement in Mr. Crabbe's fortune was, in a great measure, owing to himself. While Lord Thurlow was in office, he overcame his reluctance to asking favours of a political enemy, and urged that Chancellor to encourage genius by giving Mr. Crabbe some preferment. Lord Thurlow did something for him; and the Duke of Rutland, who had been applied to by Lord John Townshend, did more. His success in the Church, though very moderate, seemed for awhile to check rather than animate his ardour for poetry. He passed several years without publishing anything; and it was not till after an accidental conversation with Mr. Fox, who met him while shooting in Suffolk,* that he confessed that he had written some poems, but never printed them, and agreed to send them in MS. for Mr. Fox's perusal and judgment. These were the poems which I read to Mr. Fox.

" The rest of my time with him was chiefly passed in conversation. Immediately after Lord Lauderdale's departure for Paris, we had many discussions on the

* At Mr. Dudley North's.

negotiation. The demand of the French that we should give up Sicily, irritated and disappointed him exceedingly. He considered it not only as an inadmissible pretension, but as an indication of bad faith and insincerity on the part of the French Government. Indeed, when I somewhat foolishly imagined that an equivalent might be found for the King of Naples—that a retreat either in South America, or on a large pension, might be offered to the King of Sardinia, and a kingdom of islands formed of Sardinia, the Balearic islands, and some other small islands in the Mediterranean as an exchange for Sicily, he answered me by saying, ' No, no! Bad as the Queen and Court of Naples are, we can, in honour, do nothing without their full and *bonâ fide* consent; but even exclusive of that consideration, and of the great importance of Sicily, which you, young one, very much underrate, it is not so much the value of the point in dispute, as the manner in which the French fly from their word, that disheartens me. It is not Sicily, but the shuffling, insincere way in which they act, that shows me they are playing a false game ; and in that case it would be very imprudent to make any concessions, which by possibility could be thought inconsistent with our honour, or could furnish our allies with a plausible pretence for suspecting, reproaching, or deserting us.' He generally used to break off such conversations very abruptly by saying, ' And now no more politics.' In truth, he seldom allotted more than a quarter of an hour to such topics.

" There was, indeed, one subject relating to

patronage on which he was extremely uneasy : he thought, that till he had provided for the person whom I allude to, he had left undischarged a long arrear of obligations. That person, by very obtrusive and unreasonable conduct at the formation of the Ministry, had embarrassed, irritated, and even exasperated him. But it was not easy, even by misconduct, to cancel a debt of gratitude in the mind of Mr. Fox, if he thought that he had ever contracted it. He was miserable till he could requite the former zealous services of this person.

"When Lord Howick very handsomely devoted a place in his gift to that object, Mr. Fox was perfectly satisfied ; he told me more than once after that arrangement was completed, that he had nothing of the same sort on his mind, no reason to complain of others, or to reproach himself. Indeed throughout, he seemed to me pleased and gratified with the conduct of his colleagues both about men and measures.

" There were indeed two votes during the Session, of which he did not cordially approve—the income tax, and the additional allowance to the Royal brothers. ' I suppose,' (said he, of the first) ' it is necessary, for those who are most conversant with financial matters tell me so, and no man, I think, would like to propose it unless he thought so.' To the additional income of the Princes, he found the Government pledged, and he observed that he could hardly withhold or obstruct a favour to the younger Princes, who had supported his Opposition, and were now support-

ing his Ministry, which his predecessor, Mr. Pitt, had
promised them, when arrayed against him, to grant.
Indeed, his objection was not to the allowance, but to
the fund from which it was to be derived.   The
King's Civil List ought, he thought, to have defrayed
it. Since I have spoken of the concurrence of opinion
on most subjects, both of principle and detail,
between him and his colleagues during his life, I
owe it to those who survived, and to myself to add,
that with the exception of one, I knew of no measure
adopted subsequently by Lord Grenville's administration, to which, from my knowledge of his principles
and feelings, I think he would have been averse.   To
the dissolution of Parliament, I think he would have
been.   The motives which induced Lord Grenville's
Cabinet to adopt it will be mentioned hereafter; and
it must be acknowledged, that the *ratio suasoria* for
it became stronger after the event which deprived the
Government of its chief assistance in the House of
Commons.   On all public matters he had more
repugnance, during the latter part of his illness, to
talk, than his colleagues had reluctance to consult
him. The truth is, that they sought every opportunity
of doing so, and I never observed the least indifference
to his opinion, even when he was quite disabled from
enforcing it; or the slightest neglect of any advice he
gave, much less of any request which he was disposed
to make.

"Numbers of letters were written from every
quarter of the kingdom to suggest the means of
preserving his life. The warmth and eagerness with

which they were urged, expressive of the public interest taken in his recovery, were gratifying in the extreme. One remedy, an exterior application of snails and (I think) colewort to the belly, was, with the permission of the physicians, tried for a day or two. At first, it seemed to relieve him, but its effects soon subsided, and the unfavourable symptoms recurred and increased. His pulse and stomach would no longer bear much mercury. On the other hand, the state and distension of his skin were such, as to deter the physicians from allowing it to be rubbed in, a mode of applying it for which Mr. Fox had some predilection. At length the water had accumulated so much, that the operation of tapping became necessary. I was requested to apprise him that, though neither painful nor dangerous, it could only be rendered useful by keeping both his body and mind in a state of the greatest tranquillity for two or three days afterwards. If therefore he had any subject on which he felt anxious, or any directions to give in case his complaint should take a more unfavourable turn, it would be prudent to mention every such circumstance before the operation. He had, at an earlier stage of his illness, exacted from me a promise to apprise him of any approach of danger, and added with emotion, ' We are neither of us children, and it would be ridiculous to conceal anything :' he then resumed his gaiety, and added, ' I don't mean to die though, young one ; and above all not to give the thing up, as my father did.'

" It was, I believe, at that period that he spoke to

me about the *Fox-Glove*.   He expressed a strong repugnance to it, but added emphatically, 'I do not
mean, however, that I will not take *that* too, rather
than leave anything untried; but I prefer some of
these quack medicines, and if it once comes to the
Fox-Glove, I shall think very ill of it indeed.'   He
never took it.   When in one of our most despondent
moments, it was suggested, Dr. Vaughan said, ' It
would be of no service; it ought not even to be tried
in this case.'   This opinion probably arose from the
intermission of the pulse, which the physicians had
observed with some dismay, on administering drastic
medicines in an early stage of the complaint.   I wrote
down, in 1811, my recollection of Mr. Fox's own in-
junctions and wishes on the subject of the Fox-Glove,
and they prove that Mr. Trotter, his secretary, in his
insinuations against the family and the physicians for
allowing medicines too strong to be administered,
was as unwarranted in his conjectures on Mr. Fox's
own notions and wishes, as he has been shown by a
letter of Dr. Moseley to be incorrect in his supposition
of facts.

" To return to my narrative : I told him about an
hour before the first operation was performed, that
there was neither pain nor immediate danger to be
apprehended, but that great quiet of mind and body
was deemed necessary to give the operation all its
beneficial consequences ; that the efforts of the constitution to support the frame after a large portion
of water was suddenly drawn off, required the very
utmost repose ; and that any exertion, mental or

bodily, soon afterwards, would impede the endeavour of the constitution to resume its tone. He understood me. He gave me directions where to find his Will. The situation and feelings of Mrs. Fox seemed to be the chief, and indeed the only, occupation of his mind on that occasion, and on every other where he spoke of the probability of his disease terminating fatally. He could speak of nothing regarding her without strong and sensible emotion. He contrived, however, to explain his wishes and expectations about a provision for her after his death. They were as nearly fulfilled as the state of the pension laws would admit. He had hardly finished what he had to say on that painful subject, when he abruptly said, ' Now change the conversation, or read me the 8th Book of Virgil.' I did so. He made me read the finest verses twice over, spoke of their merits, and compared them with passages in other poets, with all his usual acuteness, taste, memory, and vivacity. He had no desire that I should be present at the puncture, and I declined it from a dislike to the sight of any operation. It was hardly over, however, when he called me into the room, and telling me that it was right, and might some day or other be useful to me to know what the operation of tapping was, he sat looking at the water as it spouted from him, and with good humour, and even pleasantry, commented on the figure he made.

" For some few days he seemed to revive. With the propensity to deceive ourselves, which seems to haunt a sick room, we began to entertain some faint

hopes that the medicines and treatment might ward
off the necessity of a second operation. In this interval, he took, if I mistake not, one or two airings;
and in a few days he was removed to Chiswick. The
weather was fine, and the garden through which he
was wheeled, and the pictures, and large apartments
of that magnificent villa, seemed to refresh his spirits.
A remark of Bacon quoted in the Spectator, that
poetry, sculpture, painting, and all the arts of imitation, relieve and soothe the mind in sickness, while
other occupations fatigue and harass it, struck him
exceedingly. He applied it, no doubt, to his own
situation, and after some reflection, he observed, that
he could not see the reason, but acknowledged the
truth of it. He found the employment of the mind
in the contemplation of a landscape, or the perusal of
a poem, refreshing; and all other exertion in business,
private or public, irksome.

" It was not long ere he was tapped a second
time. In the morning of the 7th of September, he
grew much worse, and Mrs. Fox sent for me over to
Chiswick, which I did not quit till after the termination of his illness. One day he sent for me, and
reminded me of my promise, not to conceal the truth.
I told him that we had been much alarmed, but
that he was better. I added, however, that he was
in a very precarious state, and that I must acknowledge his danger, though I perhaps over-stated it
from a fear of allowing myself to deceive him after the
promise I had given. He then repeated the injunc-
tions he had given me before, and said once or twice,

' You have done quite right—you will not forget
poor Liz : what will become of her ! ' As he had
now been twice apprised of his danger, and seemed
to me to have said all that he wished, I henceforth
endeavoured to encourage his hopes as much as I
could, and infinitely beyond my own judgment of his
situation. He was, however, somewhat stronger and
easier that night; he conversed more than he had
done for some time : seeing his servant in the room,
he spoke to me in French, and his thoughts still
dwelt exclusively on Mrs. Fox. ' Je crains pour
elle,' said he ; ' a't'elle la moindre idée de mon
danger ? si non, quelle souffrance pour elle ! ' I
answered him (what was indeed the truth) that she
was sufficiently aware of his danger to prevent the
worse termination of his illness being a surprise ; but
that she had not been so desponding that morning as
my sister, General Fitz Patrick, and others ; and I
ventured to add, ' et à cette heure vous voyez qu'elle
avait raison ; for in spite of what I then said to you,
" dabit Deus his quoque finem." ' ' Ay,' said he,
with a faint smile, ' but *finem*, young one, may have
two senses.'

" Such was our last conversation. He spoke,
indeed, frequently, in the course of the next thirty-
six hours, and he evidently retained his faculties
unimpaired ; but he was too restless at one time, and
too lethargic at others, to keep up any conversation
after that evening, which I think was the 11th of
September. About this period of his illness, Mrs.
Fox, who had a strong sense of religion, consulted

some of us on the means of persuading Mr. Fox to
hear prayers read by his bedside. I own that I
had some apprehensions lest any clergyman called in
might think it a good opportunity for displaying his
religious zeal, and acquiring celebrity by some exhibition to which Mr. Fox's principles and taste would
have been equally averse. When, however, Mr.
Bouverie, a young man of excellent character, without pretension or hypocrisy, was in the house, I
seconded her request, in the full persuasion that
by so doing I promoted what would have been the
wishes of Mr. Fox himself. His chief object throughout was to soothe and satisfy her. Yet repugnance
was felt, and to some degree urged, even to this, by
Mr. Trotter, who soon afterwards thought fit to
describe with great fervour the devotion it inspired,
and to build upon it many conjectures of his own
on the religious tenets and principles of Mr. Fox.
Mr. Bouverie stood behind the curtain of the bed,
and in a faint but audible voice read the service.
Mr. Fox remained unusually quiet. Towards the
end, Mrs. Fox knelt on the bed and joined his hands,
which he seemed faintly to close with a smile of
ineffable goodness, such as can never be forgotten
by those who witnessed it. Whatever it betokened,
it was a smile of serenity and goodness, such as
could have proceeded at that moment only from a
disinterested and benevolent heart, from a being
loving and beloved by all that surrounded and by
all that approached him. From that period, and not
till that period, Mrs. Fox bore her situation and

apprehensions with some fortitude; and I have no
doubt that her confidence in religion alone enabled
her to bear the scene which she was doomed so soon
to undergo.

" During the whole of the 13th of September, no
hopes could be entertained. For the last two hours
of his existence his articulation was so painful and
indistinct, that we could only occasionally catch his
words, and then very few at a time. The small
room in which he lay has two doors, one into the
large saloon, the other into a room equally small
adjoining. In the latter Mrs. Fox, during the last
ten days, constantly sat or lay down without un-
dressing. Her bed was within hearing, and indeed
within a very few feet, of that of Mr. Fox. The
doors were always open, for the weather was extremely hot. Of those who had access to him during
the last melancholy days, it was at any one moment
a mere accident who were actually in the bedchamber
with him, who were pacing the adjoining rooms, or
giving vent to their grief in the distant corners of
the apartments. Each was actually by his bedside
during some part of the day, and all, of at least
seven or eight * persons, were constantly within call
of the room in which he lay, or in attendance upon
him. The impression, therefore given, (whether in-

---

* " Mrs. Fox, Miss Fox, Miss Willoughby, Lady Holland, General Fitz
Patrick, Mr. Hawkins, Mr. Trotter, Dr. Moseley, or one of the other
physicians, and often all three, and myself : other intimate friends, such
as Lord Robert Spencer, Lord John Townshend, Lord Fitzwilliam, frequently called. Some, I think, approached his bedside, all were admitted
and stayed in the adjoining apartments for a considerable space of time."

tentionally or not, I cannot say) with respect to the persons present at his death, in Mr. Trotter's book is quite incorrect.   The last words which he uttered with any distinctness were, 'I die happy;' and 'Liz,' the affectionate abbreviation in which he usually addressed his wife.   He attempted indeed to articulate something more, but we none of us could accurately distinguish the sounds.   In very few minutes after this fruitless endeavour to speak, in the evening of the 13th of September, 1806, he expired without a groan, and with a serene and placid countenance, which seemed, even after death, to represent the benevolent spirit which had animated it.

" With some pain to myself, and with some hazard of wearying those who may at any distance of time peruse these Papers, I have thus related all the minute particulars concerning the last illness and death of the best and greatest man of our time, with whom the accident of birth closely connected me, from whose conversation and kindness I derived the chief delight of my youth, and veneration for whose memory furnished me with the strongest motive for continuing in public life, as well as the best regulation for my conduct therein.   I noted down these details, *currente calamo*, without stopping to select a word, or polish an expression, in the year 1811, five years and a few weeks after the period of his death.   I did so because I was then fresh from the perusal of a book written by his secretary, Mr. Trotter, in which the author, possibly without any evil intention, conveys

very false impressions of the opinions of Mr. Fox,
and still more so of the conduct of his relations and
friends. If a consciousness of being beloved and
almost adored by all who approached him could ad-
minister consolation in the hour of death, no man
could with more reason or propriety have closed his
career with the exclamation of—' I die happy!' for
no man ever deserved or obtained that consolation
more certainly than Mr. Fox.

" His character could be best delineated by a narrative of the leading events of his public life, by a
reference to his speeches and writings, by a publication of many of his private letters, a description of
his domestic life, and such fragments of his conversation as the memory of his friends might supply.
Such a work I have long meditated. If I have
leisure and health, I trust that I shall, some day,
accomplish it in a way, I will not say worthy of the
subject (for to that I do not aspire), but, at least, in a
manner which shall do him no discredit, which shall
offend against no one principle which I have imbibed
from him, and which shall give no unnecessary pain
to any one, and, above all, none to such as command
my regard and affection, by having shared some portion of his."

POSTSCRIPT.

In the volumes now brought to a close, I have printed the materials which Lord Holland had collected, with a view to illustrate the life of his uncle.

I hope to be able soon to execute in some degree the design which Lord Holland had formed, of giving a connected narrative of Mr. Fox's life, with extracts from his speeches.

In concluding these volumes, however, I propose to point out shortly the main principles and the chief measures of which Mr. Fox was the foremost champion.

1. Mr. Fox held the doctrine that the King ought always to be guided by the advice of Parliament, in opposition to the opinion, that he might rule without regard to party connection, by separate influence and by innate authority. Although his views may seem to have been defeated in 1784, yet they have in the end prevailed, and are now the established practice of the Constitution.

2. Mr. Fox maintained that theory of religious liberty which requires that religious faith should not be made a qualification for office or for seats in Parliament. Although he failed during his lifetime in emancipating either Protestant Dissenters from the fetters of the Test and Corporation Acts, or Roman Catholics from the disabling statutes of Charles the Second, yet his efforts were not unfruitful, and in 1828 and 1829, both these kinds of disability were removed.

3. The African Slave Trade which Mr. Pitt at once denounced and extended, received its death blow from Mr. Fox at the termination of his life. The abolition of slavery was a corollary of that act.

4. Parliamentary Reform, which Mr. Fox supported in 1782, 1783, 1785, and 1797, was finally accomplished by his friend and disciple Lord Grey, in 1832.

5. Economical Reform had its chief promoter in Mr. Burke, but Mr. Fox contributed his powerful aid to the destruction of the corrupt system which flourished during the ministry of Lord North, and which Lord North had inherited from his predecessors.

6. The most powerful speeches of Mr. Fox, both in youth and middle age, were made in favour of Peace. Not that the great orator was for peace at all times, and at any price. When France attempted to destroy the independence of Holland, in 1787, Mr. Fox applauded the vigour with which Mr. Pitt resisted the design. When Napoleon, flushed with the victory of Austerlitz, burst all the bounds of

moderation, Mr. Fox preferred the continuance of the war to dishonourable concession. Still the favourite predilection of his heart, was love of peace. Neither the pride which carried the nation forward in the assertion of dominion over America, nor the passion which sought to punish the crimes of the French people by the invasion and desolation of France, led him away from the great aim of honourable peace.

This disposition left him in a small minority in the House of Commons at the beginning of the American war, in a still smaller minority at the commencement and during the course of the French war. The loss of all prospect of power, the invectives of vulgar politicians, he was content to bear; the loss of friends, dearly loved, and of the national confidence, honourably acquired, were sacrifices more painful to his heart. But he never faltered, and never swerved from his purpose. The nation, inflamed by animosity, lifted up by arrogance, and deluded by the eloquence of men in power, assailed him as an enemy to his country, because he opposed measures injurious to her interests, and inconsistent with the great laws which regulate the relations between man and man. In this deluge of folly and of fury, he sought in a return to literary pursuits an occupation and an amusement. Other times may see the renewal of wars as unjust and as imprudent as those which Mr. Fox opposed; but while the many will be carried away by the prevailing hurricane, those who can keep their feet will recur to his example as that of a great man who preferred the welfare of his country, and of mankind, to the power and popularity which were acquired by the wanton sacrifice of human life, and the disregard of justice, charity, and mercy. By such his memory will be revered to all future generations.

THE END.